COLONIAL GENOCIDE AND REPARATIONS CLAIMS IN THE 21ST CENTURY

COLONIAL GENOCIDE AND REPARATIONS CLAIMS IN THE 21ST CENTURY

The Socio-Legal Context of Claims under International Law by the Herero against Germany for Genocide in Namibia, 1904–1908

JEREMY SARKIN

PSI Reports

PRAEGER SECURITY INTERNATIONAL
Westport, Connecticut • London

Library of Congress Cataloging-in-Publication Data

Sarkin-Hughes, Jeremy

Colonial genocide and reparations claims in the 21st century: the socio-legal context of claims under international law by the Herero against Germany for genocide in Namibia, 1904–1908 / Jeremy Sarkin.

p. cm.

Includes bibliographical references and index.

ISBN 978-0-313-36256-9 (alk. paper)

1. Herero (African people)—Reparations. 2. Namibia—History—Herero Revolt, 1904–1907—Reparations. 3. Reparations for historical injustices—Namibia. 4. Germany—Trials, litigation, etc. I. Title.

KSY2695.S27 2009

345.6881′0251—dc22 2008033452

British Library Cataloguing in Publication Data is available.

Library of Congress Catalog Card Number: 2008033452
ISBN: 978-0-313-36256-9

First published in 2009

Praeger Security International, 88 Post Road West, Westport, CT 06881
An imprint of Greenwood Publishing Group, Inc.
www.praeger.com

Printed in the United States of America

The paper used in this book complies with the Permanent Paper Standard issued by the National Information Standards Organization (Z39.48-1984).

10 9 8 7 6 5 4 3 2 1

Contents

Acknowledgments vii

Introduction 1

1. The Legacy of the Herero Genocide on Namibia Today 25

2. The Legal Implications of Gross Human Rights and Humanitarian Law Violations Committed from the Nineteenth Century Onward 63

3. The Developing Norm of Reparations and Apologies for Historical Claims: Past, Present, and Future 124

Conclusion 182

Program for Commemoration of Ohamakari Battle 195

Notes 199

Bibliography 259

Index 299

Acknowledgments

THIS BOOK EMERGES out of my work in Namibia over a number of years, which came about as a result of a lecture I gave to the law faculty at the University of Namibia in Windhoek on transitional justice in 2001. I was visiting the country as an external examiner for the University of Namibia. A number of former students, including two former directors of the Legal Assistance Centre in Windhoek, attended that lecture and recommended that I pay the Chief of the Herero a visit at Namibia's Parliament, which I did. The Chief and I spent a number of hours talking then and on many subsequent occasions. I thank him for the information he has provided and the access he has granted me to the many Namibians who have provided insights and information.

This book is the product of extensive research, including numerous interviews I conducted in Namibia, Botswana, Germany, South Africa, and elsewhere. The interviewees included members of the Herero, Damara, and Nama communities in Namibia, South Africa, and Botswana.

The book itself emerges out of a paper I delivered at the Centenary Commemoration of the Ohamakari Battle of August 11, 1904. This event was commemorated on August 14, 2004 at Ohamakari, Namibia. At that event, the German Minister for Economic Development and Cooperation, Heidemarie Wieczorek-Zeul, delivered an apology to the Herero on behalf of the German government. When I was asked to deliver an address to that gathering I realized that there was little written about the issues with which the Herero court cases were concerned (see the Program for Commemoration of Ohamakari Battle on page 195). It was around that time that I was contacted by other groups who wished to take up issues concerning claims for historical human rights violations. I delivered a paper to the Hero's Day Commemoration in Okahandja,

Namibia in 2005 and also presented another paper to traditional chiefs in August 2005. I have also worked with the Namibian Human Rights & Documentation Centre at the University of Namibia in Windhoek on developing their National Human Rights Institution.

However, my involvement in the field of transitional justice began more generally when I played a role as commissioner (from 1991) and then national chairperson (from 1994 to 1997) of the Human Rights Committee (formally the Human Rights Commission and before that the Detainees' Parents Support Committee) in South Africa. This organization lobbied and focused part of its work on dealing with the past and the establishment, appointment processes, and workings of the Truth and Reconciliation Commission (TRC). During the life of the TRC, I had different interactions, including attending various hearings and meetings and running a monthly seminar (together with a TRC staff member) on topics related to the TRC's work. My work has also dealt with the past, and with other transitional issues, in a number of countries, including Rwanda, Angola, Burma, the Democratic Republic of Congo, Sierra Leone, and Ethiopia.

There are many people who have helped in the process of writing this book. One person who assisted me enormously on the Herero issues in general is Malcolm Grant, who has assisted the Herero for many years. He has been generous with his time and his knowledge of the issues. Others who have assisted include Ryan Schneeberger (photographs), Casper Erichsen, Bob Kandetu, Werner Hillebrecht (Namibian National Archives), Ester Muinjangue, Kae Matundu-Tjiparuro, and Jatah Kazondu. William Kentridge graciously provided his artwork for use in the book. Attorney Phil Musolino, who has represented the Herero in the United States, has been a pleasure to work with. Maresa de Beer assisted with the editing, and I owe her a debt of gratitude.

I would like to thank my former home institution, the University of the Western Cape, in Cape Town, South Africa, and the Fletcher School of Law and Diplomacy at Tufts University in Medford, Massachusetts, where I was Visiting Professor of International Human Rights from September 2006 to June 2008. I would also like to thank the Law School at Washington and Lee University in Lexington, Virginia, who appointed me Scholar-in-Residence from January to April 2006. The then-Director of the Law Center, Professor Blake Morant, and Administrator Terry Evans were extraordinary in their hospitality and assistance to me and my family. I thank them enormously. The months I spent there gave me a considerable amount of time to research and write. I had access to a superb library, where the staff assisted me, above and beyond the call of duty, in working on this and other projects. I also want to thank the following people whose assistance was invaluable: Yousri Omar and Stephanie Yost at Washington and Lee University and Amy Cook, Joie Chowdhury, and Amy Senier at the Fletcher School at Tufts University. I would also like to thank the United Nations Development Program and the Sur Human Rights University Network for funding this project.

Greenwood Press has been wonderful, and I am indebted to them for their professionalism. I thank Robert Hutchinson for pushing this project and being a pleasure to work with.

Finally, I would like to thank my family, Rosanne, Eryn, and Hannah for their love and support.

Jeremy Sarkin
May 2008

Introduction

Until relatively recently colonial human rights abuses were regarded as morally problematic, but they did not seem to have any legal relevance. The treatment of colonial subjects was largely seen as part of the lawful process of "civilizing." Yet today there is a growing acceptance that colonial abuses may have belated legal implications, and that some of the colonizers' actions do not merely retrospectively qualify as violations but were already violations under the laws of that time.

While specific codified instruments were in their infancy in international law in the nineteenth century, international agreements existed even in international criminal law instruments such as the 1878 Lima Treaty to Establish Uniform Rules for Private International Law and the 1889 Montevideo Treaty on International Penal Law. Already at that time various branches of international law, especially international humanitarian law (1864 Geneva Convention), provided protection for individuals and groups. Additionally, international protection for individuals and groups at the time was found not only in international humanitarian law but also in other international legal regulations such as those governing slavery and piracy. The possibility of humanitarian intervention where human rights violations were occurring in other states also existed. Accordingly, there is considerable acceptance today that a number of historical occurrences are actionable as gross human rights and/or humanitarian law violations. In this regard, Elazar Barkan has stated: "Indigenous peoples have only recently become candidates to be considered victims of genocide, rather than merely vanishing people."[1]

Some would argue that colonialism's main intention was often the annihilation of indigenous peoples, but colonialism was primarily about control. The

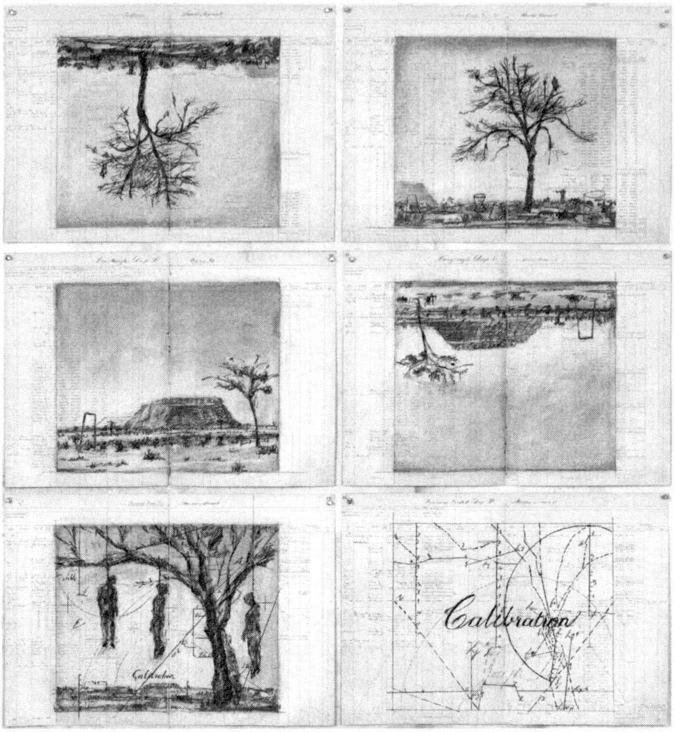

Drawing for Black Box/Chambre Noire 2005. Courtesy of William Kentridge.

predominant objective was not to exterminate, but to bring the local population under control of the colonial administration using the quickest, cheapest, and most deterring forms of violence. However, on occasion, part of the objective was to take land, and in these cases the removal or extermination of the local population was part of the intent. Interestingly, some commentators do not consider colonialism itself as a violation of international law until at least 1945,[2] and probably much later. In an attempt to establish control, the colonialists often killed hundreds of thousands of indigenous peoples as they brutally squashed rebellions. In most cases the intent of the colonialists does not meet the criteria for genocide, but their behavior could qualify today as crimes against humanity.

This book will explore issues of historical human rights violations and the possibility for reparations through the case of German colonial abuses against the Herero in then-German South West Africa (GWSA) at the turn of the twentieth century. This work will examine whether there is support in international law for the Herero claims for accountability and reparations at the time the atrocities occurred. What will be explored is whether, as some claim, by the beginning of the twentieth century various forms of genocide were already proscribed in customary international law as well as various international instruments.[3] The present work examines these issues against the background of the socio-political issues in Namibia today.

DEALING WITH THE PAST

The end of the twentieth century brought major advancements in democratization around the world. In Europe, Africa, Asia, and Latin America huge changes in the political landscape occurred, including—and partially because of—the fall of the Berlin Wall. The initial euphoria was soon counterbalanced by the imperative to address pressing and thorny issues, including how to deal with the past. For some countries, this legacy occurred recently, while in others the legacy of violence, dispossession, and abuse was of a much older vintage. The latter, those newly democratic countries with centuries-long histories of occupation and abuse, are and were forced to choose whether to deal with the past, and, if so, how.

Addressing the past is in many ways unavoidable due to its dramatic influences on the present. In the words of Faulkner: "The past is not dead. It is not even past."[4] In Namibia, as in other countries, history pervasively colors the current political landscape. As Jared Diamond has stated, Namibia "is struggling to deal with its colonial past and establish a multiracial society. Namibia illustrated for me how inseparable Africa's past is from its present."[5] Pertinent issues concern the rights, roles, and needs of minorities, especially indigenous communities; access to land and the need for land reform; and the nature of the state.

In the wake of democratization, countries with histories of undemocratic, authoritarian, and repressive rule typically have had to address past human rights violations. How the former authoritarian regimes in Eastern Europe, Latin America, and Africa were dealt with has become an international issue. Some countries, such as Chile, El Salvador, Argentina, Burundi, the Democratic Republic of the Congo, South Africa, Ghana, Morocco, Peru, Sierra Leone, and others set up truth commissions to reckon with the past. Truth commissions are constructive as they encourage victims, offenders, and the community as a whole to confront the past, and each other, in order to gain new or more comprehensive insights into what happened and why. Other countries have prosecuted violators of human rights, and some have done nothing at all.

The advent of independence for Namibia in 1990 introduced the possibility of undertaking this process and righting the wrongs committed in its past. Namibia's past reflects an atrocious history of human rights abuses as a result of German colonialism and South African apartheid that spanned more than a century. This legacy continues to haunt Namibia in many and varied ways, yet the country has chosen not to deal with the past directly, supposedly for the sake of reconciliation between the resident communities.

For a variety of political, economic, and logistical reasons the possibility to pursue claims for what had happened in the past did not present itself for Namibians before 1990. In terms of the development of relevant law at international, regional, and local levels the possibility did not exist, and such precedents as the claims of Nazi victims from WWII had not yet occurred. The arrival of independence, however, overlapped with major growth in international justice, including justice and reparations for past human rights violations in the domestic context. Accordingly, independence brought rights, and with them responsibilities, for the rehabilitation of the communities of Namibia. Among the most in need of this reckoning with the past are the Herero, who suffered severe human rights violations at the hands of their German colonizers.

For many, the need to deal with Namibia's past human rights abuses and the issue of the historical claims cannot be wished away. There have been various calls for a truth commission,[6] but the new government has resisted this pressure, claiming that dredging up the past would negatively affect the reconciliation process.[7] They even denied a request by the South African Truth and Reconciliation Commission, in 1997, to hold hearings in Namibia.[8] Some believe that the ruling party's (the South West African Peoples Organization; SWAPO) disinclination was motivated by a fear that their position might be compromised if the atrocities committed by members of their group during the fight for liberation, especially in their treatment of detainees, were exposed. Some years after independence, the fight for a truth commission has died away. As Gwen Lister argued, "The time for Namibia to have a truth commission along the lines of that in South Africa has long passed."[9] The only resurgence of this idea came in 2005 when mass graves were uncovered near the border with South Africa. These graves are believed to hold the bodies of SWAPO soldiers killed by South African security forces, although the circumstances behind the killings and the identities of those buried there remain shrouded.

Most Namibians see the land issue in Namibia as political: because the ruling party has a seventy-five percent majority and were not as affected by dispossessions as the Herero, they are not as consumed by matters of land access. The minority groups, on the other hand, are, but their position as the political opposition has allowed the ruling party to dismiss these complaints as political tactics. In truth, land questions from a hundred years ago are still very relevant today in many ways. Access to land is not only an economic issue for those dispossessed during colonial times, it is also psychological and should be interpreted within the context of "reclamation and restitution of identity and history."[10]

THE HERERO GENOCIDE

In this context, it is nearly unanimously agreed upon today that between 1904 and 1907/1908 Germany committed genocide, as legally defined, against the Herero of then-German South West Africa (GSWA), today Namibia.

The Herero genocide is unique in that the order to annihilate the Herero was publicly proclaimed and specifically made known to the target group in their own language. The official proclamation initially sought the extermination specifically of the Herero. However, other groups, especially the Nama, were later targeted because of their rich land holdings and their intransigence against the Germans. The severe treatment meted out to the Nama and the major reduction in their population numbers may also fit the definition of genocide.

German settlers in the territory who wanted the land and cattle of the indigenous Herero, and the public in Germany, incited by propaganda that the Herero were conducting a race war, bayed for Herero blood. German troops, many of whom had previously exercised brutal treatment on indigenous populations in different parts of the world, killed men, women, and children without distinction. Many other atrocities were also committed, including the rape of Herero women. These events initially occurred under the command of General Adrian Dietrich Lothar von Trotha, most likely at the instruction of Kaiser Wilhelm II—both had a history of ordering and conducting brutal extermination-type practices. von Trotha embarked on a planned, announced, systematic, and indiscriminate extermination of the Herero community.

The order to wipe out the Herero community became the first genocide of the twentieth century.[11] Between 60,000 and 100,000 people, almost all civilians and non-combatants, many of whom were women and children, were executed by German troops in various ways or were forced into the desert to die of starvation and thirst or by drinking water at water wells poisoned by German troops.

Maybe 20,000 of the original Herero population of about 100,000 were left in the end. The extermination order (*Vernichtungsbefehl)* was issued on October 2, 1904. Due to pressure on him, Kaiser Wilhelm reluctantly, and after a

German soldiers at a waterhole. Courtesy of National Archives of Namibia.

Herero hangings. Courtesy of National Archives of Namibia.

long delay, rescinded the order in December 1904; however, the acts of genocide were not limited to those few months from October 1904 to December 1904, when the official extermination order was operative. A policy of taking no Herero prisoners was in force before the official order was proclaimed, and the genocide began at least as early as August 1904. Furthermore, the eradication of the Hereros continued after the genocide order was lifted.

Herero emerging from the desert. Courtesy of National Archives of Namibia.

Initially, the genocide of the Herero would be achieved by means of German bullets and clubs, by hanging, by burning the huts where they lived, or by forcing them into the desert to die.[12]

When the order was amended, the extermination continued in a less overt manner. A few thousand Herero were captured and placed in concentration camps, where thousands died due to ill treatment, disease, and starvation. Different and smaller diet rations were given to Herero prisoners than to prisoners from other communities.

In addition, Herero prisoners were used as slave labor for both public and private enterprise. Some of the concentration camps were run by the colonial authorities, whereas others were run by private companies, such as Woermann shipping lines and Arthur Koppel Company (companies now being sued by the Herero).[13] The latter ran their own concentration camps and paid a rental fee to the German authorities for the right to use Herero slave labor in their own enterprises.

DEALING WITH THE GENOCIDE

Very little has been written about the events in then GSWA, today's Namibia, from a legal point of view. Instead, most studies have emanated from an historical or sociological standpoint.[14] Similarly, until quite recently there has been limited evaluation of historical human rights issues from a reparations and claims point of view. While the literature has grown in recent years, much work remains to be done, especially by those directly affected by the legacy of abuse. Because there are often few survivors, victims are generally neglected in genocide studies. They are hardly ever primary subjects in these studies and rarely share equal subject status with perpetrators. Referring to the lack of legal writing on the Herero genocide, Comevin has asserted that

> studies published before World War I were almost all by German authors and have essentially a documentary and didactic character. They aim at instructing the metropolitan country about the economic importance of these colonies, so rapidly acquired during the course of 1884 and 1885. Those published after 1918 are written by Germans, English, French, Americans, and Belgians, who are all more or less biased and pass moral judgements on German colonization of Africa. From 1945 onward the communist writers of East Germany come to confirm, in works written from the archives in Potsdam, the charges against German colonialism published between the two wars by English and French authors, and to utter a cry of alarm against the neocolonialism of West Germany.[15]

This was noted in 1969, but it remains the case regarding scholarship on this matter. Equally relevant to this case is the recognition in reference to the Holocaust that neglect to study atrocities is extremely harmful:

> In some ways, the effect of this academic neglect may be comparable to the damage done by those who deny the Holocaust. While I am by no means suggesting a moral

> equivalency between those who, for various reasons, omit reference to genocide and those who actively work to mislead and repress truth, I am asserting that both behaviors have somewhat similar results. That is, the failure of social scientists to adequately address the study of genocide contributes to perceptions and attitudes that, through exclusion, minimize the importance and significance of genocide. That is essentially what Holocaust denial is all about.[16]

The court cases the Herero are bringing against Germany and other actors involved at the time have brought the issues of legality to the fore. This book therefore accentuates the use of law as a means of attaining redress and reparations in the absence of a political or negotiated resolution between the parties. It examines the specific political context, which precluded a negotiated settlement but which recently saw a few tentative steps towards finding some accommodation. For example, the German government offered an apology at the hundredth anniversary of the major battle between the Herero and Germany at the Waterberg on August 11, 1904. Yet the apology was tentative and limited in scope, as Germany sought to avoid opening a Pandora's Box of possible legal consequences, which a comprehensive apology admitting guilt might have caused. The apology is examined against the theoretical and contextual issues that surround apologies and forgiveness. Despite the attention brought by the Herero court cases, the plethora of research on the genocides of Europe over the last century would indicate that European genocide is thought more worthy of study than genocide in other, often less developed, regions of the world.[17]

The present study surveys the legal interpretations of the events that took place between 1904 and 1908, acknowledging that much research remains to be done. While many studies address the question of whether the events constitute genocide, they do not evaluate these claims in terms of legal principles and international law. This book aims to rectify the common misconception that genocide and other international crimes did not constitute crimes at the time they were perpetrated on the Herero.

The historiography on Germany and GSWA has often been biased against the Herero by relying almost exclusively on German sources. Even authors with a more expansionist and critical view have often relied on German sources. Bley, for example, noted that the sources for his 1971 book were "almost entirely derived from the European side."[18] Since then there has been a growth in research on colonialism and specifically on the Herero War, but many of the accounts still depend and focus on the writings and testimonies from the German side. Very recently, a more balanced picture has emerged, drawing from a wider array of sources, including the accounts of indigenous persons. However, a distinguishing feature of the Herero genocide (and most other African genocides or those that occurred in the political south[19]) is the absence of accounts given by victims. Among the European examples, such as the Armenian genocide, survivors on the other hand often constitute the main source material on the genocide.[20] In this case, the German efficiency and penchant for good administration yielded numerous reports. Until recently, this documentation formed the bulk of source material available to authors. Because they are perpetrator accounts they are accompanied by justificatory rationalizations as well as insight into the thinking and intent behind specific deeds.

A few eyewitness accounts do exist, and some victim accounts are found in the Blue Book that recorded accounts of the atrocities committed during the Herero War.[21] Since the British produced the Blue Book during World War I, in which they fought against the Germans, reservations about its objectivity remain. However, the sentiments contained in the 1918 report were already present in a British report of 1909, which stated:

> The great aim of German policy in German South West Africa, as regards the native, is to reduce him to a state of serfdom, and, where he resists, to destroy him altogether. The native, to the German, is a baboon and nothing more. The war against the Hereros, conducted by General Trotha, was one of extermination; hundreds—men, women, and children—were driven into desert country, where death from thirst was their end; whose [sic] left over are now in great locations near Windhuk, where they eke out a miserable existence; labour is forced upon them and naturally is unwillingly performed.[22]

In August 1912, another British foreign office official commented:

> In view of the cruelty, treachery, [and] commercialism by which the German colonial authorities have gradually reduced their natives to the status of cattle (without so much of a flutter being caused among English peace loving philanthropists) the [Portuguese] S. Thome agitation in its later phases against a weak [and] silly nation without resources is the more sickening. These Hereros were butchered by thousands during the war & have been ruthlessly flogged into subservience since.[23]

Given that many British government reports predating World War I mention these same issues, the contents of the Blue Book cannot solely be regarded as the propaganda of a nation at war. Certainly, the timing of the report directly relates to the war. If the war had not taken place, the reports of the atrocities might not have been collected and chronicled in this way, but the war context per se does not reduce the veracity of its findings.

Thus, this book examines the legal and socio-legal issues around these matters. The analysis is guided by the position that the killings were not only international crimes from a present-day perspective, but were already international crimes at the time. Therefore, reparations for what occurred are due to the victims today. The present study views these atrocities in the context of the developing norms of reparations internationally, regionally, and domestically, and the development of historical claims in general. It appraises the Herero genocide events in light of the current critical legal issues regarding the extent to which international law affects historical claims for reparations.

The book also examines the effect of the genocide on Namibia today and what the Herero are doing to attain redress. It will explore the state of reparations theory and practice around the world, as well as the role of apologies in coming to terms with the past, referencing the apology Germany gave to the Herero in 2004. Critically, the genocide had a major effect on Herero population numbers. Today Herero number about 100,000, roughly the same as they did before the genocide. As a result of the genocide, they constitute less than ten percent of the Namibian population, which puts them in a hugely inferior position in relation to the majority Owambo group, which constitutes about fifty-five percent of the population and is the predominant support base of the ruling SWAPO political party. It is estimated that had the genocide not taken place, Herero numbers would be four or five times greater today, and they would thus be a major political force in Namibia.[24] In this way the genocide dramatically influenced current political power positions in Namibia. It has had, and still has, major economic effects on the land and cattle, and the identity of those groups who depend on them. Clearly and inevitably, the genocide has had dramatic effects on the Herero and on Namibia. As a result, the possibility of reparations for historical violations of human rights has emerged. In determining the likelihood that this could become reality, the reasons for the genocide, how it took place, and the impact it has had and continues to have today are all highly relevant factors.

INTERNATIONAL LAW TODAY AND IN 1904

In light of the cases the Herero have filed in the United States of America against Germany and German corporations, this book focuses on the legal interpretations of the terms and events that are likely to be applied by the various courts or tribunals. It looks at the legal definitions of genocide, crimes against humanity, and other international crimes, and both factually and legally considers whether the events indeed constitute genocide and/or other international crimes. This consideration involves determining whether the intentions were genocidal, whether genocide actually occurred, and what crimes the events would represent in today's legal terms. The central question is accordingly addressed: were the atrocities committed against the Herero by Germany already violations of international law and thereby considered international crimes at the time? It will be argued that they indeed were, both in terms of customary law and the various international treaties that were in force at the time. The present study argues that applicable international law, international human rights law, international humanitarian law, and international criminal law existed by 1904.

The classical view of the protection of the rights of individuals is that while international humanitarian law and international human rights law have much in common, they stem from completely different roots. Humanitarian law originates from the relations between states, whereas human rights law is derived from the relations between a government and the people of a particular state.[25] It is often argued that human rights law only recently developed, out of the conduct that occurred during World War II. Others counter this extremely limited view of the development of international law and proclaim that the origins of human rights law go back a few hundred, if not a few thousand, years. Although one could refine the argument by stressing that it was only since World War II that a formal system for enforcing the protection of individual rights existed, the rights themselves have had a long vintage. Thus, while few international mechanisms to protect rights or prosecute perpetrators existed before World War II, it was accepted that rights were protected at the very least in customary law. The mechanisms predating World War II will be explored later.

Despite this classical view of the distinct geneses of international humanitarian law and international human rights law, the two sets of legal principles actually derive from similar origins and overlap to a large degree. In this regard, the African Commission on Human and Peoples Rights has observed that both types of laws are based on the same principles and that "human rights and IHL [international humanitarian law] have always, even in different situations, aimed at protecting human beings and their fundamental rights."[26] Similarly, Mazzeschi argues that "the protection of human rights is, after all, the ultimate goal of the rules of international criminal law and humanitarian law."[27] Consequently, the principles of both may apply simultaneously in the sense that the law relating to international and domestic human rights protection remains in force even in times of war "as long as it is not superseded by the law of armed conflict or derogated according to the applicable rules of international human rights law."[28] There are crucial reasons why the laws of war and those that apply during times of peace differ and require distinct legal classifications. Yet it must be understood that they overlap and that, at times, both sets of principles may apply. Dolzer suggests, "The special status of the laws of war in international law entails that damages arising out of war must also be considered to be distinct and separate from damages that occur in peacetime."[29] However, damages are obtainable for harm that occurs during both.

This book will argue that crimes against humanity and genocide already constituted crimes at the time of the Herero genocide, although they were not known by those names. The word "genocide" entered usage in the 1940s, but the concept of the crime dates back thousands of years and was certainly an internationally accepted violation by the turn of the twentieth century. Furthermore, although crimes against humanity and genocide did not lead to criminal liability, specifically for individuals, civil liability and state responsibility for their commission were already in existence. The principles from which these crimes emerged existed in international law, were acknowledged by the international community, and were called upon periodically by 1900. This does not mean that the law only applies retrospectively (although it can), but that these norms were applicable at the time either through treaty or customary law obligations. Select supporters of historical reparations argue that some legal rules ensure retrospective liability for states, as they have become *jus cogens* norms.[30]

According to Jochnick and Normand, "Until the nineteenth century, the residual remains of chivalry, the non-binding theoretical treatises of the publicists, and the slow accretions of customary restraints derived from state practice comprised the legal framework governing conduct in war."[31] The various Hague Conventions and Geneva Conventions including those of 1864, 1899, 1906, and 1907, all of which were signed and ratified by Germany, as well as customary law already in force, protected against certain types of conduct during wartime. Although treaty law was somewhat deficient at the time, customary law was a critical component of these protections.

Although the 1949 Geneva Conventions and their "Common Article 3" detailing basic humanitarian rules, which must be respected in internal armed conflicts,[32] were not in force, the Conventions are a codification of customary law that existed long before 1949. These rules offered protection to those who had already laid down their arms and to others, including civilians, who were never part of the conflict.

Another question the book will examine is the jurisdiction of various courts and tribunals to deal with and apply laws to crimes that supposedly did not exist at the time of their commission, and whether such treatment is a retrospective application of the law. A number of courts, including the International Court of Justice and the European Court of Human Rights, have determined that they will examine issues predating their founding. While the Human Rights Committee (HRC), the treaty body of the International Covenant on Civil and Political Rights (ICCPR), has not been willing to apply its jurisdiction quite so widely, it has been willing to examine matters which occurred even before a particular state party accepted its jurisdiction to do so, provided that the violation is ongoing. The possibility of approaching such bodies is evaluated in Chapter Three in order to gauge the probability of success for the Herero claims, as well as for historical claims in general.

Germany's international obligations were governed by the many treaties it was party to, including the Hague Conventions of 1899 and its regulations as well as the Convention for the Amelioration of the Condition of the Wounded and Sick in Armies in the Field of July 6, 1906 (updating the 1864 Convention), which Germany signed on July 6, 1906 and ratified on May 27, 1907. The effects of those treaties are examined in the context of the Herero killings to establish what obligations were violated at the time.

The context and content of the Martens Clause in the 1899 and 1907 Hague Conventions are examined in detail to determine its effect on the development of protections available at the time, specifically as it represented the origin of the notion of crimes against humanity and genocide. By 1899 (and before), there were major concerns about the growing horrors of war, so much so that the 1899 Peace Conference was regarded as "epochmaking."[33] The various treaties that entered into force were designed to regulate what types of war states could conduct and to ensure that certain types of warfare were prohibited. In the 1950s, Hersch Lauterpacht noted: "We shall utterly fail to understand the true character of the law of war unless we are to realize that its purpose is almost entirely humanitarian in the literal sense of the word, namely to prevent or mitigate suffering and, in some cases, to rescue life from the savagery of battle and passion. This, and not the regulation and direction of hostilities, is its essential purpose."[34] Similarly, Josef L. Kunz emphasized that "the whole law of war, including the norms regulating its actual conduct, is humanitarian in character; it is in the truest sense a part of the law for the protection of human rights."[35] In light of the Hague Conventions, Chapter Two will probe whether the *si omnes* clause, which provided that the treaty would not apply if one of the parties in a conflict was not party to it, renders the Convention inapplicable to the Herero situation—given that the Herero were not a party to that treaty.

Some additional questions the book takes up are whether the events happened in the context of a war and whether the conflict was international or domestic in nature. This is important because the status of the conflict (i.e., whether it was an international armed conflict) governs which protections apply. Humanitarian law is widely seen to apply in international armed conflict, but insurgent groups involved in non-international armed conflict are not entitled to the same protections as combatants.[36] It is proposed that the war was indeed an international armed conflict because most of the peace treaties signed with the local inhabitants, including some of the Herero chiefs, never entailed the loss of sovereignty. The concept of sovereignty and its relevance to the Herero at the beginning of the twentieth century will be discussed in Chapter One. Although Germany claimed control over the territory under international law, clearly the whole territory was not under its sovereignty. For example, the area in the North where the Owambo live, which Germany was not able to bring under control, other territories where specifically negotiated protection treaties applied—with limited effect, and areas in which no protection treaties were in force were not subject to German authority. At least until 1904, many parts of GSWA were not under German sovereignty. In many parts of the territory, even within German-controlled areas, a dual legal system operated. In fact, the Germans were still signing protection treaties for tracts of land with various communities in GSWA in 1908.[37] The issue of sovereignty is further discussed below.

The debate over whether events constitute a crime against humanity when the armed conflict is of an international character (and not merely an internal one) is, thus, ongoing.[38] Previously, an international war context might have been a prerequisite for violations to be considered crimes against humanity, but that is no longer the case. The link to war is no longer necessary. In fact, the very existence of such a requirement in the past is currently questioned. This nexus requirement emerges from interpretations of the Nuremberg Charter, the statutes of the International Criminal Tribunal for Rwanda (ICTR), the International Criminal Tribunal for Yugoslavia (ICTY), and the International Criminal Court (ICC). While the debate often centers on the way these statutes have changed the requirement over the years, only the Nuremberg Charter, which was drafted after World War II, contained the war nexus requirement, as the crimes to be prosecuted at Nuremberg were those that had occurred specifically during that war. Furthermore, as Fenrick has argued: "No treaty or statutory instrument defines crimes against humanity in such a way that the offence specifically applies to conduct of hostilities situations."[39]

WAS IT A REBELLION OR A WAR?

Much of the debate in the academic literature centers on the reasons for the Herero rebellion, specifically whether it was a planned revolt. Most writers accept that what happened between 1904 and 1908 constitutes genocide. Yet a few denialists maintain that the events in question were no different from what happened to other indigenous groups in various colonial territories occupied by the French, Dutch, Belgians, British, Italians, and the people in today's United States. Given these opposing views, the precise nature of these events is evaluated.

The categorization of the German-Herero conflict has significant legal ramifications. Whether it was a rebellion, a war, an uprising, civil war, or an international armed conflict affects what legal principles apply. The term "rebellion" is especially problematic, as it implies that German supremacy and sovereignty existed.[40]

Gewald argues that the conflict was the result of misunderstandings prompted by the panic of a colonial official and "the self-fulfilling prophecy of Herero War that existed within the mind of settler paranoia."[41] According to him, the Herero did not initiate the war, but took up arms in response to actions taken against them. Melber concurs that the "uprising" was an act of self-defense.[42] Lundtofte also remarks that "it may be advanced that it was not the Herero, but the Germans themselves who conjured up the conflict."[43] Gewald further contends that the Germans not only instigated the "war" without provocation or cause, but also prolonged it after the conflict had essentially spent itself.[44] The uprising concluded by April 1904, but negotiations between the parties were barred because von Trotha and German troop reinforcements had yet to arrive. In effect, the war restarted after von Trotha arrived in June 1904. If these views have any validity, then the indigenous population did not rise up or capriciously prolong the war. If the Germans had indeed started the war in January 1904, Germany would certainly be liable for violations of the terms of various protection treaties. As Shelton has noted, this would fall under the state action doctrine.[45]

Regardless of whether the Herero started or continued the war, they had cause to rise up. Not only were they poorly treated, but they were rapidly losing their land, and the threat of losing even more land and being forced into small reserves loomed large.[46] Some recent literature contends that the Herero were not in danger of losing their land, but this danger was no mere perception on their part. There were clearly moves afoot to place at least some of the Herero in reserves. While it might be argued that placing the Herero in reserves was for their protection, Berlin and the settlers undoubtedly envisioned a much more drastic land policy. In fact, the settlers in GSWA and Germans back home generally demanded a much more draconian policy towards the African population than the more humane and accommodating policy adhered to and enforced by Governor Theodor Leutwein. The colonialists vociferously attacked him and his lenient policies, and demanded his replacement. Leutwein recognized that his political strategies were in danger,[47] and the Herero knew of the demands for change. They were aware of the meetings taking place in GSWA and Germany, and they knew about the public pronouncements. With the knowledge that it was only a matter of time before Leutwein would be removed, the threat to the Herero land holdings intensified. Perhaps the settlers' objectives would not have been carried out immediately, but the manifest intent was to dispossess increasingly more Herero and give their land to the settlers. The threat perceived by the Herero preceding the rebellion was not paranoia but a certainty that materialized swiftly and to such an extent that the Herero lost all their land and cattle, and the majority lost their lives. As Pakendorf has noted, Germany sought to take the Herero's land for white settlers, because theirs was the most suitable for agriculture. Documents in the Windhoek Archives indicate that this was the intention of the colonial administration from early on, when various initiatives were aimed at subjugating those living in the territory.[48]

As stated earlier, establishing whether the events legally constituted a war, and if so whether it was international or domestic, will determine what laws are applicable. If there were no war, the laws of war would clearly not apply. In historical documents, the German authorities referred to the events as a war, but also described the insurrection as a rebellion and the Herero as rebels. An important factor in determining the legal status of the conflict is whether GSWA was under the sovereignty of Germany. The determination is complicated because of the many peace treaties signed between chiefs and the German authorities, some of which permitted the chiefs to retain authority. Questions arise as to the extent of those treaties and whether they permitted sovereignty to be exercised over the Herero. Certainly the treaties permitted trade and other types of developments and gave the Germans authority over the white people in the area, but whether they extended or limited control over the Herero is debatable. GSWA was a German protectorate, but it is questionable whether all of its parts were considered German territory. One could make the argument that it was under German control because the territory had been given to Germany at the Berlin Conference. Were this the case, the hostilities would have constituted a non-international armed conflict and the Herero warriors would be considered rebels. Under the law of war, they could not be classified as combatants. Of importance is that martial law was declared over the whole of the protectorate,[49] even before von Trotha arrived. It would appear, therefore, that the German authorities considered the conflict a war.

Melber has termed the events between the Germans and the Herero the "German-Namibian War."[50] Acknowledging that the use of the word "Namibia" did not emerge until the 1960s, his preference is motivated by political reasons.[51] Alexander has called it "the first war of anti-colonial resistance."[52] It was undeniably a resistance conflict, but given the size of the force that was eventually pitted against the Herero and the type of arms and methods used against them, one can hardly classify such a one-sided affair as a war. Other terms, such as "massacre," "slaughter," and "annihilation" seem more apt, as would the term "genocide." Although the first few months of the conflict might fit the description of a war, thereafter the conflict involved a superior force hunting down its opponents and wiping them out by all means possible. As von Trotha stated, "any means fair or foul" were used. Thus, some analysts, the Herero, and others in Namibia regard the conflict as a war of resistance, but for the Germans it was a war of conquest and subjugation.

The issue over labeling the Herero conflict as a war has other consequences. Were it defined as a war, then if the Herero were thought to also violate the rules of war, Germany could claim that Herero warriors could lawfully be denied various protections afforded by the law of war. Thus, captured Herero would not have had to be treated as prisoners of war, for example, because they did not conduct operations in accordance with the laws and customs of war as laid down in article 1 of the 1899 Hague Convention (11).

von Trotha insisted all along that Germany was fighting a "race war."[53] However, the veracity and extent of the alleged Herero atrocities on settlers and German troops are questionable. In fact, evidence shows that the Herero went out of their way to avoid killing women and children. In the first months of 1904 the colonial authorities and the government in Berlin went on a propaganda offensive in Germany regarding the conduct of the Herero. The alleged widespread mutilation of German corpses seems to have been mere propaganda. The Rhenish Missionary Kuhlman investigated the majority of such reports and found them to be false. Even Hauptman Francke, who in a 1920 lecture stated that he had seen many corpses, argued that the allegations had no basis. Although there might have been isolated cases of such conduct, it would appear that these allegations were predominantly racist propaganda.[54] It is likely that members of the German media propagated these supposed mutilations in order to promote a racial dimension to the events in GSWA, thereby ensuring support for the intended actions of the German authorities.

In reality, the abuse and mutilation came mostly from the German forces. Bringing back severed hands and other body parts was a method approved by the field commanders and sanctioned by German officials, uniformly carried out by soldiers under German control as a way of proving to their commanders that they had killed who they said they had.[55] In an unpublished manuscript titled *The Germans in Africa*,[56] Raphael Lemkin, thought by many to be the author of the word genocide and the impetus behind the Genocide Convention, notes that before the events in GSWA in 1904, mutilations practiced by local soldiers against the indigenous population were sanctioned by the German officials who ordered the soldiers to bring back the ears of those they killed to prove the number killed. Lemkin writes that because the ears of women were used to increase the numbers, German commander Dominik ordered that the heads of those killed be brought back instead. The difficulty of accomplishing this led to the use of genitals instead. This practice so horrified the British government that it complained to the German Ambassador in London in 1902. The Imperial Chancellor wrote to the Governor of the Cameroons asking for an end to this practice and "to abstain in all instances from illegal acts and cruelties towards the natives and during any necessary punitive expeditions to abstain from all habits incompatible with the civilized state, such as the mutilation of corpses."[57]

WHEN DID THE WAR START AND FINISH?

Determining the beginning and end dates of the war is legally relevant, as the regulations of the 1899 Hague Convention and the 1907 Hague Convention may be applicable. Under these two instruments, which demarcated permissible behavior during wartime, certain types of conduct perpetrated in 1904 or later might have already been illegal. The relevant question is whether these regulations could apply, given that the Convention required both parties in the conflict to be party to it. Although Germany was a party to the Convention, the Herero were not. Having said that, these issues must, and will be, examined through a much wider lens. The Hague Conventions, as well as other instruments from before 1899, were indicative of customary international law. Thus, the principles contained in the treaties were already proscribed in both treaty law and customary law. Even if one successfully argues that the treaties did not apply, customary law did. Furthermore, the Martens Clause is applicable, given that it was considered the minimum standard that must be applied in the absence of treaty law provisions.

Another important question is whether international law covered conflicts of a non-international nature. The war certainly had international dimensions because many of the Herero were not under the sovereignty of Imperial Germany. The fact that the Herero were supplied arms by other countries also affords the conflict international status. Even if all the above arguments are cast aside, the protection treaties render the war "state action" and Germany is therefore liable in terms of its domestic law.

The end date of the war is significant because Germany adopted the 1907 Hague Convention while the war was ongoing. The Convention makes provision for individual reparations to civilians for damage suffered during wartime. Ironically, the German delegation to the conference proposed this provision.

The generally accepted dates of the Herero War (or genocide), derived from German reports and accounts, are 1904 to 1907. But these dates are questionable. Although the genocide primarily occurred in 1904, the extinction continued well into 1905 through actions such as maintaining the military cordon, which forced the Herero into the desert to starve. Even though the war officially ended in 1907,[58] killings of Herero and other indigenous people took place until 1908. Only at that time were Herero prisoners released. In fact, the period from 1907 to 1915 is described as a period of suffering and misery.[59] Dreschler described it as the "peace of the graveyard."[60] By then, Herero society had collapsed and the Germans "made sure that the Herero were widely dispersed, that all tribal connections, both political and cultural, were destroyed, and that their symbols, the oxen, the insignia, and chiefs were destroyed. Towns and settlements which had carried Herero names were renamed."[61]

The traditional view is that the Herero rose up in revolt in January 1904. According to Du Pisani the war occurred between 1902 and 1907, though he groups the Nama[62] and Herero rebellions together.[63] However, the questions of who instigated the war and when it commenced are further complicated by earlier instances of indigenous resistance to German occupation. In March 1896, the Mbanderu and the Khaus, two other indigenous groups living in Namibia at the time, rebelled. Other tribes also rebelled, including the Bondelswartz in 1903.[64] In 1904, in addition to the rebellions by the Herero, Nama, and Bondelswartz, the Franzmanns, the Red Nation, and the Veldschoendragers also rebelled. For strategic reasons, others, like the Berseba and the Keetmanshoop, refused to participate. The Bethanie chief initially refused to participate as well, but his tribe defied him and joined in. The Rehoboths, however, decided it was more advantageous for them to support the Germans.[65]

Despite the general belief that the Owambos did not rebel or participate in the uprising, they in fact did. On January 28, 1904, 500 Owambo attacked Fort Namutoni, which was defended by seven German soldiers. These seven soldiers managed to defend the fort; only one of them was wounded, but 150 Owambos were killed. Presumably this crushing defeat caused the Owambos to withdraw from further participation in the rebellion.[66]

As mentioned before, the supposed end date of the war—1907—is subject to debate. Sole, for example, claims that the war ended in 1908.[67] Although the Bondelswartz stopped fighting in late 1906, others, such as the Franzmanns, continued thereafter. In February 1907, the commander of the German troops stated that he was not against the "lifting of the state of war in South West Africa until the end of March."[68] This decision was motivated by the negative impact that the war was having on the economy and the belief that the protracted nature of the war was denting the pride and prestige of the German military. Therefore, even though combat continued, the state of warfare was publicly rescinded on March 31, 1907. However, resistance leaders such as Jakob Morenga and Simon Kooper continued their attacks.[69] In fact, the battle waged by Jakob Morenga continued until he was killed on September 20, 1907. Masson notes this date and the death of Jakob Morenga, arguing that this was "to the Germans the final act in the suppression of the great Herero-Nama insurrection of 1904–7."[70]

Yet a further viewpoint is that of Jan-Bart Gewald, who argues that 1908 is the more accurate end-of-war date because it marked the last activity against

Chief Witbooi, Governor Leutwein, and Chief Maherero. Courtesy of National Archives of Namibia.

Simon Kooper[71] and the closure of the concentration camps.[72] The war certainly continued into 1908 when the Bondelswartz resumed attacks and carried out numerous operations. On December 22, 1908, Deputy Governor Oskar Hintrager noted that there was a "current state of constant insecurity".[73] Simon Kooper only agreed to enter into a peace agreement brokered by the British Bechuanaland police in February 1909. Furthermore, there is even evidence of German patrols against the Herero in the Omaheke desert until 1911.[74] In summary, the evidence and viewpoints cited above clearly challenge claims that the war ended definitively in 1907.

Part of the difficulty in determining when the war ended is the question of what constitutes an end to a war. Does it require all hostilities to have been concluded or only the major conflicts? What does it mean when no end to a war is announced or no peace treaty is signed? Alternatively, does the closing of concentration camps signify the end of a war? Even if the latter applies, in this case it is still problematic as hostilities and acts of aggression continued beyond 1908. One further bit of evidence pointing to 1908 as the end of the war is Germany's own position as reflected in the 2005 announcement, in which Germany had agreed to give Namibia $25 million for development and reconciliation "in order to heal the wounds left by the brutal colonial wars of 1904 to 1908."[75]

INDIGENOUS RIGHTS

In recent years, attention to the rights of indigenous people has dramatically increased. On September 13, 2007, the UN General Assembly adopted the UN Declaration on the Rights of Indigenous Peoples.[76] Further, the fate of indigenous groups, specifically the continuing impact of historical legacies, is frequently addressed in contemporary academic writing. Determining which groups should be classified as indigenous people remains controversial, but Paul Keal argues that such groups define themselves and are defined by others "in terms of a common experience of subjection to colonial settlement."[77] Thus, the link to colonial times is viewed as a critical component. The effect of that common denominator, as James Anaya has noted, is that today indigenous peoples around the world usually live in circumstances of severe disadvantage in relation to others living around them. He argues that "historical phenomena grounded on racially discriminatory attitudes are not just blemishes of the past but rather translate into current inequities," and that common to most indigenous peoples was the dispossession of their enormous landholdings and other resources.[78]

Anaya's comments apply directly to the situation of the Herero in Namibia today. Although this study does not squarely address the rights of contemporary indigenous peoples, it explores the pervasive impact of the German-Herero conflict on Namibia and specifically on the Herero in terms of land, poverty, and development. It evaluates the status of indigenous states during the colonial era to determine the relationship between colonialism and international law. The present book looks at the effects of the historical events and how they pertain to the Herero's rights and current claims for reparations.

REPARATIONS

While the literature emerging from former colonized countries remains limited, there have been momentous developments for victims' reparation theory over the last few years. However, these theoretical advances have not always translated into real payments to victims of gross human rights abuses, particularly of historic human rights violations. Despite growing sentiment about the need to prosecute the perpetrators, even in states other than where the abuse occurred, victim compensation has not received much practical attention, especially not for historical claims. Although victims are able to sue, a range of obstacles hamper the prospects of success in any case. Additionally, victims in the less privileged parts of the world have difficulty raising the necessary finances to bring such cases, as few systems permit lawyers to act on contingency fee arrangements, and where they do, lawyers often refuse to enter into such arrangements unless there is some guarantee of success. Even if victims successfully sue a perpetrator, the likelihood that they will be able to collect on such a judgment is very small. Hardly any of the few successful cases brought in a small number of jurisdictions have resulted in specific payments to the victims.

As developments are occurring with regard to reparations, those who seek redress for historic human rights violations committed in the colonial era are examining the relevant origins and applicability of international law. As the number of such cases increases, various courts around the world have been asked to apply international law to these matters to determine whether reparations are due for atrocities committed long ago.

Claimants use international law in these court applications, partly for political reasons, partly because it is often easier to use international law when trying to comply with the jurisdictional requirements of certain courts and partly because claimants seek various alternative and novel routes to achieve success in such cases. Though the abuse of the Herero occurred decades before World War II and the protections that followed that war, complainants can use customary international law norms and early treaty law to show that the crimes committed against their ancestors were just that—crimes in violation of international law. Using this as a foundation, the descendants of the indigenous peoples who were exploited, abused, and even murdered on the command of foreign governments can seek redress and request reparations in the courts today.

While many claim that international law in its infancy failed to provide protections to individuals, it did in fact provide such protections more than a hundred years ago. International protection for individuals and groups was found then not only in international humanitarian law, but in other branches of the law as well, such as the international legal structures providing protection for minorities and against slavery and piracy. Humanitarian intervention in fact took place where human rights violations occurred against minorities within other states during the 1800s. Accordingly, there is considerable acceptance today that a number of historical occurrences are actionable as gross human rights and/or humanitarian law violations for what happened in the past.

Thus, by the turn of the twentieth century, the international community enjoyed the synergistic benefit of two forces at work. On one hand, there was increasing state practice in the domestic punishment of violations of the laws of war. Contemporaneously, the international community had reached an agreement at the Hague Peace Conference for the first multilateral conventions regulating the conduct of war. The combination of these developments resulted in a growing recognition and acceptance of the principle of individual culpability for violations of the international law of war crimes.[79]

The Herero cases, as well as the recent growth in the number of other claims relating to historic human rights violations, indicate that other such cases will likely be brought in the future. It is also probable that claimants will access other new forums besides the United States, as the courts there are generally conservative and relatively indisposed towards these types of cases. It is equally likely that the public relations aspects of these cases will increase as the lessons of the successful Holocaust litigation strategies of the 1990s are absorbed. It is already apparent that Germany has been forced to deal with the Herero because of the sustained pressure the Herero have brought to bear over at least the last ten years. The Herero realize that these cases may take time to succeed and are seeking alternative strategies and forums to bring their case. The Namibian government also has a key role to play in determining the direction of the case. While it has been historically unsympathetic to the case, there seems to have been a recent thaw due to new Namibian President Hifikepunye Pohamba's closer historical ties to the Herero. His unwillingness to sign an agreement with Germany over a reconciliation fund without first consulting the affected groups could indicate this new direction.

In this context the Herero claims for reparations are examined not only in terms of their historical validity but also in terms of the current political landscape. How does the historical and current relationship between Germany and Namibia impact the Herero claims for reparations from Germany? What priority do the Herero and their claims assume in present-day Namibia, given the precedence accorded by the Namibian government to issues of national reconciliation? The final chapter addresses the developing norm of reparations around the world and the cases brought by the Herero. It also looks at the possibilities of future cases by the Herero and other victims of international crimes in various fora. The chapter examines the developing norms of reparations for historical claims and argues that reparations by states to individuals are not new; they have existed in international law for at least a century. The belief that international law only applied between states, and that individuals must obtain reparations through their state, is re-examined revealing a contrary view, as is the notion that 100 years ago international law did not permit individuals to make claims directly to foreign states and other relevant bodies. The chapter also addresses the related issue of when claims become superannuated and shows that in cases where atrocities occurred more than fifty years ago it is relatively common for such claims to be paid. In addition, claims pertaining to events dating back to 150 years have recently been granted. While these payouts have occurred due to settlements and not court judgments, the process of court filings has assisted them. This is particularly true of the Holocaust cases filed in the 1990s, which saw huge payouts to victims of World War II. The Holocaust cases are significant given that Germany has paid over $100 billion to World War II victims. It continues to pay out more than a billion dollars annually. Furthermore, Germany even paid claims in 1904 to settlers living in GSWA.

The influence of the past and specifically the Herero-German war on the socio-economic climate of present-day Namibia cannot be overstated. Land holdings remain one of the major sources of tension and conflict in the country. German farmers still hold the majority of large arable farms. Land issues, the current political context, and the enduring effects of the genocide on the Herero, their memory, and identity are explored.

At present, gross human rights abuse is addressed globally with new vigor. The last ten years have seen major developments in international criminal processes.[80] Internationally, regionally, and domestically, accountability for these violations, a major problem in the past, has improved to some degree.[81] With the establishment of the ICTY,[82] the ICTR,[83] the ICC,[84] and the African Court of Human Rights[85] the prospects for prosecuting perpetrators of gross human rights violations are increasingly likely.

While it has virtually become a platitude, it bears repeating that colonialism, its ideologies, and its practices left indelible imprints on the physical, social, political, economical, and psychological landscapes of the colonized territories.[86] The colonial legacy is invariably one of poverty, underdevelopment, and marginalization.[87] Recently, human rights agendas have seen dramatic transformations, with apologies and reparation for the abuses of colonialism, slavery, and other violations firmly established. Due to these new sensibilities and possibilities, many former colonies are reappraising the past in order to establish what was done to whom, by whom, and at what cost. This retrospection has spawned a great number of truth commissions. In Africa alone truth commissions have been held in South Africa, Nigeria, Ghana, Chad, the Democratic Republic of Congo, Burundi, Liberia, Morocco, Sierra Leone, Zimbabwe, and Uganda. Algeria and Kenya are presently considering similar institutions.

Despite this push by once colonized peoples to seek reparations and compensation from past colonizers, it is unlikely that these countries will give effect to such claims.[88] Most regard such tactics as political rather than legal, and many believe that if there is in fact any liability, obligations are met through development aid. However, in many cases, including Namibia, development aid does not equal reparations. Moreover, aid is often used to fund projects in areas that are not primarily populated by the victimized groups, such as the Herero, the Nama, and the Damara.

Both the former-colonizers and their victims recognize that state immunity remains an encumbrance in exacting accountability. As a result, it has become practice for victims to target the multinational corporations that conducted business in these territories historically, claiming they benefited directly or indirectly from the violations. The increased likelihood that national courts even in third countries will permit this type of litigation has increased the number of cases targeting these institutions.

Finally, given that the Germans took much of the Herero's land before, during, and after the war, their claims not only relate to the atrocities perpetrated on them but also to land claims against the Germans and Germany. Certainly, major questions about the indigenous land rights of the Herero remain.[89]

TERMINOLOGY

The terms "reparation" or "compensation" are in use here, although other terms can and have been used. "Reparation" and "compensation" are appropriate in a legal context, as courts usually award victims damages for harm suffered in the form of a financial payment. "Reparation" can encompass a variety of concepts, including damages, redress, restitution, compensation, rehabilitation, and satisfaction. Each of these concepts has a unique meaning, although they are often used as general terms to encompass all the different types of remedies available to a victim. "Compensation" or "damages" typically signify an amount of money awarded by a court or other body for harm suffered. "Restitution" signifies a return to the situation before the harm occurred, "rehabilitation" denotes provision of medical or other types of treatment, and "satisfaction" indicates acknowledgements, apologies, and the like.

The word "reparation" was first used in the Versailles Treaty at the conclusion of World War I, but the notion of payment for harm caused is an old concept. Throughout the ages many peace agreements contained provisions that forced one side to pay the other some type of damages or give up land or some other item to compensate a state that suffered damage.

1

The Legacy of the Herero Genocide on Namibia Today

> Past atrocities visited upon a people linger in the collective memory of humanity as if mass death takes on an ethereal life of its own.[1]

This chapter contextualizes the current situation in Namibia in terms of what occurred 100 years ago, as the present position of the Herero and other minority groups directly relates to the legacy of German colonialism. The most prominent effects are seen in population numbers: had the genocide not occurred, the Herero and the Nama would almost certainly have amounted to more than ten percent of the current Namibian population.

The chapter looks at how the history, geography, and demography of Namibia shaped and produced the genocide. A brief history of Namibia is given, concentrating on the circumstances preceding the arrival of the Germans, particularly the demographic and land possession patterns of indigenous groups. These are then compared to the present land holdings of indigenous groups to determine the contemporary legacy of German colonialism. The land ownership theme runs through most of this book, as it is argued that the German interest in the territory, especially toward the end of the nineteenth century and the beginning of the twentieth century, was determined by land. The dominant motivation of the Herero-German War was to dispossess the Herero of their land and cattle and for these to be given to German settlers who were to create "a new Germany" in Africa.

The current patterns of land ownership, wealth, and poverty show a huge disparity between white and black people. These patterns mirror land dispossession by confiscation in 1904 and 1905. Present land ownership by German farmers is examined in the context of the slow pace of land reform and the Namibian government's ambiguous position: it supports land reform, but is seemingly unwilling to address the historical dispossession of various minority groups. The merits of the government's position, namely that reconciliation takes priority and opening the wounds of the past would be counterproductive, is explored.

This chapter also looks at which indigenous groups exist in Namibia, where they live, and from where they originate. The status of these groups is examined in terms of the current political situation and key political issues that are part of the legacy of the Herero-German war. These issues are critical as they affect the Namibian state's response (or lack of a response) to the court cases the Herero have filed in the United States. The scrutiny of the current Herero community encompasses the influence of the genocide on population numbers, identity, community make-up and memory, political status, and access to land, particularly the legal struggles regarding access to the land taken away by the Germans.

Acknowledging its historical relationship and obligations to the indigenous Namibian groups, Germany argues that past debts are currently addressed by means of German overseas development aid. Many question whether this aid is as generous as Germany avers (specifically in comparison to Germany's grants to other countries) and whether the aid reaches the minority groups targeted by German repression, i.e., the Herero, Nama, and Damara.

This chapter also explores whether the Herero nation was an international entity in the nineteenth century. Did it qualify as a state under international law and did it lose its sovereignty before 1904? Interestingly, at the time many used the word "nation" when referring to the Herero. Even General von Trotha referred to the Herero on a number of occasions as a "nation." Regarding the question of a Herero state at the time Rachel Anderson has noted that "the Hereros' sociopolitical structure was that of a state. The Hereros had a population, a territory, and a government, which are the core elements of a state under contemporaneous international law."[2] The answers to these questions will determine whether the Herero qualified for the legal protections afforded by the international humanitarian law of the time or whether they were merely protected by customary international humanitarian law. It will be argued that even under the rules that existed then, the Herero qualified as a state under international law. Although interpretation of the principle at the time might not have recognized the Herero as a state, it is the legal principle that is important and not its limited historical interpretation. The argument relates to such international law questions as whether the area was unoccupied when German settlers arrived, which laws applied to the territory, and when did Germany attain sovereignty over the territory. These questions are critical to the remainder of the book, as contemporary issues in Namibia are fundamentally affected by the past.

NAMIBIA'S GEOGRAPHICAL LOCATION

Before it attained independence from South Africa on March 21, 1990, Namibia was called South West Africa, after its geographic location. Its current name derives from the desert on its western coastal plain—the Namib.[3] While the name Namibia was in use before the 1960s, it was only in 1968 that the UN accepted that name for the country.[4] Professor Mburumba Kerina, a Herero politician of long standing, seems to have coined the name. He was a member of the Namibian Parliament, some of the time as a representative of the National Unity Democratic Organization (NUDO). The NUDO was founded by the Herero Chiefs' Council and has its major support base in the Herero community.[5] Kerina has subsequently fallen out with the NUDO but is one of the named plaintiffs in the court cases.

Namibia comprises an area of 824,269 square kilometers.[6] This represents roughly three percent of the land area of Africa, yet its population represents less than 0.2 percent of the continent.[7] It is, however, larger than Germany and France combined.[8] By 1914, German colonies were collectively four and a half times larger than Germany itself.[9] These are important contextual issues in relation to Germany's needs and aspirations during its colonial times.

Namibia is bordered by Angola to the north, South Africa to the south, and Botswana to the east, although the Caprivi Strip stretches further east and touches Zambia and Zimbabwe.[10] On the west is the Atlantic Ocean. The Namib Desert parallels the west coast and comprises 15 percent of the country. The eastern part is also predominantly desert, the Kalahari. Given these two large deserts, water and rainfall were, and still are, the major determinants of the country's demography and agricultural patterns. (Due to the lack of dams and specific droughts, this was even more so in German colonial times.) The northern and central parts are the sought-after areas, as they have higher rainfall and are therefore more suitable to farming. In the nineteenth century the northern areas were mainly under Owambo control, and the central region primarily belonged to the Herero. The Germans were unable to subjugate the Owambo. By the early twentieth century German companies and settlers did not own much land, and, therefore, the Herero farmlands became a key confiscation target.

Namibia's current borders reflect what Packenham[11] called "the scramble for Africa."[12] The territory was allocated to Germany at the Berlin Conference of 1884–1885, but the specific borders were determined in 1886 in an agreement with Portugal and in 1890 in an agreement with the British.[13] These arbitrary border placements agreed to by the colonial powers have been particularly problematic in terms of the Caprivi Strip.[14] This strip of land stretches 450 kilometres to the east, along the northern tip of the country, and became part of GSWA in 1890 after Germany insisted that the colonies in the southwest need access to those in east Africa via the Zambezi River. The strip was, therefore, exchanged with Britain, without considering the impact of this decision on the people living there. As the Caprivians have no ethnic, linguistic, or other connection to the Namibians,[15] they attempted to secede from Namibia by staging a *coup d'etat* in 1999. More than a hundred are on trial for this attempt. The instability of the Caprivi Strip, therefore, relates directly to the arbitrary drawing of borders.[16]

Regular droughts and variation in rainfall make most of Namibia a fairly hostile environment.[17] While the weather is generally favorable, much of the country gets little rain (a major revelation to the settlers), making crop farming unfeasible. Agriculture therefore relies primarily on animal farming, especially cattle. Rainfall has significantly shaped Namibia's history, as access to water determined which land was desirable for farming purposes. Although the current population measures only 1.8 million people, competition for land endures, specifically for the areas with adequate rainfall.

Namibia is also endowed with diamonds, copper, zinc, lead, uranium, silver, vanadium, tin, lithium, magnesium, arsenic, cadmium, germanium, bismuth, beryllium, tungsten, salt, semi-precious stones, natural gas, oil, and possibly other deposits.[18] These riches have made Namibia attractive to many, so much so that is has led to conflict, oppression, and dispossession.

Land is a critical and ongoing issue for Namibians, as the vast majority depend on it for income, either through subsistence or commercial farming, mining, or wildlife tourism.

NAMIBIA'S DEMOGRAPHY

Namibia recognizes various ethnic groups[19] according to its own national census: (Rehoboth) Baster, Caprivi, Colored, Damara, Herero, Kavango, Nama, Owambo, San, Tswana, and Whites.[20] Today the size of each group is approximately as follows (indicated as a percentage of the total population): Owambo (50 percent), Kavango (10 percent), Damara (7.5 percent), Herero (7.5 percent), Whites (6.5 percent), Nama[21] (5 percent), Colored (4 percent), Caprivians (3.5 percent), San (3 percent),[22] Rehoboth Basters (2.5 percent), Tswana (0.5 percent) and "others" (1 percent).[23] As the Owambo constitute half the population (with no other minority group exceeding ten percent) they dominate the political landscape.

Contemporary Namibia displays enormous disparities in wealth and unemployment is very high—less than half of those who could work are employed.[24] On average, German speakers earn ten times more per year than Otjiherero speakers.[25] In turn, Otjiherero speakers' annual income averages double those of Oshiwambo speakers. A 2000 report showed that Namibia had the worst equitable wealth distributions of all member states of the United Nations, with the top one percent earning more than the bottom fifty percent. According to the 2005 United Nations Development Programme *Human Development Report*, Namibia remained the worst country in the world in terms of inequality.[26] The income ratio for the poorest to the richest ten percent of the population is greater than one to ninety-four. Race correlates directly with income, with the top one percent being almost entirely white and the bottom fifty percent being black.[27] This is a direct legacy of colonialism and land appropriation. It has critical bearing on attitudes today in Namibia and may become a greater issue in the future.

Today, the Herero community consists of several groups: the Herero who live in the central and eastern regions of the country, the Mbanderu in the east, and the Himba and Tjimba in the northwest. In the past, areas were named after the ethnic group living there, but in 1992, the emerging democratic government of Namibia created new regional names to de-link the colonial association of ethnicity and area.[28] The original Herero reserves of Aminuis, Epukiro, Eastern, Waterberg East, Otjohorongo, and Ovitoto created by the German colonial authorities were later reconstituted into Hereroland East and Hereroland West.[29] Today Hereroland East forms part of the Omaheke region and Hereroland West is the Otjozondjupa region.[30] (The "make-up"—background, political situation, and political affiliations—of the Herero and the Nama in pre-colonial times are examined below in the section on their sovereignty under international law.) Owamboland's name also changed in 1992, and it was divided into four regions: Oshikoto, Ohangwena, Omusati, and Oshana. Some of the name changes were merely cosmetic, as the various ethnic groups still live in the same areas, and the boundaries frequently remained the same, as with Owamboland which was simply divided into four regions—apparently for political reasons. Equally, ethnicity is still a major issue in Namibia, affecting many facets of economic, political, and social life.

NAMIBIA'S HISTORY AND ITS LEGACY

Namibia is one of a group of southern African countries that became independent toward the end of the twentieth century. Besides Namibia (1990), others that gained "independence" during this period are Angola (1975), Mozambique (1975), Zimbabwe (1980), and South Africa (1994).[31] The histories of these five countries intersect in many ways. One of the similarities was the involvement of Cecil John Rhodes in South Africa, Nyasaland (now Zimbabwe and Zambia), and Namibia, after the Germans were expelled during World War I.

Namibia's long history of colonialism, oppression, and violence reflects domination by numerous other states. It has been under the control of the Dutch, the British, the Germans, and the South Africans. In 1773, the Government of the Cape Colony proclaimed Dutch authority over today's Lüderitz, Halifax Island, and Walvis Bay. The Dutch lost the Cape to the British in 1793 and then again in 1806, resulting in a British takeover of the three territories mentioned above.[32] In 1878, the British took further land around Walvis Bay and, in 1884, incorporated the area into the Cape of Good Hope. Subsequently, Germany took control, although Walvis Bay and some islands off the coast remained part of the Cape of Good Hope and were not given to Namibia until the 1990s.

Even before Germany annexed the territory, German interest in the area took on various guises. One of the first Germans in GSWA was Heinrich Schmelen, who was sent to Bethanie in Namaqualand in 1814 by the London Missionary Society.[33] The German Protestant Rhenish Missionary Society was working there from about 1842.[34] Direct German government interest only emerged after the 1870s when colonialism came under consideration. The formation of the Central Association for Commercial Geography and the Promotion of German Interests Abroad and the West German Association for Colonization and Export, in 1878 and 1881, respectively, gave impetus to the idea of Germany acquiring colonies. This concept was given further momentum when Friedrich Fabri of the Rhenish Missionary Society published the document *Does Germany need colonies?* in 1879. A German Colonial Association was formed in 1882.[35] To prevent the annexation of the territory by the Cape of Good Hope, Bismarck announced, in 1884, that it was under the protection of Germany.[36]

Germany occupied GSWA until World War I, when it was lost to South African and British forces who marched into the territory. Under the Treaty of Versailles, Germany formally lost its colonies in 1919. After the war, a mandate to rule the territory was given to the British but administered by South Africa. On May 7, 1919, SWA became a Class C mandate administered by South Africa. In the latter part of the century, South Africa did not want to give up its mandate, and the International Court of Justice (ICJ) was asked to rule on the matter.[37] In 1971, it ruled that South Africa's continued hold over Namibia was illegal.[38] However, South Africa only permitted Namibia to gain independence in 1990 after a violent war fought by SWAPO. It is, therefore, not surprising that Namibia has been described as a nation "plucked from the shadows of history by calamitous fate."[39]

Colonialists often claim that when they arrived in the soon to be colonized areas the land was "empty." In GSWA, the settlers believed that the land ought to be emptied of the local people to establish farms for themselves. Benjamin Madley explains that policies "of *tabula rasa*, or 'creating a map scraped smooth,' to facilitate dispossession and ethnic cleansing" occurred to permit the removal of the locals, and the notion of "empty" land and unworthiness allowed genocide and dispossession to be rationalized.[40] Accordingly, Germany asserted (and others have attempted similar claims) that much of GSWA was unoccupied when the Europeans arrived. Yet, the reality is that the territory had been populated for thousands of years. The Khoi and the San are thought to have been present in Namibia as far back as 27,000 to 30,000 years ago.[41] The Bantu-speaking people are thought to have migrated down from the north from about 1100, and Nama speakers entered from the south. The Herero are thought to have come from around the area of the Great Lakes.[42] It seems as if they had been in Namibia from at least the year 1500, but they only moved to the specific area known as Hereroland in the 1750s. Thus, even before the eighteenth century many of the different ethnic groups were already in Namibia, and the Germans certainly did not find empty uninhabited land.[43] In fact, the Herero and others controlled much of the land when Germany determined that it had protectorate status over the region in 1884 and annexed the coastal area (except Walvis Bay, which was under British control). The land was and still is sparsely populated, but the Germans were determined to go after the already populated parts which were the most fertile.

In the mid-nineteenth century, dramatic shifts in patterns of settlement followed after a series of wars between the Nama and the Herero. The longest and most influential of these was the so-called "Herero War of Freedom" of 1863 to 1870, which resulted in the ascendancy of the Herero.[44] (Lyn Berat has coined it the "Herero War of Liberation."[45]) The war ended with the signing of the Peace of Okahandja, but instability continued thereafter. Critically, this treaty is seen as giving the Herero the specific right to that area. Many base the validity of the Herero granting Walvis Bay to the British in 1876 on this treaty. In the Palgrave-Maherero treaty of September 9, 1876, specific rights were given to the British.[46] Some view this treaty as ceding title or sovereignty over Walvis Bay, yet its provisions were specific: land was given, but there is controversy about the extent to which the treaty affected sovereignty.

LEGAL STATUS OF THE HERERO IN THE NINETEENTH CENTURY

Critical questions concern the Herero's status in international law at the time of the Germans' arrival, the dates of the various protection treaties and the point at which Germany gained sovereignty over the territory. If Germany only obtained sovereignty over the Herero areas after it had subjugated them during the Herero-German war, then the war itself constituted an international armed conflict, with all the rules that apply to this designation. In addition, nineteenth-century international law did not allow sovereignty to pass to the victor until the war was over,[47] giving prime importance to the end date of the war (as discussed in the Introduction). However, the question of "effective control" enters into the determination of when sovereignty passed hands, specifically when no reasonable chance remained for the defeated to regain their land.[48] The status and impact of the protection treaties are therefore important—whether they cede sovereignty is a critical determinant of the Herero's status in international law after the treaties were signed. Detter has stated:

> The concept of equality in international law is, of course, inferred from the idea of sovereignty. For sovereignty implies, *inter alia*, not equality of power, which would be a fiction, but "legal equality, equality in law and before the law applicable to all States, great or small...." Thus, this means legal equality as opposed to political equality. Legal equality, however, has two aspects. On the one hand, it means that States, whatever political influence they may be, are all alike before international law; this is what McNair calls "forensic equality in international law"; such equality is known by all legal systems and should not create any particular problems even in an "under-developed" legal order, such as international law. But equality also means that States shall have the same capacity to exercise their rights and to assume obligations.[49] [footnotes omitted]

Many writers of the time held that only states containing Christian peoples of Europe had the capacity to create valid treaties in international law.[50] In 1884, W. E. Hall argued that non-Christian states had to be formally admitted to the international community of nations. Westlake was less rigid: in 1914, he reasoned that a state with the ability to produce a government which could provide protection could be deemed a civilized society and international law had to take account of it. However, he dismissed African chiefs as primitive and argued that, apart from European countries, international law only deemed Japan, Abyssinia (Ethiopia), Liberia, and the Congo State as members of the International Club.[51] Yet, he recognized that Turkey, Morocco, Muscat, Siam, Persia, and China did enjoy some international legal rights.

At the time, many regarded international law as governing only "civilized States,"[52] with the accepted criterion being "the standard of civilization."[53] (If this was the yardstick, the Herero did qualify as members of the international society or group of states.) While it has been assumed that the European view of Africa in the nineteenth century was that Africans had no rights in international law and did not possess sovereignty rights over their territory, many have argued differently. While some interpreted the standard of "civilization" to exclude most groups in Africa, this interpretation was clearly limited by the patently biased attitudes of the time. As Wallace-Bruce points out, the Eurocentric perception that there was an absence of state-organization in Africa and that there was a legal vacuum before colonialism is not true, nor was the contention that they were just "tribal units" and not sovereign states.[54] As John Flint has pointed out, the members of those societies expressed

> loyalties to a common language, common forms of social organization, and a sense of belonging to a wide community which in European history would be characterized as nationalism. Many of these so-called tribes number millions of people and are larger than the smaller nationalities of Europe.[55]

In his 1926 book, Mark Frank Lindley noted that for more than 300 years "there had been a persistent preponderance of jurisprudence of juristic opinion in favor of the proposition that lands in the possession of any backward peoples who are politically organized ought not to be regarded as if they belonged to no one" and argued that even the Berlin Conference and its Agreement recognized "African Sovereigns."[56] Berman notes that even before colonialism the rights of indigenous peoples were widely recognized by many, including in the works of Grotius, Pufendorf, and Vattel.[57]

Perhaps a distinction can be made between sovereignty and international legal personality, or having status in international law. Yet many recognize that at that time the territory in question was not *terra nullius*, or belonging to no one. It belonged, and was recognized to have belonged, to the different communities residing there, including the Herero, Nama, and the Owambo (in the north). State practice at the time clearly indicates that Africa in general was not regarded as *terrae nullius* that could be acquired by occupation, and cession—signing agreements with indigenous leaders—was the primary means of obtaining legal title.[58] Various court decisions, for example in Kenya and Nigeria, substantiate this view. Even the Privy Council in the *Re-Southern Rhodesia* decision in 1918 found that Britain recognized the sovereignty of local leaders.[59] In the High Court of the Bechuanaland Protectorate in 1926, in the case *Tshekedi Khama and another v The High Commissioner*, Justice Watermeyer found that "it seems quite clear that from the years 1885 for a period of about four or five years, the British Government recognized the Sovereignty of the Chiefs...."[60]

Regarding colonialism, Alexandrowicz has stated that the intent behind the process "was in the first instance not a race for the occupation of land by original title, but a race for obtaining derivative title deeds, which the European powers had to acquire according to the rule of international law relating to negotiation and conclusion of treaties."[61] In the Western Sahara case, the ICJ held that

> whatever differences of opinion there may have been among jurists, the State practice of the relevant period indicates that territories inhabited by tribes or peoples having a social and political organization were not regarded as terrae nullius. It shows that in the case of such territories the acquisition of sovereignty was not generally considered as affected unilaterally through "occupation" of terra nullius by original title but through agreements concluded with local rulers.[62]

For Malcolm Shaw and others, these protection treaties effectively recognize the international legal personality of both the leader and the people; these agreements constitute acknowledgment that such a people were a part of the community of nations. Shaw also argues that the General Act of the Berlin Conference of 1884/85 explicitly stated and recognized that there were sovereign African entities.[63]

Part of the disagreement on the international status of African states or nations revolves around the question of what constituted a state, and which elements made up such a determination. In this regard, Wallace-Bruce notes that until the twentieth century there were no clearly defined rules that determined when statehood had accrued and that in fact "a number of well-organized political units were in existence in Africa" in pre-colonial times. He lists examples of more than twenty-five of these units, arguing that by the arrival of the colonialists more than twenty stable governments existed in Africa.[64] According to him "It is palpably clear that Africa had various independent states on the eve of colonialism. These kingdoms, empires, and city-states varied enormously in territory, population, and organization."[65] Wallace-Bruce contends that precisely due to the absence of clearly defined rules determining statehood in international law, many of these "political units" qualified. The commonly cited parameters for statehood include such factors as a defined territory, a permanent population, effective government, and independence.[66] In 1931, the Permanent Court of International Justice noted the connection between independence and sovereignty:

> Independence ... is really no more than the normal condition of States according to international law; it may also be described as sovereignty (*suprema protestas*) or external sovereignty, by which is meant that the State has over it no other authority

> than that of international law. The conception of independence, regarded as the normal characteristic of states as subjects of international law, cannot be better defined than by comparing it with the exceptional, and to some extent abnormal, class of states known as "dependent States".... It follows that the legal conception of independence has nothing to do with numerous and constantly increasing States of *de facto* dependence which characterize the relation of one country to other countries. It also follows that the restriction upon a State's liberty, whether arising out of ordinary international law or contractual engagements, does not as such in the least affect its independence. As long as these restrictions do not place the State under the legal authority of another State, the former remains an independent State, however extensive and burdensome those obligations may be.[67]

However, Wallace-Bruce has stated:

> The effect of colonialism, therefore, was to interrupt temporarily the sovereignty of those African States which were existing on the eve of colonialism. When they began to achieve statehood in modern times, the African states were, in fact, regaining the independence which they had enjoyed for centuries previously.[68]

This view equates independence and sovereignty and contends that the loss of sovereignty amounted to the loss of independence—which was regained only when these states became independent from the 1960s onward.[69] However, the two concepts are not always intrinsically linked, seen to be the same, or have the same effect. Shaw sees territorial sovereignty as concerning the type of authority a State exercises over its territory, and that title is linked (both) to sovereignty and effective control.[70] There are different modes of title acquisition in international law—occupation of *terra nullius*, prescription, cession, accretion, and subjugation or conquest.[71] Whether title is held affects the options available for another state to acquire the right to that territory.

James Crawford contended that a state met the necessary conditions for statehood as long as it had a degree of governmental authority capable of maintaining law and order.[72] This was confirmed by the International Court of Justice in the *Western Sahara* case, which held that international law did not require a particular structure of a state.[73] According to Shaw, the following principle can be derived: as local leaders could cede territory, a dual system of international law existed—those within and those outside of the European system of states.[74] Critically, he argues that international law accepted the role of local leaders. Shaw therefore postulates a three-level structure of international law: (1) European states, (2) other states, and (3) non-state entities.[75] Regarding the last category, Shaw argues that this group had only limited personality in international law, but it included "the capacity to hold title to territory and territorial sovereignty."[76] Regardless of whether different states had different levels of international status, his view clearly acknowledges that not only European states were subjects of and incorporated in international law at that time.

PROTECTION TREATIES OR RELINQUISHING SOVEREIGN RIGHTS

The role and extent of the protection treaties signed between the Herero and the Germans are vitally significant in determining Germany's legal liability for events that occurred in GSWA during the time under review. If the protection treaties ceded sovereignty, the war between the Herero and the Germans would only be covered by customary international law, as the rules of war did not cover internal armed conflict at the time.

Several questions pertain: Were there treaties that covered the whole territory? Were all the treaties valid, as some appeared to have been obtained under fraudulent circumstances? Did all Herero fall under the agreements, as not all chiefs signed peace agreements? To what extent did these agreements give sovereignty to the German colonial authorities?

Many authors have addressed the relationship between the protection treaties and (maintaining or surrendering) sovereignty. Goldblatt maintains that the Herero did not intend to give up their sovereignty or to transfer it to the Germans.[77] Similarly, Pendleton has argued that the Herero throughout German rule clearly resisted encroachment on their territorial sovereignty.[78] Huaraka recognizes that besides the northern part of GSWA (where sovereignty was only achieved later), Namibia came under German sovereignty only in the early part of the twentieth century and then only by conquest. He refers to the wars fought by the Germans against the Herero and Nama and argues that no title passed before the war or through any of the protection treaties.[79] Similarly Dinah Shelton maintains that the Herero did not relinquish their full sovereignty but simply control over foreign affairs and the right to trade without interference for which Germany was to "respect native customs and abstain from any act that would be illegal in its own country. At a minimum, therefore, German law should have applied to state action in Namibia."[80]

While it is argued by some that the Herero purportedly lost their sovereignty by signing various treaties, it will be argued that most of these treaties, including the ones signed by the Herero, did not amount to loss of sovereignty. There were so many agreements that it had been remarked that they were signed by the "cartload."[81] That so many treaties were signed indicates that states, including Germany, recognized the multiplicity of traditional authorities in the area. By 1886, a number of treaties had been signed, and, while some chiefs may have ceded their sovereign power, others had concluded only limited protection treaties; yet several had even rejected these limited protection treaties.[82] It is doubtful whether most or even more than just a few of the chiefs gave up their sovereignty. Some took salaries to enforce peace and order among their communities or for an agreement to sell land. Although they often had to enforce peace in the name of the Emperor, which could be *perceived* as surrendering sovereignty, it clearly is arguable that they ever *did* so.

Most of the treaties signed between the Herero and the Germans were protection treaties, not treaties relinquishing sovereignty. This was the case with the first treaty signed in 1884 with the Bethanie community. The Bethanie agreed not to sell land to another country, and the treaty did not abdicate control or authority in word or intent. It is also significant in whether sovereignty changed hands that Germany agreed not to get involved in the administration or judicial system of the Bethanie.

The words of Chancellor von Caprivi confirm that Germany did not, even in its own view, have sovereignty over the whole area. In 1893, he stated in the *Reichstag*: "we do not intend to become masters of the country and to consolidate our sovereignty without bloodshed. We possess South-West Africa once and for all; it is German territory and must be preserved as such."[83] Von Caprivi's statement clearly acknowledged that while they possessed GSWA, they did not have sovereignty over all parts of it and that they intended to consolidate their sovereignty over the territory.

Last known photograph of Chief Witbooi. Courtesy of Klaus Dierks.

Hendrik Witbooi, chief of the (Nama) Witbooi tribe,[84] understood the issue of treaties and sovereignty. That he did not surrender his rights to sovereignty is evident from a letter to Leutwein in 1894 in which he wrote: "I have not given up my independence, because I alone have the right to that which is mine, which I can give or withhold if someone asks me for it, as I wish. Francois[85] has waged war against me because I did not give what was mine."[86] Thus, Witbooi made it clear he was aware that his tribe's sovereignty was at stake and that he was not prepared to surrender it. When the German troops later took up arms against the Witbooi, they were unable to defeat them, which meant they were unable to enforce sovereignty, as international law demanded that conquered territory had to be held on to militarily.[87] Later that year, Witbooi did sign a protection and friendship treaty and agreed to provide military assistance to the Germans, which he did until 1904. Whether he gave up his sovereignty is debatable, but doubtful. That the Witbooi were and remained independent can be seen from the following comment by Kurd Schwabe, a *Schutztruppe* officer who participated in the war against Witbooi. In his book, *Mit Schwert und Pflug in Deutsch-Südwestafrika: Vier Kriegs- und Wanderjahre*, he wrote:

> When the details of the peace treaty became known in Germany, many opinions were expressed to the effect that the war should have been continued, to the complete annihilation of the Witbooi tribe. Some ignorant people with no insight even demanded that the brave chief should have been hanged or shot.... Hendrik Witbooi has never broken his word, he has sworn an oath of truce and to render military assistance, and has proven with deeds that he is a man of his word. There was not the slightest legal justification to punish him with death, as *he was not a treacherous, dishonourable rebel but a free tribal chief*, who defied us in open combat![88] [my emphasis]

The limited extent of the sovereign control of the area is demonstrated by the fact that the Germans never attempted to take control of the Owambo area in the north, as they realized that this was not militarily possible. From an international law perspective, it is significant that Germany did not control Owamboland and other areas. Cohrssen confirms this when he states that in the 1890s "Germany's hold on the territory was still tenuous at best...."[89] Even after the Herero War, GSWA was still not entirely under German rule. In this regard, John Wellington noted that Germany did not obtain complete authority until 1907 when Owamboland was brought under their control.[90] It is even argued that control of the northern parts was only attained in 1908.[91] In the southern and central parts, GSWA officials attempted to ban the Herero from importing weapons, but Berlin lifted this ban, citing that "friendly" people ought to be able to get weapons.[92] This is important from the standpoint that the Herero, during the war with Germany, while getting guns from Swedish and British traders as well as German missionaries,[93] got their ammunition during the war from the Owambo chief of East Ondonga Chief Nehale, who was also behind the attack on the German troops at Fort Namutoni on January 28, 1904.[94] Thus, it is clear that even if the Herero are deemed not to have been sovereign, the fact that they got their munitions from the Owambo, who were sovereign, ensures that the hostilities were an international armed conflict to which those rules applied. To return to whether the issue was control, if this were the case then the authorities would not have been willing to allow weapons. It was only in June 1889 that a unit of 21 soldiers under Captain Curt von Francois attempted some type of control. Although ordered not to take "hostile action," von Francois took troops to Windhoek to make it his "headquarters" and attempted to prevent arms and ammunition from entering. This soured the relationship with the local inhabitants and caused huge rifts and unhappiness. The Windhoek issue was particularly controversial, as the Herero maintained they had only "lent" Windhoek to Jan Jonker, and it was still theirs. However, von Francois claimed that, since Jan Jonker had been killed, Windhoek belonged to no one, and he could therefore take it.[95] von Francois' argument that Windhoek belonged to no one confirms the Germans' lack of sovereign power. Regarding the methods to be employed and the motivation for such methods, von Francois stated that "occupation," not "protection," was needed to get land out of the hands of the local population—and that rifles, not words, were needed.[96] His statement implies that there was merely protection at the time, not occupation, and to achieve the latter action was necessary. He challenged Samuel Maherero "to come and drive him out."[97] At this time, the relationship between the Herero and Nama was not good. In fact, Hendrik Witbooi[98] was willing to attack the Herero on the request of the Germans, but wanted to subjugate all the Nama first.[99] One of von Francois's tasks was to delineate the borders of the Herero and the Owambo land, so the (German) South West African Company could get the land in between.[100]

Of significance, in terms of the treaties signed by the Herero and the Nama, is the fact that these communities were not composite groups with a single chief ruling over them. The Namas consisted of eight tribes,[101] including the Rooinasie or Red Nation, the Franzmanne (after the name of the chief), the Swartboois (after their chief), the Topnaars, and the Bondelswartz. While the other tribes paid tribute to the head of the Rooinasie, he was not a paramount chief, as he had no real powers over them. His status was not of much significance as clan loyalty prevailed over tribal loyalty.[102] The Damaras were similarly fragmented and resided in eleven regional groupings.[103] The Herero, too, were a "disjointed" political group "laced together by a unique double-clan socio-religious system."[104] The divisions between the Herero were based on economic status as well as historical migration patterns and location within Hereroland. The largest and wealthiest Herero group, the Ovaherero (Herero), came from the Kaokoveld in the north and resided in western Hereroland. The poorest group, the Ovatjimba (Tjimba), remained in the Kaokoveld. The third group had entered the area from Botswana and resided in eastern Hereroland; they were known as the Ovambanderu (Mbanderu) or Eastern Hereros. In turn, each of the three groups consisted of clans (called Otjikutu) in which each person was bound by roughly eight different ties of matrilineal descent and twenty separate ties of patrilineal descent. Matrilineal ties governed inheritance of property, while the patrilineal lines governed the religious aspects. These matrilineal clans of the Herero-Mbanderu formed a "loose kind of confederation."[105]

As mentioned before, a single chief did not rule the various communities. One group often had many leaders, none of whom were in full command. The subordinate or superior status of chiefs was a common issue at that time, not only in Namibia. One example concerns a treaty between Britain and the ruler of Boussa, regarding territory on the Niger. France established that the chief whose signature had been obtained was a subordinate one, and so a race between the two countries began to obtain the signature of the superior chief.[106]

The question of the rights and responsibilities of a paramount leader was addressed in the Barotse arbitral award, in 1905, in which the boundary of the Barotse kingdom was in dispute. In that matter, it was held that "a Paramount ruler is he who exercises governmental authority according to [customary law], that is by appointing the subordinate chiefs or by granting them investiture, by deciding disputes between these chiefs, by disposing them when circumstances call for it and by obliging them to recognise him as their Paramount Ruler."[107] These powers did not seem to apply to the Herero paramount chief of that time.

The Herero did not always have a national leader. Even today the *ombara* (paramount chief) is not recognized by all. The Mbanderu have always opposed such a position and have, in the recent past, attempted to revive the status of the Herero royal houses. Today, the position of paramount chief is an elected post, and the choice is determined by factors such as personality, intelligence, organizational ability, and education.[108] Before the war there were five major chieftainships—those of the Okahandja, Otjimbingwe, Omaruru, Otjozondjupa, and Okandjoze.[109] Consequently there was not a single chief who could sign away the rights of the community at large. In 1885, Germany, represented by three German officials, including Ernst Göring (the father of Herman Göring), signed a protection treaty with Maherero. However, it is improbable that that treaty could be regarded as binding for all Hereros. At the time, Göring even expressed doubts about whether Maherero was in a position to sign that treaty on behalf of all the Herero chiefs.[110] In fact, so unconvinced were the Germans that Maherero was the supreme leader that they went to get a second signature, that of Manasse, another chief.[111] A German jurist of the time, Dr. Felix Meyer, viewed as the foremost authority in Germany on indigenous law, indicated then that the other Herero chiefs, including Kambazembi, Muretti, Tjetjoo, Zacharias, and others, did not view Maherero as in any way a supreme leader and that they were not bound by his agreement.[112] Thus, the extent of the treaty's effect is questionable.

In order to gain an advantage over the Nama, some Herero entered into a protection treaty with the Germans in 1885. But again, as Herero power was decentralized, agreements with some of the chiefs were not applicable to or binding for all Hereros.[113] Many Herero groups did not enter into such agreements, and those who did only bestowed the right to determine foreign policy to the Germans—they did not cede their sovereignty.[114] These treaties only dealt with issues of the different groups living in the same area, although the Herero gave the Germans jurisdiction over the white people living in the area.[115]

While Maherero signed a protection treaty, his status at the time was not that of overall chief. Thus, even if the treaty involved cession of sovereignty, as Lindley argues, it would not been valid if the grant of cession was not in the power of the person granting it.[116] A cession would also be voidable if obtained fraudulently, for example when the Germans used different mile lengths when buying land from the Herero (the Germans used the longer German mile, but the Herero were under the impression the agreed areas were measured in shorter English miles). Moreover, the treaty he signed was a protection treaty, not a peace treaty or one that surrendered sovereignty. In any event, he later revoked the treaty.

Chief Maherero. Courtesy of Klaus Dierks.

Of importance are the *intentions* of the Herero when entering into these treaties, as it is the intent of the parties that determines its effect. If one party interprets a treaty as more broad than the other party, the intent would be where the two meet—in other words, on the narrower basis. In this regard, Goldblatt forcefully argued that the Herero did not intend to cede sovereignty; their intentions were for the Germans to provide protection against other groups, such as the Nama, who were attacking them.[117] For instance, Maherero agreed to a German protection treaty in October 1885 because he needed assistance (arms and ammunition) in his conflict with Hendrik Witbooi of the Nama.[118] That this treaty did not cede sovereignty can be seen in the fact that he shortly afterward signed another one, giving mineral concessions to the Germans.

It has often been argued that the Herero did not appreciate what they were agreeing to in many of these agreements; yet, the contrary view holds that their alleged "ignorance" is irrelevant, as without the requisite intent no such agreements were valid. It is clear from the wording of most of the signed treaties that the intent was much narrower than would be required for cession or ceding title. Except for a few examples, such as the cession of Walvis Bay to the British, the general intent was to gain protection against local communities with whom they were in regular conflict. Certainly most of these treaties were not expansive in terms of foreign representation, treaty making, giving up governmental control, or ceding judicial functions (except where Europeans were concerned). As Lindley confirms, many of the treaties between the Herero and the German colonialists recognized that prior treaties remained in force, that chiefs could levy taxes, and that they retained their right to apply justice to their own people.

The treaties were not all identical in content and effect. It could be argued that some might have had implications for sovereignty, while others did not. One treaty signed by the Bethanie contained sales of land. Regarding civil and criminal jurisdiction, the treaty with the Basters and the Bethanie provided for a joint tribunal where settlers were involved. The early Maherero treaty gave jurisdiction to the German authorities, but that jurisdiction had to be exercised in consultation with a member of the Chiefs' Council. Thus, when only indigenous people were involved, jurisdiction was not handed over; where settlers were concerned, both groups had to act together. In the main, the process of justice was a joint one. Only a few other treaties, such as the one signed with the Berseba, made provision for a German jurist to rule in cases between the settlers and the Nama.[119] However, some groups, such as the Rooinasie, completely rejected the provision on jurisdiction.[120]

Often, one of the implications of the treaties was that Germany was given a most-favored-nation treatment or status,[121] rather than sovereignty over the territory. This is further indication that the wording of the treaty or the intent of the Herero was not to hand over sovereignty. This complies with Antony Anghie's view that "protectorates were a common technique by which European States exercised extensive control over non-European states while not officially assuming sovereignty over those states."[122] In fact, it has been argued that even if the colonial administration intended these treaties to result in cession of the territory from the indigenous groups (which they probably did), many groups in Africa were not aware that these treaties had such implications (or could have such consequences).[123] If this is true, the question arises whether legal cession occurred when the parties did not intend such cession. Hence, sovereignty would only pass through conquest. The Herero undoubtedly had no intent to relinquish sovereignty; moreover, the wording in many treaties was limited to achieving "protection" in its real sense, rather than granting Germany authority over the Herero.

Often, European powers signed protection treaties with local leaders not specifically to attain sovereignty, but simply to indicate a sphere of influence to other European powers and their intent to gain the particular territory. The protection treaties only constituted steps in a broader process, and they seldom changed the territory's status.[124] While the ultimate objective of the Germans was to attain sovereignty, they too regarded the protection treaties as steps toward this goal—not as conclusive agreements of cession. With the Herero, the Germans hoped that providing humanitarian services to them would assist in winning their favor.[125] Fredrick Lugard, a British Governor in what is today Nigeria, outlined this stepwise progression toward absolute power:

> The evolution of colonial empires ... follows a well-known process.... First, travellers, missionaries, and traders; then treaties of commerce and friendship; then a kind of protection agreement half-conceded under the form of an unequal alliance; afterward the delimitation of spheres of influence and the declaration of a right of priority; then a protectorate Treaty properly so-called, the establishment of tutelage, the appointment of Resident Magistrates ... and finally annexation, pure and simple.[126]

Likewise, Uzoigwe charts nine stages in the process of formally acquiring colonial territory: (1) Settlement, (2) Exploration and Discovery, (3) Slave-Trade Suppression, (4) Commercial Posts and Chartered Companies, (5) Missionary Settlements, (6) Occupation of Strategic Areas, (7) Treaties, (8) Hinterland Doctrine, and (9) Effective Occupation.[127]

Another question pertains to the implications and effects of a colonial power declaring a protectorate, as Germany did in the 1880s. There are different types, as Lindley showed in 1926:

> In the early instances the weaker state might gain the advantage of protection without losing its sovereignty. In the later examples of the older type of protectorates, however, an essential feature of the arrangement has been that the protected state has handed over the conduct of its external affairs to the Protecting Power, or accepted its dictation in regard to those affairs and thus parted with part of its sovereignty without however losing the whole of its independence.[128]

One, therefore, has to distinguish between the different types of protectorates: some were designed simply to be protective, with both parties agreeing to this objective; these protectorates were not designed to lead to absorption. The second type was a much more extensive arrangement in which the parties agreed that the State providing protection be given greater authority, which included at least some cession of authority. Only in this type of protectorate was sovereignty potentially ceded; although the protectorate might not simultaneously or directly have lost its independence, the agreement was designed to lead to absorption.

Lindley calls these two types "protectorate proper" and "colonial protectorates." According to him, a colonial protectorate was meant to indicate to other European states that the protecting State was taking steps toward annexing the territory in question. The effect was to declare the intent to acquire the land, but no change in sovereignty actually occurred. Drawing up a treaty with a local leader was often merely the first step in establishing a protectorate. In fact, many treaties contained "no direct reference to the sovereignty or protectorate of the European contracting Power, although they comprise provisions which imply some kind of paramountcy on the part of that Power."[129] According to Lindley the treaties of protection and friendship entered into by the German authorities in GSWA were the older type of protectorate arrangement. He maintains that treaties entered into with the Red Nations, Rehoboth, and the Herero guaranteed the validity of preceding treaties with others and allowed the chief to continue to levy taxes. Germany was given most-favored-nation treatment but was not given control of foreign relations. The agreement only determined that no treaty could be entered into with another state, and that no land could be ceded to another state or individual without Germany's consent.[130] The only control given to Germany was that it would have some say in whether land could be sold or not. (This, however, applied only to some treaties.)

Even in the 1890s, Governor Leutwein recognized that the Herero areas were still under the control of the Herero. In his book, *Elf Jahre Gouverneur in Deutsch-Südwestafrika*, published in 1906 in Berlin, he commented that the dispute over who was to become chief provided "an excellent opportunity to intervene in the affairs of Hereroland."[131] At the time, Leutwein was permitted to station a garrison of troops in the area, not for control, but to protect Samuel Maherero (the new chief) and his community.[132] While it could be argued that such military presence affected Herero sovereignty, and although the German authorities probably used this presence to gather knowledge and to extend their influence, the troops were merely providing protection to the Herero. Leutwein often attempted to obtain information, sometimes by sending emissaries to learn where troops were stationed and gather other intelligence. Further evidence that the Herero did not submit to German authority is the fact that Samuel Maherero was paid a salary to ensure respect for the German and other agreed borders. This again proves that Herero boundaries were being honored—and that they did not surrender sovereignty. In fact, in 1893, Samuel Maherero wrote to the Kaiser asserting his right of governance over Hereroland.[133]

The most important issue emerging from the treaties was the right it gave the Germans to trade without interference. However, the Germans did not adhere to the terms of the treaty. Their limited observance of the agreement seemed to have been predetermined, as Governor Leutwein noted that the "high minded promises" were a diplomatic ruse by the Germans forced by their "weak strategic position at the time."[134] Thus, the content of the German peace agreements must be understood in the context of the Germans viewing GSWA as a possible new Germany in Africa, one that, if peaceful, could attract German settlers. Leutwein specifically mentioned the question of security in a letter to Hendrik Witbooi in 1894:

> To your last letter of 17th August, I have to say: It is neither a sin nor a crime that you do not want to submit to the German Empire. *It is, however, a threat to the safety of the German Protectorate.* There is no point, therefore, to any further letters which do not offer your surrender. I hope we shall agree to conduct this campaign, which has become inevitable thanks to your truculence, humanely; I also hope it may be brief. I shall also gladly give you any explanation you seek, even while we are at war if thereby I may hope to shed no more blood than is strictly necessary. Signed: Leutwein.[135] [my emphasis]

Accordingly, in 1894, the German authorities saw brokering a peace agreement with the Herero as a short-term solution. They believed that the Herero would continue to be a problem unless dealt with once and for all. In addition, obtaining Herero land and cattle must have been more attractive than the benefits of using the Herero for labor purposes. Already in that year, Governor Leutwein was being pressured into ensuring that Herero land was available for occupation by arriving settlers.[136] The clearing of Herero land took place in the context of warfare. While it was not the Germans but the Witbooi who were responsible for driving the Hereros off their land, the Germans took advantage of the opportunity this provided.[137] From 1895, other types of land clearance or "forced removals" followed: the land was needed for settler occupation and the authorities did their utmost to drive the Herero off their land. The Germans threatened force to gain land signed over by indigenous chiefs in preceding agreements.[138] As this occurred more frequently, the Herero were forced onto less and less land. While some chiefs benefited individually from these developments, the pressure on Herero communities grew, because as "access to water, grazing game and lands became ever more contented, tension rose."[139]

Another treaty was signed in 1895 with Samuel Maherero, which provided that if cattle were found on the wrong side of the border, five percent of the animals were to be confiscated, with half of those confiscated going to Maherero. This treaty caused a rift between Maherero and other chiefs, but once again evidences the respect for the borders of Hereroland.[140] In 1896, the borders of Herero territory were extended after Leutwein sided with Maherero against others who disputed the border.[141] As a result of losing that conflict, the Eastern Herero were made to pay 12,000 cattle as a penalty for going to war against the Germans. This, in turn, indicates the division between different Herero communities—confirming that a peace treaty with one group or chief was not binding for all Hereros. Once again, Leutwein recognized the borders of the Herero. He wrote: "Both occurrences reduced the herds of the Herero to such an extent that they could not even think of violating the borders any longer."[142]

Leutwein used a policy of diplomacy throughout his 11 years as governor. He avoided use of military means unless he thought it absolute necessary, and even then not to subjugate or to achieve control. Leutwein did not want to follow the wishes of the settlers because he doubted whether he was able to defeat the Herero militarily; neither did he want to transgress the various protection treaties. This he admitted directly.[143] Leutwein recognized the treaties as protective agreements and realized that they did not allow for subjugation of the Herero. This, again, challenges the perception of possible loss of sovereignty by all groups. In 1904, Rhenish missionary Pastor Anz noted that "the Germans have come into the country under the guise of friends and protectors, whereas it has always been and will remain their opinion that they are the masters here."[144] Yet many recognized that Germany was not in control in the territory—neither in theory nor in practice. In a letter to Chancellor Bulow, the German envoy to Lisbon recognizes Germany's limited control over the territory. In this letter, written in early 1904, he comments on the uprising:

> Unfortunate though the Herero uprising may be, it will lead to the seizure and possession of the whole expanse of the territory, so that German South West Africa can cease to be a so-called sphere of interest and become an orderly and promising colony.[145]

This comment confirms that the treaties offered friendship and protection, not control or loss of sovereignty, and that the German authorities recognized this. Sovereignty occurred only after von Trotha arrived in June 1904, and Leutwein's approach of negotiations was rejected. It is clear that, until that time, the German forces could not militarily control some communities, especially some Herero groups, and, therefore, these communities had not yet lost their sovereignty.

The crux of the matter is that the treaty with at least some of the chiefs was a legal agreement, the terms of which were not in doubt, despite the fact that from the beginning the Germans did not always intend to stick to the terms of the agreement. Nevertheless, the treaty was binding and its terms were relevant—and they still impact current legal issues. Gewald identifies the specific trigger for the events of January 12, 1904 onward as a misunderstanding by a Lieutenant Zürn, who panicked and started the war. If the Germans attacked the Herero and initiated the war, this would have been in violation of the peace treaties in force at the time. Furthermore, if the Germans did not have sovereignty, the war could be deemed an international armed conflict, which would have been covered by the well-developed laws of war relating to that type of conflict. (This issue will receive further attention in due course.)

THE IMPACT OF THE GENOCIDE ON HERERO IDENTITY

The memory of what occurred a century ago is central to understanding the Herero and their situation today. It defines them and is inculcated in almost everything in which they are collectively involved. As Gewald notes: "The immensity of the catastrophe that befell the peoples of central Namibia between 1904 and 1908 was such that it could not, and still cannot be banished from public memory and debate."[146]

The memory of the past is a focal point of Herero psyche. The court case is part of the attempt to keep that alive in a context in which the perpetrators have neither acknowledged nor accepted responsibility for what they have done. In reaction to the indifference of the current government, the memory of the past spurs on the legal challenges. What Elie Wiesel wrote about the Holocaust is equally relevant for the Herero: "I have tried to keep memory alive, I have tried to fight those who would forget. Because if we forget we are guilty, we are accomplices."[147]

Gewald suggests that various people are using the memory of what occurred for their own ends. According to him, the genocide has been "deployed for varying and, at times, contradicting interests by German Social democrats and English imperialists through to anti-Apartheid activists and post-colonial tribalists."[148]

Memory can be seen in the most familiar symbol of Herero identity: their clothing. At their functions the men wear turn-of-the-century German soldier uniforms and Herero women dress in long brightly colored Victorian dresses. The Ovambanderu wear green and black Victorian dresses, the Ovaherero women wear red and black, and those from Objimbingwe wear white dresses.[149] The dress of Herero women is exactly what the wives of the missionaries wore[150] and represents a key component of Herero history and identity.[151]

The origin of the *Truppenspieler* (troop players) movement, with its military structure and practices based on the German colonial army, is not clear. Some writers claim it dates from the time of the Herero War and represents a means of establishing a Herero organization, as well as unity and solidarity in the community.[152] Others believe the movement only developed at the time of World War I, when there was an "awakening of a national consciousness among the Herero after Germany was forced out of GSWA."[153] As a result, the Herero have taken to wearing German army uniforms and conducting army drill routines at important functions. Military ranks are allocated and insignia worn. From 1938, the movement has been called the Red Band Organization (*Otjira Tjotjiserandu).*[154] Appropriating and reinterpreting these uniforms and the army drill routines can be interpreted as a means of transforming elements of colonial subordination into symbols of liberation and resistance.

Similarly, the development of their own church in 1955, *Okereka Jeuangelie Joruuano* or the Protestant Unity Church, evidences the appropriation and adaptation of colonial practices. The church is believed to have roots in the 1920s when people claiming to represent the Marcus Garvey movement from the

United States urged the Herero to leave the mission churches. The new church was established in reaction to the segregation and racism of the time, the lack of educational and leadership opportunities for the Herero, and because the mission churches condemned the Herero traditions of traditional marriages, circumcision, ancestor worship, and the holy fire. The new church was thus established to serve Herero needs, and it absorbed Herero traditions into its practices and added Herero ancestors to the Holy Trinity.[155] The church celebrated its 50th anniversary and invested its bishop on Heroes' Day (August 26) 2005.

Thus, not only was the genocide a turning point in the history of the Herero, but it has also defined them ever since. Their population size and lack of resources are the primary reasons for Herero marginalization and ostracism from mainstream Namibian politics. Their tradition, culture, and outlook have all been influenced, if not redefined, by what occurred a century ago.

Although the genocide dates back a century, and was not directly experienced by the last generation(s), its memories are clear and specific, and very much part of the collective group memory. Pierre Nora explains collective group memory as "what remains of the past in the lived reality of groups, or what these groups make of the past."[156] History, as Elazar Barkan has noted, often informs identity intimately. He argues that history

> changes who we were, not only who we are. In this sense, history has become a crucial field for political struggle. Yet the politics of memory, as it is often referred to, operate according to particular rules and tempo. For a "new" history to become more than a partisan "extremist" story, the narrative often has to persuade not only the members of the in-group who will "benefit" from the new interpretation, but also their "others": those whose own history will presumably be "diminished," or "tainted," by the new narratives."[157]

The pervasive impact of the Herero War and the genocide on Herero identity can partly be attributed to the fact that they remain marginalized in a newly democratized country. The (contributing) irony is that their suffering was exploited to achieve independence—sentiments regarding the genocide proved useful in motivating the local communities to work together and in mobilizing international support. Despite this, and despite the necessity of acknowledging the past when establishing a new democratic legal order,[158] the Namibian approach has been to ignore it and simply move on.[159]

Forgetting the past is not easy. It is essentially an illusion: a society that decides to ignore the past will invariably be confronted with it at some stage.[160] Indeed this holds true for Namibia, where issues from the past still determine relations between groups today, especially in terms of land.

The extent to which the Herero honor the memory of their past was demonstrated in the efforts of the Omaruru community to get the Krugersdorp municipality in South Africa to disinter and return the remains of King Michael Tjiseseta. The King had led the fight against the German forces and led more than 130 fellow prisoners in a breakout from the Swakopmund concentration camp,[161] before fleeing to Botswana in 1904. He died in South Africa in 1927. It took three years to return his remains, and he was reburied in Namibia in 2004. On this occasion one of the Herero leaders commented: "This is indeed an emotional but also a joyous moment for the people of Omaruru, and of course all Namibians. Our leader deserved a proper and dignified funeral in his land now that Namibia is free."[162]

THE LEGACY OF THE GENOCIDE TODAY

It goes without saying that the genocide and the confiscation of their land and cattle have had a major impact on the identity and culture of the Herero.[163] Regarding the loss of their cattle, Luttig commented: "Due to the loss of these sacred animals the tribal religion fell into decay and naturally with it a great part of the tribal culture."[164] For the Herero selling cattle was "a sin against the forefathers, from whom they had been received as an inheritance."[165] The custom of worshipping their ancestors was dependent on having cattle, and having lost their cattle, this custom was jeopardized.[166] Land was also regarded as sacred,[167] and its loss hurt the Herero deeply. Accordingly, the war, their memories of it, and the loss of their land and cattle still affect the Herero profoundly today. This memory is demonstrated in various traditions, behaviors, and responses. Accordingly, when the Namibian Government refused to recognize a number of Herero traditional leaders, the spectre of General von Trotha's extermination order and interning the survivors in concentration camps was used as a rallying call against actions that compromise the community.[168] This type of reaction is represented in the following statement by the leader of the Democratic Turnhalle Alliance (DTA), a party supported by the Herero community, in the Namibian National Assembly: "For how long is your SWAPO Government going to treat the Hereros as foreigners in their own country? Are you going to imitate von Trotha in your suppression of the Herero People?"[169]

The matter of traditional authorities and their recognition has been an issue of major concern. Formal recognition is important not only for the sake of identity but also because it affects a group's access to land. Some representatives of groups such as the San and Herero have not yet been recognized by the State.[170] This has been a source of tension between the Government and the Herero, as the Government has only recognized a small number of the more than 40 Herero traditional leaders through the Traditional Authorization Act of 1995. Even the Paramount Chief of the Hereros has not received state recognition in terms of the Traditional Authorities Act 25 of 2000. On the other hand, the six Herero royal houses, the Maherero, Mbanderu, Kambazembi, Otjikaoko, Vita, and Zeraua have been recognized. Should the Herero community be given more recognition, status, and a more important role in Namibia, it would help to increase their sense of self-worth and restore their dignity. The economic and political marginalization[171] of the Herero today also impacts the question of repatriations. They have been so excluded from the political structure that there have been calls for a Herero state or at least some federal system with extensive regional powers.

The Herero War is generally regarded as a crystallizing point in Namibian history.[172] The year 2004 was not only the centenary of the start of the war, but also the 160-year anniversary of missionary involvement in Hereroland, 120 years of direct German colonialism, 90 years of direct South African involvement in Namibia, and 15 years after UN Resolution 435 was completed.[173]

THE COMPLEX LAND QUESTION TODAY

Land acquisition was a prime motivation for the genocide. Due to this legacy, access to land remains a dominant issue in contemporary Namibia. This section explores current issues relating to land, with the understanding of its link to the genocide and its significance in terms of reparations. (Reparations will be addressed in Chapter Three.)

As "an obvious projection area of potential social conflicts, the complex and emotional land question has the potential to create or even deepen racial mistrust and hatred."[174] Correspondingly, the Namibian Constitution takes account of property rights in general and the expropriation thereof and land ownership specifically.[175] Article 16 provides:

> (1) All persons shall have the right in any part of Namibia to acquire, own, and dispose of all forms of immovable and movable property individually or in association with others and to bequeath their property to their heirs or legatees: provided that Parliament may by legislation prohibit or regulate as it deems expedient the right to acquire property by persons who are not Namibian citizens.
>
> (2) The State or a competent body or organ authorized by law may expropriate property in the public interest subject to the payment of just compensation, in accordance with requirements and procedures to be determined by Act of Parliament.

Article 100 provides:

> Land, water, and natural resources below and above the surface of the land and in the continental shelf and within the territorial waters and the exclusive economic zone of Namibia shall belong to the State if they are not otherwise lawfully owned.

The Constitution manifestly provides for ownership and expropriation but does not provide for dealing with the historical dispossession of land. In this regard, Clement Daniels argues that Namibia's Constitution perpetuates the colonial situation of land dispossession, as it provides that land, water, and natural resources not lawfully owned belong to the state.[176] According to him, these provisions have dispossessed the majority of Namibians of their land.

When Namibia gained independence, more than half of all agricultural farmland was owned by white farmers who constituted six percent of the population.[177] Yet, while land reform has been on the agenda in Namibia since independence, it has not been addressed with the expected urgency. The same applies to other countries such as Zimbabwe, where land redistribution took twenty years before it gained momentum. In Namibia, land reform has distinctive political ramifications because most of those who had been dispossessed form part of the political opposition today. In addition, the farm owners are mostly from important trading and development partners, namely South Africa and Germany. Land reform or redistribution is a major political issue for the Namibian government, as it could appreciably affect the economy. Although agricultural production is a relatively small part of the economy, it has major effects on other parts of the nation.

Germany is purportedly Namibia's most important partner for development aid and trade, and Namibia has looked to Germany to help resolve its land problems. It needs Germany to support the expropriation process by facilitating agreements and possibly compensating German farmers who still occupy the largest and most arable parts of Namibia.[178] If many of these white farms are expropriated too rapidly, the economy could be affected both in terms of agricultural production and in terms of investor confidence. In addition, the 1993 Protection of Investment Agreement between Germany and Namibia stipulates that Namibia would be liable to compensate German farmers at market value if their land is expropriated—paying them the difference between the market value of the land and what they get, in German currency.[179]

The political dimension is further complicated by the fact that land confiscation in the colonial era did not take place in Owambo areas.[180] The Red Line, a fence for control of animal disease, cut the territory in two: about two thirds of the country fell below the Red Line, and one third above. It was the rich arable land south of the Red Line belonging to the Damara, Herero, and Nama that was lost to the colonizers. The land north of the Red Line belonging to the Owambo and others, some of the richest land,[181] was virtually left untouched. Although the latter, particularly the north, had more reliable rainfall, the population density was greater, so the possibility for military success was remote. Therefore, one third of the land (that above the Red Line) was governed by indirect rule, while direct rule occurred in the two thirds below the Red Line. (This is addressed further below.)

Currently, there are about 20,000 Namibians of German origin. It is estimated that Namibians of German origin own about one third of the big farms, and there are approximately 400 Germans who own farms but live outside Namibia.[182] Many of the white farms are south of the Red Line. Breytenbach notes: "In Namibia today, white commercial farmland is the only land earmarked for redistribution. Communal lands, whether underutilized or not, are not intended for resettlement—which gives the appearance of double standards."[183]

One element of the colonial legacy is that the pressure for land reform is not equally strong in all communities. As Hunter notes, "the former liberation movement, the South West African People's Organization (SWAPO)—now the ruling SWAPO Party of Namibia—does not urgently need the land campaign in order to convince its voter base."[184] This is because SWAPO enjoys popular support now, even beyond its original Owambo constituency. Since independence SWAPO has increased its electoral support from fifty-seven percent in 1990 to nearly eighty percent in 2005.[185] This does not mean that there is no pressure for access to land.[186] There is great demand among many Namibians who either have not owned land and/or were unable to acquire land during both the colonial and apartheid administrations. While Namibia is a very large country with a relatively small population, only about a third of the territory gets sufficient rainfall to sustain agriculture—so there is little land for agricultural use.[187] Large land holdings by white farmers starkly contrast with those of commercial black farmers. Whites account for about one percent of the Namibian population, but whites own 4,128 of the 6,300 farms comprising the commercial land held in terms of freehold title. These farms constitute forty-four percent of the available land and seventy percent of the most productive agricultural land. On average, white-owned farms are about twenty-five times larger than black-owned farms. Besides the commercial farming, 33.5 million hectares, or forty-one percent of the available land, are farmed communally by 138,000 households.[188]

These figures clearly show the need for land reform to provide a more equal distribution of land to all Namibians. By 1999, fifty-one farms, compromising 305,556 hectares, had been purchased by the government for resettlement. By 2003, only 118 farms, totaling 710,000 hectares, had been purchased by the government.[189] This increased to 134 farms in 2005, amounting to a total cost of U.S. $105 million. By 2005, the state had resettled 37,100 people out of an estimated 243,000 "land-hungry" citizens.[190] To assist in its land reform program, the state had also embarked on an extensive land valuation process, in order to impose a land tax on the 12,700 farms on the valuation roll.

While the Namibian government has blamed the slow reform process on the unwillingness of white farmers to sell at reasonable rates, this is a half-truth that ignores the unequal deprivations of the past. The pressure on the government to achieve land reform is not as significant as it would have been had the Owambo suffered greater losses during colonialism and apartheid. Since land deprivation primarily affects the minority groups, it has not been addressed with sufficient urgency. Furthermore, SWAPO's roots in the late 1950s and its formation in April 1960 arose out of the belief that the Owambo were excluded from the process undertaken by the Herero Chiefs' Council (established in 1945). After the acceptance of the Organization of African Unity (OAU) principle that it could only support one liberation organization, the South West African Liberation Front was formed in 1963 as a coalition between SWAPO and the South West African National Union (SWANU; established in 1959). However, due to much rivalry between internal and external factions, this coalition was short-lived.

The government's reluctance to deal with historical claims by the Nama, Herero, and Damara is also attributed to "the attitude of some of the SWAPO

[South West African People's Organization] leadership ... that these groups did not participate in SWAPO's armed struggle and thus do not deserve to be awarded in any way."[191] Yet this is not entirely valid, as SWAPO had many high-ranking Herero and Damaras during the liberation period.[192] Additionally, there seems to be lingering resentment because the Herero Chiefs' Council formed the National Unity Democratic Organization (NUDO) in 1964, ending its cooperation with SWANU. The formation of NUDO was regarded as a strategy to compete with SWANU and SWAPO.[193]

There is further animosity because NUDO's leader, the Paramount Chief of the Herero, Chief Clemens Kapuuo, led NUDO into the Turnhalle Conference in 1975 and then into the Democratic Turnhalle Alliance (DTA; an alliance of groups) in 1977. When independence came, they competed in the elections as an opposition party. In that election (1989), the DTA won twenty-nine percent of the vote (twenty-one seats), while SWAPO received fifty-seven percent (forty-one seats). Paramount Chief Kuaima Riruako was President of the DTA from 1982 to 1990. NUDO broke away from the DTA in 2004 and now has three seats in the Namibian Parliament. According to Suzman, there is a widespread perception that SWAPO has intentionally neglected areas traditionally hostile to it.[194]

While SWAPO and the Namibian government are resistant to acknowledging the role of the Herero in the liberation struggle, it must be remembered that the Herero resisted German colonial domination in the war of liberation from 1904 onward. Later, the Herero Chiefs' Council (formed in 1945) was one of the first groups to bring the question of Namibia's future before the United Nations. It was the Herero leader Hosea Kutako who led the successful fight to ensure that then-South West Africa was not incorporated into South Africa. The major reason for the current animosity toward the Herero seems to stem from the occurrences since the 1970s. The relationship between SWAPO and the Herero soured when Hosea Kutako's successor, Clemens Kapuuo, began to seek and attain a role internationally. This was exacerbated when Kapuuo attempted to overturn the international community's recognition of SWAPO as the sole representative of the Namibian people. His objection to the fact that only SWAPO was receiving funding added to the prevailing tensions between the groups.[195] When this campaign was unsuccessful, he attacked SWAPO frequently, driving further wedges between them.

When Kapuuo agreed, in 1978, to participate in the Turnhalle constitutional process designed by the South African government, SWAPO was indignant, as they did not believe his claim that he was acting on behalf of the Herero; they saw it as an anti-SWAPO maneuver. By the same token, Kapuuo's decision was rejected by some Herero groups, such as the Tjamuaha-Maherero Royal House, who argued that he was not recognized by all Hereros.[196] (The Turnhalle process still enjoys recognition in the Namibian political milieu, and the DTA has endured as a political party into the twenty-first century.[197])

In 1978, Clemens Kapuuo was succeeded by Kuaima Riruako after Kapuuo was assassinated by unknown persons. Disputes over whether Riruako is the legal paramount chief of the community have fueled divisions among the Herero. Riruako was president of the opposition DTA, which has been perceived as an ally of South Africa during the war of liberation. Riruako remains an opposition member of Parliament and leader of the Herero political party NUDO. The dispute about his status as paramount chief is part of a long history of protracted succession contestations. These disputes continue to divide the Herero, some of whom argue that Riruako cannot be a political leader as well as the paramount chief.

When Maherero Tjamuaha died in 1890, the dispute over who was to succeed him lasted four years. It was only because of the intervention of the German colonial forces that Samuel Maherero, the son of the former chief, who actually did not have a right to this position, became the new chief.[198] The role of the German authorities in proclaiming Samuel the Paramount Chief is seen by some to have had a lasting effect on how the Herero viewed the German Colonial administration. The determination as to who was the Paramount Chief also contributed to the uprising that occurred in 1896, which resulted in the shooting of the lawful heir of Maherero, Nikodemus, and his subchief, Kahimema, by the German authorities because of their role in the uprising. Nikodemus's half-brother, Asa Riasura, is thought to have harbored resentment about these executions, which contributed to the 1904 uprising.[199]

The matter of the paramount chieftainship continues to be an issue. It led to the formation of The Association for the Preservation of the Tjamuaha/Maherero Royal House in 1970, to oppose Kapuuo's succession of the deceased Chief Kutako.

Given the above-mentioned context, it is not surprising that the return of land confiscated during colonial times has not been a priority since independence.

Herero Day Commemoration in Okahandja: Ovaherero Chief Kuaima Riruako at the grave of Chief Hosea Kutako. Courtesy of Klaus Dierks.

Land reform, as such, has not been off the agenda—within a month of independence, a parliamentary resolution called for a national conference on the issue. The consultative National Conference on Land Reform and the Land Question was held in 1991, but a resolution achieved by consensus stated that "given the complexities in redressing ancestral land claims, restitution of such claims in full is impossible."[200] It was reasoned that giving historical claims validity would limit land access by all Namibians who had experienced discrimination during the pre-independence years.[201]

Although the state is less than keen to address these historical claims, various communities have attempted to claim their land and gain greater roles in the state. Not only the Herero have asserted claims for land restoration and/or compensation for land dispossession—the San, the Rehoboth Basters, and the Kavango have done so too.[202]

Before the independence elections in 1990, the question of whether Namibia was to become a federal state was very important to minority groups, as the dominance of the Owambos (and therefore SWAPO) was problematic to them. The rejection of a federal state during the constitutional process saw the Basters withdraw from that process and declare Rehoboth independent. The Basters occupied government buildings for more than a year. In June 1995, the Basters went to court to reclaim their traditional land. However, the High Court found against them, and the decision was confirmed on appeal by the Supreme Court in 1997. The Basters then decided not to pursue their claim further because of high legal costs and the ill health of their chief. When their chief died, the new chief adopted a more conciliatory attitude. However, concerns about the transfer of ownership of the Basters' communal land to the state again heightened tensions.[203]

The unhappiness and antagonism about a range of issues, including the status of minority groups and land ownership, could possibly lead the Herero and other groups to pursue their indigenous and historical land claims in Namibia—against the Namibian government.[204] Land reform has not been entirely ignored. The Agricultural (Commercial) Land Reform Act, 1995 (No. 6 of 1995) provides that land be acquired on a willing buyer-willing seller basis while government had a preferential right to purchase the land. A Land Reform Advisory Commission was established and the government of Namibia designated 192 farms, supposedly owned by German and South African absentees, for transfer. All of these farms were below the Red Line.

While, officially, relatively few land transfers have occurred as transfers are still based on the willing buyer-willing seller principle, *The Namibian* reported in March 2005 that it had established, on a visit to the Maize Triangle, that more than forty-five percent of the farms in that area had been sold. This news came at the same time that the new President of Namibia was being sworn in. He cautioned that Namibia may face "a revolution" if white farmers did not agree to sell their land and stated that the country could become "ungovernable."[205]

THE NAMIBIAN GOVERNMENT'S VIEW OF THE HERERO COURT CASES IN THE UNITED STATES

The Namibian government has not supported the claim of the Hereros. At times, they have provided mixed messages about the claims and whether these claims ought to succeed, especially more recently. In 2000, then Prime Minister Hage Geingob criticized the Herero leaders for seeking compensation for Herero-speaking Namibians only,[206] saying that they (the Government) "are being condemned by the Chief for not taking action. But we cannot just say we want money for the Hereros. Not only the Hereros suffered the consequences of war. All Namibians suffered and the best would be to help all Namibians by providing roads and schools."[207] On another occasion, the Namibian Prime Minister said it was unfortunate that the issue of reparations had been politicized and questioned why the issue of Herero reparations had not been brought before the Namibian Parliament. This has not happened because the Herero accuse the governing SWAPO party of diverting $500 million in German aid to Owambo voters.[208] Therefore, they want Germany to establish a fund to allow Hereros to purchase land and cattle. According to Gottlob Mbaukaua, an opposition party Herero leader in Okahandja, "What we are saying is that the Germans, because they only killed the Herero and no one else, must uplift us."[209]

The Namibian government declares that it has not supported the Herero claim because, while the "Herero and Nama lost all their lands, the inhabitants of the Ovambo kingdoms were never driven off their lands by either the German or South African colonial presence. As such, the present government does not feel itself called upon to fight for something that is not part and parcel of its shared historical experience. In addition, the government is at pains to ensure that its heroes, and not those of another sector of society, receive recognition."[210] Furthermore there are concerns that about half of the development aid and much technical and other assistance come from Germany and that arrangement ought not to be affected.

Although the government does not support the Herero, the Herero genocide was extensively used by SWAPO as a political tool during the resistance to South African rule and the process to achieve independence. Herero ideologies, the loss of land, and the genocide gave impetus to the development of formal resistance politics and the formation and growth of the political parties SWANU and SWAPO. In the exile years the Herero genocide was used as propaganda to rid Namibia of South Africa and move toward independence.[211]

The way that different histories are interpreted and valued can be seen in the celebration of Hero's Day, August 26. While it is a national holiday in Namibia, its origins and significance are contested. For SWAPO and its supporters, it is a commemoration of August 26, 1966, when SWAPO operatives attacked the South African police at Ongulumbashe in the north of then South West Africa. For the Herero, it marks the remembrance of August 26, 1923, when the body of Samuel Maherero was brought back from Botswana where he had been living in exile since the extermination order in 1904. Each year on this date the Herero hold commemorations in Okahandja where the graves of various Herero leaders are located.

The role of the Herero War in Namibian history was recognized by former Namibian President, Sam Nujoma, in his capacity as President of SWAPO in exile (before independence). In the preface to the Dreschler book, he said: "Without a sound grasp of these past events which lie behind the present difficulties in our country, Namibian revolutionaries and patriots would not be in a position to formulate appropriate strategies for dismantling of the previous social order as well as for its replacement."[212] Thus, before independence, the Herero War and the status of the Herero victims were politicized and adopted as key issues to lobby world opinion to support the Namibian people in their fight for liberation and independence from South Africa.

While the genocide was a unifying factor in the battle for independence, after 1990 it reverted back to being "only" a Herero issue. Independence politics saw the Owambo majority of the population assume control of the government, while minority groups such as the Herero were relegated to the opposition.[213] The SWAPO government has "tried to ensure that Herero claims for reparations would remain muted or couched within the demands of the nation-state, which they controlled."[214] Nonetheless, the government has made some pro-reparation statements. One such statement came from Theo-Ben Gurirab, the Namibian Prime Minister in 1995, who said that the atrocities committed by the Germans remained a "festering sore" and reparations needed discussion "at some stage, but that it was not a government priority at that stage."[215]

In recent times, however, the Namibian government has adopted a more open stance to the reparations claims. In fact, on October 26, 2006, the Namibian National Assembly unanimously (and therefore with SWAPO support) adopted a motion acknowledging the genocide and supporting the reparations claims. On the thawing of relations between SWAPO and the Herero, see Chapter Three.

COMMEMORATIONS OF THE GENOCIDE

The twenty-first century has seen regular commemorations of genocide events. In 1995 the Armenian genocide was commemorated, and in 2005, the sixty-year anniversary of the liberation of the Nazi concentration camp, Auschwitz, was celebrated.

In 2004, the centenary of the Herero genocide was commemorated with various ceremonies in Namibia, including conferences and anniversaries to observe specific events that had occurred exactly 100 years ago. While the Auschwitz and Armenian events were internationally celebrated, the Namibian event was primarily a national celebration, although it included the German government. The Armenian and Namibian scenarios are similar in that both experienced genocide while they were not independent states, and both countries have recently obtained independence.

In Namibia, two complementary groups or committees decided to hold commemorative events throughout the year. One, The Coordinating Committee for the Commemoration of the Ovaherero Genocide, 100 Years After, was established as a community-based, non-political organization.[216] Two events were held in January 2004 to commemorate the official beginning of the war: one in Windhoek and one in Okahandja (Waterberg), where the battle of Hamakari took place. The Namibian government did not officially take part in the January commemorations, apparently because of the differences among the two committees, but individuals, ministers, and high-ranking government officials did attend one or the other function. At the later events, various government officials participated more fully and even delivered addresses. The controversial nature of the commemorations gave rise to a perception that President Nujoma did not want to be part of these events and had declined several invitations to attend and participate.[217] However, at times, President Nujoma[218] has seemingly been sensitive to the war and the atmosphere it can and has caused. In August 2003, when a German Scout group, the *Deutsche Pfadfinder Bund*, wanted to commemorate the war (as they had done annually) by touring the burial ground of German soldiers, President Nujoma prohibited it, arguing that the event was "provocation of the highest order." Minister Ngarikutuke Tjiriange also stated that the commemoration would have seen "a breakdown of peace, law, and order in the country."[219]

At the Okahandja event in 2004, Germany's ambassador to Namibia and Chief Riruako spoke, both conveying messages of peace, reconciliation, and development. After these commemoration events, the two committees vowed to

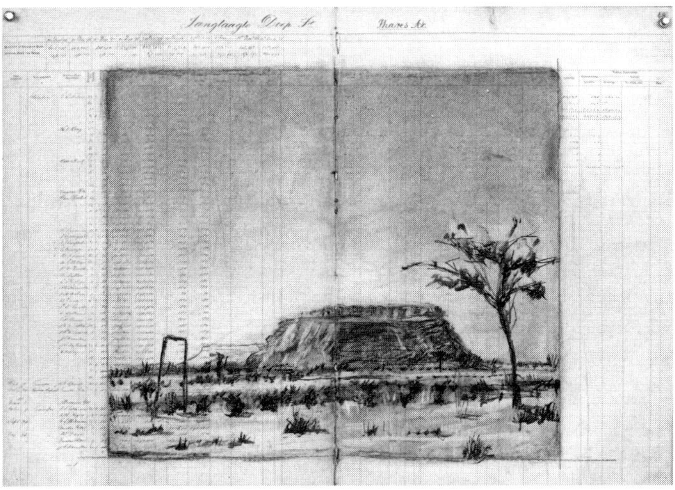

Drawing for Black Box/Chambre Noire 2005. Courtesy of William Kentridge.

work toward a single agenda, dispelling perceptions that the two were at odds. Subsequently, later events, i.e., the anniversary of the battle of Waterberg in August 2004 and the commemoration of the issuing of the extermination order in October 2004, involved both committees.

Hence, the Namibian genocide was commemorated with a number of events in 2004. One of these was a conference at the University of Namibia, themed "Decontaminating the Namibian Past." It aimed to reduce the misrepresentations and ignorance that exist about the Herero, achieve greater tolerance among the various communities in Namibia, and "promote empathy in Namibia's historical discourses."[220] One panel of the 2004 University of Namibia conference focused on Damara history.

Not all the conferences and events of the centenary year have been unreservedly positive. One conference that caused heated debate and controversy in both Germany and Namibia was a symposium held in Bremen in November 2004 to discuss the reconciliation process between the German Government and the Herero. Among the delegates were the German Minister for Economic Development and Cooperation Heidemarie Wieczorek-Zeul (who had offered the German apology three months before), and Namibia's Minister of Information and Broadcasting, Nangolo Mumba. This conference did not promote the reconciliation process, as the Herero leadership did not feel it was a useful or legitimate attempt to address their concerns. On the contrary, they perceived it to be retarding the efforts to establish dialogue. The Paramount Chief emphasized that reconciliation had to happen between the German Government and the Herero, and voiced his concern that "reconciliation cannot be the exercise of an academic conference" and that he detected attempts to divide the Hereros.[221] He urged delegates to "Stop adding insult to injury by encouraging division amongst our people. Any continuation of such evil designs will be viewed by all Ovahereros as a second round of genocide being perpetuated against our people. We shall resist that with all legitimate means at our disposal."[222] Chief Riruako listed the conditions for reconciliation as being (1) a genuine apology by the Government of the Federal Republic of Germany (FRG); (2) acceptance of that apology by the descendants of the victims of the war of extermination against the Ovaherero; (3) willingness by the FRG government to engage the leadership of the Ovaherero in looking for practical and meaningful ways to make good for the physical, material, emotional, and psychological damage done to the Ovaherero by the German colonial authorities.[223]

According to newspaper reports Minister Wieczorek-Zeul was visibly upset by this response and commented: "I heard very well what the Chief said, and I think that some of his remarks are detrimental to the process of reconciliation. It is unacceptable to use the word genocide in this context."[224]

Hence, key issues which remain stumbling blocks for both sides include the use of the word "genocide" and whether reconciliation is possible in the absence of a program of reparations. An additional tension that emerged from the Bremen conference is that the involvement of others results in the perception that the Herero are being told what to do. Critically, the Herero were not officially consulted in the process of setting up the conference, nor were they involved in determining the agenda or program.[225] Such omissions can only cause further resentment and anger.

Another issue is the failure of exhibitions and events reflecting on the histories of those countries that had colonies to include reflections of their colonial endeavors. In 2000, Smith noted that a new German History Exhibition in Berlin did not even mention the Herero Genocide at all. In contrast, a 2005 exhibition in The Royal Museum for Central Africa in Brussels examined the relationships between Belgium and the Congo. This exhibition focused on the Belgium Congo and attempted to paint a picture from all perspectives, including a focus on the abuses that were committed.

Attempts to gain recognition of the occurrences at the beginning of the twentieth century have a long vintage. Even in Namibia, the only memorials that exist are for the Germans who died in the Herero War.[226] Remarkably, there are no memorials to honor the Herero who died during that war. Even though Namibia is now independent, the statues to the former German colonialists still remain. According to Gewald and Silvester, the most photographed statue in Namibia is *Der Reiter*, a statue unveiled on Kaiser Wilhelm II's birthday on January 27, 1914, memorializing the 1,633 Germans who died in the Herero War.[227]

Leadership of the Nama, including Chief Witbooi and Simon Koper. Courtesy of Klaus Dierks.

The statues are only part of the colonial legacy still visible in contemporary Namibia. Places, streets, etc. still bear the names of conquerors from colonial history. Many of the huge farms are still occupied by German farmers,[228] whose farms carry German names (although some of these farms have English, Afrikaans, or even local names). One example of renaming is that of the Windhoek main road, which has been changed from *Kaiserstrasse* (after Kaiser Wilhelm II) to Independence Avenue. In certain cases names have been changed, but often only to accommodate other leaders requiring acknowledgment. With many colonial names remaining, the issue of names is significant. Despite numerous proposals to change various names, the sticking point has often been which language to use for new names, given the multitude of languages in use in Namibia.

Most names in Herero areas have not been changed from those in use before independence. While proposals have been submitted to revive traditional Herero names in Herero areas, the Namibian Parliament rejected them in mid-2005, arguing that it would be at variance with reconciliation and would be perceived as such by white members of the community. One minister argued that the name Otjomuise for Windhoek was a name that "nobody knows how to pronounce."[229] The Herero responded that the same applied to Ouagadougou, the capital of Burkina Faso, to which Namibian ministers often travel.[230]

As mentioned before, the statues of some leaders are also controversial. The statue of the Herero chief Hosea Kutako outside the Parliament buildings in Windhoek was wrapped in black plastic bags and under armed guard for many years on government orders. Only recently was the plastic removed. Even today, the status of some traditional leaders is highly politicized, and only some leaders are formally recognized. The perception lingers that recognition is in large part contingent on links to and support of the ruling party.

GERMAN DEVELOPMENT AID TO NAMIBIA AS A SUBSTITUTE FOR REPARATIONS

For many years, Germany has countered claims that it is liable for reparations for its past conduct using the argument that it has a special relationship with Namibia and anything it owes to Namibia is given by way of development aid. This section will evaluate that relationship and whether Germany's obligations are indeed met by way of development aid.

There certainly is a close relationship between Germany and Namibia. In this regard Heike Becker has noted: "Namibia is not just any country. Seventy-four years after the end of colonial rule in German SWA, a wide ranging network between Germans and their favorite colony exists from family ties to German politicians and organizations."[231] While Germany espouses this notion of its special relationship with Namibia, a comparison of its relationships and development aid packages[232] to other countries does not support this claim. Although Germany has been Namibia's biggest donor, this does not mean that its support has been commensurate with their historical relationship. Germany disburses about 7.5 billion dollars a year in official development aid (ODA), which is about 0.28 percent of its gross national income (GNI). In proportion to gross national income disbursed, it is twelfth on the list of countries giving such aid. This figure has decreased from 0.42 percent in 1990.[233] In terms of the amount given, Germany was the fifth highest in the world, behind the United States, Japan, France, and the United Kingdom. It was also third on the list of countries granting debt forgiveness over the period 1990 to 2003.[234] Yet it allocated only 1.4 percent of government spending to ODA, compared to 7.3 percent on the military.[235]

That being said, Germany hardly imports or exports to Namibia. In fact, less than one percent of imports and only about two percent of exports flow between Germany and Namibia.[236] In addition, Germany's claim that Namibia receives the highest levels of aid seems to be false. Between 1985 and 2001 Namibia was in absolute terms only twenty-third on the list of African receivers[237] of development aid from Germany. The amount given has been about $20 million per year, while Egypt as the highest recipient received more than $220 million per year. If only the post-independence years are considered, Namibia's position as a receiver of aid from Germany improves to twentieth position.[238] During these years the amount given to Namibia has been about $29 million dollars per year, compared to the more than $250 million per year received by Egypt. In both periods, Egypt, the highest African recipient of German ODA, received approximately ten times more than Namibia. Another of Germany's former colonies, Tanzania, ranks third in the first period (receiving an average of $61 million per year) and fifth in the shorter period (on average $65 million per year).[239]

It could be argued that a more realistic measure of aid distribution requires evaluating the numbers on the basis of population size, i.e., per capita. Due to Namibia's small population, this calculation for the period 1985 to 2001 places Namibia second on the list ($13 per capita per year on average) behind Cape Verde ($22 per capita per year on average). Namibia still does not top the list, as Cape Verde receives about double the aid per capita. Only if one looks at ODA from a relative point of view, i.e., considering both the population numbers and the percentage of ODA that Namibia receives from Germany compared to donations from other countries, does Namibia top the list. Interestingly, aid to Namibia has peaked each year following visits to the country by Chancellor Helmut Kohl and President Roman Herzog.[240] Equally significant is the fact that the one area in which Germany contributes appreciably to the Namibian economy is tourism. According to Schuring, "German tourists flock to Namibia for a simple reason: they can find a little bit of Germany on the African continent; being far away but nevertheless at home."[241]

To complicate this picture, German aid to Namibia does not go specifically to the minority groups that suffered at the hands of German colonialists, such as the Herero or Nama.[242] At the same time, aid is not reparations nor is it a measure to restore the Herero to the position they held at the beginning of the twentieth century.

CONCLUSION

In 1914, soldiers from South Africa took control of German South West Africa. Under the Versailles Treaty, the territory became a League of Nations mandate exercised by South Africa after the war. This had little effect on Herero land ownership patterns: despite a degree of hope that their confiscated land would be returned to them, this did not happen. Reservations for the Herero and other minority groups were embraced as a means to ensure control over these groups. Resistance to outside rule, be it German or South African, was not simply accepted. It was, however, the Herero who initiated the response to colonial rule and led the campaigns to oust both the Germans and the South Africans. During the liberation struggle, century-old Herero resistance and dispossession was used politically. Today, again for political reasons, this history is no longer respected, and the plight of the Herero in modern Namibian society is not a priority. Regardless, the memory of what occurred is very much alive in the Herero community today, even if there is not always consensus on who represents this community, nor on the steps required to address the legacy of German rule.

2

The Legal Implications of Gross Human Rights and Humanitarian Law Violations Committed from the Nineteenth Century Onward

> ... if the Hague Convention represented customary international law, then its rules should have applied because the Herero had not relinquished their full sovereignty. Their chief had signed an agreement giving Germany control over their foreign affairs and the right to trade without hindrance. In return, the German government promised to respect native customs and abstain from any act that would be illegal in its own country. At a minimum, therefore, German law should have applied to state action in Namibia.[1]

Though drafted in 1899 (and contained in the 1899 Hague Convention), Martens' "principles of humanity" are still an appropriate expression of what may be called the "common denominator" of international humanitarian and human rights law. The principle of humanity, which requires that the inherent dignity of any human being be recognized and protected, is the first and foremost yardstick for both bodies of law.[2]

This chapter examines the legal origins, interrelationship, and dimensions of international law, the law of armed conflict, international human rights law, and international criminal law to determine what the law proscribes and from when these proscriptions were valid. While one could claim that these questions are not relevant, as the violations occurred and redress ought to be given regardless, they bolster the argument that reparations are payable for the harm caused. It reinforces the idea that what occurred then was unlawful, and thus legally reparations are due. Questions relating to reparations will be addressed in Chapter Three, where it will be argued that individual reparations were known and accepted in international law at the beginning of the twentieth century and that at that time individuals were even able to take up these questions without relying on their own state.

This chapter explores what the applicable legal regime is, when it came into being, and when the protections against these types of conduct became available. It is argued that by the turn of the twentieth century many laws were already available and in force. While it is commonly held that international protections against human rights violations were activated in the World War II era, they actually were accessible much earlier. Without having to resort to natural law or other schools of thought that claim such protection was available since ancient times, the legal history shows that a system for protecting groups' and individual's human rights was available from at least the nineteenth century. Some argue that individuals could not access this system at the time, but regardless, there were indeed measures protecting minorities, protecting people against slavery and the slave trade, and protecting people against certain types of warfare long before the 1940s. In fact, international law originated centuries before the 1800s. Various authors have noted that international law precedes the Peace of Westphalia of 1648.[3] Both the fields of humanitarian law and international human rights law certainly developed considerably in the nineteenth century. This chapter will also show how the international system of rights protection, even outside the rules of war, was not only present in the nineteenth century, but developing rapidly. It will therefore be proposed that an international system of human rights to protect people existed, although there was no real mechanism to enforce or realize those protections.

This chapter evaluates whether the atrocities committed against the Herero, Nama, and Damara would today be classified as crimes, or civil wrongs such as in delict or tort law, and whether they would constitute a violation of international human rights and international humanitarian law. It will further examine what the relevant legal systems were in 1904. Some of the critical questions are whether the events constituted war, whether war crimes were committed, and if so, whether the law of war was applicable at the time. Additionally, this chapter will consider whether there were transgressions of international human rights law, such as genocide or crimes against humanity, and whether that body of law applied at the time. Other than tracing the pertinent legal issues to determine what crimes were committed against the Herero, the early history of customary law and ways of interpreting customary law are examined to show that by the twentieth century customary international law was indeed in force and is relevant to the events in GSWA. That system is explored to indicate that there was a war at the time and thus some humanitarian protections were available which would apply in the Herero case, but also that non-war-related protections applied as well. Specifically, the history of genocide is assessed. Although it is generally accepted that genocide as a crime genre only materialized during World War II, it is shown that the concept existed long before the actual term was born. It will be argued that genocide has been classified as a crime for hundreds of years and has functioned under multiple names in many languages, including English. Although some believe the historical origins of genocide as a crime stretch back even further, it at least dates back to the nineteenth century.

To determine Germany's direct liability for the events between 1903 and 1908 in then GSWA, various treaties are examined, as well as the standing of certain international crimes in international law. In 1958 Michael Scott wrote that, "the conduct of von Trotha and the German army in Tanganyika, Togoland, and the Cameroons were important factors in the development of international accountability at that time."[4] By then there was already legal liability for such acts, but the absence of mechanisms or procedures to bring people to book resulted in no accountability for such crimes.

This chapter also surveys some of the specific international treaties adopted by Germany and its predecessors to determine for which other historical crimes Germany would be liable. The inquiry includes questions regarding prescription or legal barring of such claims: would such crimes be barred by time because they happened so long ago, or does the nature of the crime preclude time-barring, i.e., would some interruption in the time-period be permitted? Appreciably Lord Anthony Gifford has noted that it was not possible for the people in a country that was subjected to colonialism to pursue those responsible for atrocities. How could they make such claims when their nation was seen only as a possession of the state that had committed the atrocities? Even after independence the colonial legacy and other forms of dependency have limited the ability of Africans in this regard.[5] As a result, Geraldine van Bueren has noted, "the passage of time has made Western States cozy with injustice."[6]

It will be argued that the massacre of the Herero people constituted genocide as defined in the Genocide Convention, was a crime against humanity, and violated the laws of war as found in various treaties as well as in customary international law. Critically, the German-Herero conflict amounted to a war, although one could debate whether it was an internal or an international war. This debate is complicated by the fact that while crimes against humanity and other crimes have their origins in codified law from 1899, they are also found independently of these treaties in customary international law. Yoram Dinstein has noted that crimes against humanity are a part of customary law, but their definition is "not free of doubt."[7]

A specific focus of this chapter is the Martens Clause, adopted into the Hague Conventions of 1899 and 1907 by unanimous vote. Germany was a party to the 1899 Convention, which entered into force on September 4, 1900.[8] The Conference was attended by twenty-seven states. Twenty of these were European countries, namely Germany, Austria, Belgium, Denmark, Spain, France, the United Kingdom, Greece, Italy, Luxembourg, Montenegro, the Netherlands, Portugal, Romania, Russia, Serbia, Sweden, Norway, Switzerland, and Bulgaria. Only seven countries—the United States, the Ottoman Empire, Mexico, China, Japan, Persia, and Siam—represented the rest of the world.[9] The Martens Clause constitutes the origins of international law in the positivistic sense, is considered applicable to the whole of international law,[10] and has shaped the development of customary international law, aspects of which are relevant to the Herero case. It will be argued that the Martens Clause is a specific and recognized provision providing protection to groups and individuals during both war and peace time. Judge Weeramantry has stated that "the Martens Clause clearly indicates that, behind specific rules as had already been formulated, there lay a body of general principles sufficient to be applied to such situations as had not already been dealt with by a specific rule."[11] Professor Martens originally introduced this clause at the Hague Peace Conference of 1899 because the delegates could not agree on the status of civilians who took up arms against an occupying force. Although the notion was specifically focused on protecting civilians, a much wider use was also intended and accepted by many. A small number have argued that it was merely a "diplomatic ploy to paper over strong disagreement between states by skillfully deferring the problem for a future discussion."[12] However, a much wider view of its significance is that it allows international law, particularly customary law, to continue to grow and develop progressively, and to deal with emergency situations and crises within the law (such as those arising from the current "war on terror") without having to wait for slow and sometimes fiercely resisted developments within the flawed world of state practice and treaty law. While it may be contended that this clause is applicable to international armed conflict only, it will be argued that it has relevance beyond that body of law and is in fact the recognition of principles of humanity and other notions found in international human rights law.

The wording of the Martens Clause is seen as the origin of the international legal concept of "crimes against humanity." In fact, Bassiouni asserts that the term "crime against humanity" originates in the preamble to the Hague Convention, and only the Nuremberg Charter brought it into positive international law. He argues that the notion of "crimes against humanity" has been part of the "general principles of law recognized by civilized nations," and that it originated in the Preambles of the First Hague Convention of 1899 and was expanded in the Fourth Hague Convention of 1907.[13] Nelayeva similarly notes that the concept of humanity is closely linked to the Martens Clause.[14] According to Jean Pictet, the notion of humanity means

> capture is preferable to wounding an enemy, and wounding him better than killing him; that non-combatants shall be spared as far as possible; that wounds inflicted be as light as possible, so that the injured can be treated and cured; that wounds cause the least possible pain; that captivity be made as endurable as possible.[15]

In this regard Ticehurst argues that this did not "append much to the existing laws of armed conflict as the protection extended by the principles of humanity appears to mirror the protection provided by the doctrine of military necessity."[16] He thus believes these protections to have already been available and that the clause merely codified them. However, while the Martens Clause is specific about the issue of humanity, the law of war—at least from 1899—also considered the necessity of actions taken during a war and the effects of the war. In the preamble to the 1899 Hague Convention (II), State parties agreed that the purpose of the Convention was "to diminish the evils of war, as far as military requirements permit."[17] Fundamentally, these protections relate to crimes against humanity in that they limit the targeting of civilian groups and prohibit causing "widespread or systematic" harm. While these provisions were meant to apply in times of war, they are applicable in the sense that they also reflect customary law (as will be discussed).

A critical question in any discussion of the legal consequences of what happened a hundred years ago concerns what legal action could have been taken at the time. Would the domestic law of the country where the claim is made apply, or would international law apply? If an international court or a UN tribunal hears the case, then certainly international law will be applied, but in relation to the specific country that is brought before such an institution. Thus, if Germany was brought before an international institution, that institution, after determining that it had jurisdiction, would apply international law to Germany from the time they became bound by the agreements they were party to. Claims can also be brought under various headings, such as international law in general, humanitarian law, human rights law, etc. Various aspects of international law or even domestic criminal law could be used to indicate the illegality of the conduct for which Germany is being sued. A claim could also be brought under general civil law, in which case the general principles of private law would apply. The specific private law applied would depend on the country in which the claim is brought, or which law the adjudicating court applied. As noted earlier, a central question is whether the Herero were sovereign or under German administration. Yet this would not rule out the application of either international or domestic law: even if, for example, it is found that the Herero were not sovereign, a court could apply international law such as the Genocide Convention.

The claims can also be brought before either a domestic or international court that could apply either international law (as stated) and/or public and/or private law principles. In private law, a court could and should apply principles such as torts or delict, as well as principles of unjust enrichment, depending on who the defendants were. Thus, if a case were brought in Namibia it might for example be possible to sue those beneficiaries who are in possession of land that was taken from the Herero on the basis of unjust enrichment. Obviously, the question of compensation might be complicated by cases where the current owners acquired such property much later, and by questions as to whether market value was paid or not. There may also be questions of unjust enrichment relating to the benefits attained by using slave or forced labor.

THE ORIGINS OF INTERNATIONAL LAW, INCLUDING CUSTOMARY INTERNATIONAL LAW

While it has often been argued that international law originated fairly recently, it has actually existed from the time that organized communities dealt with one another on a consistent basis. What has changed is the definition and meaning of the concept "international." What the ancient Egyptians or Greeks would have considered "international" would have been very limited, but it reflected the world as they knew it.[18] From a "Western" perspective, the "world" only really consisted of what we today know as the Middle East, North Africa, and Europe. But as technology developed to enable people to travel more widely, and as they began trading with more or less formalized societies on different continents, the term "international" gradually acquired a global dimension, and international law came to govern many states and societies. At various times, different movements in philosophy and legal theory interpreted international law to mean the law governing all members of humanity (natural law), different states and their governments (positivistic state law), or some combination thereof.[19] International law originally grew from a combination of the relations between two or more societies or states and the basic societal norms that had emerged in them.[20] In other words, local customs gave rise to the rules that governed trade and other interactions between states. When the customs of two states clashed, conflict ensued; alternatively, customs often adapted to smooth relationships between the conflicting parties. In many cases, societies found that their general practices and customs were sufficiently similar to be reconciled to the satisfaction of all parties involved. These practices slowly solidified into the fabric of what we now call international law. Nearly all of the great empires and societies have literature that established in writing regulations for dealing with other states and visiting diplomats (although the terms utilized may be different than those used today). The current "law of nations" owes its birth to Hugo Grotius, who, in the seventeenth century in the aftermath of the Thirty Years War and the fall of the power of the church in favor of the nation-state, developed a theory of law that extended beyond the individual state.

International law is said to arise from a variety of sources. Scholars commonly articulate its definition as "a set of rules generally regarded and accepted as binding in relations between states and nations."[21] This statement is consistent with a positivistic legal tradition in which a sovereign exists to posit laws governing subjects, and those sovereigns would determine international law (given that there were some enforcement mechanisms). Yet other scholars maintain that international law includes not only state law and practices and the "law of nations," but also a rich tradition of societal and cultural customs, statements and pronouncements made by states and their representatives, universal rights and duties, and other sources such as judicial declarations and commentaries.

Article 38 of the ICJ identifies the sources of international law as being general principles, custom, and treaties between states (state governments).[22] International treaty law is composed of obligations states voluntarily accept between themselves and express in treaties.[23] According to Pustogarov "international law is not merely a device for recording the formation of relations between states, but is also a manifestation of the moral values of the human race."[24]

Yet the focus of this study is also customary law, particularly what was applicable at that time and the role and impact on customary law of the Martens Clause that was found in both the 1899 and 1907 Hague Conventions. In this regard the Statute of the International Court of Justice describes "custom" as "evidence of a general practice accepted as law."[25] It should be noted that "general practice" does not specifically refer to state practice but could include religious, ethnic, cultural, or other practices that are commonly accepted as law. Further, by whom the practice(s) should be accepted is not specifically articulated. This implies that any of the following could potentially accept a practice as customary law: a small group of highly trained legal professionals and judges, the more powerful nations capable of effecting enforcement, a majority of state governments, or even a majority of humanity. Arguments have been made in favor of each of these entities. In addition, one could take the position that through acquiescence by states, groups, and individuals, a practice could become part of customary law.

Customary law can be said to consist of established patterns of behavior (practices or statements) that can be objectively verified within a particular social setting. The modern codification of civil law developed out of the customs of particular religious and cultural groups, expressions of law (social norms) that developed in particular communities and were gradually collected and recorded by local jurists.[26] Such customs acquired the force of law when they became the undisputed rule by which certain entitlements (rights) or obligations (duties) were regulated between members of a community.[27] It could therefore be said that all law utilized today has its origins in custom and customary law.

In international law, traditionally (since the Grotian period and specifically since the middle of the nineteenth century), customary law referred to the "Law of Nations" (other than treaty law) or the legal norms developed through the customary exchanges between states over time, whether based on diplomacy or aggression.[28] Essentially, legal obligations were said to arise between states and state governments to regulate relationships and ensure the managing of mutual affairs ran consistently with accepted state conduct and universally accepted basic norms and practices. These regulating customs could also change depending on the acceptance or rejection of particular acts by states, peoples, or the international community as a whole. Yet in practice for the most part, prior to the introduction of individual rights in international law and the Universal Declaration of Human Rights (1948), only state practice was used to determine custom.

There are two main conflicting positions regarding the categorization of what constitutes customary law. Roberts refers to these opposing stances as the "traditional" and "modern" positions of interpreting customary law.[29] She also identifies the conflict between those scholars who support customary law as defined narrowly by general state practice (what she terms "action") and *opinio juris*[30] (what she terms "statements").[31] According to Brierly, "the best evidence for the existence of international law is that every actual state recognizes that it does exist and that it is itself under obligation to observe it. States may often violate international law, just as individuals often violate municipal law, but no more than individuals do states defend their violations by claiming they are above the law."[32] This statement could be expanded to include cultures, religions, ethnic societies, and non-state actors (groups, corporations, etc.).

THE INTER-RELATIONSHIP[33] OF HUMAN RIGHTS LAW AND HUMANITARIAN LAW

The general view is that international humanitarian law and international human rights law have been independent of each other. While there has always been some degree of overlap, at the beginning of the twentieth century the two legal dominions were distinct: the laws of war (humanitarian law) applied only to the handling of combatants and non-combatants by their enemies in wartime, while international human rights law governed the relationship between states and their citizens in peacetime.[34] On the basis of this distinction many argue that the prohibitions articulated in the laws of war would only apply to the "enemy" and suggest that in peacetime a state had relative freedom regarding the treatment of its own people.

However, while humanitarian and human rights laws have ostensibly been discrete, they do intersect.[35] They have shared characteristics and convergences stretching back more than a hundred years—and even further back if one embraces the view of the natural law school and others that these concepts have a long and deep tradition in international as well as domestic law.

Accordingly, there is recognition that human rights and humanitarian law coincide on the concepts of dignity, humanity, and necessity, which were specifically introduced into the laws of war, and elsewhere, by the Martens Clause. At this point in treaty law, and possibly earlier in customary law, these different bodies of law began to intersect. Josh Kastenberg notes that the developments post-World War II simply codified existing law.[36] Similarly, Best asserts that a large part of the modern law of war has developed simply as a codification and universalization of the customs and conventions of vocational/professional soldiering.[37]

INTERNATIONAL HUMANITARIAN LAW TODAY

That Germany was at war with the Herero from 1904 does not seem to be in doubt. However, of concern is whether Germany committed war crimes in terms of current law, and whether their conduct amounted to violations of the legal regime of 1904. Hence it is imperative to determine what war crimes encompass and whether the same or similar standards or legal designations existed at that time.

International humanitarian law comprises two parts: the law of Geneva, which concerns the protection of those who are not or are no longer part of the war; and the law of The Hague, which deals with the way warfare is conducted. Dugard notes that the "law of Geneva distinguishes clearly between international and internal conflicts in respect of criminal sanctions. 'Grave breaches' are committed only in international conflicts and they alone can give rise to prosecution or extradition."[38] Yet he does not mention civil liability, a major question in regard to the liability of those not criminally liable but liable to repair the harm caused. He also focuses on treaty law and not customary law. He is certainly correct in noting that "the most significant extension of criminal sanctions to acts involving the systematic violation of human rights in internal conflicts has been brought about through the broadening of the scope of international crimes."[39] However, this omits the issue of civil liability that occurs once the act is committed. Thus, the act could be a tort or delict at the same time of its commission, in addition to or independent of whether it is a crime.

While Dugard suggests that "human rights law is different as it is primarily concerned with relations between States and their nationals in time of peace,"[40] human rights law does indeed apply even in times of war, as certain wartime issues are still governed by this law. Further, while human rights law is often primarily concerned with the relationship between states and individuals, this too can be challenged on the basis that human rights is now also concerned with relationships between individuals, and between individuals and other non-state actors. Dugard further maintains that "human rights treaties are largely designed to deal with individual and not systematic violations of protected rights."[41] Again, this cannot be supported, as human rights law is concerned with genocide and other types of systematic violations; because these types of violations can occur outside of warfare, they often fall under human rights law.

Regarding the way war can legally be conducted, the laws of war today are found in the 1949 Geneva Conventions[42] and the two Optional Protocols,[43] which are basically the codification of humanitarian law. That which occurs outside of what is permissible is classified as a war crime. The four Geneva Conventions deal with the wounded and sick on land, the wounded and sick at sea, prisoners of war, and civilians. Some of the prohibited conduct relevant to the Herero situation includes willful killing, torture or inhumane treatment, willfully causing great suffering or serious injury to body or health, and unlawful confinement of a civilian. Today the law regulates who constitutes illegitimate targets: those who are not or are not anymore part of the conflict, including civilians; military staff no longer part of the combat; medical personnel, etc. The law also circumscribes which methods and means of attack are permitted and which are deemed illegal. The latter include giving no quarter orders and perfidy.

In the case of GWSA, perfidy occurred when von Trotha invited the Herero to come and make peace and then shot them.[44] The prohibition on perfidy is found in the 1863 Lieber Code in Article 16,[45] and in the 1899 Hague Regulations, which allowed what is commonly called "ruses," but prohibited perfidy or treachery.[46]

Executions committed during the period 1904–1905. Courtesy of Klaus Dierks.

Other provisions include that prisoners must be treated humanely, that reprisals against prisoners of war are illegal, and that all prisoners of war be treated alike by the detaining power, without any adverse distinction based on race, nationality, religious belief, political opinions, or any other distinction founded on similar criteria. For civilians, murder, torture, corporal punishment, etc. are prohibited.

Again, some argue that the Hague Regulations are only applicable between contracting parties and that the *si omnes* provisions[47] of the Hague Convention ensure that the protections available do not apply to other groups that are not party to the Conventions, but as will be argued throughout this book, the acts can be judged as war crimes on the basis of customary international law.

INTERNATIONAL HUMANITARIAN LAW IN 1904

The idea of 'war crimes' has a long vintage.[48] The question here is the extent to which it was developed by 1904 as well as its applicability in the Herero case. International humanitarian law would apply in its conventional form if the conflict was considered an international armed conflict at the time. If the Herero-German war was considered an international armed conflict, then the rules of humanitarian law would apply to it. On the other hand, it has been argued that the Herero are not able to rely on these provisions, as they were not party to the Conventions. Yet many agree that this is not necessarily fatal, as customary international law then often mirrored what the treaties contained.

One of the debates within international law relevant to the Herero claims is whether individuals are subject to, and can legitimately claim rights under, international law.[49] Dugard, for example, has noted that international law is "a body of rules and principles which are binding upon states in their relations with one another"; yet he concedes that although early on international law was once concerned only with states, this is no longer the case.[50] Other actors now fall within its purview. Certainly, there is a commonly held view that when it comes to insurgents and belligerents, international law was deemed relevant a long time ago.[51] However, this aspect is not directly significant to the Herero case, as they were undoubtedly involved in a war. The question is rather: if the laws of war were the only body of law that existed then, did they only apply to international armed conflict or also to internal armed conflict? The general consensus is that all humanitarian law treaties before the 1949 Geneva Conventions did not deal with internal armed conflicts because it was thought that insurgents should only be entitled to the protection of law when in control of territory and if they had sufficient support from the population to permit them to "exercise government-type functions."[52] Cassese notes there must be effective control over the territory and that the conflict should endure for some time and attain a particular scale of intensity.[53] In such a case, belligerent status would be conferred on the insurgents with the concomitant international legal protection. Thus, in these circumstances, international legal personality would be attained. This was indeed the case with the Herero: they were in control of significant territories and exercised their own form of governing over these territories. It could be argued that some of these principles are of a more recent vintage, having arisen out of the legitimization of the struggles against colonial rule, only during the twentieth century. Regardless, the precepts are not new. They were already in existence then, as evidenced by the debates during the Hague conferences about rules applying to belligerents and insurgents.

Another heavily debated question is whether humanitarian law protected civilians before the Geneva Conventions of 1949. Many contend that before 1949 a member of the armed forces of one state could not commit a war crime against a civilian of another state in the context of an armed conflict.[54] In support of this view it is argued that the 1907 Regulations did not even mention civilians.[55] However, as Plattner notes, "Curiously enough, the governments of that time were so sure that it was impossible to intern nationals of a belligerent State who were resident in the territory of the adverse party that they refused to include any such prohibition in those Regulations."[56] Thus, civilians were not mentioned because it was deemed unnecessary, as those protections already existed.

Another argument justifying the notion that no protections for civilians existed at the time was the lack of dissension in response to a call for an instrument to protect civilians in periods of war, which came after World War II, specifically because protection for civilians was so undeveloped.[57] Yet, while there were no specific codified protections, they can be found in the 1868 Declaration of St. Petersburg and the 1899 Hague Convention. These instruments manifestly embrace the idea that "the only legitimate object which States should endeavor to accomplish during war is to weaken the military forces of the enemy."[58] In addition, as noted above, there existed customary law to this effect as well as *opinio juris*. The only question that can legitimately affect the provisions of these two instruments is whether the norms of the 1864 Geneva and the 1899 Hague Convention apply to non-international conflicts,[59] and therefore to the conflict in German South West Africa, if it were deemed as such.

Regarding permissible conduct during wartime, many argue that restrictions on types of warfare date back to the some of the earliest civilizations, and that these limitations could already be found in ancient Greek, Roman, Indian, Chinese, and other societies', as well as religious, texts.[60] Between 1581 and 1864 European governments signed roughly 294 treaties regarding wounded soldiers.[61] An early non-war instrument was the *Paris Declaration Respecting Maritime Law* of April 16, 1856. However, at least from 1864, international law in its codified form made certain types of conduct illegal during wartime.[62] This was when the *Geneva Convention for the Amelioration of the Condition of the Wounded in Armies in the Field* entered into force.[63] Crucially, in 1949 the ICJ found in the *Corfu Channel* case[64] that Albania's obligation to notify others of the presence of mines was "based, not on the Hague Convention of 1907, No VIII, which is applicable in time of war, but on certain general and well-recognized principles, namely: elementary considerations of humanity, even more exacting in peace than in war."[65] The decision shows that the notion of humanity came not only from the Martens Clause, but also from customary law, which determines these principles to be equally applicable in times of peace. This has been confirmed by the ICTY, which in a *Tadic* ruling in 1995, held:

> It is by now a settled rule of customary international law that crimes against humanity do not require a connection to international armed conflicts. Indeed, as the Prosecutor points out, customary international law may not require a connection between crimes against humanity and any conflict at all. Thus, by requiring that crimes against humanity be committed in either internal or international armed conflict, the Security Council may have defined the crime in Article 5 more narrowly than necessary under customary international law.[66]

Interestingly, Dugard notes that at the time of the Anglo-Boer War, which took place in South Africa between 1899 and 1901, humanitarian law was in its infancy, but nevertheless applicable.[67] He further observes that, as in the case of GSWA, neither party to the Anglo-Boer War was a party to the 1864 Geneva Convention or the 1899 Hague Convention, yet customary international law applied.[68] Humanitarian treaties existed only between states and often contained *si omnes* clauses that confirmed their application only to states governed by that treaty. Thus, obligations were based on reciprocity: for such an instrument to apply to a particular conflict, all parties in the conflict had to be state parties to that particular treaty.[69] Others argue, however, that while international law itself was then based on these notions, human rights and humanitarian law "have been said largely to escape from reciprocity because both essentially aim to protect the interests of individuals rather than states."[70]

Furthermore, Eide has suggested that because the laws of war are international in origin and human rights law emerged in the domestic context and was then internationalized, the reciprocal obligations of international humanitarian law do not apply to human rights law.[71] Thus, the reach of the *si omnes* clauses in general should not be overstated, as after 1907 these clauses were commonly rejected in treaties. In addition, while *si omnes* clauses went out of favor in treaties after 1907, their loss of favor is thought to have occurred even earlier in customary law.[72] Even though *si omnes* clauses were contained in international treaties, some commentators do not regard their provisions as applicable to human rights or humanitarian protections, and therefore they do not see these clauses as limiting the effect of the 1899 Hague Convention or other relevant treaties in protecting those not party to these conventions. It is argued, rather, that human rights obligations guarantee individual rights and are not about reciprocal relations between states.[73]

Crucially, customary international law also applied to the events of the time, and the notion certainly existed that civilians were protected, regardless of the type of conflict. In fact, in 1900, Baty stated: "the standard in customary law falls somewhat short of the provisions of the Conventions, otherwise no Conventions would have been needed; though it is probably true to say that since the date of the earlier agreements, and to a certain extent in consequence of it, the general law has been sensibly instigated."[74] Baty's observation about the shortcomings of customary law followed months after the drafting of the 1899 Convention. Today, it is generally recognized that treaty law and customary law converged substantially and that customary law was often more advanced in some areas. At the minimum, as Shelton has stated, "it should be noted that both Hague Conventions declared or stated principles and rules that, in essence, represented then existing customary international law."[75]

The Herero's situation in GSWA was similar to the situation in South Africa during the Anglo-Boer War between the British and the Boer Republics of the Orange Free State and the South African Republic (Transvaal) in the years between 1899 and 1902. The two Boer republics were not signatories to either Convention. Therefore, as Baty noted in 1900:

> the South African Republic is not a party to the Geneva Convention, nor to that of The Hague; and therefore that the conduct of the parties to the present hostilities must be estimated independently of those treaties and tried by the standard of ordinary belligerent propriety.[76]

However, this may not alter their influence, as the two treaties, as well as the St. Petersburg Declaration, the Lieber Code, the Protocol that emerged from the Brussels Conference, and the Oxford Manual, reflected to some extent customary law and were therefore applicable even to non-signatories.

Many view the Hague Convention as applicable regardless of its reflection in customary law because Germany was bound to the Convention in 1904. Hinz comments that the Convention "protected the Herero although they were formally not party to it. Protective norms in international humanitarian law entitle even non-government claimants as much as the language directly reflects rights and interests of individuals."[77] According to Hinz, "In view of von Trotha's extermination order and the manner in which the fleeing Herero were treated, the German army violated the quoted obligations under the Hague Convention."[78] Article 6 expressly provided that combatants who were wounded regardless of "whatever nation they may belong, shall be collected and cared for." This did not happen; the wounded and even civilians were often executed. Nonetheless, this clause would limit the effect of the *si omnes* clause if applied, as it appears to apply to all, including individuals not citizens of a state party to this treaty.

Moreover, the International Court of Justice held in its decision *Military and Paramilitary Activities in and against Nicaragua* (*Nicaragua v. United States of America*), Merits, Judgment, ICJ Reports 1986, p. 14 (June 27), that the idea contained in common Article 1 of the 1949 Geneva Conventions that the "High Contracting Parties undertake to respect and ensure respect for the present Convention in all circumstances" was indicative of customary law. Thus, as Meron has pointed out, this contradicted the notion that reciprocity was essential to the availability of protection in treaties. He argues that the Commentary on the First Convention, which notes that "a State does not proclaim the principle of the protection due to wounded and sick combatants in the hope of saving a certain number of its own nationals. It does so out of respect for the human person as such," implies that reciprocity is not a prerequisite and the obligations are unconditional—both in the article and by implication in customary law.[79] Thus, the ostensible prerequisite of reciprocity contained in the Hague Convention may not be as sacrosanct as previously believed.

While many suggest that civilians, as a category of protected "victims" of armed conflicts, were brought rather slowly into the ambit of modern international humanitarian law[80]—generally speaking protecting civilians was kept off the agenda until the 1930s[81]—the origins of their protection can be found in the nineteenth century. The protection of the victims of war was the basis of the laws of Geneva and The Hague. While the Hague Conventions are primarily concerned with the way war is conducted and the methods of war, the distinctions between it and the laws of Geneva have become blurred. Both have their origins in protecting those involved in the warfare and those considered victims of certain types of conduct. For example, Article 155 of the U.S. Lieber Code, drawn up in the 1860s, states:

> All enemies in regular war are divided into two general classes—that is to say, into combatants and non-combatants, or unarmed citizens of the hostile government.[82]

When it was drafted, the Lieber Code, an early attempt to codify the laws of land warfare, was thought to reflect customary law.[83] Thus, at least from the 1860s those involved in establishing the law of warfare were concerned with humanizing war and protecting civilians and others. The Lieber Code, which recognized the existence of the "law of nations"[84] as well as the "principles of justice, honor, and humanity,"[85] yielded a manual known as the *Instructions for the Government of Armies of the United States in the Field*. The Code was not only intended for application in civil war but in all armed conflict.[86]

The term "humanitarian law" reflects the extent to which these issues became part of the discourse. Interestingly, some even include human rights law under the notion of humanitarian law.[87] From 1863 onward the law of armed conflict was a matter of major international importance and discussion. Numerous conferences, declarations, and discussions were organized. The Lieber Code of 1863 reflected these concerns and began a national trend. Germany adopted the Lieber Code and used it to govern the way its forces operated in the Franco-German war of 1870.[88] Thus, it would seem that even Germany accepted the customary law position of the Lieber Code. In fact, Meron notes that the Lieber code anticipates the subsequent provisions of the Geneva Conventions that prohibit murder, enslavement, and the carrying off to distant parts. As Green notes, these principles were so accepted that similar codes were issued by Prussia (1870), The Netherlands (1871), France (1877), Russia (1877 and 1904), Serbia (1878), Argentina (1881), Great Britain (1883 and 1904), and Spain (1893).[89]

As can be seen above, the Lieber Code was domestic in nature before the 1860s but became international between 1870 and 1904.[90] Green argues that this is evidence of the customary international law position.[91] The historical context and the events surrounding the 1874 Brussels Conference are significant. The United States did not attend the Brussels Conference. At that time the United States was not quite considered a world power and was initially not invited. When invited at the last minute, the United States felt snubbed and decided not to attend. That they did not accept the outcome of the conference must be understood against this background. However, U.S. practice is demonstrated by the fact that several of their soldiers were tried for atrocities committed in the Philippines following the end of the Spanish-American war, when during the brutal suppression of a rebellion in the Philippines hundreds of thousands of Filipinos were killed.[92] At the time there was no war, so the crimes committed did not constitute war crimes under the law of the time. They are more adequately termed "crimes against humanity," and the tribunals used phrases like "laws of man," "principles of humanity," etc., to describe them.

The various manuals states used for their armed forces, essentially copying the Lieber Code, did not try to exempt certain conduct through the distinction that international law drew between international and non-international armed conflict. Thus, international law, at least at customary law level, accepted that particular types of warfare were prohibited regardless of the status of the war in which they occurred. Article 71 of the Lieber Code provides:

> Whoever intentionally inflicts additional wounds on an enemy already wholly disabled, or kills such an enemy, or who orders or encourages soldiers to do so, shall

> suffer death, if duly convicted, whether he belongs to the Army of the United States, or is an enemy captured after having committed his misdeeds.

The relevance of this clause is still apparent today; it is seen as "the forerunner of what is today accepted as universal jurisdiction over those guilty of committing war crimes."[93] Specifically concerning civilians, Article 155 of the Code states:

> All enemies in regular war are divided into two general classes—that is to say, into combatants and non-combatants, or unarmed citizens of the hostile government.[94]

Some notion of the standards that applied can be found in the first international instrument relating to weapons, the 1868 St. Petersburg Declaration *Renouncing the Use, in Time of War, of Explosive Projectiles under 400 Grammes Weight*, which stated that the

> progress of civilization should have the effect of alleviating as much as possible the calamities of war; that the only legitimate object which States should endeavor to accomplish during war is to weaken the military forces of the enemy; that for this purpose it is sufficient to disable the greatest possible number of men; that this object would be exceeded by the employment of arms which uselessly aggravate the sufferings of disabled men, or render their death inevitable; that the employment of such arms would therefore be contrary to the *laws of humanity*....[95] [my emphasis]

This Declaration codified a "fundamental customary rule" and thus the protection of civilians and others was already regarded as part of international law. The principles stated in the Declaration have had an enduring influence on the development of international humanitarian law. These principles were already applicable at the time of the Herero conflict in 1904, and the Germans violated several of them. The German army did not only aim to weaken the Herero army by disabling the greatest number of men, but aimed to completely destroy the Herero nation. Therefore. one can conclude that at the very least Germany violated customary international law at the time.

The Brussels Conference of 1874 followed the St. Petersburg Declaration. This conference, called for by the Russian government, adopted the *International Declaration Concerning the Laws and Customs of War*. This document contained many sections intended to make warfare more compassionate, but it never received the required ratifications, and thus never had a direct effect. However, as Meron[96] notes, it became one of the foundations for the Regulations attached to the 1899 Convention (II) with Respect to the Laws and Customs of War on Land that was drafted by the (first) International Peace Conference in The Hague. In fact, the 1899 Convention specifically discussed[97] and brought into its realm the 1874 Brussels Convention in terms of the status of belligerents, the treatment of POWs, as well as the limitations extended on occupied territory.[98] Thus, what had been accepted in the St. Petersburg Declaration at least in part became codified and recognized in the Hague Convention.

The content of the declaration is therefore significant in the development of international law. The Final Protocol of the Brussels Conference of 1874 states that

> a further step may be taken by revising the laws and general usages of war, whether with the object of defining with greater precision, or with the view of laying down, by a common agreement, certain limits which will restrain, as far as possible, the severities of war. War being thus regulated would involve less suffering, would be less liable to those aggravations, unforeseen events, and the passions excited by the struggle; it would tend more surely to that which should be its final object, viz., the re-establishing of good relations, and a more solid and lasting peace between the belligerent States. The Conference could respond to those ideas of humanity in no better way than by entering in the same spirit into the examination of the subject they were to discuss....[99]

While the Conference resolution was never ratified, it certainly indicates the customary position at the time. This can be seen in the *Oxford Manual of the Laws of War on Land*, which was adopted by the Institute of International Law in 1880. This manual served as a blueprint for the Regulations that are annexed to the Hague Conventions of 1899 and 1907.[100] The Manual states the following:

> [i]t may be said that independently of the international laws existing on this subject, there are today certain principles of justice which guide the public conscience, which are manifested even by general customs, but which it would be well to fix and make obligatory.... The Institute ... feels it is fulfilling a duty in offering to the governments a Manual suitable as the basis for national legislation in each State, and in accord with both the progress of juridical science and the needs of civilized armies. Rash and extreme rules will not be found therein. The Institute has not sought innovations in drawing up the Manual; it has contented itself with stating clearly and codifying the accepted ideas of our age so far as this has appeared allowable and practicable. By so doing, it believes it is rendering a service to military men themselves. In fact, so long as the demands of opinion remain indeterminate, belligerents are exposed to painful uncertainty and to endless accusations. A positive set of rules, on the contrary, if they are judicious, serves the interests of belligerents and is far from hindering them, since by preventing the unchaining of passion and savage instincts—which battle always awakens, as much as it awakens courage and manly virtues—it strengthens the discipline which is the strength of armies; it also ennobles their patriotic mission in the eyes of the soldiers by keeping them within the limits of respect due to the rights of humanity. But in order to attain this end it is not sufficient for sovereigns to promulgate new laws. It is essential, too, that they make these laws known among all people, so that when a war is declared, the men called upon to take up arms to defend the causes of the belligerent States, may be thoroughly impregnated with the special rights and duties attached to the execution of such a command....[101]

The International Court of Justice has noted that these nineteenth century processes developed and reflected the customary international law position. In the

Advisory Opinion on the Legality of Nuclear Weapons of July 8, 1996[102] the Court found:

> A large number of customary rules have been developed by the practice of States and are an integral part of the international law relevant to the question posed. The "laws and customs of war" as they were traditionally called were the subject of efforts at codification undertaken in The Hague (including the Conventions of 1899 and 1907), and were based partly upon the St. Petersburg Declaration of 1868 as well as the results of the Brussels Conference of 1874.[103]

Thus, state practice helps establish the principles of the Lieber Code in customary law, along with the fact that the Code was the greatest influence on several international treaties of the 1800s, including the Brussels Declaration, the Hague Conventions, the St. Petersburg Conference and Declaration, and the Oxford Manual. The Russian Proposal to the Brussels Conference was the inspiration for fifty-two of the sixty articles of the Brussels Declaration, and Prof. Martens of the Russian delegation acknowledged the impact the Lieber Code had on the Russian Proposal.[104] In 1907 George Davis also stated that Dr. Bluntschli of the German contingent and chairman of the committee on codification at Brussels admitted that his chief reliance in the performance of his duties was on the Lieber Code.[105]

The Lieber Code had a very specific influence on the drafting of the Hague Conventions in which the Martens Clause is found.[106] According to Paust the "Lieber Code became widely accepted as a codification of customary international legal principles and prohibitions," is still seen to influence international law and was referred to by the ICTY in the *Tadic* decision.[107] Paust also makes the following point:

> It is a serious historical error to argue that customary laws of war reflected in the Hague Conventions apply only to "international wars" between states and not also to civil war upon recognition of insurgents as "belligerents," as in the case of the U.S. Civil War. Lieber's codification was meant to apply to a belligerency but also to reflect law applicable in wars between states. Previously, and thereafter, laws of war were also applicable in wars with Indian nations. Violations in each instance have long been recognized as "war crimes."[108]

WHICH WAR CRIMES PERPETRATED ON THE HERERO WERE VIOLATIONS OF INTERNATIONAL LAW AT THE TIME?

One of the major violations of the law of war committed by the Germans in GSWA (which was the essence of the extermination order) was the instruction that no quarter was to be given. Its prohibition was found in the Lieber Code. It was copied by many other countries and was probably indicative of customary law. The prohibition was also included in the Land Warfare Regulations annexed to the 1899 Hague Convention,[109] Articles 4 to 20. While the 1899

Convention was replaced in 1907, its provisions were incorporated into the 1907 Convention. Further, the 1899 Convention was adopted unanimously[110] and was in force until it was supplanted by the 1907 Convention, which remains very much part of international law today. It is still often referred to; for example, UN Security Council Resolution 1483 called on states to observe their obligations under the four Geneva Conventions of 1949 and the Hague Regulations of 1907.[111]

Article 60 of the Lieber Code states that "it is against the usage of modern war to resolve, in hatred and revenge, to give no quarter. No body of troops has the right to declare that it will not give ... quarter ..." This provision not only states the U.S. position, but the use of the term "modern war" indicates a more universal application. The Code goes even further in Article 61, stating: "Troops that give no quarter have no right to kill enemies already disabled on the ground, or prisoners captured by other troops." It also stipulates that

> the unarmed citizen is to be spared in person, property, and honor as much as the exigencies of war will admit ...[112] [and] ... private citizens are no longer murdered, enslaved, or carried off to distant parts, and the inoffensive individual is as little disturbed in his private relations as the commander of the hostile troops can afford to grant in the overruling demands of a vigorous war."[113]

The Code also states that "in modern regular wars of the Europeans, and their descendants in other portions of the globe, protection of the inoffensive citizen of the hostile country is the rulc...."[114]

GERMANY'S OBLIGATIONS UNDER INTERNATIONAL HUMANITARIAN LAW AT THE TIME

Germany was a contracting party to the Second Hague Convention on the Laws and Customs of War on Land of July 29, 1899, which entered into force on September 4, 1900.[115] It was enacted into German law when it was published in the official gazette in 1901.[116] A number of provisions in that Convention proscribed certain types of actions and activities,[117] many of which relate to what the Germans did to the Herero. Article 3 of the Convention stated that the "armed forces of the belligerent parties may consist of combatants and non-combatants. In case of capture by the enemy both have a right to be treated as prisoners of war." Article 4 stipulated that prisoners of war "are in the power of the hostile Government, but not in that of the individuals or corps who captured them. They must be humanely treated. All their personal belongings, except arms, horses, and military papers remain their property." Article 6 held that while prisoners of war could be made to work, the work could not be excessive and they had to be paid for that work. Article 7 noted that the "Government into whose hands prisoners of war have fallen is bound to maintain them. Failing a special agreement between the belligerents, prisoners of war shall be treated as regards food, quarters, and clothing on the same footing as the troops of the Government which has captured them." Article 23 of the Annex notes that

> it is especially prohibited
>
> (a) To employ poison or poisoned arms;
> (b) To kill or wound treacherously individuals belonging to the hostile nation or army;
> (c) To kill or wound an enemy who, having laid down arms, or having no longer means of defence, has surrendered at discretion;
> (d) To declare that no quarter will be given …;
> (e) To destroy or seize the enemy's property, unless such destruction or seizure be imperatively demanded by the necessities of war.

Thus, many of the actions taken against the Herero in German South West Africa were in violation of these articles. However, the difficulty is that Article 2 of the Convention states that the "provisions … are only binding on the Contracting Powers, in case of war between two or more of them. These provisions shall cease to be binding from the time when, in a war between Contracting Powers, a non-Contracting Power joins one of the belligerents." The terms were therefore not binding against parties not contracted to the Convention. Nonetheless, the intent to outlaw certain conduct is unmistakable. While Dinah Shelton argues that the Hague Convention of 1899 did not apply to those events because of the *si omes* clause, but because that treaty represented customary international law its rules should apply. She also argues that in any case German law should have applied to state action that occurred in Namibia at the time.[118]

While it could therefore be argued that the Convention does not specifically cover the events in question, it is clear that the conduct described in the various articles was already thought to be proscribed by international agreement. In addition, as Harring has pointed out, the "Herero were not represented at The Hague, and could not, therefore, sign the convention. Thus, the issue is not the literal application of the Hague Convention to the Herero War. Rather, it is the Convention as a statement of international customary law."[119] Therefore, at the minimum, international customary law recognized these violations as transgressions of international law. Germany's knowledge of their transgressions at the time, and von Trotha's attitude that they would not abide by the Geneva Conventions and other international treaties, will be returned to later.

INTERNATIONAL HUMAN RIGHTS LAW

It is often argued that before the twentieth century international human rights did not exist as a distinct set of rules within the law of nations, and that it was not recognized as a branch of international law. This is an extremely narrow view. Doswald-Beck and Vite have pointed out that "[i]nternational humanitarian law is increasingly perceived as part of human rights law applicable in armed conflict."[120] Although it could be argued that these are contemporary positions, their arrangements were applicable before, as evidenced from customary international law in force at the time.

Some commentators differ about when international human rights law and humanitarian law came to the fore. Most agree that international humanitarian law came into being around the middle of the nineteenth century and that international human rights law is a post-World War II development. But international human rights law considerably predates World War II: not only can it be found in various non-war agreements before World War II,[121] it can also be found in various societies in ancient times. The clearest examples of international criminal law in the nineteenth century were piracy and the slave trade,[122] as well as the protection of minorities that was occurring in the international sphere.

An important issue often raised regarding the role of international law at the beginning of the twentieth century is the claim that it only applied to states and not to individuals or groups. It is argued that various treaties in the nineteenth century provided protection of human rights but did not create enforcement provisions at the international level for individual human rights, only for international obligations between states with respect to the treatment of individuals and groups. Judge Richard Goldstone contends that before World War II "individuals had no standing in international law."[123] Again, this is a limited perspective, as already at that time individuals could approach some international courts and could certainly raise such issues before domestic courts (as is the case today).[124] Furthermore, this view does not take into account that individuals enjoyed certain rights at the international law level in the beginning of the twentieth century, many years prior to World War II and before the establishment of international courts. The argument that, given the absence of the recognition of individual rights, human rights did not exist in international law before World War I does not hold.[125] The Hague Conventions of 1899 and 1907 had no specific or stated provisions on punishing individuals who violated their articles[126] and because there was no international criminal court system or procedure to hold individuals accountable, prosecutions primarily took place at the international level before Nuremberg. Yet, there were a few prosecutions at the domestic level of crimes deemed violations of those Conventions. It was not the case that international law on these issues did not exist, but rather that the prevalence of a strong philosophy of nation-state sovereignty meant that individual states were expected to deal with the crimes of their own nationals and those in their custody who committed crimes against them.

A further problem arising from the absence of an enforcement mechanism is that the provisions of human rights and humanitarian law regarding international crimes, and responsibility and accountability for such abuses, have been nebulous and controversial in meaning.[127] Before Nuremberg and until the 1990s there were no courts to interpret the provisions or give deterrence sufficient to stop such abuses. This does not indicate that the proscribed conduct was not considered crime—it was, and what was outlawed in 1899 is even clearer today because of subsequent interpretations. Whether the 1899 Hague Conventions afforded rights to individuals does not obviate the fact that crimes were committed after these Conventions entered into force, and those states party to such instruments would be liable under those Conventions—despite the absence of a mechanism to examine or adjudicate these matters.

Another argument is that there was no protection for individuals at the time, as human rights protections only became part of international law much later and crimes against humanity require that the individual is a subject of international law, yet the individual only obtained protection by international law much later.[128] However, the absence of international enforcement machinery does not negate the existence of the law itself. Before the establishment of the ICTR, the ICTY, and more recently the ICC, the rules of customary international law and the Hague Conventions were recognized and applied in domestic courts. The latter, at times, used these international standards in the same way in which many international cases applied these standards. For example, the standards were applied to prosecute prisoners of war responsible for committing violations during World War I. France and later Germany had already applied these standards during World War I.[129] Thus, international law, and specifically international criminal law relying on the Hague Convention, was applied even by Germany shortly after the early Hague Conventions came into being. That the Hague Convention contained no enforcement mechanism was not even then seen as a hindrance to prosecuting or punishing those found guilty of crimes under these bodies of law.[130]

While some doubt the connection between humanitarian law and human rights law, Draper states that the humanitarian consideration that infused the law of war contains the "parentage" of human rights law.[131]

GERMANY'S OBLIGATIONS UNDER SPECIFIC TREATIES TO UPHOLD HUMAN RIGHTS

Besides the obligations contained in international customary law, Germany was also party to a whole host of treaties that prohibited the violations it committed against the Herero. In this regard Rachel Anderson has noted that her analysis of the historical sources of customary international law indicates that from 1884 on, European states had obligations to those they colonized under natural law but also in terms of various treaties, such as the Berlin West Africa Convention, the Anti-Slavery Convention, and the 1899 Hague Convention. She argues that the European states were obliged to protect and look after the welfare of the indigenous inhabitants and that while the term "genocide" was not known, other conceptions of it such as "wars of annihilation" were a violation of customary international law from 1878.[132]

One of the most important treaties Germany was obligated to follow was the Berlin Conference Treaty of 1885. Various obligations flowed from the General Act, the most relevant of which was contained in Article 6:

> *Provisions Relative to the Protection of the Natives, of Missionaries and Travellers, as well as to Religious Liberty.*
>
> All the Powers exercising sovereign rights or influence in the aforesaid territories bind themselves to watch over the preservation of the native tribes, and to care for the improvement of the conditions of their moral and material well-being, and to help in suppressing slavery, and especially the Slave Trade. They shall, without distinction of creed or nation, protect and favor all religions, scientific or charitable institutions, and undertakings created and organized for the above ends, or with aim at instructing the natives and bringing home to them the blessings of civilization ... Freedom of conscience and religious toleration are expressly guaranteed to the natives, no less than to subjects and to foreigners.

The 1885 Berlin Act therefore promised to "watch over the preservation of the native tribes, and to care for the improvement of their moral and material well-being, and to help in suppressing slavery."[133] The obligations contained in the Berlin Treaty were not the only relevant ones; the 1890 Anti-Slavery Convention, also known as the Brussels Act of 1890, noted these same concerns and committed seventeen nations to "efficiently protecting the aboriginal population of Africa."[134] Germany was a signatory to both these agreements. The fact that so many states signed both of them indicates that these states shared the conviction that slavery was prohibited under international law. This is therefore evidence of an *opinio juris* as a necessary element of customary international law.

Although the Herero were not signatories to these treaties, they are thought to have been protected by them. Anderson contends that the various Conventions conferred rights on the Herero because of the third-party beneficiary doctrine. She argues that the parties to these treaties intended to grant specific protections to the African populations. While Anderson does not deal with the questions of reciprocity or *si omnes* clauses (which determine that such treaties are applicable only to the signatories), the understanding that human rights clauses would not be limited by such questions seems to be implicit. If that is the case, then certainly the notion of a third-party beneficiary doctrine could be relevant, if such a notion was known at the time. However, more relevant is Anderson's argument that the signatories of these treaties specifically intended to protect the local population and to provide a means for redress when this did not occur. She shows that the drafting process of the 1885 Convention clearly confirms that the intention of the treaty was to create "a duty of protection under international law that *de facto* criminalizes the intentional annihilation of indigenous peoples of Africa."[135]

THE ORIGINS OF CRIMES AGAINST HUMANITY

Although many argue that crimes against humanity entered international jurisprudence as a result of the Nuremburg Charter, its origins can be found much earlier. In 1945, Justice Robert H. Jackson, the Chief Prosecutor at Nuremburg, argued this point. When referring to "crimes against humanity," Jackson noted that "atrocities and persecutions on racial or religious grounds" were already outlawed under general principles of domestic law of civilized states and that "[t]hese principles [had] been assimilated as a part of International Law at least since 1907."[136] According to Paust, Jackson relied on the Martens Clause for this assertion.[137] The ICTR, too, has noted that "the concept of crimes against humanity had been recognized long before Nuremberg."[138]

The roots of crimes against humanity have been traced to the teachings of Socrates, Plato, and Aristotle and the notion of natural law.[139] The origins certainly date back further than 1864 and 1899. In the Middle Ages and without doubt by the nineteenth century, international law was developing a doctrine in support of the legitimacy of "humanitarian intervention" in cases in which a State committed atrocities against its own subjects that "shocked the conscience of mankind."[140] Jorgensen notes that from the Enlightenment[141] the principles protecting "humanity began to seep into the international system."[142] In the sixteenth century it was stated:

> [Taking prisoners] is permissible. This fact is evident by the *jus gentium*. No (authority) censures this practice, nor does any condemn the captor to make restitution, on the contrary, such captors may retain these men until the latter are ransomed. Secondly … it is no longer permissible to slay them, for they are captives; nor is slaughter needful to the attainment of victory.[143]

This is not an isolated example—there is evidence aplenty of generally accepted and respected codes regarding the way war should be conducted and who could be attacked.

Although William Wallace was tried and convicted in 1305 by an English court for "crimes offending humanity" and "excesses in war," "sparing neither age nor sex, monk or nun,"[144] the trial of Peter von Hagenbach in 1474 is generally regarded as the earliest known international trial for war crimes or crimes against humanity,[145] and this represents the origins of the enforcement of international law forbidding certain types of conduct again humanity. Von Hagenbach was prosecuted for having "trampled under foot the laws of God and man."[146] Dugard agrees that von Hagenbach's trial is considered the "first international war crimes trial," citing that he was tried "for atrocities committed during an attempt to compel Breisach to submit to Burgundian rule—by a tribunal comprising judges drawn from different States and principalities."[147] Ögren sees the Articles of War decreed in 1621 by King Gustavus II Adolphus of Sweden as providing for us "an idea of what existed in the way of humanitarian law before the publication of Grotius' *De Jure Belli ac Pacis* in 1625 and appear to have been inspired by Gentili's 1612 *De Jure Belli*."[148] The Peace of Westphalia, which ended the Thirty Years' War in 1648, also represents one of the origins of the international community's censure for such persecution.[149]

European nations entered into various treaties agreeing to the protection of the rights of various peoples. These include the Treaty of Augsburg of 1555, the Treaty of Olivia of 1660, the Treaty of Nymegen in 1678, the Treaty of Ryswyck in 1697, and the Vienna Congress in 1815. Other similar agreements include the Treaty of Paris of 1856, which created obligations to the people of Walachia, Moldavia, and Serbia, and the Treaty of Berlin in 1878, which included a guarantee by Turkey to protect Armenians and defend religious liberties. The Treaty of Paris of 1898, which ceded Puerto Rico and the Philippines from Spain to the United States, also provided protection to minority groups.[150]

The nineteenth century saw the notion of the protection of humanity contained in the St. Petersburg Declaration of 1868. This *Declaration Renouncing the Use, in Time of War, of Explosive Projectiles under 400 Grammes Weight*[151] stated:

> [T]he progress of civilization should have the effect of alleviating as much as possible the calamities of war; that the only legitimate object which States should endeavour to accomplish during war is to weaken the military forces of the enemy; that for this purpose it is sufficient to disable the greatest possible number of men; that this object would be exceeded by the employment of arms which uselessly aggravate the sufferings of disabled men, or render their death inevitable; that the employment of such arms would therefore *be contrary to the laws of humanity*....[152] [my emphasis]

Subsequently the Brussels Conference of 1874 adopted a protocol that repeated and expanded the Principles of the St. Petersburg Declaration.

Even before 1899, the expressions "crimes against humanity" or "laws of humanity" were used in various other contexts. In 1775, in similar wording to the Martens Clause, the Declaration by the Representatives of the United Colonies of North America, Now Meeting in General Congress at Philadelphia, Setting Forth the Causes and Necessity of Their Taking Up Arms declared that

> a reverence for our great Creator, principles of humanity, and the dictates of common sense, must convince all those who reflect upon the subject, that government was instituted to promote the welfare of mankind, and ought to be administered for the attainment of that end.[153]

Similar language was used in various other contexts in the United States, including in a number of court cases. Another example of its usage occurred when African-American lawyer and historian George Washington Williams wrote to the U.S. Secretary of State that King Leopold's Belgium was guilty of committing "crimes against humanity" in the Congo.[154]

The British Secretary of State, John Thossell, explaining the reasons for the British intervention in 1860, noted: "It is hoped that the measures now taken may vindicate the rights of humanity."[155] In 1874, George Curtis likewise referred to the "the laws of humanity" with respect to slavery in the United States.[156] When revolts against misrule and persecution in the Ottoman Empire in the late 1870s were met with killings, looting, rapes, burning, pillaging, and torture, it was noted that these were the "most heinous crimes that had stained the history of the present century."[157] William Gladstone, the future British Prime Minister, condemned these actions and specifically used the term "humanity."[158] Already in 1877 Gladstone noted that:

> A little faith in the ineradicable difference between right and wrong is worth a great deal of European diplomacy, bewildered by views it dare neither dismiss nor avow.... What civilization longs for, *what policy no less than humanity requires*, is that united Europe, scouted, as we have seen in its highest, its united diplomacy, shall pass sentence in its might, upon a Government which unites the vices of the conqueror and the slave, and which is lost alike to truth, to mercy, and to shame.[159] [my emphasis]

Certainly, some recognized and accepted the concept of crimes against humanity at the beginning of the twentieth century. In 1901, the non-governmental organization (NGO) the *Ligue des Droits de l'Homme* published its first document for "all humanity."[160]

THE MARTENS CLAUSE—CONNECTING WAR CRIMES AND CRIMES AGAINST HUMANITY

The legal origin of the concept of crimes against humanity in international law is the Martens Clause of the 1899 Hague Convention II and the 1907 Hague Convention IV. It has been "hailed as a significant turning point in the history of international humanitarian law."[161] That the clause was unanimously adopted indicates the consensus of participating states on the matter. It stated:

> Until a more complete code of the laws of war is issued, the High Contracting Parties think it right to declare that in cases not included in the Regulations adopted by them, populations and belligerents remain under the protection and empire of the principles of international law, as they result from the usages established between civilized nations, from the laws of humanity, and the requirements of the public conscience.

The 1907 version of the clause saw "populations" replaced by "inhabitants," "law of nations" replaced by "international law," and "requirements" changing to "dictates."[162] The "laws of humanity" referred to in earlier versions of the Martens Clause later became the "principles of humanity."[163] Some believe that these terms are not identical or interchangeable. However, de Guzman comments on the link between "laws of humanity" and "crimes against humanity."[164] Ticehurst, among others, has claimed that the expression "principles of humanity" is identical with "laws of humanity."[165] Orentlicher has noted that "the most important legal wellspring of crimes against humanity

... is the Martens Clause."[166] Cassese states that the main principal and importance of the Martens Clause is that it "proclaimed for the first time that there may exist principles or rules of customary international law resulting not only from state practice, but also from laws of humanity and the dictates of public conscience."[167]

The role, meaning, and extent of the Martens Clause have been debated extensively and it has been described as "ambiguous and evasive."[168] Various meanings have been ascribed to the clause and its effects.[169] Primarily due to the wording of the clause, many see the Martens Clause as the official originator in positive conventional or codified international law of the notion of "crimes against humanity." Further support for this view is that the provisions of this clause are now found within the notions of "crimes against humanity" and "genocide." Before 1899, issues of morality were not governed by international legal rules in the positivist tradition; however, this seems to have changed subsequently.

The specific link between the Martens Clause and the notion of "crimes against humanity" is apparent from the events of World War I. The May 1915 declaration from Great Britain, France, and Russia about the occurrences in Armenia used the term "crimes against humanity."[170] The joint declaration condemned the massacre of Armenians as "crimes against humanity and civilization for which all members of the Turkish Government will be held responsible together with its agents implicated in the massacre."[171] The Commission on the Responsibilities of the Authors of War and on Enforcement of Penalties for Violation of the Laws and Customs of War also used this concept to describe the occurrences. The Commission found that "in spite of the explicit regulations, of established customs, and of the clear dictates of humanity, Germany and her Allies have piled outrage upon outrage."[172] Thus, it used the Hague Conventions, the Martens Clause, and customary law as the basis for concluding that prosecutions would be justified. It also found within the concept of the "laws of humanity" that violations could be prosecuted as "crimes."[173] Hill, in 1917, noted that "even in the efforts to overcome an armed foe the principles of humanity are considered by all civilized peoples to have a binding authority."[174] The Versailles Treaty provided for the prosecution of the Kaiser for these types of crimes. Article 227 of the treaty provided for the creation of a tribunal and established the individual responsibility of the Kaiser for "a supreme offence against international morality and the sanctity of treaties." Thus, the provision was not for war crimes, but other international crimes, which the Versailles Treaty did not specify in name. The lack of specificity was due to the United States and Japan opposing the criminalization of this type of conduct, believing that crimes against the laws of humanity were only violations of moral law and not contained in positive law, and therefore could not be legally defined.[175] This does not mean that such laws did not exist and does not detract from their recognition by these states. In fact, it is clear from the Versailles Treaty that such crimes could in the eyes of the international community be prosecuted, although there was no agreement from where they specifically flowed. The only reason the Kaiser was not prosecuted was that the Netherlands, where he was in exile, refused to hand him over.

Dadrian notes that it was the 1915 declaration that specifically created the use and international norm of "crimes against humanity."[176] At a minimum the term "crimes against humanity" was in vogue in 1915, and the Martens Clause of 1899 and 1907 functioned as the basis of determining such crimes. Hence, if the Martens Clause constituted the foundation of this principle, and it was in force at the time, then the notion of these crimes in fact became operative from 1899.[177]

The Treaty of Sèvres, signed on August 10, 1920, also indicates the acceptance of the notion of such international crimes and the ability to prosecute those responsible for their commission. In Article 230 the Treaty provides for the punishment of individuals who committed crimes on Turkish territory against persons of Turkish citizenship (even if of Armenian or Greek origin). While the Treaty was not ratified and thus did not come into force, it was supplanted by the Treaty of Lausanne in 1923, which implicitly recognized these crimes as it provided for an amnesty for offenses committed between 1914 and 1922 (which would have been superfluous had these offenses not been considered crimes). As the date recognized was 1922, many years after the conclusion of World War I, it also recognized that such crimes could be committed outside of war.

Nonetheless, there are different views on the role of the Martens Clause in international law. The "narrow" view holds that it has merely "motivated and inspired" the development of international law.[178] The broader view maintains that the Martens Clause prevents the argument that nothing not mentioned specifically in the 1899 Convention, regardless of how problematic it was, could be carried out during a war. As Judge Weeramantry stated in his dissent in the ICJ *Legality of the Threat or Use of Nuclear Weapons* case: "The Martens Clause clearly indicates that, behind such specific rules as had already been formulated, there lay a body of general principles sufficient to be applied to such situations as had not already been dealt with by a specific rule."[179] Cassese has criticized this view, arguing that it gives no value to the clause, because that principle already existed when it was drafted, and discounts the role of custom, thereby making the meaning of the clause redundant.[180]

Another trend to which some authors ascribe is that of the clause as an interpretative tool. Interpreting the legal principles would be done in the context of the principles of humanity and public conscience. Yet another comparable view suggests that the value of the clause is in ensuring that humanitarian principles are regarded when new rules of international law are considered. This can be linked to the view that natural law ought to be considered more often as international law develops. As some have pointed out, the Martens Clause reflects the notion that humanitarian law is not only a "positive legal code ... [but] also provide[s] a moral code" that guarantees that it is not only the view of the large military nations that determine the growth of the law. Thus, the point of view of other states and individuals would be allowed to impact to a larger degree on the development of international law.[181] This affords the clause a vital role in the development of international law and ascribes to it new sources of international law, a moral code—that of the laws of humanity and the dictates of public conscience. Various authors have endorsed this view and a number of cases subscribed to it.

The Martens Clause has been discussed in several decisions emanating from the Nuremberg Tribunal[182] and the International Court of Justice. The Opinion of the International Court of Justice on the Legality of Nuclear Weapons mentions the Martens Clause a number of times in its decision.[183] In one instance it notes that "[i]n particular, the Court recalls that all States are bound by those rules in Additional Protocol I which, when adopted, were merely the expression of the pre-existing customary law, such as the Martens Clause, reaffirmed in the first article of Additional Protocol I."[184] Cassese argues that the "reference to the clause is far from illuminating" and that the court does not give reasons for finding that the Martens Clause is a part of customary law.[185] Nonetheless, he accepts by implication that this is the finding of the ICJ. He examines and rejects the notion that the Martens Clause only applies to international armed conflict and not to internal armed conflict. Yet while it may be argued that this distinction was applicable at the beginning of the twentieth century, the current views do not necessarily reflect the historical position regarding the Martens Clause. Even in the dissenting opinion in *Advisory Opinion on Nuclear Weapons* it was held that

> the Martens Clause provided authority for treating the principles of humanity and the dictates of public conscience as principles of international law, leaving the precise content of the standard implied by these principles of international law to be ascertained in the light of changing conditions, inclusive of changes in the means and methods of warfare and the outlook and tolerance levels of the international community. The principles would remain constant, but their practical effect would vary from time to time: they could justify a method of warfare in one age and prohibit it in another.[186]

The relevance and role of the clause are also found in the decisions of human rights bodies, as well as in many treaties, such as the 1949 Geneva Conventions, the 1977 Additional Protocols, and the Preamble to the Convention on Prohibitions or Restrictions on the Use of Certain Conventional Weapons. It also forms the basis, in paraphrased form, for Resolution XXIII of the Tehran Conference on Human Rights of 1968.[187] In fact, the Geneva Conventions of 1949 and the two Protocols additional thereto of 1977 reaffirmed the Martens Clause.[188] In addition, the 1977 Diplomatic Conference which drafted Additional Protocol I emphasized the ongoing significance of the Martens Clause by shifting it from the preamble and making it a specific provision of the

Protocol.[189] It is also significant that the ICTY in its decision in the *Kupreskic* trial referred to the Martens Clause and held that it

> enjoins, as a minimum, reference to those principles and dictates any time a rule of international humanitarian law is not sufficiently rigorous or precise: in those instances the scope and purport of the rule must be defined with reference to those principles and dictates.[190] In the light of the way States and courts have implemented it, this Clause clearly shows that principles of international humanitarian law may emerge through a customary process under the pressure of the demands of humanity or the dictates of public conscience, even where State practice is scant or inconsistent. The other element, in the form of *opinio necessitatis*, crystallizing as a result of the imperatives of humanity or public conscience, may turn out to be the decisive element heralding the emergence of a general rule or principle of humanitarian law.[191]

In the *Martic* case the ICTY, in its ruling on procedural matters in 1996, found that "the prohibition against attacking the civilian population as such, as well as individual civilians, and the general principle limiting the means and methods of warfare also derive from the 'Martens Clause'."[192] The tribunal went on to state that "these norms also emanate from the elementary considerations of humanity which constitute the foundation of the entire body of international humanitarian law applicable to all armed conflicts." Thus, the ICTY's view was clearly that the Martens Clause rose to a source of law, and that, since 1899, protections existed, at least for civilians. Although it remains debatable, international practice therefore seems to confirm that the Martens Clause is a part of customary international law and has been recognized as such for many years. At least from 1899, crimes against humanity have been acknowledged too. Hence, while the exact terms were not yet in use, the notions of crimes against humanity and genocide were recognized from the beginning of the twentieth century.

The Martens Clause has played and continues to play an extensive role. As Allen remarks, the "crucial core of principles of civilian protection are often described as flowing directly from the principle of humanity."[193] The International Military Tribunal noted in the *Krupp* decision after World War II one example of the way the clause is seen to influence international law. The Court stated that:

> The Preamble is much more than a pious declaration. It is a general clause, making the usages established among civilized nations, the laws of humanity and the dictates of public conscience into the legal yardstick to be applied if and when the specific provisions of the Convention and the Regulations annexed to it do not cover specific cases occurring in warfare, or concomitant to warfare.[194]

Thus, certain activities were already regarded as objectionable to humanity, and crimes against humanity emerged out of what was deemed unacceptable types of conduct during wartime. The remaining issue was whether this conduct was also unacceptable in the absence of war. This appears somewhat contradictory: it does not seem logical to argue that certain types of conduct were not accepted during war but were permitted during times of peace. If anything, one would expect there to be greater scope for harmful activities during wartime than during times of peace. In fact, the International Court of Justice ruled in the *Corfu Channel* case that certain principles existing in the Hague Conventions were also to be found in the general principles regarding humanity. The Court found that these were "based, not on the Hague Convention of 1907, No VIII, which is applicable in time of war, but on certain general and well-recognized principles, namely: elementary considerations of humanity, even more exacting in peace than in war."[195] Thus, while it is clear that the laws of war provided for protections of various classes of persons, those provisions did not protect everyone. However, it was clearly already accepted that during wartime for those not covered by the principles, and in times of peace, customary law already provided some measure of protection. This was recognized by the ICJ.[196] According to Bassiouni, crimes against humanity began as an extension of war crimes; he thus recognizes that these types of violations were initially seen as part of the law of war, but then became part of international law generally through the Martens Clause and customary international law.[197] Bassiouni also notes that Nuremburg Charter's crime against humanity articles come from the preambles to the 1899 and 1907 Hague Conventions, and thus, the Martens Clause is critical. It is, however, possible to argue legitimately that the origins of these crimes predate these conventions, in the context of customary law. There is, therefore, a clear link between crimes committed during wartime and crimes against humanity committed in peacetime.

Crimes against humanity seem to have been recognized even before the Convention specifically criminalized them. In 1891, in the sixth edition of a treatise on international law, Woolsey noted:

> One or two recognized branches of duty between nations deserve a brief notice.
>
> 1. The duty of humanity, including hospitality. This duty spends itself chiefly in the treatment of individuals, although suffering nations or parts of nations may also call for its exercise. The awakened sentiment of humanity in modern times is manifested in a variety of ways, as by efforts to suppress the slave trade, by greater care for captives, by protection of the inhabitants of a country from invading armies, by the facility of removing into a new country, by the greater security of strangers. Formerly, the individual was treated as a part of the nation on whom its wrongs might be wreaked. Now this spirit of war against private individuals is passing away. In general any decided want of humanity arouses the indignation even of third parties, excites remonstrances, and may call for interposition.... But cruelty may also reach beyond the sphere of humanity; it may violate right, and justify self-protection and demand for redress.[198]

As Shelton points out, "as early as 1904 the Imperial Chancellor, Count von Bulow, called the extermination order issued respecting the Herero a 'crime against humanity'."[199] President Theodore Roosevelt in his 1904 State of the Union Address asserted that

> … there are occasional crimes committed on a vast scale and of such peculiar horror as to make us doubt whether it is not our manifest duty to endeavor at the least to show our disapproval of the deed and our sympathy with those who have suffered by it.…[200]

Further, in the same year, the United States came out against the practice of crimes against humanity and genocide when the Secretary of State of the United States forcefully argued against Jewish persecutions that were occurring in Romania 'in the name of humanity' and stated that the U.S. government would not stand idly by while such international wrongs were being committed.[201]

It was at this same time that Germany, and people such as the Social Democratic MP Ledebour, even condemned what was occurring in GSWA, stating that von Trotha ought to be prosecuted for his methods "before the tribunal of the German people and the judgment of History."[202] Similarly, various governments and others accepted as criminal what was happening to the Herero and Nama. President Woodrow Wilson, acknowledging the intent to exterminate and the goal of acquiring the land of the colonized, commented that Germany had

> *brought intolerable burdens and injustices on the helpless people of some of the colonies, which it annexed to itself; that its interest was rather their extermination* than their development; *that the desire was to possess their land for European purposes,* and not to enjoy their confidence in order that mankind might be lifted in those places to the next higher level.[203] [my emphasis]

Thus, clearly the concept of crimes against humanity formed part of the international vocabulary by World War I,[204] and conduct that fell within its purview was often condemned.

Genocide, as it is now understood, was specifically labeled as a crime in a report by an international commission of inquiry regarding atrocities committed against national minorities during the Balkan wars.[205] The report identifies these acts as violations, and Schabas points out that a section of the report entitled "Extermination, Emigration, Assimilation" indicates that these acts would today be categorized as genocide or crimes against humanity.

The aforementioned 1915 declaration by the governments of France, Britain, and Russia condemning the Armenian atrocities as "crimes against humanity and civilization"[206] shows that these powers recognized that international crimes were being committed and that the individuals involved would be held accountable. As a result, some postulate that this declaration gave the impression that the category of "crimes against humanity" was separate from "war crimes." Bassiouni states that this declaration was "responsible for the origin of the term 'crimes against humanity' as the label for a category of international crimes."[207]

Despite the controversy regarding the interpretation of the Martens Clause and its relevance for international law, it is indisputable that the 1899 Convention took important steps in humanizing the laws of war and extended the Geneva Convention of 1864, indicating that the participating states were in agreement that further protection was necessary during wartime.[208] Certainly, as well, the Martens Clause introduced into the treaty laws of international law concepts, the extent of which is still debated today, which had not been previously recognized in positive law but were available in customary law.

CRIMES AGAINST HUMANITY

The proscription and definition of crimes against humanity today is found in Article 5 of the Statute of the International Tribunal for Yugoslavia (1993), Article 3 of the Statute of the International Criminal Tribunal for Rwanda (1994), and Article 7 of the Rome Statute of the International Criminal Court. It is also still found in international customary law. Crucially, the provisions on the idea of crimes against humanity were developed within the framework of the law of the armed conflict.[209]

As noted above, the origin of crimes against humanity in their codified form is the Nuremburg Charter,[210] which defines them as

> atrocities and offences, including but not limited to murder, extermination, enslavement, deportation, imprisonment, torture, rape, or other inhumane acts committed against any civilian population, or persecution on political, racial, or religious grounds whether or not in violation of the domestic laws of the country where perpetrated....

According to the Nuremberg Charter acts to be defined as crimes against humanity had to be committed against "any civilian population."[211] The use of the term "civilian" as opposed to "combatant" signifies the inclusion of all non-combatants. At the time of the battle of Waterberg in August 1904 the Herero were predominantly a civilian population,[212] as there were many women, children, and men without arms. In fact, there were about 6,000 to 8,000 combatants and about 40,000 woman and children at Waterberg.[213] Those Herero men who tried to flee from the Waterberg region into the desert were a defeated army that did not offer resistance; as such, they were no longer combatants. Evidence of their attempts to surrender, which were ignored by the Germans, supports this claim. Thus, even if the Hereros were initially thought to be resisting the Germans, only a small portion of them were involved.

The ICTY finding in the *Vukovar Hospital* case, where soldiers had lain down their arms, is applicable: "Crimes against humanity must target a civilian population, individuals who at one time performed acts of resistance may in

German troops below the Waterberg. Courtesy of National Archives of Namibia.

certain circumstances be victims of crimes against humanity."[214] The *Tadic* decision also found that such a crime is committed if those targeted are of "a predominantly civilian nature. The presence of certain non-civilians in their midst does not change the character of the population."[215]

In the *Tadic* decision the ICTY specified when murder in the context of international crimes constitutes a crime against humanity or a war crime

> if classified as a crime against humanity, the murder possesses an objectively greater magnitude and reveals in the perpetrator a subjective frame of mind which may imperil fundamental values of the international community to a greater extent than in the case where that offence should instead be labeled as a war crime.[216]

The ICTR made it clear that customary international law does not require crimes against humanity to take place during an armed conflict:

> It is by now a settled rule of customary international law that crimes against humanity do not require a connection to international armed conflict. Indeed … customary international law may not require a connection between crimes against humanity and any conflict at all. Thus, by requiring that crimes against humanity be committed in either internal or international armed conflict, the Security Council may have defined the crime in Article 5 [of the Statute of the International Tribunal for Yugoslavia (1993)] more narrowly than necessary under customary international law.[217]

Dugard too has noted that the "blurring of the distinction between international and non-international armed conflicts and the expansion of the definition of international crimes have led to the criminalization of human rights violations, particularly where they are committed in a systematic manner or on a large scale."[218] Given the above, there is little doubt that Germany's conduct toward the Herero would constitute crimes against humanity under the current definition.

DEFINING GENOCIDE

The definition of genocide is intensely contested terrain.[219] "The term and its underlying concepts have been subject to a bewildering array of misrepresentations and distortions, both unintentional and deliberate."[220] What is indisputable is that war is not a precondition for genocide to occur. Although the events in GSWA are well-documented, even through the statements of the perpetrators themselves, a measure of denial remains about whether what occurred was genocide (even in today's terminology).

The legal definition of genocide is contained in international customary law,[221] the Genocide Convention, and the Statute of the two international criminal tribunals (ICTR, ICTY), as well as the Statute (The Rome Statute) of the ICC.[222] These international courts would, however, not be able to examine the Herero genocide, because the crimes happened before the courts came into existence and because they do not have jurisdiction, in some cases, beyond certain geographical borders.

While the legal definition of genocide is settled in treaty law, its definition in customary law is not. Many also regard the treaty definitions as insufficient and in need of amendment because the concept of genocide in the Genocide Convention is overly narrow (although expanded by the ICTR and ICTY statutes). The legal definition is seen as too limited, as political groups are excluded and, therefore, remain outside the ambit of the Convention. This limited scope, regarding which groups are included within the Genocide Convention, has even been criticized by the ICTR, who in examining the Tutsi group found that they did not constitute a racial or ethnic group. Hence the ICTR argued that the definition of the term "group" includes "permanent and stable groups." This view has been criticized by, among others, William Schabas,[223] who argues unconvincingly that it would amount to a watering down and overuse of the term genocide, thus leading to a trivialization of the horror of actual genocide.[224]

As a result of criticisms directed at the legal definition of genocide, numerous other definitions from a range of diverse scholars have been offered to overcome the perceived problems and limitations of the legal definition.[225] As a result, enormous definitional debates on genocide still pervade non-legal disciplines. Although the *de facto* reality is that these remain academic definitions, with little immediate practical applicability, it does not negate their academic relevance for the study of genocide and their complementary function in finding ways of preventing or reducing future genocides. Yet the legal definitions will prevail, as determining liability and the payment of reparations will ultimately be determined using the legal definitions.

However, the Herero are not seeking criminal prosecution for the acts of genocide and other international crimes committed; they seek to achieve civil liability and attain damages. Accordingly, the definitions of these crimes are not examined in the context of criminal liability; in fact, the Genocide Convention does not deal with redress and reparation to victims of genocide and does not provide for any civil remedies.[226] Yet the definition is important in that it would establish a transgression of the rights of those affected. If harm has been caused, it is a clear principle of international and domestic law that damages or reparations are payable.

Within the legal debate, some scholars have raised the question of a hierarchy of genocide and seek to classify genocidal events by the number of people killed. The UN Whitaker report notes that "It could seem pedantic to argue that some terrible mass-killings are legalistically not genocide, but on the other hand it could be counter-productive to devalue genocide through over-diluting its definition."[227] However, under the legal definition numbers are unimportant, and technically one killing or even the attempt to do so, could constitute genocide.

Article 2 of the Genocide Convention provides that there is genocide when there is factually (the *actus reus* requirement):

1. killing members of the group;
2. causing serious bodily or mental harm to members of the group;
3. deliberately inflicting on the group conditions of life calculated to bring about its physical destruction in whole or in part;
4. imposing measures intended to prevent births within the group; and
5. forcibly transferring children of the group to another group which is committed with intent (the *mens rea* requirement) to destroy, in whole or in part, a national, ethnical, racial or religious group.

Each group enjoying protection in terms of the Convention (and now elsewhere) has been specifically stipulated, but it has taken the various recent decisions of the two international criminal tribunals to determine the composition of these groups. Thus, the International Criminal Tribunal for Rwanda has declared

- an ethnic group is constituted by people who share a common cultural traditions, language or heritage[228];
- a religious group is defined as people who "share the same religion, denomination or mode of worship"[229];
- a national group is constituted by members with a common citizenship "coupled with reciprocity of rights and duties"[230];
- a racial group can be distinguished by hereditary physical traits that are often linked to a geographical region, "irrespective of linguistic, cultural, national or religious factors."[231]

Thus, genocide is composed of three elements:

1. The commission of any of the acts in Article 2
2. The direction of that act at one of the enumerated types of groups
3. The intent to destroy the group in whole or in part

It is also important to note that Article 1 of the Genocide Convention states that genocide is an international crime that can be committed either in times of peace or war. The language and provisions of the Genocide Convention have been imported into the Statutes of the ICTR[232] and the ICTY[233] as well as the ICC.[234] However, it is generally accepted that the provisions outlawing genocide have assumed the status of customary international law. Article 4 of the Convention provides that individuals committing genocide shall be punished, regardless of whether they are constitutionally responsible rulers, public officials, or private individuals. A number of provisions impose obligations on states party to the Convention to enact domestic measures that prevent and punish genocide. The Convention also has mechanisms for states to call upon organs of the United Nations to take action to prevent and suppress genocide and to refer disputes concerning the "interpretation, application or fulfilling" of the Convention to the International Court of Justice.

Article 3 of the Convention states that the following acts shall be punishable:

1. Genocide
2. Conspiracy to commit genocide
3. Direct and public incitement to commit genocide
4. Attempt to commit genocide
5. Complicity in genocide

The difficulty of determining what constitutes genocides stems partly from the fact that genocide is not only a factual question; the specific intention of the perpetrator(s) must be also be determined before a crime legally constitutes genocide.[235] As was noted in the ICTR Trial Chamber case in *Akayesu* (the first ever genocide conviction, which occurred on September 2, 1999):

> Genocide is distinct from other crimes inasmuch as it embodies a special intent or *dolus specialis*. Special intent of a crime is the specific intention, required as a constitutive element of the crime, which demands that the perpetrator clearly seeks to produce the act charged. Thus, the special intent in the crime of genocide lies in the intent to destroy, in whole or in part, a national, ethnical, racial or religious group, as such."[236]

When the orders or goals of perpetrators are not committed to paper, as was common in the past, intention can be difficult to ascertain or prove. Accordingly, many countries and individuals guilty of genocide refuse to accept responsibility for the crime.[237]

DO THE HERERO KILLINGS LEGALLY CONSTITUTE GENOCIDE?

The first three provisions of the five *actus reus* (factual) situations in Article 2 of the Genocide Convention (and elsewhere) are applicable to the Herero War. The ICTR in the *Akayesu* decision[238] noted that for genocide to be present the acts

> must have been committed against one or several individuals, because such individual or individuals were members of a specific group, and specifically because they belonged to this group. Thus, the victim is chosen not because of his individual identity, but rather on account of his membership of a national, ethnical, racial, or religious group. The victim of the act is therefore a member of a group, chosen as such, which, hence, means that the victim of the crime of genocide is the group itself and not only the individual.[239]

The Hereros were targeted as a group. As an ethnic group, with common ties of ancestry, language, and culture, they would have been protected by the Convention. In the *Akayesu* decision the ICTR accepted that

> [t]he primary criterion for [defining] an ethnic group is the sense of belonging to that ethnic group. It is a sense which can shift over time. In other words, the group, the definition of the group to which one feels allied, may change over time. But, if you fix any given moment in time, and you say, how does this population divide itself, then you will see which ethnic groups are in existence in the minds of the participants at that time.[240]

Tens of thousands of Herero people were killed, and the life conditions of the few survivors changed radically. Their cattle and land were seized, and they were confined to concentration camps where they had to provide forced labor and sexual favors because of their ethnic status.

Having established that the Herero were targeted as an ethnic group, the next question concerns the intention to eradicate a significant proportion of the population. In this regard the International Law Commission has stated that

> it is not necessary to intend to achieve the complete annihilation of a group from every corner of the globe. Nonetheless the crime of genocide by its very nature requires the intention to destroy at least a substantial part of a particular group.[241]

Similarly, the ICTY in the *Jelisic* case stated that "it is widely acknowledged that the intention to destroy must target at least a *substantial* part of the group."[242] The ICTR Trial Chamber has also noted in the *Akayesu* decision that for genocide to have occurred legally does not require

> the actual extermination of a group in its entirety, but is understood as such once any one of the [enumerated] acts ... is committed with the specific intent to destroy "in whole or in part" a national, ethnical, racial or religious group.[243]

Since the Herero population was diminished by about eighty percent, leaving approximately 16,000 survivors, genocide could be proclaimed.

Although the number of deaths does not determine genocide, Thomas Simon has noted that "we must acknowledge that the higher number of killings, the easier a *prima facie* case for genocide may be made."[244] The number of fatalities may also contribute to proving the intent to commit genocide. According to Helen Fein intent can be demonstrated "by showing a pattern of purposeful action."[245] Similarly, the ICTY held that the specific intent to achieve genocide

> may be inferred from a number of facts such as the general political doctrine which gave rise to the acts possibly covered by the definition in Article 4, or the repetition of destructive and discriminatory acts. The intent may also be inferred from the perpetration of acts which violate, or which the perpetrators themselves consider to violate, the very foundation of the group—acts which are not in themselves covered by the list in Article 4(2) but which are committed as part of the same pattern of conduct.... [T]his intent derives from the combined effect of speeches or projects laying the groundwork for and justifying the acts, from the massive scale of their destructive effect and from their specific nature, which aims at undermining what is considered to be the foundation of the group.[246]

While Steinmetz argues "it is unambiguously clear that the Ovaherero were neither exterminated physically nor decimated culturally, even if their suffering was enormous and the changes in their culture extensive,"[247] they were indeed nearly exterminated, and following their physical destruction much was done to destroy their cultural identity. Thus, although the Herero were not completely exterminated, a substantial enough proportion of the population was killed for the German campaign to constitute genocide. In the *Sikirica* case the ICTY noted that: "This part of the definition calls for evidence of an intention to destroy a substantial number relative to the total population of the group."[248] Additionally in the *Kristic* ICTY Appeal case handed down in 2004 the Court noted that "the substantiality requirement both captures genocide's defining character as a crime of massive proportions and reflects the Convention's concern with the impact the destruction of the targeted part will have on the overall survival of the group."[249]

While specific intent to destroy the group or part thereof is required in Article 2 of the Genocide Convention and in customary law, it has been argued that it is difficult to conceive of a state with specific intent.[250] However, it has been held that the required level of control (and hence responsibility) of state authorities over armed forces is "*overall control* going beyond the mere financing and equipping of such forces and involving also participation in the planning and supervision of military operations."[251] In *Prosecutor v Tadic* the Appeals Chamber of the ICTY noted that

> [t]he requirement of international law for the attribution to States of acts performed by private individuals is that the State exercises control over the individuals. The

> degree of control may, however, vary according to the factual circumstances of each case. The Appeals Chamber fails to see why in each and every circumstance international law should require a high threshold for the test of control.[252]

Thus, according to *Tadic*, even the acts of private individuals could fall under state responsibility and (therefore) liability. Von Trotha and his men were *public* officials, and therefore the state certainly could be held liable for their conduct.

Regarding state liability for genocide, the ICJ in the case *Yugoslavia v United Kingdom* found that Yugoslavia had failed to allege or prove that the NATO states had acted with genocidal intent[253]; however, the implication was that evidence could have been found. There have been suggestions for resolving the problem of proving genocidal intent by a state (if that is indeed a problem). Some suggest that, as in corporate liability in domestic law where the question of intent or *mens rea* is transferred from the corporate leader to the company, the liability of a state for genocide would depend on whether its leaders had perpetrated the crime. Thus, the mental element (of intent) would not be overlooked, it would be simply transferred.[254]

The ICJ decision in 2007 in the case *Bosnia v Serbia* is now the most instructive on state responsibility and liability for genocide.[255] In this decision the Court extends the traditional view of what states duties are under the Genocide Convention. The Court finds that the Convention gives rise to state responsibility for genocide.[256] It finds that states have a duty to not conspire to commit genocide, and may not attempt, aid, abet, or incite genocide. The Court finds that states can be found civilly liable for acts of genocide. Crucially, and relevant for the Herero cases, the Court holds that

> [g]enocide will be considered as attributable to a State if and to the extent that the physical acts constitutive of genocide that have been committed by organs or persons other than the State's own agents were carried out, wholly or in part, on instructions or directions of the State, or under its effective control.[257]

Critically, genocide is hardly ever spontaneous or accidental. According to Smith (and many others), it as usually premeditated and planned.[258] In this regard the ICTY Appeals chamber in the *Jelisic* decision held that

> [t]he existence of a plan or policy is not a legal ingredient of the crime. However, in the context of proving specific intent, the existence of a plan or policy may become an important factor in most cases.[259]

The Germans' intent to effect genocide is evidenced by their specific plans to destroy the Herero. The Germans took many steps over six or eight months to set in motion a process that culminated in the genocide. Their intent is further evidenced by the systematic destruction of the Herero's life support system by burning down their kraals and confiscating their cattle. They did little as well to stop the genocide when it was in motion.

In the *Akayesu* case, the ICTR stated:

> It is possible to deduce the genocidal intent inherent in a particular act charged from the general context of the preparation of other culpable acts systematically directed against the same group, whether these acts were committed by the same offender or by others. Other factors, such as the scale of atrocities committed, their general nature, in a region or a country, or furthermore, the fact of deliberately and systematically targeting victims on account of their membership of a particular group, while excluding the members of other groups, can enable the Chamber to infer the genocidal intent of a particular act.[260]

Given these findings, the *mens rea* and state responsibility of Imperial Germany is clear. At a minimum the Kaiser was aware of the ongoing acts of his agents and actively supported them; he may even have ordered the genocide. In addition, General von Trotha, who directly ordered and participated in the atrocities, was the highest direct representative of the German authority present in German South West Africa. His actions were either officially sanctioned or ordered by the Kaiser, and as such represented the actions of Germany itself. In this regard Trial Chamber II of the ICTR in *Kayishema and Ruzindana* held as follows:

> ... individuals of all ranks belonging to the armed forces under the military command of either the belligerent Parties fall within the class of perpetrators. If individuals do not belong to the armed forces, they could bear the criminal responsibility only when there is a link between them and the armed forces. It cannot be disregarded that the governmental armed forces are under the permanent supervision of public officials representing the government who had to support the war efforts and fulfill a certain mandate. On this issue, in the Akayesu Judgment, Trial chamber I was correct to include in the class of perpetrators, "individuals who were legitimately mandated and expected as public officials or agents or persons otherwise holding public authority or *de facto* representing the Government to support or fulfill the war efforts."[261]

At a minimum, Germany was complicit in the exercise of genocidal conduct. Regarding the intent required for accomplices to genocide, the ICTR has noted:

> The *mens rea*, or special intent, required for complicity in genocide is knowledge of the genocidal plan, coupled with the *actus reus* of participation in the execution of such plan ... an accused is liable as an accomplice to genocide if he knowingly aided or abetted or instigated one or more persons in the commission of genocide, while knowing that such a person or persons were committing genocide, even though the accused himself did not have the specific intent to destroy, in whole or in part, a national, ethnical, racial or religious group, as such....[262]

The Israeli court held in the *Eichmann* case that the following acts constituted the infliction of serious physical or mental harm[263]:

> ... the enslavement, starvation, deportation, and persecution of Jews and their detention in ghettos, transit camps, and concentration camps in conditions which were

> designed to cause their degradation, deprivation of their rights as human beings, and to suppress them and cause them inhumane suffering and torture.[264]

The way the Herero were treated satisfies the definition of genocide and fits the requirement of conditions calculated to bring about the destruction of a group in whole or in part. Thus, as Berat states: "Today, a strong case can be made that under international law Germany is liable for genocide committed in Namibia against the Herero and Nama/Orlam."[265] Hochschild agrees: "The killing there was masked by no smokescreen of talk about philanthropy. It was genocide, pure and simple, starkly announced in advance."[266]

Genocide has been classified into the following categories:

- Retributive (to avenge some event)
- Utilitarian (as a means to gain access to land and other resources)
- Monopolistic (to monopolize power)
- Institutional (massacres that are carried out a part of conquest)
- Ideological (for ideological reasons, such as the genocide in Cambodia or Rwanda)

From a non-legal definitional point, the genocide perpetrated on the Herero would fall into all these categories, except perhaps ideological. Weitz argues that the genocides in the Soviet Union, Nazi Germany, Cambodia, and Bosnia must be seen to have occurred in the pursuit of national utopias.[267] Victims of genocide are frequently dehumanized by those who attack them. They are depicted as vermin—lice, rats, and cockroaches—and often not perceived as individuals but only as part of the group.[268] Hence, perpetrators seek means to blame the victim and rationalize the genocide, as was the case with the Herero.

The foregoing demonstrates that what happened in 1904 conforms to the legal requirements of genocide today. Lyn Berat agrees, noting that the evidence on the way the Herero and other groups were treated indicates that the criteria for genocide were met. She notes that there was the intent to destroy the groups by way of killing, the causing of serious harm, and the infliction of conditions calculated to cause their destruction.[269]

It is interesting to note that Raphael Lemkin, the father of the term genocide and known by many as the person who led the campaign to create a Genocide Convention, produced two unpublished manuscripts that deal with the Herero extermination. Schaller, who examined these manuscripts, argues that Lemkin does not specifically state that genocide had occurred, but he believes these two documents imply that it had.[270] Interestingly, the document dealing specifically with the Herero is missing a number of pages, but the start of a section about the effects of the von Trotha proclamation is entitled "Genocide."[271] This confirms that Lemkin believed that the Herero case met his definition of genocide, namely:

> ... a coordinated plan of different actions aiming at the destruction of essential foundations of the life of natural groups, with the aim of annihilating the groups

Herero prisoners in chains. Courtesy of National Archives of Namibia.

> themselves. The objectives of such a plan would be disintegration of the political and social institutions, of culture, language, national feelings, religion, and the economic existence of national groups, and the destruction of the personal security, liberty, health, dignity, and even the lives of the individuals belonging to such groups.[272]

In his unpublished manuscript about the Herero, Lemkin records the factual evidence of genocide:

> After the rebellion and von Trotha's proclamation, the decimation of the Hereros by gunfire, hanging, starvation, forced labor, and flogging was augmented by prostitution and the separation of families, with a consequent lowering of the birthrate.[273]

GENOCIDE AS A SPECIES OF CRIME AGAINST HUMANITY

Crimes against humanity and genocide are part of the same "species" of crime. Many view genocide as part of crimes against humanity, and a number of scholars have pointed out that the two share a single source. Greenawalt has noted that scholars normally view genocide as a specific type of crime against humanity rather than an entirely separate crime. He argues that these concepts overlap more today than in the past and that it is "virtually certain that any act of genocide will also constitute a crime against humanity."[274]

Similarly, Fenrick notes that genocide is the "supreme crime against humanity," and others have similarly described it as the gravest form of crime against humanity.[275] Lippman has called genocide "an aggravated crime against humanity"[276] and according to Stoett "mass murder and/or genocide are, of course, the principal and most outrageous crimes against humanity."[277]

Schabas also cites a whole host of authorities supporting the overlap between these crimes.[278] Theodor Meron, one of the most respected international criminal law academics and a member of the ICTY, has written that crimes against humanity overlap considerably with genocide. He argues that genocide can be seen as a "species and particular progeny of the broader genus of crimes against humanity."[279] The difference between the two concepts is noted by the ICTR in the *Kayishema* case:

> The crime of genocide is a type of crime against humanity. Genocide, however, is different from other crimes against humanity. The essential difference is that genocide requires the aforementioned specific intent to exterminate a protected group (in whole or in part) while crimes against humanity require the civilian population to be targeted as part of a widespread or systematic attack. There are instances where the discriminatory grounds coincide and overlap.[280]

Schabas points out that recent cases emerging from the tribunals have "tended to insist upon the distinctions rather than the affinities between the two categories"[281]; however, the ICTY has noted the overlap and similarity. Schabas, himself has noted that "[f]or fifty years, crimes against humanity and genocide co-existed in parallel, so to speak. Most authorities treated genocide as a sub-category of crimes against humanity."[282] Thus, in the *Kupreskic* case, the Court noted that

> the Trial Chamber wishes to stress that persecution as a crime against humanity is an offence belonging to the same *genus* as genocide. Both persecution and genocide are crimes perpetrated against persons that belong to a particular group and who are targeted because of such belonging. In both categories what matters is the intent to discriminate: to attack persons on account of their ethnic, racial, or religious characteristics (as well as, in the case of persecution, on account of their political affiliation). While in the case of persecution the discriminatory intent can take multifarious inhumane forms and manifest itself in a plurality of actions, including murder, in the case of genocide that intent must be accompanied by the intention to destroy, in whole or in part, the group to which the victims of the genocide belong. Thus, it can be said that, from the viewpoint of *mens rea,* genocide is an extreme and most inhuman form of persecution. To put it differently, when persecution escalates to the extreme form of willful and deliberate acts designed to destroy a group or part of a group, it can be held that such persecution amounts to genocide.[283]

In the *Tadic* decision, the ICTY found that "genocide is itself a specific form of crime against humanity."[284] In the *Sikirica* decision, the ICTY noted that "genocide is a crime against humanity, and it is easy to confuse it with other crimes against humanity, notably, persecution."[285] Thus, the ICTY clearly claims that genocide is a crime against humanity but also intimates the affinity between genocide and persecution. Persecution, another type of crime against humanity, can in fact amount to genocide (as shown in the *Kupreskic* citation above).

Frulli notes that the "crime of genocide belongs to the class of crimes against humanity but may now also be considered as a separate crime."[286] Thus, she seems to argue that they derive from the same origin, but through developments over the last few years and through their codifications in various instruments they are now considered different crimes. So much overlap occurs that some, such as Green, have argued that the distinctions between genocide, "grave breaches," and war crimes ought to be abolished as they are all "but examples of the more generically termed 'crimes against humanity.'"[287]

Thus, while distinctions between these crimes are made today, the international tribunals have even recognized that they are interconnected and derive from the same roots, which are characterized by prohibitions about the ways in which to engage in war.

GENOCIDE: A NEW TERM FOR AN OLD CRIME OR A NEW CONCEPT?

Genocide has occurred throughout human existence. Thus, Jean-Paul Sartre has claimed that "the fact of genocide is as old as humanity."[288] Yet it is not just "the fact" of its existence for ages that is important; it has also been recognized as a crime for centuries. Some arguments from Greek and Roman times still resonate today, namely that a universal law of nature existed by which individuals had to abide. Certainly, the origins of specific international law criminalizing the persecution of individuals because of their ethnic, national, racial, or religious origins date back at least 350 years.[289]

While the word genocide is a relatively recent term, neither the concept nor the fact that the conduct constitutes a crime is new. As the UN Whitaker report on genocide in 1985 noted, the word "is a comparatively recent neologism for an old crime."[290] Raphael Lemkin, who coined the term, stated: "Deliberately wiping out whole peoples is not utterly new in the world. It is only new in the civilized world as we have come to think of it."[291] Roger Smith agrees that the phenomenon is ancient, but disagrees that it was always a crime. He states that "[a] recent study of genocide begins with the statement 'The word is new, the crime ancient.' This should read 'The word is new, the phenomenon ancient.'"[292] According to Smith, it is only in the last few centuries that genocide has produced a sense of "moral horror" and certainly there has been an implicit admission of the criminality of the conduct in the twentieth century, because not one state engaged in such conduct has admitted to it.[293] Thus, even though Smith disagrees about how long ago genocide became a crime his acknowledgment that it evoked "moral horror" over the last few centuries suggests that he recognizes it as a crime under customary international law.

Many argue that genocide only became a crime when Raphael Lemkin gave it a name in the 1940s. However, genocide was recognized as a crime long before Lemkin. The conduct was proscribed by custom from the Middle

Ages[294]; Lemkin merely gave it a name.[295] Lemkin only coined the term "genocide," because he regarded the term "mass murder" (in use at the time) as insufficient. He felt it failed to account for the motive of the crime, which arose solely from racial, national, or religious considerations and had nothing to do with the conduct of war. He believed the crime of genocide required a unique definition, as this was "not only a crime against the rules of war, but a crime against humanity itself" affecting not just the individual or nation in question, but humanity as a whole.[296] Even he recognized that the atrocities constituting genocide committed until then were indeed crimes of a specific genus, and part of crimes against humanity.[297] Thus, Lemkin coined a new name for something that had been subsumed under the general mantle of "crimes against humanity" for many years. In fact, the Charter of the International Military Tribunal of Nuremberg in Article 6(c) described crimes against humanity as: murder, extermination, enslavement, deportation, and other inhumane acts committed against any civilian populations, before or during the war; or persecutions on political, racial, or religious grounds in execution of or in connection with any crime within the jurisdiction of the Tribunal, whether or not in violation of the domestic law of the country where perpetrated.

Thus, already then the notion of genocide was contained in codified form and was thought to be part of crimes against humanity. In this regard, Nagan and Rodin have noted that "the Charter of Nuremberg defined crimes against humanity as covering many of the circumstances that today would fall under the legal label of genocide."[298]

Some Nazis, such as Herman Goering, were convicted[299] at Nuremburg for conduct aimed at exterminating Jewish people that amounted to genocide,[300] and the judgment in the *Justice* Case described genocide as "the prime illustration of a crime against humanity."[301] Schabas notes that while genocide was not charged at Nuremberg, because it was not enumerated in the Charter, it was dealt with indirectly as a crime against humanity.[302] In fact, at the time Winston Churchill called it "a crime without a name,"[303] recognizing that although it was not specifically identified, it was indeed a crime.[304] At the domestic level, some individuals were prosecuted and convicted for genocide even before the Genocide Convention came into force. Poland convicted Amon Goeth, Rudolf Hoess, and Arthur Greiser for genocide under Polish law,[305] specifically using the term genocide.[306]

However, the debate continues on whether there could be genocide if the word itself was only coined by Lemkin[307] in 1943[308] and was only legally defined by the 1948 UN Convention on the Prevention and Punishment of the Crime of Genocide. The "modern" history of genocide is tied to the actions of the various colonial powers and what they did to the respective indigenous populations in the colonies.[309] Yet Howard-Hassman and others have argued that there were no international legal rules prohibiting genocide and ethnic cleansing in "the early modern capitalist world."[310] She maintains that at a time when even in Europe very few people enjoyed human rights protections there was little concern about what happened in the colonies. While this is true, one must question what is meant by the "early modern capitalist world," and whether the indifference of Europe regarding the colonies meant that international law did not apply to the colonies. In fact, by the 1860s the laws of war were formulated in international law, and from 1899 human rights issues were incorporated into international law through the Martens Clause. Not only is the contention that this only applied to humanitarian law erroneous, it also represents a myopic view of treaty law and does not account for customary law, which was also well developed by then.

There is additional evidence that genocide as we know it today existed before Lemkin. In English, the term "murder of a nation" had been in use since 1918.[311] In French, the term *populicides,* or the killing of a population, was coined by Gracchus Babeuf in 1795, describing the massacre of 117,000 farmers in the Vendée region during the French Revolution.[312] In German, the term *Völkermord* was used from 1831 to describe the killing of a people. In fact, at the time the Herero were deemed and called a *Volk* by members of the *Reichstag.*[313] In Polish, the term *ludobojstwo* means killing of a people. In Armenian *tseghaspanutiun* means to kill a race, and in Greek *genoktonia* is an ancient term denoting the killing or death of a nation.[314] The word was even known in indigenous languages. In the South African language Zulu the word *izwekufa* means "death of the nation."[315] *Izwekufa* was a word known in the 1830s when there was huge turmoil in the region and hundreds of thousands fled because of the violence caused by Zulu leader Shaka. The word *izwekufa* comes from two words: "*izwe* (nation, people, polity), and *ukufa* (death, dying, to die). The term is thus identical to "genocide" in both meaning and etymology."[316]

The word genocide comes from the Greek word *genos*, connoting race, tribe, or species, and the Latin suffix *cide*, meaning killing.[317] The term Holocaust could have been used to denote the concept of genocide, but clearly that would be contentious. The word stems from the Latin term *Holocaustrum,* used in biblical times to refer to the killing of Jews.[318] Hence the word genocide is a new term but not a new concept or a new crime. The word only emerged in the 1940s because the widespread mass killings by states at that time were seen to require new terminology to describe these occurrences.[319]

Critically, the debate over what constitutes "genocide" concerns its specific definition and application, not its existence or its prohibition under international law. The ICTR recognizes that the crime of genocide was inherent in the laws defining war crimes and crimes against humanity long before the Genocide Convention, but had not been given a specific name. There is ample evidence prohibiting the slaughter of peoples for their cultural makeup or religious preference. Certain scholars still debate whether this applies only to the context of war, arguing that since the prohibitions are found in laws governing the act of war and apply to those peoples outside the sovereign realm of a nation or those actively joining in a rebellion, the concept is not universally applicable.

GENOCIDE BEFORE THE GENOCIDE CONVENTION

In 1946 before the Genocide Convention was even drafted[320] (or acceded to by any states) genocide already was recognized as an international crime. This is verified by the text of a 1946 General Assembly resolution, which stated:

> The General Assembly therefore:
> Affirms that genocide is a crime under international law which the civilized world condemns ...[321]

The preamble of the Genocide Convention states that "at all periods of history genocide has inflicted great losses on humanity." Thus, in 1948, it was recognized that genocide had already been a crime for a long time. Even when the move began to draft a Genocide Convention, Saudi Arabia described genocide as "an international crime against humanity."[322] In 1946, genocide was already accepted as a crime, which many claimed was linked to crimes against humanity. The 1948 Convention did not "create" the crime, but merely codified and clarified this type of criminal conduct. According to Freeman it was only with the adoption of the Genocide Convention that the crime became dissociated with "its original military context."[323] In other words, one view is that, before the Convention, genocide was linked to the context of war, and its separation from the laws of war only occurred from 1948.

Genocide as a crime pre-1948 is corroborated in Article 1 which states that "[t]he Contracting Parties confirm that genocide, whether committed in time of peace or in time of war, is a crime under international law...." The word "confirm" indicates that genocide was a pre-existing crime, and incorporating it into the treaty merely formalized its prohibition. This was also recognized by the ICJ in the *Reservations to the Convention on the Protection and Punishment of the Crime of Genocide* case in 1951. The ICJ held that genocide was a crime beyond the Convention and noted "the principles underlying the Convention are principles which are recognized by civilized nations as binding on States, even without any conventional obligation."[324] In fact, it could be argued that, as genocide was a crime in customary law, the Convention has a valid retrospective effect because it simply confirmed that genocide was a crime before the Convention, and it can, therefore, be applied to events predating its coming into force.

Retrospectivity is not unknown in either international or national law. While, generally speaking, it is frowned upon and seen as a violation of the rights of an accused, in certain cases there are accepted exceptions to this position. One such exception concerns international crimes such as crimes against humanity and genocide. While there has been no international court ruling on this matter, this position is widely accepted; Courts in Australia[325] and Canada[326] have found that the prosecutions of such cases, even before legislation on these crimes was adopted, are not retrospective as they were considered crimes in international law before a new law was adopted.[327]

While many feel that various international crimes were controversially adopted in the London Agreement of August 8, 1945, which established the Charter of the Nuremberg Tribunal, the counterpoint of their use then was that no new crimes were enacted; the Charter merely codified existing international law. Critically, retrospectivity is contained today in modern international treaties, including the Convention on the Non-Applicability of Statutes of Limitation to War Crimes and Crimes against Humanity of 1968 and the Vienna Convention on the Law of Treaties of 1969. While one could argue that *nullum crimen sine lege, nulla poena sine lege praevia* (no crime without law, no penalty without previous law) is a basis for non-retrospectivity and validity for not pursuing events that occurred before the treaty came into force, this norm is not always applicable. For example, while the applicability of this norm is contained in Article 15(1) of the International Covenant on Civil and Political Rights, it is limited in its operation by Article 15(2) which states:

> Nothing in this article shall prejudice the trial and punishment of any person for any act or omission which, at the time when it was committed, was criminal according to the general principles of law recognized by the community of nations.

In other words, if a crime was criminalized under customary law before the treaty came into effect, it is not limited by the retrospective nature of the operation of the treaty. This same limitation on the operation of *nullum crimen* is contained in Article 11(2) of the Universal Declaration of Human Rights, which provides that retrospective application of the criminal law is not prohibited if the event that is the basis of the prosecution was a crime in national or international law.[328] Regarding the question of retrospectivity and the Genocide Convention it has been noted:

> The language of the Genocide Convention neither excludes nor requires its retroactive application. In other words—there is nothing in the language of the Convention that would prohibit its retroactive application. By contrast, there are numerous international treaties that specifically state that they will not apply retroactively.[329]

Precisely the fact that some statutes find it necessary to stipulate they are not retrospective implies the possibility that retrospectivity might exist in others.

As noted above, it may not even be necessary to apply the Convention retrospectively as the *travaux preparatoires* of the Convention has numerous references to genocide as a crime before the Convention.[330]

Lyn Berat too has written that "genocide always constituted an international crime"[331] and in 1955 Professor Hersch Lauterpacht stated in his treatise that "[i]t is clear that as a matter of law the Genocide Convention cannot impair the effectiveness of existing international obligations."[332] This view has been supported by the UN Commission on Human Rights, which, in 1969, stated: "[i]t is therefore taken for granted that as a codification of existing international law the Convention on the Prevention and Punishment of the Crime of Genocide did neither extend nor restrain the notion of genocide, but that it only defined it more precisely."[333] This does not imply that the Genocide Convention itself in its treaty form applies retrospectively; it probably does not as it simply codifies what was in existence before 1948. But genocide as a prohibited legal act existed before 1948. According to Steinmetz it "remains to be seen whether courts and publics find the U.N. genocide convention to be retroactively applicable to events such as the German assault on the Ovaherero which happened before the mid-20th century."[334] However, the Vienna Convention on the Law of Treaties states:

> Unless a different intention appears from the treaty or is otherwise established, its provisions do not bind a party in relation to any act or fact which took place or any situation which ceased to exist before the date of the entry into force of the treaty with respect to that party.[335]

Though the Vienna Convention did not enter into force until 1980, it is accepted that its provisions primarily delineate what customary international law was and is, and that, unless the notion of genocide as a punishable crime before the entry into force of the convention is read by a court, it will not apply retrospectively. Before the Vienna Convention came into force, the ICJ noted in the *Ambatielos* case:

> To accept [the Greek Government's] theory would mean giving retroactive effect to Article 29 of the Treaty of 1926, whereas Article 32 of this Treaty states that the Treaty, which must mean all the provisions of the Treaty, shall come into force immediately upon ratification. Such a conclusion might have been rebutted if there had been any special clause or any special object necessitating retroactive interpretation. There is no such clause or object in the present case. It is therefore impossible to hold that any of its provisions must be deemed to have been in force earlier.[336]

However, while the Convention may not itself be retroactive in its effect, it does not mean that prohibitions of genocide did not apply before the Convention; they did, as the principles predate the Convention. As was found in the ICJ decision, the "principles underlying the Convention are principles which are recognized by civilized nations as binding on States, even without any conventional obligation." Interpreting this decision, Schabas has argued that while the ICJ advisory opinion is usually viewed as authority for the proposition that the Genocide Convention is a codification of customary norms, this is not the situation.[337] Schabas's point is that the Court is not saying that the entire Genocide Convention codifies customary norms, but that the prohibition of genocide is a norm of customary law. Schabas also admits that the Convention does indicate that genocide was a crime before the Convention was drafted and even before the General Assembly Resolution of 1946. Thus, it is clear that genocide was considered a crime before, and the Convention recorded and clarified international opinion on it at the time.

The ICTR has taken this point even further, stating in its *Akayesu* decision that the "Genocide Convention is undeniably considered part of customary international law."[338] This was also the view of the United Nations' Secretary-General in his 1993 Report on the establishment of the International Criminal Tribunal for the former Yugoslavia.[339] These recognitions are important as the UN Convention on the Non-Applicability of Statutory Limitations to War Crimes and Crimes against Humanity,[340] to which Germany is a party,[341] plainly and consciously pronounced its retroactive application. Article 1 stipulates: "No statutory limitation shall apply to the following crimes, *irrespective of the date of their commission* ... the crime of genocide as defined in the 1948 Convention...." Thus, genocide can therefore form the basis of prosecution even now for events that were legally deemed to be genocide in customary law when committed. Supporting this is the finding in the *Eichmann* trial where the Court held that the

> crimes created by the Law and of which the appellant was convicted must be deemed today to have *always borne the stamp of international crimes*, banned by international law and entailing individual criminal liability.... [T]he rules of the law of nations are not derived solely from international treaties and organized international usage. In the absence of a supreme legislative authority and international codes, the process of its evolution resembles that of the common law; ... its rules are established from case to case, by analogy with the rules embodied in treaties and in international custom, on the bases of the "general principles of law recognized by civilized nations," and in the light of the vital international needs that impel an immediate solution. A principle which constitutes a common denominator for the judicial systems of numerous countries must clearly be regarded as a 'general [principle] of law recognized by civilized nations ...[342]

One of the real effects of the drafting of the Convention is that from the late 1940s crimes against humanity, war crimes, and genocide were defined in distinctive ways through the various instruments drafted at that time.[343] This does not, however, imply that there was and remains no degree of overlap between these crimes; a person could be guilty of one or more of these distinct crimes for the same act.[344]

SLAVERY AND THE PROTECTION OF MINORITY GROUPS

In GSWA the Herero men, women and children were kept as prisoners and made to work without pay; i.e., they were subjected to slavery or forced labor.

Before 1900, and even before the coalescing of customary law on this issue, Germany was bound by obligations regarding slavery. Prussia was a signatory to the 1815 Vienna Declaration, in which the European Powers condemned the slave trade in principle and called slavery "repugnant to the principles of humanity and universal morality." However, many believe that this agreement

Herero women washing German soldiers' uniforms. Courtesy of National Archives of Namibia.

was insufficient to make the practice a *crime jure gentium*.[345] More importantly, in terms of Germany's obligations, it was party to the 1841 Treaty for the Suppression of the African Slave Trade (Treaty of London). This Treaty established a duty to prohibit, prevent, prosecute, and punish those involved in slavery. The United Kingdom prohibited slave trafficking in its colonies in 1807. Yet according to Geoffrey Robertson, the slave trade and slavery were abolished in international law only between 1885 (when the Berlin Treaty was signed) and 1926 when the slavery convention specifically gave states the jurisdiction to prosecute those engaged in the practice of slavery.[346]

Thus, although slavery was outlawed in the 1885 General Act of the Conference Respecting the Congo (General Act of Berlin), of which Germany was also a signatory, many question whether this act made slavery an international crime. Bismarck chaired the Berlin Conference and was therefore able to effect decisions made at the conference, which later assisted Germany in gaining its colonial share. The prohibition of the slave trade was contained in the German Act of the Berlin Conference of 1884 to 1885. In fact, Bismarck used the pretext of the Arab slave trade to intervene in East Africa.[347] Yet it has been noted that the slave prohibition and other "humanitarian and philanthropic clauses of the Berlin Act, mainly intended for home consumption, played no part in the thinking of founding fathers of German colonialism, and the later senior colonial administrators."[348]

Germany was also a party to another agreement that obligated them with respect to slavery, the 1890 Convention Relative to the Slave Trade and Importation into Africa of Firearms, Ammunition, Spirituous Liquors (General Act of the Brussels Conference). In fact, in 1895 a German law provided for the punishment of slave trading.[349] The 1904 International Agreement for the Suppression of the White Slave Traffic was settled in the same year that the Herero genocide began.[350]

The Annex to the 1899 Convention contains its Regulations, and Article 4 of these regulations states the most basic principle regarding the protection of prisoners of war: "Prisoners of war are in the power of the hostile Government, but not of the individuals or corps who capture them. They must be humanely treated...." Already at the beginning of the twentieth century there was a conventional duty on a detaining power to guarantee humane treatment. Article 6 of the Regulations contained in the Annex states that "the State may utilize the labor of prisoners of war ... their tasks shall not be excessive, and shall have nothing to do with the military operation...."[351] Thus, the use of slave or forced labor was proscribed in certain instances, and what was occurring in 1904 to 1908 certainly transgressed these regulations. Additionally, the prohibition of slavery is seen also to "have achieved the level of customary international law and have attained *jus cogens* status."[352] Article 7 of the Regulations declares: "The Government into whose hands prisoners of war have fallen is bound to maintain them." Thus, the Germans had a duty to maintain the combatants who fell into their hands; likewise, the captured civilians had to be treated in accordance with the recognized rules. Article 8 held that "Prisoners of war shall be subject to the laws, regulations, and orders in force in the army of the State into whose hands they have fallen."

In spite of these regulations, Herero men, women, and children were subject to slavery and forced labor. Hence the status of slavery and forced labor at the time, including whether either constituted crimes or violations of international law, are key issues. Bassiouni's comment that "slavery is unique in that it has almost been totally eradicated since the beginning of the 1900s without reliance on international enforcement machinery"[353] demonstrates that there was at least some measure of prohibition of slavery in force by then. He believes that this was primarily due the fact that "the commonly shared values of the world community had coalesced, and concurred with the political will of states...."[354] This certainly indicates that by 1900 the prohibition of slavery was so widely accepted that it complied with the necessities of customary law. Many countries had by then abolished slavery, and states generally accepted the position that international law forbade slavery, even if there is some doubt about whether the various international agreements on slavery were clear on the matter before 1926. Already in Britain in 1772 Lord Chief Justice Mansfield ruled that English law does not accept slavery; in 1775 slavery was abolished in Madeira; in 1807 England and the United States prohibited their citizens from engaging in the international slave trade; in 1823 slavery was abolished in Chile; in 1824 in Central America, 1829 in Mexico, 1831 in Bolivia, 1838 in all British colonies, 1842 in Uruguay, 1848 in all French and Danish colonies, 1851 in Ecuador, 1854 in Peru and Venezuela, 1863 in all Dutch colonies, 1865 in the United States, 1873 in Puerto Rico, 1886 in Cuba, and 1888 in Brazil.[355] In 1993 Lord

Anthony Gifford, a proponent of reparations for slavery, acknowledged that subjecting Africans to slavery was a crime against humanity.[356] According to Geraldine van Bueren, Britain and the United States' agreement to classify slavery as a form of piracy amounted to their acceptance of legal guilt.[357] Germany's violation of the norms relating to slavery in German South West Africa will be returned to later in this chapter.

Another area in which there was development in international human rights before the nineteenth century is in the matter of the protection of minority groups. Eide argues that human rights law emerged in the seventeenth and eighteenth centuries, and that this internationalization partly occurred due to concerns about the protection of minority groups.[358] At a minimum this issue dates back to the Vienna Congress (1815), but additionally a number of treaties protecting national minorities were concluded before the twentieth century. In fact, by the nineteenth century international law had developed a doctrine on the legitimacy of "humanitarian intervention" in cases where a state committed atrocities against its own subjects that "shocked the conscience of mankind."[359] This is evidenced in various examples, including the resolution in 1827 of the Great Powers to intervene in the Ottoman Empire to halt the slaughter of Greek Orthodox Christians.[360] In fact, in the Treaty of Kutchuk-Kainardi Russia "claimed" to protect the Christian minority living in the Ottoman Empire.[361] The London Treaty between Great Britain, France, and Russia for the Pacification of Greece, July 6, 1827, noted that they were "putting a stop to the effusion of blood" so as to re-establish "peace between the Contending Parties by means of an arrangement called for, no less by sentiments of humanity, than by interests for the tranquility of Europe."[362]

An early nineteenth century example of humanitarian intervention for human rights reasons is the intervention that took place in 1827 by Great Britain, France, and Russia into Greece because of the oppression of Greek Christians by the Ottoman Empire. The document authorizing the intervention, the London Treaty,[363] claimed that this was being done because of "sentiments of humanity." In fact, abuses perpetrated by the Ottoman Empire saw interventions a number of times during the nineteenth century, including when France invaded Syria in 1860, and when Russia invaded territory today considered part of the former Yugoslavia in 1877. The Russian intervention was in fact authorized by a number of European states.

In the 1860s Austria, France, Britain, Prussia, and Russia, with the consent of the Ottomans, had authorized a force of 6,000 to restore order and protect the Christians, even though "state sovereignty" was paramount at the time. This example, like the others, indicates that by the nineteenth century state sovereignty was no longer the inviolable principle it had been before.[364] The Treaty of Berlin of 1878 required various states amalgamating into the Concert of Europe to recognize the rights of religious minority groups in their countries.

As noted above, the notion of humanitarian intervention is an old principle. Although state sovereignty is still an issue in the twenty-first century, there were already a number of historical cases that indicated state sovereignty was less than sacrosanct, and occasionally breached when necessary. Further, the establishment of the International Commission in 1860 to investigate the causes of the atrocities committed by the Ottoman Empire, the extent of the persecution, and how to punish those responsible[365] substantiates acceptance of these atrocities as punishable. Accountability for these crimes already constituted an accepted part of international law; in fact, international criminal law existed to punish offenders even before the twentieth century. In summary, from 1815 states had convened numerous times to devise many instruments prohibiting slavery and the slave trade, and developing protections for minorities.[366]

DID THE GERMANS KNOW THAT WHAT THEY DID TO THE HERERO WAS ILLEGAL?

Relevant to determining liability for the harm perpetrated on the Herero is the question of whether the Germans knew at the time that they were violating international law, and whether others objected to the German conduct.

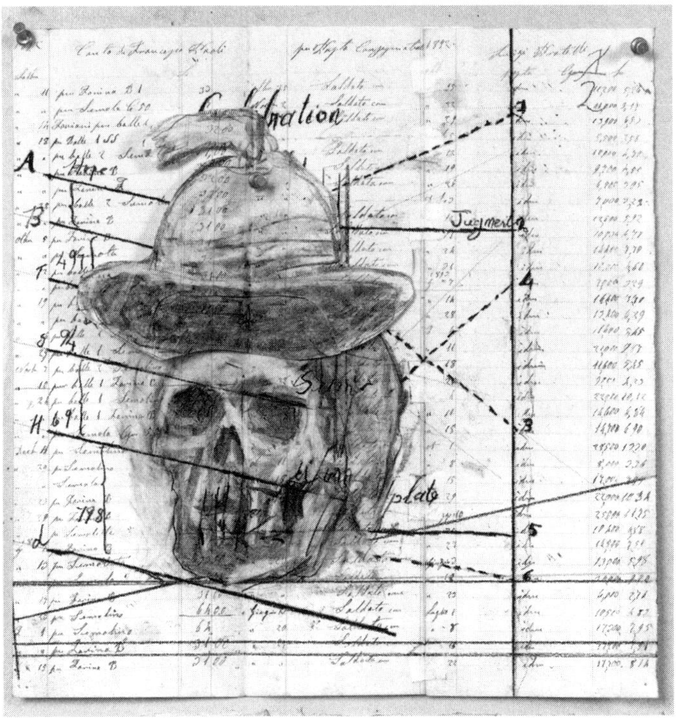

Drawing for Black Box/Chambre Noire 2005. Courtesy of William Kentridge.

According to B.D. Bargar some British humanitarians did protest, but "the notorious campaign against the Hereros ... did not arouse British opinion of the time."[367] In response, Kenneth Mackenzie notes that there was a

> long, coherent, and inflexible opposition to German methods. British and colonial officials, and commentators well qualified to remark on German colonial activity did so in definite and generally uncomplimentary terms long before 1914. Overwhelming evidence of the widespread dislike and hostility of what occurred is contained not only in unpublished private papers, but also in a steady stream of articles and comments in the published journals and newspapers of the time.[368]

Public comment abounded despite the fact that states themselves often abstained from commenting on the treatment meted out by the colonizers, mostly likely because they feared reciprocal criticism for the various abuses conducted in their own empires. There were, however, exceptions. In 1904 the British published a highly critical report of abuses committed by the Belgians in the Congo. The report, compiled by Roger Casement, noted that the events in the Congo were in violation of the 1885 Berlin Act.[369] The report was sent to a number of the Berlin Act signatories. As a result the Congo administration ordered an investigation, which led to the arrest of various officials. It follows that if what happened in the Congo violated the Berlin Act, the actions of the Germans in GSWA did as well. Thus, international opinion was against the abuses suffered in the colonies, as they were thought to violate acceptable standards.[370] Mackenzie points to an article that appeared in 1888 in the journal *Nineteenth Century,* which criticized the German conduct in Samoa.[371] The article reflected on the "constant aggression," arson, and land confiscations waged against the Samoans. The events were deemed to be a series of outrages, and "the action of the Germans is not only indefensible but worthy of condemnation."[372] Three months later an Archdeacon in East Africa also published an article in the *Fortnightly Review*, complaining about how Germany operated in a brutal and clumsy manner toward Africans. Already then it was argued that "the native races which were quietly settling down to peace and industry, are now taking up their weapons again to fight the hated Germans."[373]

In two articles in 1889 and 1890 Joseph Thomson stated that Germany's introduction "of civilization to the semi-barbarous people who inhabit those parts is being joyously celebrated by the thunder of artillery, the demolition of the towns, and human bloodshed."[374] He condemned Germany's disregard for "international law and equity."[375] In the 1890 article Thomson remarked that "the Germans have leveled every town on the East Coast and bespattered the ruins and the jungles with the lifeblood of their inhabitants."[376]

An article by V.L. Cameron noted that Carl Peters, the German explorer, shot Africans with little or no provocation.[377] Another article in the same journal by E.W. Beckett also attacked Peters. Beckett detailed a whole list of newspapers that had denounced German behavior.[378] In his book *Britain and Germany's Lost Colonies 1914–1919*, William Rogers Louis argued that "the doctrine of Germany's guilt as a uniquely brutal and cruel colonial power originated in the First World Wars and not before"[379]; yet he concedes that "in justice to the humanitarians, some did protest the treatment of the Hereros."[380] O. Eltzbacher launched an especially virulent attack on Germany, saying that the Germans' "ill-treatment of the South West Africa natives undoubtedly constitute, not a private injury, but a public wrong ... and ... an offence against justice and humanity."[381] Articles in various publications are evidence that criticism of Germany's conduct toward the Herero was clearly widespread.[382]

Germany and its forces were aware that their conduct was illegal and understood that others thought so too. That the Germans knew the Herero were supposed to be treated according to the Geneva and Hague Conventions is clear from its recognition at the time that Herero captives were prisoners of war. The colonial department on January 7, 1905 in a communiqué to the Governor of Cameroon (then Kamerun) specifically recognized these captives as prisoners of war.[383] There was some debate in the *Reichstag* on this matter, yet this does not repudiate the recognition of the issue. The 1904 statement about the GSWA atrocities by Colonial Director Stubel evidences that Germany was conscious of and felt governed by the 1899 Hague Convention and its Martens Clause:

> In any event, we have no authentic information in this connection, and in my opinion, our German character does not tend to do cruelty and brutality. Even if a temptation to trespass against the laws of humanity might have arisen, the troops in question would not in fact have contravened the laws of humanity.[384]

This was not an isolated statement. On May 9, 1904, Colonial Director Stubel reported in the *Reichstag* that Chancellor von Bülow wrote to Governor Leutwein on March 28 of the same year:

> Press reports of letters from the protectorate cause me to point out that steps are to be taken to prevent violations against humanity, against enemies incapable of fighting, and against woman and children. Orders in the sense are to be issued.[385]

These statements show that the Chancellor and the Colonial Director both knew about and accepted the provisions of the Martens Clause and felt it applied even in GSWA. Hull interestingly notes that no record of the cable from the Chancellor to the Governor has been found, and there is no reference to it in any part of the diaries, hence it must be presumed that it was never transmitted.[386] If the cable was indeed not sent, it would suggest that the Germans did not want to temper their conduct and that the brutality was in fact supported and condoned.

In the German Parliament the founders of the German Social Democrats, Wilhelm Liebknecht and August Bebel, accused the colonial troops of crimes against the locals in the colonies and the "handful of Hottentots"[387] in their South West colony. They specifically objected to the suppression of the Hereros, but also to the steps taken in East Africa (today Tanzania,[388] Rwanda, Burundi).[389] They certainly foregrounded these issues in the *Reichstag*,[390] and their objections contributed to the awareness of the German populace and people around the world about what was happening in the colonies.[391] Despite these efforts, at the time some questioned the extent to which German citizens knew the details of what was happening.[392] G.A. Krause, an eyewitness to events occurring in 1905, wrote in the *Berliner Tageblatt*:

> Each time a war with the natives breaks out through the fault of some official, the people back home are told nothing but that a war has taken place, that it is over now, and that they have to foot the bill. There is never any mention of the whys and the wherefores.... According to the telegraphic message all is quiet in the protectorate. Everything is indeed quiet, the dead lie peacefully in their graves and the wounded on their sick-beds, and the rest have been put to rout.[393]

Germany's development aid minister, Heidemarie Wieczorek-Zeul, acknowledged the opposition in Germany a hundred years ago to the treatment of the Herero. She delivered an apology to the Herero at Waterberg on August 14, 2004. In her speech, the Minister stated the following:

> Even at that time, back in 1904, there were also Germans who opposed and spoke out against this war of oppression. One of them was August Bebel, the chairman of the same political party of which I am a member. In the German parliament, Bebel condemned the oppression of the Herero in the strongest terms and honored their uprising as a just struggle for liberation. I am proud of that today.[394]

When Bebel was told "unsatisfactorily" that women and children were being killed because the combatants were using them as shields,[395] this met with skepticism. Crucially, there was no denial that women and children were being killed. In fact, when these atrocities became known in Germany, Chancellor von Bülow demanded an explanation. Not denying the occurrences, the Chief of the General Staff, Alfred Graf von Schlieffen, replied that women had taken part in the fighting and "were the chief instigators of the cruel and awful tortures."[396]

That the Hague rules applied to Germany and that they were accepted in the military is evidenced by the British understanding of their obligation and responsibility just before the Herero War. During the Anglo-Boer War (1899–1901) Major-General Sir John Ardagh, who had represented his country at the Hague Conference, told the war Secretary, Lord Landsdowne, that the rules had merely codified "custom and usages" and that it applied even to those states that were not signatories to the treaty.[397] It was repeated in the British Parliament that Britain would conduct the war against the Boers, who were not signatories to the Convention, under the Hague Rules. While their conduct did not always comply with those rules, the point is that even then it was accepted that the Hague Rules applied, and even against non-signatory parties.[398]

At the time, even von Trotha knew that they were violating international law. He wrote an article in the *Deutsche Zeitung*, stating that

> [it]t is obvious that the war in Africa does not adhere to the Geneva Convention. It was painful for me to drive back the women from the waterholes in the Kalahari. But my troops were faced with a catastrophe. Had I made the smaller waterholes available to the women, then I would have been faced with an Africa Beresina.[399]

The above citation illustrates a few points: Firstly, von Trotha knew about the Geneva Convention, and knew Germany was obligated to it and what it entailed, but admitted that he was not going to comply with its provisions because what occurred in Africa does not "adhere" to these provisions. It is not known on what legal basis he based his pronouncement, but it is obviously both legally and ethically problematic. Even if another force does not observe its obligations, or has no obligations because certain treaties do not bind it, it does not give Germany as a signatory party the right to be excused. In this regard George Steinmetz has argued that the "insistence by Governor Leutwein in 1896 (during the first campaign against the rebellious Ovaherero) and again by General von Trotha in 1904 that the (first) Geneva Convention was *irrelevant* to the colonial context indicates precisely the opposite, namely, that its relevance already fell within the bounds of plausibility for both of these men."[400]

Further, von Trotha also makes it clear that the German forces stopped the Herero from accessing water, and even prevented the civilian population from doing so. This in itself was an international crime. While von Trotha makes reference to what happened to Napoleon at Beresina in 1812, that event occurred a century before von Trotha's activities, when no international law regarding war crimes existed. Not only were the Beresina circumstances very different, but the events of 1812 did not target civilians. It also seems as if even von Trotha was aware of the legal issues concerned conducting war humanely. He stated to Leutwein: Against non-humans (*Unmenschen*) one cannot conduct war "humanely."[401]

In defense of the Germans Nordbruch argues that

> [u]nlike the European combatants, the Herero did not wear uniforms, but wore their traditional civil clothes (*Räuberzivil*). They were everywhere, in thick bushes and on farms, day and night—it was impossible to make out whether it was a civilian or partisan. There were lots of German patrols that dreadfully lost their lives to such bands of partisans. Torture and mutilation was common. The Herero never took prisoners. Hence, the General's proclamation is also to be understood as a protective measure for his own troops.[402]

Although Nordbruch claims that civilians could not be distinguished from combatants, von Trotha's *Deutsche Zeitung* article indicates he knew they were dealing with civilians and this did not make any difference to him. This is supported by his reference to the Geneva Convention—if he was in doubt about whether they were civilians, he would not have mentioned it. Because he knew they were civilians he made reference to the lack of compliance with the Convention in

Africa and that he was not adhering to the provisions regarding civilians. Nordbruch's other point is that von Trotha was justified in his troop's action toward the Herero, because the Herero were killing, mutilating, and torturing German troops; Nordbruch portrays these actions as self-preservation. However, the literature and accounts from eyewitnesses do not support the accusations that the Herero were mutilating and torturing the German soldiers. Even if one accepts that they did, it still did not give the Germans license to persecute the Herero in this way, and certainly not civilians.

There is enough evidence to show that even those in leadership (including von Trotha) knew they were violating international law. Yet another example is from the Kaiser's July 1900 Hun speech. His advisors "heard his oration with concealed horror" and tried to limit its effects by providing the press with an altered version of his speech.[403] It is not clear whether his advisors were appalled by what the Kaiser said or were upset because his original unedited speech later emerged. Be that as it may, that the Kaiser's advisors attempted to conceal what he had said shows that even in the nineteenth century Germany recognized the illegality of the conduct and feared as a result how the speech would be received. Interestingly, the Kaiser did not see his conduct as problematic, and was in fact dismissive of the concerns regarding his speech. If he did not recognize the immorality of his conduct then, there is little reason to believe that he would have had qualms giving a similar order a few years later.

Importantly, the Chancellor von Bülow knew that Germany's actions were illegal and a "crime against humanity."[404] He opposed von Trotha's conduct, arguing that it "will demolish Germany's reputation among the civilized nations and feed foreign agitation against us."[405] His words show that already at that time he, and therefore the highest level of the German government, understood the concept of "crimes against humanity." The 1902 German Army manual on land warfare made no specific reference to the Hague rules,[406] but stressed that "certain severities are indispensable to war," and that "humanity" was best served by the "ruthless application of them."[407] The use of the term "humanity" is presumably a reference to the obligations of the 1899 Convention and/or the 1868 St. Petersburg Declaration. One could argue that it indicates a degree of awareness by Germany of the notion of humanity in the context of war just before the Herero genocide.

As far back as 1878 and 1879 Prussian General Julius von Hartmann wrote a series of three influential articles on "Military necessity and humanity/humanitarianism: A critical inquiry."[408] According to him the "strict enforcement of military discipline and efficiency ultimately achieved the most humane results."[409] While he criticized the trend toward humanitarianism in the laws of war, his articles demonstrate an awareness of the acceptance of humane practices in war. Even at that time there was therefore an understanding in Germany of the international expectations and norms regarding the way war should be fought. Jochnick and Normand note that "Many European law scholars complained that the German war manual ignored the Hague Conventions, to which

Germany was bound by agreement.... It is quite clear that the authors of the German manual regard military effectiveness rather than considerations of humanity the test of the legitimacy of an instrument or measure."[410] The German notion of *Kriegsraison geht vor Kriegsmanier*, which means "the necessities of war take precedence over the rules of war" (or *Not kennt kein Gebot*—"necessity knows no law") was very much part of the system[411] and supports the argument that Germany believed they could ignore the accepted customs on war. Thus, although Germany was bound by certain conventions, their war manual did not reflect these obligations. This contradiction means that to some degree the state is to blame for the conduct of the troops in carrying out their assignments.

By the end of World War I the laws of humanity found their way into German *jurisprudence,* and could only have been derived from the Martens Clause. The Leipzig War Crimes Court on May 30, 1921 found that Captain Emil Muller had committed offenses while he was the commandant of a prisoners of war camp: "His acts originated, not in any pleasure in persecution or even in any want of feeling for the sufferings of the prisoners; but in a conscious disregard of the general laws of humanity."[412] Significantly, Chancellor von Bülow, in his attempt at the end of 1904 to revoke von Trotha's order, called the methods used "inconsistent with the principles of Christianity and humanity."[413] According to Berat, this indicates Germany acknowledgement that it was committing international crimes.[414] While one could argue that this statement was not meant to convey a legalistic intent, it is implicit that the Chancellor knew the conduct was beyond acceptable limits. This awareness is also made clear by the fact that the order was eventually revoked, in part because of the bad press Germany's conduct received back home and in part because of the negative view of Germany it generated in other states.

Ultimately, the German government knew that others deemed their methods unacceptable. Yet their concern was not about the conduct, but about the criticism that ensued. Another piece of evidence comes from a 1907 report by Paul Rohrbach, a former German colonial official, who stated that there was a "strong inner resistance of our officers and men against literal obedience to this blood order (*blutbefehls*)."[415] Similarly, Goldblatt reports that there "were many German soldiers who did not strictly carry out von Trotha's orders,"[416] while Wellington notes that it was common knowledge that some soldiers refused to obey the order and were consequently sent to Togoland and Cameroon by von Trotha.[417] Clearly, some (and possibly many) German soldiers regarded the order as illegitimate and illegal at the time, indicating that there was indeed recognition, even at the level of the soldiers, that the measures employed were exaggerated and in violation of the law.

3

The Developing Norm of Reparations and Apologies for Historical Claims: Past, Present, and Future

> Does Namibia, as many Namibians have done in the past, seek to emphasize ethnically based claims for redress, or will Namibians seek to acknowledge and commemorate the national character of the war? That is, that the Namibian War affected and determined the course of Namibian history as a whole, and not just sectors of Namibian society. We would contend that the war and its consequences had a fundamental impact on the subsequent history of Namibia. Access to land, population distribution, economic power, urbanization, and political power have all been shaped, and are only understandable, in terms of the Namibian War.[1]

> Law serves to channel vengeance, thereby both discouraging less controlled forms of victims' justice, such as vigilantism, and restoring the moral and social equilibrium that was violently disturbed by the offender.[2]

Until recently, claiming reparations for historical violations has been extremely difficult. This was due in part to the limited number of rights afforded to individuals and a lack of specific means to obtain damages or reparations within the international legal system dealing with human rights law or humanitarian law violations.[3] While hitherto opportunities for redress were quite limited, this has changed dramatically. The last decade of the twentieth century saw "a remarkable, and in some respects revolutionary, attempt to restructure the classical approach to peacemaking and the resolution of matters relating to the international consequences of war."[4] Thus, human rights, human rights protection, and reparations for human rights and humanitarian law abuses have never received more attention than at present. Yet it remains difficult for individual victims of gross human rights violations to achieve redress. For many reasons it has been almost impossible for victims to bring these cases to courts in their own states. In addition, victims struggle to find forums at international and regional levels (in courts and other adjudicating bodies outside their own countries) to which to bring their reparation claims.

While it is clear that around the world countries are coming to terms with their pasts in many ways and the question of reparations for victims has often been high on the agenda,[5] this typically happens only for internal violations in the state in question. Very few states are addressing past "external" violations, i.e., what their country did in or to another country, particularly in relation to historical human rights violations. Europe, for example, has not come to terms with its colonial past, or the present system of neo-colonial dependence that continues in many former colonies. While Europeans may be attending to the past in their own countries, to the benefit of their people, by having conferences and exhibitions about their colonial history, they tend do so without involving those directly affected in countries where colonialism occurred. Granted, some former colonial subjects are occasionally invited to attend or speak at such events, but the focus remains inward, on how a particular European country acted in the past and how it ought to reflect on that past. This modus operandi fails to address the past from the perspective of the former colonies or those living in these colonies.

While Germany has dealt and continues to deal with two of its totalitarian regimes (the Nazi era and that which occurred in East Germany before the Wall came down), it has not addressed the violations of its third regime, under Kaiser Wilhelm II.[6] While many European and North American victims of the Nazi period have been compensated, most other victims have been ignored. Many regard this as indicative of racism, which adds fuel to the fire for those who claim that discrimination is the reason Germany will not deal with its earlier violations.

While claims for recent violations are now attainable, the prospects for claims relating to past human rights violations—what are often called historical claims—have not progressed much. There have been some developments, but certainly not to an equivalent degree. The last few years have seen major advances due, at least in part, to the successes of the Holocaust claims—claims from more than fifty years ago. Payments have been made not on the basis of successful court decisions but because the pressure generated by these cases has resulted in defendants reaching settlements. Thus, victims received payouts, but not because a court had accepted the legality of their claims. Nonetheless, these cases have provided a new impetus for other such claims, which are now being filed.

This chapter evaluates the Herero legal claims in the wide sense before the courts, as well as reparations claims filed by other applicants, and examines the probability of success and the impact such success might have. It does not, however, deal with the specific United States law in terms of cases currently being fought, but only reviews the decisions that have been handed down already. An analysis of the Alien Tort Claims Act and the cases that have flowed from it over the last twenty-five years has been the subject of a previous study.[7] This chapter therefore focuses on the wider issues relating to historical human rights claims for reparations. To determine the availability and potential for alternative strategies to attain redress, the various complaints and litigation mechanisms are explored. These mechanisms and courts exist through the International Covenant on Civil and Political Rights (ICCPR), the Convention against Torture and Other Cruel, Inhuman, or Degrading Treatment or Punishment, the Convention on the Elimination of Racial Discrimination (CERD), and the Convention on the Elimination of all forms of Discrimination against Women (CEDAW), as well as under regional human rights systems. The mechanisms of the Human Rights Committee under the ICCPR and the CERD Committee, as well as various courts internationally, regionally, and domestically, will be examined to assess whether these bodies and courts permit such issues to be brought before them. This will appraise the availability of such avenues for the Herero or other groups seeking reparations for historical claims in the future.

This chapter therefore evaluates the developing norms of reparations and apologies. While it is specifically centered on the Herero claim for reparations, it also draws on other cases to assess the general position of historical claims worldwide and the potential for success. The impact of the various cases, including the Holocaust cases, is examined, in addition to the effects these cases could have on the Herero claims for other legal actions against colonial powers.

THE DEVELOPING NORM OF INDIVIDUAL REPARATION CLAIMS FOR HUMAN RIGHTS AND HUMANITARIAN CLAIMS

In the past, international instruments did not comprehensively deal with remedies or reparations, yet various instruments made reference to the possibility. Although individuals have not historically been given much status in international law, the possibility of obtaining compensation exists in many international instruments, including some from a hundred years ago. This is true specifically in humanitarian law treaties. However, within customary law individual compensation apparently existed in the nineteenth century. For example, in 1796 the United States Supreme Court found that private individuals had the right to compensation for acts that occurred during the American Revolutionary War. The Court held that rights were "fully acquired by private persons during the war more especially if derived from the laws of war only against the enemy, and in that case the individual might have been entitled to compensation from the public ..."[8] In 1891, Theodore Woolsey stated in the 6th edition of a treatise on international law: "The right of redress exists in the case of individuals, although it would seem that a person cannot with justice be his own judge.... Redress consists of compensation for injury inflicted and for its consequences."[9] Woolsey also noted a "duty to humanity," and his commentary recognized that cruelty "beyond the sphere of humanity" violated certain rights and demanded redress.[10]

The 1899 Hague Convention on Land Warfare contained sections dealing with compensation or reparations following the conclusion of the conflict.

Section III of the Regulations on "Military Authority over Hostile Territory" made provision for an occupying power to provide compensation.[11] Article 52 requires that a receipt be provided when items requisitioned during the war are not paid for. Thus, compensation or restitution was envisaged then. Article 53 of the Regulations provided that the various items requisitioned were to be restored to their rightful owners at the conclusion of the hostilities.[12] Both sections provide for items that were lawfully requisitioned, and it presumably follows that items unlawfully taken would also merit compensation. The German delegate to the 1907 Second Hague Peace Conference came to this interpretation and proposed a revamped compensation section. Major-General von Gündell argued that the earlier section ought to be narrowed to apply only to violations of the Regulations and broadened to apply to events that occurred not only in occupied territories.[13] Thus, it was recognized that the earlier section applied to events not covered by the Regulations.

The rights of individuals in international law and their right to claim compensation or reparation received further recognition in 1907 when individuals were even given standing before the International Prize Court through the Convention on an International Prize Court of October 18, 1907. Individuals were intended to be able to approach the court in relation to property. However, insufficient ratifications occurred and the treaty did not come into force. Also in 1907, Costa Rica, El Salvador, Guatemala, Honduras, and Nicaragua established a Central American Court of Justice. The Court operated from 1908 to 1918 and permitted a range of actors, including individuals, to bring complaints against states other than their own country.[14] This was no aberration in granting rights and providing procedures to individuals to claim reparations from states through international law. In 1928, the Permanent Court of International Justice accepted that international rights and duties could be conferred or imposed on individuals by treaty in its ruling *Opinion on the Jurisdiction of the Courts of Danzig*.[15] This decision recognized that individuals were within the ambit of international law.[16]

The 1918 Treaty of Versailles also afforded individuals the right under international law to claim reparations. It established tribunals through which individuals had direct access to make claims for reparations or restitution of property.[17] The 1922 German-Polish Convention created the Upper-Silesian Arbitral Tribunal which was permitted to accept claims from individuals in Trusteeship Territories.[18] A range of other situations gave rise to the right of individuals to claim directly. These include the Polish-Danzig Treaty, various minority treaties in the interwar years, and indirectly, the Mandates Commission of the League of Nations.[19] The International Labor Organization established in 1919 also permitted individuals to file private petitions for violations of human rights for labor law issues.[20] Since the 1950s it has become a norm for regional treaties, such as the European Convention, and more recently the inter-American system and the African Commission on Human and People's Rights, to allow individuals to make claims from states where the individual's rights had been violated. The recently inaugurated African Court also permits such claims.

The above examples illustrate that by 1907 individuals had standing before a number of international courts, and some states also recognized the rights of individuals in international law and before international courts. Recognition of the right of the individual in international law and the right to individual reparations is also found in Article 3 of the 1907 Hague Convention IV respecting the Laws and Customs of War. This article reads:

> a belligerent party which violates the provisions of the said Regulations shall, if the case demands, be liable to pay compensation. It shall be responsible for all acts committed by persons forming part of its armed forces.

Already then compensation was available, in treaty form and in state practice, for violations of the law of war. While some have argued that this provision only applied to reparations between states, Frulli notes that state responsibility does not exclude the possibility of the individual's right to claim. Thus, the possibility of Article 3 reflecting the right for individuals to claim compensation is apparent. Similarly, but more directly, others have argued that this right can be found in Article 3. Mazzeschi argues in this regard that the preparatory works to the article indicate that it was intended to provide reparation to individuals and that the word 'compensation' is used and signifies the intent to permit individuals to claim reparations. Mazzeschi argues further that Hague Convention No. IV, as well as a number of the laws and customs of war, is intended to create duties for states and individuals and to subject those individuals who do not conform to those rules to criminal prosecution.[21] That "compensation" refers to the right of the individual is supported by Kalshoven, David, and Greenwood,[22] who also maintain that the right of the individual to claim compensation was behind this article and is available in international humanitarian law. Thus, of critical importance for the Herero claim is that by 1904 in treaty form the intent to benefit individuals and allow them to claim was evident.[23]

In reference to the right of individuals to claim, and with specific relevance to the Herero claims, it is noteworthy that the article found its way into the text at the Second Hague Peace Conference in 1907, when the language of the 1899 Convention on Land Warfare with Annexed Regulations was amended. At the Conference, it was the German delegation who actually proposed introducing two sections concerning the liability of a state to pay reparations where a breach of the regulations occurred. The first proposal from the German delegation was that belligerent parties be responsible for all acts committed by their armed forces and that these parties have a duty to compensate neutral persons for loss suffered due to any violations of the regulations. The German delegation's second proposal was that compensation for victims of the violations from the other side of the conflict be dealt with once peace was achieved. When the article was drafted, both proposals were absorbed and, although the specific beneficiaries of compensation are not mentioned, it is clear that the German delegate intended for individuals to be covered. Critically, the notion of state liability to individuals was not opposed by other states at the Conference. What was not decided was whether states had to claim compensation on behalf of their citizens or whether the individuals could do so on their own.[24] Kalshoven notes that Article 3 was intended for the sole benefit of enemy and neutral civilians.[25]

It is important to note that Article 3 is virtually exactly replicated in Article 91 of the First Additional Protocol to the 1949 Geneva Conventions, which is accepted as reflective of international customary law. However, the International Law Association has argued that Article 91 "should be understood along the same lines as Article 3 of the Hague Convention IV of 1907, i.e., as not supporting individual claims for compensation."[26] This position is taken despite arguments that the purpose of Article 91 was to strengthen individual rights and that this can only be understood as reinforcing the position of individual victims as the ultimate beneficiaries of the compensation. If this is the case, and Article 91 of Additional Protocol I simply replicates Article 3 of the Convention, and individuals are seen to have rights in Article 91, then individual rights already existed in 1907, if not before. However, the International Law Association notes that Article 2 of Hague IV states that the treaty applies between "Contracting Parties" and that "nowhere are individuals named as direct beneficiaries or claimants of the said compensation."[27] This position is problematic, as most international humanitarian law "instruments are silent as to who are the beneficiaries of reparation for violations of international humanitarian law. They only address the *responsibility* to compensate."[28] Thus, it is somewhat problematic that the Hague Convention has traditionally been interpreted as providing the right to reparations only to states.

This is not an isolated view, as even the ICRC has argued that the 1949 Geneva Conventions did not give individuals the right to reparations. The ICRC has argued that it is the State that has rights and duties to other states and not individuals.[29] Others have relied on the dictum in the 1970 International Court of Justice decision of the *Barcelona Traction* case in which the Court held that "in interstate relations, whether States' claims are made on behalf of a State's national or on behalf of the State itself, they are always claims of the State."[30] Certainly, various domestic courts in the United States, Germany, Japan, and Italy have interpreted Article 3 as applicable and available to states only.[31] However, the ICJ decision does not rule out the possibility of individual claims. It refers to interstate claims and claims made by one state against another. It does not state that individuals could not make their own claims. Despite this, the general interpretation of the ICJ decision by others is based on the understanding that only states have been the subject of international law.

This position no longer holds true, and has not held in customary law for many years. Thus, some have argued that this narrow interpretation does not reflect the true position of international humanitarian law, which does provide such a right to individuals.[32] Georges Abi-Saab has argued that the very purpose of international humanitarian law is to go beyond the "interstate levels and [to reach] for the level of the real (or ultimate) beneficiaries of humanitarian protection, i.e., individuals and groups of individuals."[33] Critically, the right to reparation does not solely arise out of a convention but also from customary law and elsewhere. Thus, as Emanuela-Chiara Gillard notes, the obligation to provide reparation arises "*automatically* as a consequence of the unlawful act, without the need for the obligation to be spelled out in conventions."[34]

For many years the more restricted view has held sway. However, that individuals were entitled to claim reparations is clear at least at the conclusion of World War I, specifically in The Treaty of Versailles.[35] Article 297(e) provided:

> The *nationals* of Allied and Associated Powers shall be entitled to compensation in respect of damage or injury inflicted upon their property, rights or interests, including any company or association in which they are interested, in German territory as it existed on August 1, 1914.... *The claims made in this respect by such nationals* shall be investigated, and the total of the compensation shall be determined by the Mixed Arbitral Tribunal provided for in Section VI or by an Arbitrator appointed by that Tribunal. This compensation shall be borne by Germany, and may be charged upon the property of German nationals within the territory or under the control of the claimant's State. This property may be constituted as a pledge for enemy liabilities under the conditions fixed by paragraph 4 of the Annex hereto. The payment of this compensation may be made by the Allied or Associated State, and the amount will be debited to Germany. [my emphasis]

Clearly, the focus was on the individual and the right of the individual to claim reparations.

REPARATIONS FOR HISTORICAL HUMAN RIGHTS VIOLATIONS

In the years after World War II, the practice of providing reparations has evolved dramatically. Reparations have now been paid for events that date back more than half a century. As well, there is greater recognition internationally that what occurred in the process of possessing and exploiting the resources of the colonized countries cannot be ignored. There is a consciousness that the numerous human rights abuses, including *inter alia*, crimes against humanity, war crimes, genocide, extermination, disappearances, torture, forced removals, slavery, racial discrimination, and cruel, inhumane, or degrading treatment need to be addressed in some manner.

This new awareness gave rise to the 2004 Berlin Anti-Colonial Africa Conference.[36] The conference was attended by many African countries, as well as various organizations dedicated to addressing the legacy of the 1884–1885 Berlin Conference Agreement, which is partially responsible for the current situation in many previously colonized countries. The Conference explored how the state of affairs in these countries can be addressed and suggested that various strategies can be adopted to acknowledge the narratives of intolerance and suffering so often overlooked by countries in the North.[37]

Claiming reparations for damages suffered is not a recent practice. In fact, at the conclusion of warfare parties often reached agreements detailing a payment or a forfeit of land that would follow. For example, after the Franco-Prussian War of 1872, France paid Germany reparations.[38] Reparations or damages paid to individuals are, however, more recent phenomena. Only in the post-World War II era did such reparations begin in earnest. At first these reparations were negotiated, and later they resulted from the enactment of a statute or decisions of courts of law. At the level of statute, various countries, including Argentina, Chile, and South Africa, have made provision for reparations to be paid in the wake of human rights abuses.

AN APOLOGY

Offering an apology for historical wrongs is a vital starting point to achieving long-lasting reconciliation between the perpetrators and the victims. Over the years, a variety of groups and individuals has demanded apologies, official or not, for harm caused to them. This often occurred at the conclusion of conflict that entailed violations. To achieve progress and allow reconciliation, an apology is given either voluntarily or following a request. As Nicholas Tavuchis has suggested, a "proper and successful apology is the middle term in a moral syllogism that commences with a *call* and ends with forgiveness."[39] The call is essential and must entail some expression of sorrow and regret.[40] Dialogue is an important part of this process, and while it does not have to focus solely on the concept of guilt, it does have to include some recognition of past injurious behavior, acceptance of responsibility, and a commitment to the pursuit of justice and truth.[41] To be effective, an apology must be more than a mere political act—victims must believe it is genuine and sincere.

An apology can be given in a public ceremony or by some official declaration. In the recent past, there has been an increase in frequency of apologies. While all victims will not react similarly, authentic and voluntary expressions of remorse can sometimes provide a measure of closure for many.[42] Yet confessions and apologies might not be sufficient for reconciliation.

Despite world opinion or moral authority asserting that there are very valid reasons for colonizing countries to pay reparations, it is unlikely that these states will acknowledge and apologize for past human rights abuses or be willing to pay reparations. On the other hand, requests for apologies abound. African Americans have called for an apology and reparations for two hundred years of slavery, while Australian Aborigines and New Zealand Maoris have made demands on their governments for apologies and compensation for past state policies.[43] In 1995, when Queen Elizabeth II apologized to the Maori, it "was hailed as a new dawn for New Zealand by the government and Maori elders alike."[44] The Queen "acknowledged that the crown acted 'unjustly' by, among other things, 'sending its forces across the Mangatawhiri River in July 1863, unfairly labelling Waikatos as rebels, and subsequently confiscating their land,' which had 'a crippling impact' on Maori life." She expressed "profound regret and apologize[d] unreservedly for the loss of lives because of hostilities arising from this invitation and at the devastation of property and social life which resulted."[45] Despite these examples of recent apologies, others responsible for similar historical violations have refused such processes, claiming that too much time has passed.

An interesting example of an apology was that which President Havel of Czechoslovakia gave to Germany in 1990. On the fifty-first anniversary of the German invasion, Havel officially apologized to the German president, who was on a state visit to his country. The apology was for the expulsion of most Germans from Czechoslovakia after the war. When Havel rejected the possibility of compensation, the German Chancellor stated that a failure to enter into dialogue with Sudeten Germans on this question would negatively affect the Czech Republic's chances of joining the European Union.[46]

Over the years, German leaders have offered many excuses as to why the German Federal Government was not responsible for the atrocities that occurred during GSWA colonization and thus why they could not apologize to the Herero. Their justifications include the passage of too much time for the German government to lodge a formal apology, that international rules for the protection of civilian populations were not in existence at the time of the atrocities, and that Germany has over the years financially supported the Namibian government and therefore compensation for past actions was not necessary.[47]

On a visit to Namibia at the beginning of March 1998, German President Roman Herzog said that too much time had passed for Germany to give any formal apology[48] for slaughtering Hereros during colonial rule. Herzog said that German soldiers had acted "incorrectly" between 1904 and 1907 when members of the Herero group were killed for opposing colonialism. Herzog rejected the payment of compensation, stating that this was not possible as international rules for the protection of the civilian population did not exist at the time of the conflict, and no laws protected minority groups during the colonial period.[49] He also said that Germany had significantly assisted Namibia for many years and he pledged that Germany would live up to its special historical responsibility toward Namibia.[50] Germany has also stated that the issue of reparations would not be considered as Namibia was already receiving preferential financial support from Germany. (This will be explored in due course.)

In spite of the German government's intransigence on the matter, calls for an apology and reparations were made in Germany. In 2001, the German Association for Threatened People (*Gesellschaft für Bedrohte Völker*) called on the German government to take responsibility for past actions, especially the genocide on the Herero people in Namibia. They argued that at the World Conference against Racism in Durban, South Africa, the Minister of Foreign Affairs, Joschka Fischer, had signaled an acknowledgment of what had happened to victims during slavery and colonialism. They urged the German Government to call what had happened to the Herero by its name—genocide—and insisted on compensation to the Herero people. However, the need to deal with Germany's past preceding the Holocaust was not on the official agenda at all. The only issue that received attention in the past was whether Germany was willing to cooperate on the Namibian land question and the way that would affect German farmers, whom the government of Namibia sees as holding onto much of the land that should be available for land distribution.

On August 14, 2004, Germany eventually apologized when Heidemarie Wieczorek-Zeul, Minister of Development Aid, delivered an apology to the Hereros at the centennial commemoration ceremony of the battle of Waterberg (see the Program for Commemoration of Ohamakari Battle on page 195). However, this apology—one hundred years after the event—followed years of requests and multiple denials by the German government. The timing and content of an apology are critical issues. The "longer one waits following a call, the more difficult it is to apologize, the more carefully one's words must be chosen, and the less the apology is worth."[51] This was indeed the case with the apology to the Herero.

Orenstein has noted that apologies should contain eight distinct elements:

> (1) acknowledge the legitimacy of the grievance and express respect for the violated rule or moral norm; (2) indicate with specificity the nature of the violation; (3) demonstrate understanding of the harm done; (4) admit fault and responsibility for the violation; (5) express genuine regret and remorse for the injury; (6) express concern for future good relations; (7) give appropriate assurance that the act will not happen again; and, if possible, (8) compensate the injured party.[52]

As will be shown, the German apology did not (at least not according to some in the Herero community) meet these requirements. Despite a discussion between this author and one of the most senior officials of her department on what the content and tone of the apology ought to be, the German Minister of Development Aid stated that:

> A century ago, the oppressors—blinded by colonialist fervor—became agents of violence, discrimination, racism, and annihilation in Germany's name. The atrocities committed at that time would today be termed genocide, and nowadays a General von Trotha would be prosecuted and convicted.

Regardless of the discussions and the consensus that the "production of a satisfactory apology is a delicate and precarious transaction,"[53] the Herero thought the German apology was limited and that Germany did not accept responsibility in the full sense. Critically, the Minister blamed General von Trotha alone and stated that what occurred was done in Germany's name, rather than by Germany. The speech therefore did not reflect state acceptance of responsibility. Accordingly, the apology did not fully acknowledge the harm done and many perceived it as inadequate and insincere. Important components of an apology were omitted. The role of an apology is to be "an integral part of restoring a victim's self-respect and dignity. An apology constitutes something more than a legal remedy: it also speaks to moral and social justice by embracing the repentance of the perpetrator."[54] In this regard, the Minister's apology fell short.

Yet the Minister's speech did contain the following redeeming sentence: "We Germans accept our historical and moral responsibility and the guilt incurred by Germans at that time." This statement implies a broadened attitude regarding German accountability. However, while the Minister acknowledged genocide had occurred, she prefaced this by claiming that it would have been genocide only in terms of the current laws. This formulation was probably used to avoid admission of what occurred then as a crime of genocide—to circumvent liability for reparations. The German Government has held this view for some time. It was so stated by Foreign Minister Joschka Fischer on a visit to Namibia in 2003: he asserted that the court cases were the main obstacle to a German apology. The likelihood that German acknowledgment would boost the court case against genocide has been noted by the German ambassador to Namibia, who stated: "If Germany were to admit that it was genocide, then the case for reparations will find basis in merit."[55] At the time Namibian Minister for Foreign Affairs, Theo-Ben Gurirab, argued that in light of German apologies for crimes committed during World War II against Jews, Poles, and Russians, the refusal to apologize for colonial crimes was racist, as the only difference was skin color.[56]

As indicated, some people regarded Minister Wieczorek-Zeul's August 2004 apology as controversial and limited in its intent. A few days after the commemorations the Namibian newspaper *New Era* reported that the "Minister's speech fell short of an apology compelling her to clarify that most of what she said could be read as an apology. She made this clarification when someone from the audience shouted the word apology upon realizing that Minister Wieczorek-Zeul hadn't said anything to that effect. It is not clear whether the Minister responded to the shout for an apology or not."[57] The German apology lacks what Lazare delineates:

> What makes an apology work is the exchange of shame and power between the offender and the offended. By apologizing, you take the shame of your offence and redirect it to yourself. You admit to hurting or diminishing someone and, in effect, say that you are really the one who is diminished—I'm the one who was wrong, mistaken, insensitive, or stupid. In acknowledging your shame you give the offended the power to forgive. The exchange is at the heart of the healing process.[58]

For many this exchange did not transpire. Certainly, quite a few Herero believe the apology was limited and did not amount to much.

Not everyone rejected the apology, though. Some members of the Namibian government accepted it. The Namibian Minister without Portfolio and South West African People's Organization (SWAPO) Secretary General Ngarikutuke Tjiriange described the apology as a "magnanimous gesture" which was wholeheartedly accepted by the Namibian people.[59] However, the extent to which such statements by government officials are tainted by politics cannot be understated.

According to Elazar Barkan, an "apology doesn't mean the dispute is resolved but is, in most cases, a first step: part of the process of negotiation, but not the satisfactory end result."[60] While some accepted the German apology, at least some of the Herero thought it was undermined by subsequent events. Two months following the apology, in October 2004, at an event marking the 100th anniversary of the issuing of the extermination order, the Paramount Chief of the Herero stated that as genuine as the apology might have been then, it was seemingly contradicted by various statements by German officials after the apology took place and by an agreement between Namibia and Germany that the word "genocide" would not be used.[61]

In December 2004, the German ambassador responded to claims that they had been approached for an out-of-court-settlement, noting that the Namibian Government was the German Government's partner in negotiations for reconciliation.[62] The ambassador, Wolfgang Massing, stated that the "two governments are already engaged in talks. We do things in a transparent manner and not behind closed doors."[63] Yet he did not demonstrate this supposed transparency by disclosing what was discussed. Further, as the Herero community has noted, the discussions took place between the two governments and not between the victims and perpetrators. These not-so-transparent discussions led to Germany announcing a reconciliation process with the people of Namibia in 2005. As this was done without consulting the affected groups, they have not accepted the gesture as a way forward. Germany has set aside $25 million over a ten-year period for development and reconciliation in Namibia "in order to heal the wounds left by the brutal colonial wars of 1904 to 1908."[64] A committee made up of various representatives would disperse these funds, it was announced, which would be used for development projects in areas mainly inhabited by the Herero, Nama, and Damara people.[65] This may finally set the process of addressing the historical claims and improving relations underway.

While the governments of Namibia and Germany ostensibly agreed on the dissemination of these funds, the President of Namibia in 2005, when presented in Germany with the agreement for signing, stated that the agreement must be put on hold until the Herero, Nama, and Damara had been consulted. Minister Heidemarie Wieczorek-Zeul responded that she regretted this step by the Namibian government because the content of the agreement was known to them and they had agreed to it.[66] Namibian Foreign Affairs Minister, Marco Hausiku, however, stated that the German government had been too hasty with the agreement and that the Namibian government first had to consult those affected before signing. It is important to note that Namibian President Hifikepunye Pohamba had met with the Herero Paramount Chief a few weeks before his visit to Germany to discuss the reparations issue. Not surprisingly, the Ovaherero Genocide Committee supported the decision by the president to not sign the agreement, arguing that the Herero were not familiar with its terms.

The past continues to haunt Namibia today in many ways. At the end of 2005 a number of mass graves were uncovered that allegedly held the bodies of

Governor Leutwein and General von Trotha. Courtesy of National Archives of Namibia.

those fighting for the liberation of the country. They were supposedly killed by South African forces in the 1980s before the country gained its independence. In addition, former detainees of SWAPO, the ruling political party, are still agitating for a truth commission in which they can tell their stories and discover what happened to their comrades.

The historical legacy concerns not only the German government and the people of Namibia, but others were also involved in the war. Important in this regard is the role of various companies (some of whom the Herero are suing) and others who were involved in some way, including individuals such as the descendants of German settlers who occupy the land of the Herero and other tribes today. Certainly, General von Trotha's family has some responsibility regarding the events in GSWA. The role of the von Trotha family in the Herero genocide goes beyond that of the General. One account names his nephew, Thilo von Trotha, in the carrying out of killings.[67] It is reported that the issues of the Herero War and its links to the von Trotha family "haunts his German descendants."[68] The family meets twice yearly to discuss these issues. von Trotha's great grandnephew has offered his "deepest regrets" over what occurred. It is further reported that the von Trotha family supports a discussion regarding reparations between the German government and the Herero.

As far as the Herero are concerned, the matter of an apology has not concluded. They are dissatisfied with the content and wording of the apology, the context in which it was given, and the subsequent developments or rather lack thereof. The Herero did not simply want an apology; they expected it to be accompanied by some form of redress or reparations for the violations committed a hundred years ago. They demand some type of land restitution and some form of compensation, particularly for the land that ought to be in the hands of the descendants of those who were dispossessed.

GERMAN REPARATIONS IN THE PAST

Even during the Herero War the German government made reparations to some of those who had been materially affected by the war. The confiscation of Herero land and cattle was justified as a normal outcome for those defeated in war.[69] A Commission for Compensation was established in 1904 to compensate those who were not "unfriendly" to the German government. Paul Rohrbach was a chairman of the Commission.[70] Compensation was given to those who had suffered material loss during the Herero War as long as they were not "unfriendly" to the German state (this certainly did not include any Hereros).[71] Compensation was often given for specific purposes, such as to purchase cattle. The Commission for Compensation determined that the war caused 12.5 million marks worth of damage. However, the *Reichstag* was only willing to allocate 5 million marks. The new Governor, Friedrich von Lindequist, hurried to Berlin to argue for a greater allocation. As a result, the amount was increased

Propaganda photo depicting German defense. Courtesy of National Archives of Namibia.

to 10 million marks. The settlers were so vociferous in their address to the Budget Commission of the *Reichstag* that the commissioners hardened their attitude toward them. The Governor believed that without this antagonism, the settlers would have been awarded an even larger amount than was finally allocated. Thus, the Governor saw the settlers' lack of diplomacy as having adversely affected their cause.[72] This, again, indicates the strident stance the settlers took toward GSWA issues in Germany.

The Herero desire some parity or equality of treatment. For example, the farms given to the German farmers at that time might be repossessed or expropriated by the Namibian government, who needs that land for redistribution. Should Germany compensate these farmers, the local people whom Germany had disowned at the turn of the century should also receive compensation.

Interestingly, Germany accepted the principle of reparations as it related to them for events that happened in the early twentieth century. It sought reparations for its own loss of its colonies for many years. In the years just before World War II, Professor Vincent Harlow of the University of London wrote:

> yet with growing vigour Germany maintains her demand for restitution, not only on grounds of legality, but of equity and natural justice; and Englishmen continue to ponder the proposition, write books about it, and engage in earnest discussion in the press. Clearly then something happened at the distribution of the spoil on this occasion—the introduction of some strange new value in international conduct, unknown to the diplomacy of previous generations.[73]

At the end of World War II, Germany entered various agreements to pay or provide goods to the Allies.[74] In addition, at the end of the 1940s the German government discussed the issue of reparations with the Israeli government.[75] As a result of the Conference on Jewish Material Claims against Germany, the Luxembourg Treaty was signed in 1952 with Israel.[76] This treaty led to the enactment of various Federal Compensation Laws to compensate victims. In the agreement Germany contracted to pay $714 million to Israel to support the assimilation of displaced and impoverished refugees from Germany or areas formerly under German control. The treaty required individual compensation as well as payment of $110 million to the Conference of Jewish Material Claims against Germany for victims. The process ran from 1952 until 1965. There was a range of other reparation programs, such as that which emerged out of the 1959 Norwegian-German[77] Agreement.[78] In this agreement Germany consented to compensate Norwegians victimized due to their race, belief, or opinions and whose freedom or health was impaired or who died as a result of the persecution.

Since the end of the war, Germany has dealt with compensation for or the restitution of land confiscated during the Nazi period. Various laws have been enacted to address victim compensation. Even after Germany's reunification in 1990, new laws were passed and a set of new programs were put into place to deal with compensation for those in former East Germany or whose property was in East Germany. Even though it was more than forty-five years after the end of World War II, it was thought necessary because East Germany had paid no heed to these matters. Thus, programs to deal with property taken from 1933 onward were put in place. People inside or outside Germany were permitted to submit claims to either gain their land back, get comparable land, or receive the market value of the land at the time. Although these reparations addressed events dating back 50 years, there has been an unwillingness to deal with other historical claims such as those of the Herero. As mentioned, the one positive recent development was Germany's announcement in June 2005 that they would grant $25 million for development and reconciliation in Namibia.

This announcement generated harsh criticism from Paramount Chief Kuaima Riruako. He stated that no dialogue had taken place between the German government and those who suffered during its colonial rule of Namibia and that the "German government should have consulted the victims through a process of dialogue, as was agreed in Bremen [a genocide conference in November 2004] before deciding on their own to avail the N$160 million which is apparently meant to assist with the reconciliation process."[79] He urged the German government to "engage us in a serious dialogue to talk about what my people endured, something they are still suffering from, and how their suffering could be relieved through appropriate compensation."[80]

The offer was increased in 2006 under a plan known as the "special initiative" to about $25 million a year for ten years. The funds, however, are not for the Herero alone. The amount negotiated, to be administered by the German and Namibian governments, if accepted by the groups concerned, will fund development projects in areas where the Herero, Nama, San, and Damara live.

The German offer of $25 million a year pales in comparison to Germany's payments for claims relating to World War II. Since 1945, Germany has paid out approximately $100 billion to victims as compensation for World War II acts. It still distributes about $1 billion a year through various programs to victims. Of note is that not all victims of this period have been able to claim compensation, and what reparations they received often depended on where the victims were living when they claimed. Some of those excluded in the past, such as those that lived behind the iron curtain, have more recently been included in compensations.

Despite some difficulties regarding how to compensate these victims equally, the various programs Germany agreed to were so good that the UN Commission on Human Rights *Study Concerning the Right to Restitution, Compensation, and Rehabilitation for Victims of Gross Violations of Human Rights and Fundamental Freedoms*, written by Professor Theo van Boven in 1993 (before the cases of the 1990s, which dramatically improved payment of reparations), noted: "The most comprehensive and systematic precedent of reparation by a government to groups of victims for redress of wrongs suffered is provided by the Federal Republic of Germany to the victims of Nazi persecution."[81] It is important to note that the country's rationale for these reparations was that "Germany, acting on vaguely comparable motivations of perceived international interests, but also on its unique need to re-establish political and moral legitimacy, sought to repent for its sins under Nazism by reaching an agreement with its victims."[82]

Even after this, as a result of the Holocaust litigation cases[83] in the United States, Germany has paid many more reparations.[84] In addition, the German Foundation for Remembrance, Responsibility, and the Future was established by an act of the German parliament in 2000.

Critically, these are important issues from a reparations perspective, from the perspective of government action. They are also important for issues relating to ongoing or recurring discrimination or inequality of treatment, which would bring even historical violations committed even before Germany adopted various treaties such as the International Covenant on Civil and Political Rights (ICCPR) and the European Convention. Importantly, the German government finances about half of the reparations, while German business covers the rest.[85] Thus, there might be a basis for claiming inequality of victim treatment and therefore ongoing human rights violations as has been permitted by various courts to bring matters committed even before a state has adopted a treaty or consented to that court examining the state's compliance with that treaty.

The Foundation was established to make payments to several categories of Nazi victims, including former slaves and forced laborers. The German government and various corporations have distributed more than $5 billion to about 1.5 million former laborers of the World War II era. The Herero, also once used as slaves and forced laborers, received none of this. In 2005, the Foundation dispensed about $3,200 to each of more than 7,000 victims of Nazi "medical" experimentation. Again, the Herero were subjected to similar experimentation but did not benefit from such payments. The medical payments constituted a second payment for each victim, as they had received a prior amount of $5,400 each.[86] A statement issued by the United States noted that these "survivors live in the United States, Israel, and other countries in Europe and around the world."[87] Thus, it appears as if the payments went to more than 1.7 million Nazi victims residing almost entirely in the North, which not coincidently tends to command more leverage to affect these matters. It seems that the establishment of a state-funded Foundation follows a Japanese model, in which a similar

Rail construction on the Otavi railway line. Courtesy of National Archives of Namibia.

organization was established to provide payments to former comfort women. In both cases, the effect was to distance the state from direct compensation.

The Foundation at the least provides recognition that the state is liable for violations it historically committed. On this basis there is no reason why claims against the German state for slave or forced labor performed by the Herero in German businesses during the war period ought not be recognized and paid. In fact, the leading negotiator for the Foundation for Remembrance, Responsibility, and Future, Dr. Otto Graf Lambsdorff, has stated that Germany is liable for compensating those forced to perform labor because "compensation for illegal employment of civilians from occupied territories was and is considered a reparation issue under public international law."[88] Hence, the Herero would also qualify. The *Otavi Minen AG* admitted that the state supplied labor to German businesses during the Herero War, which the businesses used as forced or slave labor.

In their centennial commemorative publication (1900–2000) one paragraph reads:

> Because of the Herero War it was difficult to get enough employees to build the railway. We were happy about every Herero who registered voluntary. The Government sent us also prisoners of war (Hereros): 900 men, 700 women, and 620 children.[89]

In 1997, Bravenboer and Rusch published *The First 100 Years of State Railways in Namibia*, in which they assert that when the war began Herero workers were not initially available and European workers were hired.[90] According to this book, it later became easy to get Herero labor as "Herero prisoners of war were assigned to the railways at the beginning of 1905."[91] Photographic and other evidence also shows that the Herero were forced to build the railroad for the company. German soldiers, in fact, guarded the laborers while they worked.

Construction of the Luderitz railway line using Herero slave labor. Courtesy of Klaus Dierks.

While Bravenboer and Rusch state that the Herero workers returned only after the war and that they "were reportedly willing laborers who had endurance,"[92] this is only true from around 1908—before then the company used Herero prisoners of war, supplied and guarded over by the German authorities. It is interesting that the term "prisoners of war" is used because it indicates the recognition of the Herero as such. It could also signify recognition that a violation of the laws of war had occurred.

It has been argued that the Herero would not specifically qualify for compensation, as none of those alive today would actually have served as slave or forced labor themselves. Yet the words of Kai Hennig, the spokesman of the Foundation, apply: "The payments from the Foundation are not compensation. It was totally clear that one could never find a balance in the distribution of funds to those who were in the labor camps for one day or one year. The payments were to be a financial aid for the people that were forced to work for Germany."[93] The same would be true for the Herero, who are in greater need of financial assistance.

Other than the Foundation, the post-war Conference on Jewish Material Claims against Germany still plays its part in securing compensation from Germany and the United States. Ambassador Edward B. O'Donnell, Special Envoy for Holocaust Issues, represents the United States government on the board of the Foundation.

Germany has also recently been dealing with the gross human rights violations committed during communist rule in East Germany. This reckoning with the human rights violations of the past, or *Vergangenheitsbewältigung*, has been taking place since the Berlin Wall came down in 1989.[94] Even a few prosecutions, such as those of the "border guards," who killed people trying to escape East Germany, have occurred.[95] With the opening of the "Stasi" files, the truth emerged[96]; this process permitted individuals to find out what those files contained.[97] In addition, a commission of inquiry, composed of sixteen members of parliament and eleven citizens, was established to investigate and report on human rights abuses committed in East Germany.[98] Much has therefore been done in Germany to address the past and provide reparations for the genocide it committed during World War II. However, Germany is unwilling to deal directly with the genocide it committed forty years before that time.

Germany has clearly been inconsistent in its acknowledgment of the various gross human rights violations it has committed. For example, the Minister of State, Kerstin Müller, gave a speech at the Stockholm International Forum on Preventing Genocide on January 26, 2004. In her speech the only reference to German atrocities pertained to the Holocaust:

> The history of my country is inseparably bound up with the Holocaust, that horrific crime against humanity perpetrated against the Jews of Germany and Europe. I can assure you that we, the democratic Germany, have acknowledged our responsibility for that genocide and accepted the obligations such a responsibility entails.[99]

The speech reflects Germany's acceptance of their obligations—the duty to remedy the situation by paying reparations. The Minister also stated:

> One obligation it entails is to vigorously combat anti-Semitism and racism. Another is to pursue a foreign policy which ensures that never again will war and other horrors be unleashed from German soil, that there will be no repetition of the Holocaust, and that also in the international arena we do everything in our power to protect human rights and prevent genocide and similar atrocities.[100]

Germany signed the declaration, which in Clause 3 reads: "We are also committed to supporting survivors of genocide to rebuild their communities and to return to normal life."[101] This is directly relevant to the Herero who have, a hundred years later, not yet been able to return to a "normal" life, and are still without their land and cattle. This disparity in providing reparations for what happened sixty years ago and the massacre of the Herero a century ago has frequently drawn comment. The Herero continually relate their genocide to the Holocaust. More recently Chief Riruako, acknowledging the apology from Germany, commented: "Given the historic acceptance of responsibility by the German government and the apology rendered, it is our expectation that international trend and practice will prevail, as was the case with the Jewish people."[102]

THE DEVELOPING INTERNATIONAL NORM OF REPARATIONS

Internationally, there has been a solid movement toward recognizing a legal basis for victims of human rights and humanitarian abuses to claim reparations. The ongoing effort to establish international principles on reparations is one example. In 1989, the UN Sub-Commission on Prevention of Discrimination and Protection of Minorities selected Professor Theo van Boven to draw up a set of basic principles and guidelines on remedies for gross human rights violations. A draft version of the Basic Principles and Guidelines on the Right to Reparation followed.[103] As a result of the 1998 session of the UN Commission on Human Rights, Professor Cherif Bassiouni was appointed to prepare a draft for the next session so that the principles could be clarified and sent to the UN General Assembly for approval. This task is now complete and the *Basic Principles and Guidelines on the Right to a Remedy and Reparation for Victims of Violations of International Human Rights and Humanitarian Law* was accepted by the UN General Assembly in 2005.

The issue of compensation has become so important because reparations are seen as fulfilling at least three functions: most importantly, victims are able to cope with the financial deprivation that they have suffered; second, they allow for an official recognition of the past; and finally, reparations deter future perpetrators from committing similar violations. While it was previously believed that compensation for past abuses was not available and that the only way to secure any redress was via foreign aid and investment by the previous colonial powers (who tend to do so out of guilt), developments worldwide in the theoretical and practical field of reparation have now made it possible.

David Horowitz champions the argument that most claimants in the United States have already benefited in some way. He maintains that trillions of dollars have been given to African Americans in welfare benefits and through various affirmative action processes. He argues "if trillion dollar restitutions and a wholesale rewriting of American law (in order to accommodate racial preferences) for African Americans is not enough to achieve a "healing," what *will*?[104] Yet such an argument does not apply to the Herero, as they have not even benefited from development aid (as discussed elsewhere).

One reason for the increased focus on reparations is the growing awareness, internationally, of the need for compensation and redress for these victims. Moreover, entitlement to an effective remedy (which includes the means to full rehabilitation) is recognized by many international human rights instruments.[105] In fact, the paying of reparations for past human rights abuses is a recognized principle of international law.[106] This notion is so highly regarded that it is also recognized by regional human rights instruments, as well as in the decisions of the courts of those regional human rights instruments.[107] It is now accepted that international human rights law also extends to the exercise of control over states and private actors, including juridical bodies such as corporations. The notion of universal jurisdiction is now widely accepted.

However, most states view reparations for historical claims as a political rather than legal issue.[108] Due to the difficulties in getting states before courts,[109] victims of gross human rights violations are more readily targeting multinationals to secure reparations.[110] Multinationals usually constitute more lucrative targets because they often have large investments in countries with more relaxed rules of procedure in litigation. Due to the precedent set by the reparation cases relating to the Holocaust and the Second World War, more victims have decided to undertake litigation to secure redress. As Ellinikos has noted, "eventually as business leaders are now finding out, somebody has to take responsibility."[111] Therefore, these watershed cases are based on the assumption that the multinationals have benefited from certain illegal actions.

THE ROLE OF COURT DECISIONS IN THE DEVELOPMENT OF THE NORM OF REPARATIONS

The two international tribunals set up in the 1990s to adjudicate gross human rights violations in Yugoslavia and Rwanda have accepted the right to reparations. The governing statutes of these two tribunals[112] established such rights for victims. Indeed, the Rome Statute, which governs the International Criminal Court, provides greater rights for victims to compensation than ever before.

As far as individual claims are concerned, it is the post-World War II era that defines the movement toward granting reparations for violations of human rights. Certainly, Germany's payment of reparations and the cases brought against banks and other corporations have assisted this process. The first of these claims occurred in October 1996, when a class action lawsuit was filed in the federal district court of Brooklyn, New York, against the Swiss banks—Credit Suisse, Union Bank of Switzerland, and Swiss Bank Corporation. All the filed cases were brought together in 1997 as *In re Holocaust Victim Assets Litigation.* The consolidated claim alleged that the banks did not return assets deposited with them, they traded in looted assets, and benefited by trading in goods made by slave labor. The case was settled in 1998 with the banks paying out $1.5 billion. Not only Jews benefited from this settlement, but also homosexuals, physically or mentally disabled or handicapped persons, the Romani (Gypsy) peoples, and Jehovah's Witnesses.[113]

The Holocaust cases against the Swiss banks were followed with suits filed against German and Austrian banks in June 1998. These cases were launched by American Holocaust survivors, who filed a class action lawsuit against Deutsche Bank and Dresdner Bank, alleging profiteering from the looting of gold and other property belonging to Jews. All the cases were merged in March 1999 as *In re Austrian and German Bank Holocaust Litigation.* French banks or banks that had branches in France during the war, such as the British bank Barclays, were also sued. The parties reached a settlement agreement in 2001. Holocaust survivors also sued more than a dozen European insurers. Neither were German corporations spared. Former slave laborers also launched cases against a host of German companies. A number of these were dismissed because of statutes of limitations or due to treaties signed by Germany and the Allied powers at the conclusion of the war. However, a settlement for roughly $5 billion was reached, on condition that all other slave labor cases would be dropped. The U.S. government also agreed to intercede in any future lawsuits filed against Germany relating to claims arising from World War II.[114] Although these cases were filed, the fact that they ended in settlements means that they do not constitute legal precedent. Nonetheless, they indicate that the courts have assisted a progressive movement toward individuals obtaining reparations.

In the United States, in the first case under the Aliens Torts Claims Act, *Filartiga v. Pena-Irala,*[115] the courts recognized that aliens could sue for reparations for human rights abuses committed against them by individuals who were not U.S. citizens. The court noted that the "international community has come to recognize the common danger posed by the flagrant disregard of basic human rights and particularly the right to be free of torture."[116] This case has had momentous consequences and has spawned several other cases with successful results for victims.

The other major case that had a dramatic effect on reparations law and the ability of victims to approach the courts was the Inter-American Court of Human Rights decision of *Velásquez–Rodriguez.* In this decision, the Court held that individuals having suffered human rights violations could pursue damages claims against the perpetrators and the state where the acts had occurred, if officials of that state had carried out those violations. The Court concluded that "under international law a State is responsible for the acts of its agents undertaken in their official capacity and for their omissions even when those agents act outside the sphere of their authority or violate internal law."[117]

Yet the process is not always easy, and there have been many unsuccessful outcomes. It has been even more difficult to claim damages for events that happened fifty or more years ago. U.S. courts have been the most sympathetic to this type of litigation., hence it is not surprising that the Herero chose to bring their case there. Although there is a significant tendency to bring cases dealing with gross human rights violations (especially against multi-nationals) to common-law countries, most civil litigation has occurred in the United States. In contrast to other jurisdictions "litigation in the United States is the natural product of a legal culture that relies on private lawsuits both as a means to obtain compensation for injuries and also as a tool to address societal problems."[118] In other jurisdictions victims have had difficulty obtaining legal assistance, while in the United States, they have been able to get lawyers to handle such claims. Yet only a handful of the more than two million U.S. lawyers are willing to bring claims for gross human rights violations committed elsewhere before the courts. Even in the U.S. courts, it is exceedingly difficult, if not virtually impossible, to sue a state, let alone obtain judgment against it. Even in the case in which Iran was successfully sued in the 1980s, the U.S. State Department blocked any attempt at getting the judgment filled by going after Iranian property. This sovereign immunity is prevalent around the world, and many courts uphold it. One exception occurred in Greece in a case against Germany.[119] Yet, much like the Iranian case in the United States, the successful Greek victims were unable to collect against Germany, as Greek law demanded government authorization for a judgment that seeks to seize the assets of a foreign state, and their government refused. When these victims attempted to enforce their judgment in Germany, on the basis of a bilateral agreement on the enforcement and recognition of judgments, the German Supreme Court refused to recognize the Greek judgment.[120]

While the U.S. courts have been willing to hear claims relating to gross human rights violations,[121] the courts in many countries have been quite disinclined to deal with the events of another country.[122] Generally speaking, courts apply a limitation on the types of cases they are willing to adjudicate, based on territorial jurisdiction. In other words, courts are reluctant to hear cases that emanate from outside their country, especially when there is a political dimension to the case. This unwillingness partly stems from the fear that the decisions handed down by the courts of one country may have diplomatic and other ramifications. A court sitting in another country may not get the complete picture or fully comprehend the context and complexities in these cases, and the decisions might not be respected or honored. This view will change as universal jurisdiction becomes more widely acceptable,[123] and the Rome Statute impacts on the law in the states party to the ICC treaty.[124] These states must implement the ICC statute, which has ramifications for offenses such as war crimes and crimes against humanity and now imposes obligations on these states even if the offense did not occur in their jurisdiction.[125]

THE "REALITY" OF ACHIEVING REPARATIONS

As mentioned, it has generally been very challenging for victims to obtain reparations for gross human rights abuses from the courts. Achieving success for historical claims has been even tougher. Success has often been contingent on showing that a historical violation falls within the jurisdiction of the court on the basis that the violation is continuing in some way. (This will be discussed when dealing with actions before such bodies as the Human Rights Committee or the European Court of Human Rights.)

Despite some success in developing the law and the awarding of some reparations, there have been few actual payments to victims. Victims have been most successful in the domestic context. However, even domestically there have been few successful claims, and even fewer payments. Furthermore, the NGO Redress observes that in countries where damages for torture claims have been paid, such as South Africa and Nigeria, the amounts awarded have been comparatively low.[126] In some countries, such as Kenya and Nigeria, the enforcement of awards against the state is dependent on consent, and those governments have shown reluctance to comply with the decisions of their courts.[127] The Redress report also notes a gap in some countries between what the law permits and what occurs in practice.[128]

THE HERERO COURT CASES

One of the first cases fought on issues dating back to colonial days is the case filed in September 2001 in Washington, D.C. by the Herero People's Reparations Corporation and the Herero tribe, through its Paramount Chief Riruako and other members of the tribe.[129,130] They sued Deutsche Bank, Terex Corporation, also known as Orenstein-Koppel, and Woermann Line, now known as Deutsche Afrika-Linien GmbH & Co.[131,132]

The Herero filed suit against these parties in the courts of the United States, as the courts there have jurisdiction over activities that occurred outside the U.S.—even a long time ago. The court application states:

> Foreshadowing with chilling precision the irredeemable horror of the European Holocaust only decades later, the defendants and imperial Germany formed an alliance with German commercial enterprise which cold bloodedly employed explicitly sanctioned extermination, the destruction of tribal culture and social organization, concentration camps, forced labor, medical experimentation, and the exploitation of women and children in order to advance their common financial interests.

The Herero are suing Deutsche Bank because it is alleged that it was the principal financial and banking entity in German South West Africa. Allegedly, Disconto-Gesellschaft, which was acquired by Deutsche Bank in 1929, and Deutsche Bank controlled virtually all financial and banking operations in German South West Africa from 1890 to 1915. The case asserts that these entities were major and controlling investors, shareholders in, and directors of the largest mining and railway operations in GSWA during that time. It is further claimed that Deutsche Bank, itself and through Disconto-Gesellschaft, was a critical participant in German colonial enterprises and that Deutsche Bank committed and is directly responsible for crimes against humanity perpetrated against the Herero. The Herero allege that Deutsche Bank specifically financed the then government and companies linked with Germany's colonial rule.[133]

Terex was also sued under the assertion that it is the successor in interest to or merger partner of Orenstein-Koppel Co., the principal railway construction entity in German South West Africa from 1890 to 1915. The court papers state that Arthur Koppel, the principal of Orenstein-Koppel, was a powerful German executive. His business specialized in earth-moving technology and had contracts all over the world at the beginning of the twentieth century. The case claims that Terex and its predecessors prospered over the 125 years of its existence through organizing, participating in, and taking advantage of a slave labor system. It is further alleged that they profited enormously from the system and committed and were directly responsible for crimes against humanity perpetrated against the Herero.

The claimants later withdrew their legal claim for reparations against Terex (at least temporarily), as the corporation maintained that it had been under different management at the time the atrocities were committed.[134] However, the claimants then filed against the German government.[135] In this regard, Chief Kuaima Riruako stated: "I am suing legitimate governments and companies who happened to function in the colonial days.... We're equal to the Jews who were destroyed. The Germans paid for spilled Jewish blood. Compensate us, too. It's time to heal the wound."[136]

Woermann Line[137] is also being sued under the assertion that they controlled virtually all of the shipping into and out of GSWA from 1890 to 1915. In fact, Woermann and other business people played a considerable role in convincing Germany to take possession of its various colonies, as German control of these areas suited their business interests.[138] The plaintiff's claim avows that Woermann employed slave labor, ran its own concentration camp, was a critical participant in the German colonial enterprise, and "individually and as a member of that enterprise, Woermann is directly responsible for and committed crimes against humanity perpetrated against the Hereros."[139]

Further, complainants allege that the Otavi Mines and Railway Company (OMEG) was founded on April 6, 1900, with the legal status of a German Colonial Company whose purpose was the exploitation of copper deposits and the construction of a railway system.[140] In fact, the construction of the Otavi railway was a causative factor in the Herero "rebellion." The railway line from Swakopmund to Windhoek had a dramatic effect on the Herero: in addition to the land they had already lost, the company sought all the land necessary for the line itself as well as swathes of land up to 20 kilometers wide adjoining the tracks. While the Herero granted the essential land for the tracks, they realized that in due course the settlers would want the land bordering the railway tracks, as well.[141]

Deutsche Bank was allegedly a member of the OMEG governing board from 1900 to 1938. The applicants aver that Disconto-Gesellschaft, one of Germany's largest banks by 1903, was a principal investor in OMEG and that the Woermann Shipping Lines had by 1900 established complete control of the shipping and harbor enterprises in South West Africa. All materials for the OMEG railway were shipped by and through Woermann, who used the slave and forced labor of over 1,000 people to load and unload ships at Swakopmund.

Problematically, the complaint did not identify the specific law granting a cause of action, but simply stated that well-recognized principles of District of Columbia law, United States law, and international law provided the court with jurisdiction.[142] The case was originally filed in the Superior Court of the District of Columbia. As this was a state court (not a federal one) the Alien Tort Claims Act (ATCA) was not available as a source of jurisdiction or as a cause of action. Unfortunately, the applicability of the ATCA was not amended when the case was transferred to a federal court, after the defendants petitioned the court. The complainants unsuccessfully sought to remand the case back to a state court, contending that the defendants had failed to adequately assert jurisdiction in their removal petition. Woermann Lines claimed that there was no personal jurisdiction over it in D.C., or anywhere in the United States Deutsche Bank made the same claim, but admitted that it did substantial business in New York. When the Herero proposed transferring the case to New York, the defendants refused. The court then dismissed the Woermann case for lack of personal jurisdiction in D.C. The claim against Deutsche Bank was dismissed for failure to state a claim upon which relief could be granted,[143] and because Federal Common Law provides no cause of action for violations of customary international law.

A separate action was then filed against both defendants in federal court in New York, specifically asserting the ATCA as a jurisdictional basis. The defendants refused to accept service and were ultimately served through the Hague Convention. The defendants had raised multiple bases for the dismissal of the case in federal court in the Washington, D.C. action, but took no action in New York. In the D.C. case the judge ruled that the plaintiffs had standing but granted Woermann its motion to dismiss for lack of personal jurisdiction and later granted Deutsche Bank its motion to dismiss by concluding that violations of international law did not constitute a cause of action in U.S. Federal courts.[144] At that point, Deutsche Bank sent a proposed stipulation to the judge in New York, fixing a stay pending the outcome of the D.C. Appeal and setting a briefing schedule for issues including *res judicata*. The defendants asserted that the New York case was barred by the decision in D.C., subject to the appeal. The appeal in D.C. was unsuccessful.

The next step in the process was in April 2005 when the complainants filed against Woermann in District Court in New Jersey under the Alien Tort Claims Act and Federal Common Law for violations of international law, crimes against humanity, genocide, slavery, and forced labor. The court dismissed the claim on a simple motion to dismiss by the defendant for failing to state a claim and, in the alternative, for failing to bring a claim within the applicable statute of limitations, stating that it did not think plaintiffs "came close" to meeting the burden of proof. The court believed that the case suffered difficulties, including the "amount of time that has passed since these acts occurred, then the difficulty of identifying through witnesses who exactly committed them, which persons suffered them, how plaintiffs have the right to assert those victims' rights, and even how damages might be apportioned—issues of timeliness and justiciability that are pressed by defendant in this motion as individual bases for dismissal."[145]

The court held that the Herero did not (and could not) sufficiently prove that they were effectively barred from bringing their claim and that the statute of limitations should therefore be tolled. The court stated that plaintiff's evidence—in the form of historical documentation and class plaintiff declarations—was insufficient and problematic and that the plaintiffs did not raise any extraordinary circumstances to bring equitable tolling into operation for an 80-year period. The court held that the declarations made by various Herero plaintiffs (none of whom were born before 1915) who sought to establish extraordinary impediments required the court to examine historical documents and events to determine whether the claim was sufficiently asserted to toll the statute of limitations for 80 years. According to the court the declarations suffered from the problem of "remoteness of the declarant's personal knowledge" and that such a determination by the court was "fraught with practical problems."[146] However, historical documentation is an acceptable form of evidence and has been used in the past to prove equitable tolling in similar cases. Further, the plaintiff's case relied not only on historical documentation but also on declarations from members of the plaintiff class, who comprehensively show a history of extraordinary impediments to bringing such cases earlier.

Equitable tolling is a simple factual determination which the court could have made. The complainants' claim (substantiated with historical documentation) that they did not bring the case earlier for fear of reprisal has been accepted in other cases.[147] The court attempted to distinguish this case from *Jama v. I.N.S.*,[148] in which the court determined whether particular events occurred at a specific time as part of a continuing pattern, and held that it was "another matter entirely for a court to rely on history books, personal reminiscences that allegedly mirror the experiences of others, and the professional competence of a history professor to support equitable tolling because no other factual support is available."[149] It is inconsistent for the court to state that the

Herero claim fails for relying on historical documents and academics instead of personal knowledge, and then claim that the declarations from the plaintiffs themselves, which "allegedly mirror the experiences of others,"[150] are unreliable. However, the history of GSWA after the German-Herero War, including South Africa's harsh and violent occupation until Namibian independence, is well documented and even common knowledge, as evidenced by the International Court of Justice's decision examining South Africa's continued occupation of the country before it gained independence in 1990. There was no need to rely, as the court argued, on historical documents. Further, the respondent's two-paragraph attack on the plaintiff's equitable tolling claim did not dispute the apartheid regime or its racist policies in Namibia. Surely there would have been no difficulty in confirming the dates of the apartheid regime's control of Namibia. Critically, the complainants did present evidence from individual plaintiff class members about their personal knowledge of the life of the Herero under apartheid, their fear of reprisal, and their lack of access to courts to bring their claims. However, the court dismissed these declarations, concluding that relying on them would require the court to look into historical events to evaluate whether they sufficiently established extraordinary impediments to toll the limitations period. This reasoning is problematic, as courts often do such assessments in cases of this nature.

Regarding the question of suspending the period in which the cases ought to have been brought, the court also had a very limited view. It held that equitable tolling could be applied, but that obstacles created by fear of reprisals are accommodated by a ten-year limitation period and thus the case should have been brought within that ten-year period, i.e., shortly after the events of 1904 to 1907. The court grossly mischaracterized the dicta in *Jama* to suggest that a ten-year statute of limitations is sufficient to bring a claim for continuing human rights violations and that obstacles created by fear of reprisal are accommodated by a ten-year limitations period.[151] The court in *Jama* did not hold that a ten-year limitation period permits plaintiffs to assert claims *despite* hindrances such as gathering evidence, unavailability or hesitation of witnesses who may fear reprisal by a corrupt regime, or other delays caused by ongoing human rights violations. Rather, *Jama* declared that the statute of limitations was increased from two to ten years *because* these hindrances were commonly problematic for claimants trying to assert their claims within the two-year limitation period. Further, the court in *Jama* found that the ATCA's statute of limitations was longer than State statutes of limitations (such as the two-year rule in New Jersey) to promote fairness, primarily because aliens (foreigners) bringing claims under the ATCA usually faced greater obstacles than plaintiffs in ordinary tort cases.

If the court in *Jama* had believed that such hindrances did not unfairly bar plaintiffs from bringing a claim, as the New Jersey court interpreted, then the two-year state statute of limitations would have sufficed and would not have been extended for purposes of fairness, as the *Jama* court expressly held. *Jama* recognized that such hindrances did not allow plaintiffs to fairly assert their claims, thus having a ten-year limitation period increased the likelihood that such hindrances would become nonexistent. In addition, the court's interpretation that the ten-year limitation period is sufficient despite fear of reprisal and ongoing human rights violations directly contravenes case law that grants equitable tolling when just such hindrances prevent claimants from filing within the ten-year limitation period. Thus, the court in *Forti*[152] held that a limitation period could be tolled when "as a practical matter" the hostile military regime that controlled the courts made it impossible for plaintiffs to get a fair hearing. In *Doe v. Unocal Corp.*[153] equitable tolling occurred because the plaintiffs were unable to obtain access to judicial review under an oppressive regime in their own country, Burma. In *Hilao*[154] it was held that claims against President Marcos of the Philippines for torture, disappearance, and summary execution were tolled until Marcos left office because circumstances outside of plaintiffs' control resulted in fear of intimidation and reprisal.

Regarding the cause of action, plaintiffs alleged crimes against humanity include, but are not limited to:

1. the initiation of and implementation of a race war against the Herero;
2. the initiation of and implementation of an implicit and explicit campaign of genocide and extermination of the Herero;
3. the brutalization and enslavement of the Herero, and the systematic use of forced labor;
4. the systematic forced degradation of Herero women who were held as captives and used as comfort women; and
5. the systematic destruction of Herero culture.

Problematically, the court examined issues that would be relevant to apportioning damages alongside those matters pertinent to determining whether the plaintiff has sufficiently stated a claim for which relief could be granted. Additionally, the court relied on the cautious opinion in *Sosa v. Alvarez-Machain*,[155] which called for vigilance about private cause of actions grounded in normative international law and their implications for foreign policy and foreign relations. *Sosa* held that courts must require a plaintiff to demonstrate that the claimed violation offends "a norm of customary international law so well defined as to support the creation of a federal remedy."[156] While the court speculated about the Herero's ability to prove the facts laid out in their brief before the court, such kind of speculation is not permitted under Rule 12(b)(6), as facts pleaded in a complaint are assumed to be true, although a court may deem them legally insufficient. Thus, the court's analysis was beyond what the Rule permitted and the Herero action should have survived the motion to dismiss for failure to state a claim.

The decision in New York against Deutsche Bank was handed down in April 2006. The New York court per Judge Robert L. Carter applied *res judicata*, i.e., that the matter had been heard already, and concluded that the Washington,

D.C. decision was binding. The same argument was rejected in New Jersey, because Woermann was dismissed from the D.C. case for lack of personal jurisdiction before the merits decision.

The case then went to the U.S. 3rd circuit on appeal from the United States District Court for the District of New Jersey. Here the Herero raised two errors: the first being that the District Court erred as a matter of law when it concluded that the complaint failed to state a claim, and the second being that the claim was barred by the statute of limitations. The court held, however, that the conduct alleged did not rise to the level of violating a "specific, universal and obligatory norm of international law," though the court acknowledges that the alleged conduct may have violated some international norms at the time. The court also offered a public policy reasoning for why the claim should be dismissed. It stated that decisions like this that relate to political questions are not appropriate for the judiciary, particularly when they deal with foreign policy decisions or ones that may open the door to a flurry of related claims of human rights violations. Thus, the court relied heavily on the Supreme Court decision in *Sosa v. Alvarez-Machain*.[157] In fact, the U.S. Attorney General attempted to get the court to narrow the applicability of the ATCA to very narrow circumstances, which to some degree the Supreme Court did. The *Sosa* court attempted to ensure that states where issues had been dealt with during a transition were not brought to the courts of the United States, such as apartheid South Africa claims. Thus, the 3rd circuit was reluctant to permit new causes of action under the Alien Tort Statute. It seemed to be concerned that a looser interpretation of the statute may result in a flurry of litigation by other foreign individuals who seek to use the American courts to lay out their grievances against other foreign parties involving disputes that should be taken up in the appropriate foreign court. Thus, the court ruled that the appellants did not state a cause of action. It held that it did not need to address the second alleged error (statute of limitations) and the motion to dismiss was affirmed. However, at the end of 2007, after the 3rd circuit handed down its decision, the 2nd circuit examining the South African case referred to in *Sosa*, brought against businesses that are alleged to have colluded with the apartheid state, overturned a decision similar to the 3rd circuit decision, and returned the case to the lower court.

WHY ARE THE HERERO SUING MULTINATIONAL COMPANIES?

The Herero are seeking reparations from the various multinationals understanding that, while reparations and compensation should be sought from past colonizers, it is unlikely that these countries will allow this to happen.[158] They realize that, despite world opinion or moral authority acknowledging the need for former colonizers to pay reparations, it is doubtful that these states will apologize for past human rights abuses or be willing to pay reparations. If reparations are forthcoming in the future, this will be due to a change in the political climate which leads toward consensus regarding the obligations of states in this regard.[159] Hence the more likely targets are the multinational corporations or other companies who conducted business and benefited directly from these historical violations.

Another reason why these institutions are such pursued targets is the likelihood that international courts will accept these types of litigation before them. For these reasons, the Herero are targeting multinational corporations. However, the courts remain powerless in ensuring that redress for victims of human rights abuses occurs, and this is unlikely to change. Furthermore, victims of gross human rights violations have no access to these courts, and more importantly, non-state actors are not allowed to litigate before them: juridical persons, like multinationals, have no obligations under public international law. Essentially, in more than twenty-five years, the legal status of multinationals has not changed.[160]

PANDORA'S BOX

The Herero's case has enormous relevance[161] because they are not the only group who were victims of colonial atrocities, gross human rights violations, and dispossession of land and other resources.[162] Therefore, the Herero case may lead to a host of other litigations for events that occurred during colonial times.

Africa suffered immensely during the colonial years. About 18 million Africans were traded as slaves, and millions of Africans died during attempts to capture and transport them.[163] Consequently, while in the sixteenth century Africans constituted twenty percent of the world population, by the nineteenth century they only represented twelve percent.[164] In specific parts of Africa the death toll was particularly severe. Under King Leopold II, between five and ten million people were massacred in the Belgian Congo.[165] Yet it was not only the Belgians and Germans who exacted a high toll—most colonial powers committed gross human rights abuses. Thus, cases could be brought against Britain, the Netherlands, France, Germany, Belgium, Italy, Spain, and Portugal.[166]

Such colonial practice was not confined to the African continent. Indigenous populations in many parts of the world were severely affected by colonialism. In the Americas, the local population declined by about seventy-five percent in the sixteenth century and by ninety-five percent over a longer time period. This devastation was not only caused by killings, forced labor, and inhumane working conditions, but was also due to diseases brought from Europe to that part of the world.[167] In other parts of the world, such as Australia, New Zealand, and Hawaii, the indigenous populations were also decimated. The approximately 300,000 indigenous people in Australia in the 1700s declined to about 60,000 by 1900. Hawaiians who numbered between 300,000 and 800,000 in 1778 only numbered between 50,000 and 70,000 in 1900. The number of Chamorro people of Guam and other islands declined from 80,000 in 1668 to only about 1,500 by 1783.[168]

Clearly, the Herero case could have consequences for many societies around the world affected by similar histories. The case has great significance not only for the Herero but also for Namibian and African history. Other cases are already under consideration, and some are currently being filed. One such case relates to the massacres in German East Africa (now Tanzania) between 1905 and 1907 in what was known as the Maji Maji rebellion. It is believed that about 250,000 Ngoni, Matumbi, Waluguru, Makua, Yao, and Makonde people were killed. The Elders' Council of the Maji Maji Museum of Songea had contemplated the possibility of such a case and asked Tanzanian Chief Justice Barnabas Samatta for advice on the matter.[169]

Former Mau Mau freedom fighters from Kenya are also filing a case claiming reparations for human rights abuses committed during colonial times. They are seeking compensation from the British government for atrocities committed against the Mau Mau before Kenya's independence. Allegedly, thousands of freedom fighters were killed, others maimed and raped, and their property destroyed.[170]

Although many other communities suffered severe abuse, genocide is very difficult to prove, and thus future litigation may only be successful in claiming crimes against humanity. Many argue that the various European powers meted out different levels of atrocities. Some vow that the Germans were particularly inhumane, whereas others believe Germany's actions were either less abhorrent than those of the British or were not qualitatively different from those of other colonial powers.[171] According to Howard, the "British were often quite ruthless in their suppression of resistance. For example, every person in the market of the village of Muruka (Kenya) was slaughtered to revenge the killing of one British soldier in 1902."[172] Nonetheless, the effects of actions by all colonizing nations are felt even today, and therefore many groups and societies could benefit from a successful court decision.

The Herero case also demonstrates how the courts can be used to pursue human rights violators even in a third country.[173] The role of court action in achieving acknowledgement and reconciliation cannot be underestimated. However, it should not overestimated, and other processes such as truth commissions are also needed. In this regard former Chief Prosecutor of the International Criminal Tribunal for the Former Yugoslavia (ICTY), Justice Richard Goldstone, has also stated in the context of the tribunals—but equally relevant in the domestic context and to the Herero case—that a judicial process is "essential for reconciliation to begin, it is insufficient alone to satisfy the human need for knowing the truth of a tragic series of events. In addition to criminal prosecution, it is necessary for a damaged society to arrive at a wider understanding of the causes of its suffering."[174]

Yet many fear that the reparations claim by the Herero is the Pandora's Box for issues of the past; once opened the box cannot be closed. As Sydney Harring has argued, the Herero case embodies and is representative of cases that could be filed against the various colonial powers. Given Germany's liability for reparations for Jewish World War II claims, Harring questions why colonial genocides are considered different from later events. He argues that given the context of poverty in Africa it is not remarkable that the operation of different sets of international law, one for each continent, offends Africans.[175] Others, however, are concerned with the flood of similar cases that could result if the Herero case determines that such treatment was not permitted at the time, as many claim. Fröschle's comment represents this concern and argues that the Herero War was "a normal colonial war, not a genocide."[176]

German officials have made similar arguments. In July 2004, Germany's Ambassador to Botswana, Hans-Dietrich von Bothmer rejected calls for reparations for the Herero. He told a gathering in Tsau in northwest Botswana, where 1,000 people had gathered to commemorate the Herero uprising a century before, that Germany regretted "this unfortunate past," but was not prepared to pay reparations as it had provided R3,7bn since 1990 in aid to Namibia to the benefit of all Namibians. He reasoned that "it could not be justified to compensate one specific group."[177] Even Human Rights Watch, an international NGO, has stated that while "human history is filled with wrongs, many of which amount to severe human rights abuse, significant practical problems arise once a certain time has elapsed in building a theory of reparations on claims of descendancy alone."[178] Human Rights Watch warns that if cases go back too far in time "most everyone could make a case of some sort for reparations, trivializing the concept."[179] However, this perspective does not account for the harm suffered and its ongoing effect on these societies in a myriad of ways. It discounts the historical legacy of the North's underdevelopment of the South. Due in part to the legacy of the colonial past, the current landscape in these countries is one of extreme hardship. However, reflections and blame for the causes of the major economic, social, and cultural problems in some countries is contested terrain. Many, however, blame the effects of mismanagement in the post-independence era.

Whatever the causes (and former colonial powers do occasionally accept partial blame), those responsible for these atrocities contend that past events must be interpreted in their historical context when such conduct was legitimate. Some argue that concepts such as genocide, crimes against humanity, and others were not known then, and were not considered crimes at that time. Their rationalization is that liability for actions cannot exist if the actions were not crimes when they were "committed." In addition, many reason that these countries provide reparations for past conduct in the form of development aid.

Despite these claims, many formerly colonized groups and states maintain that the colonizers owe them compensation for the ill effects of the colonial years, as states, and even specific communities, still suffer from the consequences. It has been stated that the "roots of the poverty in central and southern Africa that persists today can be traced to colonial population and economic disasters."[180] The argument of the former colonial powers that development aid adequately addresses these problems is based on a complete misunderstanding of the crisis. Not only are the amounts and type of aid often insufficient, the aid frequently does not reach those who deserve it, and those directly damaged by the past often receive little or no assistance at all.

The desired compensation assistance is not merely about the money: it has a deeper symbolic significance. Those abused in the past feel entitled to assistance to reclaim their dignity. Therefore, it is critically important to formerly colonized countries (and particular groups and individuals residing there) that they receive compensation or some type of reparation for past human rights violations. Waldron aptly comments that, in addition to actual compensation for losses, reparations "may symbolize a society's undertaking not to forget or deny that a particular injustice took place, and to respect and help sustain a dignified sense of identity-in-memory for the people affected."[181]

Observers of these processes commonly misunderstand that the huge sums of money claimed by those who seek reparations is meant to draw attention to the claim. Often, a specific gesture coupled with a sincere, appropriately worded apology would be satisfactory. If groups are consulted, they would often be satisfied with reparations in the form of community development, the building of roads and houses, the provision of well points, and so forth. This applies to the Herero. Professor Mburumba Kerina, a Herero member of parliament, has stated that they did not want the money, but the return of their land.[182] Although the comments of Joe Feagin and Eileen O'Brien concern the American context, they also apply to Namibia:

> For many generations now, white children have inherited ill-gotten gains from the anti-black actions of whites before them. Recognition of this inheritance of privilege is key to understanding arguments for reparations, and *key* to bringing about reconciliation between blacks and whites.[183]

Part of the demand is for compensation or restitution of land. As Jeremy Waldron has observed, a "judgement about past injustices generates a demand for full and not merely symbolic reparation, a demand not just for remembrance but for substantial transfers of land, wealth, and resources in an effort actually to rectify past wrongs."[184]

Harring points out that a significant portion of the land was "stolen" from the Namibian people during colonial times in "brutal seizures."[185] He observes that some of that land is still in the hands of white people. According to him, rights to land, especially communal land transferred to Namibia by South Africa upon independence, which was never occupied by the state, could still be subject to indigenous land title. Hence, the possibility of such a claim has been raised, and the precedent case of *Mabo* in Australia is used to demonstrate that such claims may be available in law.[186]

APPROACHING OTHER COURTS OR TRIBUNALS?

One of the major questions facing litigants wishing to pursue ex-colonial powers responsible for colonial gross human rights violations (including the

Herero in the future) is which court or tribunal to approach to hear their claims. In the past, this has proven to be the biggest obstacle to getting resolution of these claims, as relatively few courts will hear such historical matters. While plaintiffs could approach the courts in their own countries, pursuing states in the domestic courts has not been possible for both political and legal reasons. Legally, pursuing a state in the courts of another country is extremely difficult, as many states have rules that make it virtually impossible to bring these types of cases. Politically, the relationship between the previous colonial power and the formerly colonized, now independent state is typically one of dependency and aid. Hence, the government of the latter is usually extremely reluctant to engage in anything that might sabotage the economic relationship between the two states and will do all it can to avoid such cases. Approaching the courts in the former colonizers' country is as difficult—if not more so—as courts there will be equally loath to accept jurisdiction on the basis of the widely accepted principle of sovereign immunity. Finally, if a court did allow the plaintiffs to surmount this obstacle, it is unlikely to rule in favor of such cases, as a successful outcome would have political ramifications and may open the floodgates for similar claims from a range of claimants.

CAN STATES BE HELD RESPONSIBLE FOR GENOCIDE?

The Genocide Convention, ratified by 138 states in 2008, was ratified by Germany in 1954, by Namibia in 1994, and by South Africa in 1998. The Convention confirms that perpetrators of genocide can be "constitutionally responsible rulers, public officials, or private individuals."[187] While some have argued that this implies that only individuals are liable under the Convention, Shaw points out that "the international community views such phenomena as ... genocide as reprehensible activities for which States are to be held accountable."[188] In addition, Article 9 of the Convention states:

> Disputes between the Contracting Parties relating to the interpretation, application, or fulfilment of the present Convention, including those *relating to the responsibility of a State for genocide* or for any of the other acts enumerated in Article III, shall be submitted to the International Court of Justice at the request of any of the parties to the dispute. [my emphasis]

While it is common to hold individuals criminally accountable, states can also be held accountable for genocide and similar crimes (as Shaw has stated). While the term "accountable" usually denotes civil liability for reparations, a wider interpretation could encompass state liability for criminal activities for which individuals could be held responsible. However, the International Law Commission has found that the Genocide Convention does "not envisage State crime or the criminal responsibility of States in its article IX concerning State responsibility."[189] Not everyone agrees with this.[190] At the time the genocide Convention was drafted, the representative of France stated:

> The theoreticians of Nazism and Fascism, who had taught the doctrine of the superiority of certain races, could not have committed their crimes if they had not had the support of their rulers; similarly, pogroms had occurred frequently only in countries where no severe legal measures were taken against the perpetrators. Thus, the experience of history showed the way it was that human groups should be exterminated while the Government remained indifferent; it was inadmissible that the central authority should be powerless to put a stop to mass assassination when homicide was the first of punishable crimes. When the crime of genocide was committed, it was committed either directly by the Governments themselves or at their behest; alternatively, they remained indifferent and failed to use the power which every Government should have in order to ensure public order. Thus, whether as perpetrator or as accomplice, the Government's responsibility—was in all cases implicated.[191]

The International Criminal Tribunal for Rwanda (ICTR) has also noted that the state usually has a role in the execution of genocide:

> although a specific plan to destroy does not constitute an element of genocide, it would appear that it is not easy to carry out a genocide without such a plan, or organization. Morris and Scharf note that "it is virtually impossible for the crime of genocide to be committed without some or indirect involvement on the part of the State given the magnitude of this crime." They suggested that "it is unnecessary for an individual to have knowledge of all details of the genocidal plan or policy." The Chamber concurs with this view.[192]

While the International Law Commission has found that genocide is not a crime for which a state can be held accountable, nor that there would be criminal responsibility of a state under Article 9, the Convention clearly intends and has been interpreted to imply civil liability for states for genocidal acts. This has been the opinion of the ICJ in the case of *Bosnia-Herzegovina v. Yugoslavia*,[193] in which Yugoslavia argued that Article 9 only covers the failure of a state to fulfil its obligations of prevention and punishment of genocide, but that the responsibility of a state for an act of genocide perpetrated by the state itself is excluded from the scope of the Convention. The court rejected this argument in its interpretation of the Convention. It found that "the responsibility of a State for genocide ... does not exclude any form of State responsibility."[194] The Special Rapporteur of the International Law Commission has stated that "the Court's reference to any form of State responsibility is not to be read as referring to State criminal responsibility, but rather to the direct attribution of genocide to a State as such."[195] While not everyone ascribes to this view,[196] there is broad consensus that genocide is prohibited under international law, including customary international law. Moreover, the normal rules of state responsibility apply in the context of an international legal obligation; an act or omission that violates that obligation, that is imputable to the state responsible and causes loss or damage resulting from the unlawful act or omission, is actionable.[197]

John F. Murphy has highlighted that "only rarely have governments been held liable for the commission of international crimes."[198] Yet he concedes that recently "the situation has changed dramatically, especially in U.S. courts."[199] Decisions have in fact been delivered against the governments of Cuba,[200] Iran,[201] and Libya.[202] There is increased acceptance that Germany is liable for what occurred in GSWA—even if the Kaiser never gave the specific order. If he did, there are no reservations. As Nollkaemper has noted, both individual as well as state liability ensues as

> a limited number of acts can lead both to state responsibility and individual responsibility. These acts include planning, preparing, or ordering wars of aggression, genocide, crimes against humanity, killings of protected persons in armed conflict, terrorism, and torture. These acts can be attributed twice: both to the state and to the individual.[203] (footnotes omitted)

In its judgment on Preliminary Objections in the Application of the Genocide Convention case, the ICJ concurred. With respect to Article 9 of the Genocide Convention, the ICJ found:

> The Court would observe that the reference in Article IX to the responsibility of a State for genocide or for any of the other acts enumerated in Article III does not exclude any form of State responsibility. Nor is the responsibility of a State for acts of its organs excluded by Article IV of the Convention, which contemplates the commission of an act of genocide by "rulers" or "public officials."[204]

In this regard, the doctrine of legal continuity and the principles of state responsibility[205] ensure that a successor government is liable for actions undertaken by a former government. The right of a state to prosecute can be seen in the 1967 *Eichmann* decision[206] in Israel,[207] which stated:

> The abhorrent crimes defined in this Law are not crimes under Israeli law alone. These crimes, which struck at the whole of mankind and shocked the conscience of nations, are grave offences against the law of nations itself (*delicta juris gentium*). Therefore, so far from international law negating or limiting the jurisdiction of countries with respect to such crimes, international law is, in the absence of an International Court, in need of the judicial and legislative organs of every country to give effect to its criminal interdictions and to bring the criminals to trial. The jurisdiction to try crimes under international law is universal.

Thus, a state with a wide criminal law jurisdiction, albeit not universal jurisdiction, could hold a state or a multinational criminally liable, and, as the U.S. example shows, it could find them civilly liable.

Concerning the situation in 1904, one could argue that international law attributed "acts of individuals who act as state organs exclusively to the state.

Although in factual terms states act through individuals, in legal terms state responsibility is born not out of an act of an individual but out of an act of the state"[208] (footnotes omitted). In this regard the Permanent Court of International Justice stated in 1923: "States can act only by and through their agents and representatives."[209] This confirms that Germany would be liable for what occurred in GSWA, whether the Kaiser or General von Trotha ordered the atrocities. Either would be sufficient to hold the state liable.[210] If the Kaiser did give the order, he would be liable on the basis of a conspiracy. The ICTR in *Akayesku* noted

> that complicity is viewed as a form of criminal participation by all criminal law systems, notably, under the Anglo-Saxon system (or Common Law) and the Roman-Continental system (or Civil Law). Since the accomplice to an offence may be defined as someone who associates himself in an offence committed by another, complicity necessarily implies the existence of a principal offence.... It appears from the *travaux préparatoires* of the Genocide Convention that only complicity in the completed offence of genocide was intended for punishment and not complicity in an attempt to commit genocide, complicity in incitement to commit genocide, nor complicity in conspiracy to commit genocide, all of which were, in the eyes of some states, too vague to be punishable under the Convention.[211]

STATE SUCCESSION

One issue claimants would have to tackle if Germany was sued in any court, even its own, is whether the Germany of today is a successor state of the state responsible for the violations a century ago. It might well be argued that Germany today is not the successor of the German state that existed then, because of the collapse of that state after the two world wars, when Germany became two separate states, which then reunified in 1990. In this regard, Du Plessis reasons that "many of the Western States singled out for reparation claims are a mere shadow of their former colonial selves. In any event, the dominant theory of rights would frustrate claims being brought against existing states for conduct committed by predecessor governments and over which they had no control."[212] However, questions of state liability today for the actions of an earlier state are governed by the rules of state succession, which has been defined as the "process during which a certain competence—usually defined as the 'responsibility for international relations of territory'—is transferred between two or more states. In other words, as a result of state succession, one state (the 'successor state') replaces another (the 'predecessor state') as the representative of a certain territory and its population in the international arena."[213] Thus, today, state succession is viewed differently regarding Germany's liability for conduct in Namibia. More recently, state succession is often viewed from the perspective of new states and their succession to treaties that were adopted by the preceding state.[214] Legally, it could be argued (although probably not very forcefully) that Germany today is not the state that committed the atrocities one hundred years ago.[215] While the old German Democratic Republic (GDR) denied that it had succeeded earlier German states, it would appear that West Germany never denied being the legal successor to the German Empire. With reunification that would be difficult to overcome, especially in the light of Germany's continued acceptance of reparation payments arising out of World War II. Various authors have argued that the German state today is the legal successor of the German state then, and therefore can be held responsible.[216] Berat has argued that because Germany is clearly a "direct legal continuation of the old Germany instead of the creation of a new sovereign entity, it, rather than South Africa and Namibia, should be accountable for acts which took place in Namibia earlier in this century."[217]

A propos state succession, the Federal Republic of Germany (FRG) perceives itself as the legal successor of the Nazi state and has accepted the legal and moral responsibilities to the victims of that state.[218] Many have argued that automatic succession by states of humanitarian treaties is the norm, despite some disagreement on this question.[219] A comprehensive examination of this matter is outside the scope of this study, but the general view is reflected in the words of Kamminga, who has argued that

> state practice during the 1990s strongly supports the view that obligations arising from a human rights treaty are not affected by a succession of States. This applies to all obligations undertaken by the predecessor State, including any reservations, declarations, and derogations made by it. The continuity of these obligations occurs *ipso jure*. The successor State is under no obligation to issue confirmations to anyone.[220]

Although state practice has changed since the break-up of the Soviet Union, this understanding of state succession was clearly the case before, and as such governs the issues addressed here.

CAN AN INTERNATIONAL COURT BE APPROACHED?

One option for claimants of colonial violations is to pursue such claims before an international court. However, generally speaking, states have been "unwilling to allow individuals immediate and direct access to an international court,"[221] and this has limited individuals' access to such courts.

Although the ICJ could potentially hear the case, the major problem is that a state usually has to bring such a claim. States accepted the right of the ICJ to adjudicate on matters when they make a declaration, in terms of section 36(2) of the statute, that the court can give a ruling on a dispute it has with another state. As noted above, Article 9 of the Genocide Convention permits the Court to hear disputes between states that have ratified the Convention. The Court may then deal with the questions concerning the interpretation, application, or fulfillment of the treaty. The Court may also be approached regarding matters such as state responsibility for genocide or any other acts as laid out in the

Convention. Namibia could therefore go to the ICJ concerning Germany's responsibility for what occurred a century ago. The problem, however, is that the Namibian government would have to bring the case. Although the new President of Namibia is much closer to the Herero than his predecessor, it remains unlikely that the Namibian government would bring such a claim against Germany, as it would jeopardize their relationship. In addition, the Herero constitute less than ten percent of the Namibian population and have little political clout in a state where another group maintains power.[222]

Yet this does not mean that no case could be brought before the Court, as the ICJ has found:

> The consent of States, parties to a dispute, is the basis of the Court's jurisdiction in contentious cases. The situation is different in regard to advisory proceedings even where the Request for an Opinion relates to a legal question actually pending between States. The Court's reply is only of an advisory character: as such, it has no binding force. It follows that no State, whether a Member of the United Nations or not, can prevent the giving of an Advisory Opinion which the United Nations considers to be desirable in order to obtain enlightenment as to the course of action it should take. The Court's Opinion is given not to the States, but to the organ which is entitled to request it; the reply of the Court, itself an "organ of the United Nations," represents its participation in the activities of the Organization, and, in principle, should not be refused.[223]

It is possible to bring such a case before the ICJ, as occurred in the case of *Legal Consequences of the Construction of a Wall in the Occupied Palestinian Territory* concerning the building of the protective wall in the Middle East. The Palestinians, as a non-state entity, could not bring this case, heard in 2004, before the court, and clearly Israel was not inclined to do so. Consequently, the UN General Assembly asked the ICJ for an advisory decision on the matter in terms of Article 96(1) of the UN Charter, which provides that the "General Assembly or the Security Council may request the International Court of Justice to give an advisory opinion on any legal question."

As far as the ICJ's capability to hear the matter, the Court held in 1982 that it was "a precondition of the Court's competence that the advisory opinion be requested by an organ duly authorized to seek it under the Charter, that it be requested on a legal question, and that, except in the case of the General Assembly or the Security Council, that question should be one arising within the scope of the activities of the requesting organ."[224]

From this, one could ascertain that there may be limits on the types of matters that a UN organ could ask the ICJ to investigate. However, the ICJ in the *Legal Consequences of the Construction of a Wall in the Occupied Palestinian Territory* decision noted widely:

> The Court would observe that Article 10 of the Charter has conferred upon the General Assembly a competence relating to "any questions or any matters" within the

> scope of the Charter, and that Article 11, paragraph 2, has specifically provided it with competence on "questions relating to the maintenance of international peace and security brought before it by any Member of the United Nations ..." and to make recommendations under certain conditions fixed by those Articles.[225]

In this case, the General Assembly would have to make the argument that international peace and security was being affected. However, the Court also has held that

> [i]n certain circumstances ... the lack of consent of an interested State may render the giving of an advisory opinion incompatible with the Court's judicial character. An instance of this would be when the circumstances disclose that to give a reply would have the effect of circumventing the principle that a State is not obliged to allow its disputes to be submitted to judicial settlement without its consent.[226]

This suggests that, should the improbable situation arise that a UN organ referred the Herero predicament to the ICJ for an advisory decision on whether what occurred was genocide, the ICJ would in all likelihood decline to hear the matter on the basis of the non-consent of both Namibia and Germany to allow a dispute concerning them to be brought before the World Court.

This does not mean that the national courts of a third country could not prosecute or hold civilly liable a state (Germany) or multinationals (involved in the perpetration of the genocide)—even successor ones—for the actions of a previous state or multinational. This would be possible under the notion of universal jurisdiction, which permits the prosecution of international crimes committed anywhere in any country whose criminal law permits such prosecutions.[227]

CAN UNITED NATIONS COMMITTEES BE APPROACHED?

Various options might be available to the Herero (or other groups/individuals) to approach structures within the United Nations system for redress. Two instruments, and their supervisory processes, that are accessible are the International Covenant on Civil and Political Rights (ICCPR) and its HRC and the Convention for the Elimination of Racial Discrimination (CERD) and its committee.

Both Germany and Namibia have ratified the ICCPR and CERD, as well as the First Optional Protocol to the ICCPR. The ICCPR entered into force on March 23, 1976. While Article 41 of the ICCPR permits inter-state complaints, this is an unlikely possibility as this procedure has not been used before. In fact, although by 2003 forty-seven states had given authorization to the HRC to consider inter-state complaints against them, no such complaint had been made.[228] Furthermore, these bodies only examine issues occurring after the date of ratification and the entry into force of the complaints procedure, but will investigate events that occurred before then if they constitute continuing violations or have continuing effects.[229]

The Human Rights Committee was established under Article 28 of the International Covenant on Civil and Political Rights (ICCPR).[230] The Committee, whose role is to monitor compliance of member states with their obligations according to the Covenant, consists of eighteen individual members. They are elected by states that are party to the instrument. There are various complaints procedures (including those from other states), but the relevant instrument here would be the individual complaint mechanism contained in the First Optional Protocol to the ICCPR. As Germany has ratified the Protocol, this mechanism is available to individual victims who believe their rights have been violated. Complaints can be raised before the Committee, as it covers "events within the territory of a State Party ... or that otherwise within the jurisdiction (under the effective control) of the State in question."[231] The Human Rights Committee has also held:

> [T]he principle of equality sometimes requires States Parties to take *affirmative action* in order to diminish or eliminate conditions which cause or help to perpetuate discrimination prohibited by the Covenant. For example, in a state where the general conditions of a certain part of the population prevent or impair their enjoyment of human rights, the state should take specific action to correct those conditions. Such action may involve granting for a time to the part of the population concerned certain preferential treatment in specific matters as compared with the rest of the population. However, as long as such action is needed to correct discrimination in fact, it is a case of legitimate differentiation under the Covenant.[232]

Claimants would have to show that they have exhausted domestic remedies as required by Article 5(2)(b) of the ICCPR Optional Protocol and CERD Article 14(2). The HRC, when dealing with matters relating to the ICCPR, has held that domestic remedies must be followed if such remedies are "available and effective."[233] While the HRC interprets this to mean that all juridical remedies must have been exhausted,[234] administrative remedies must also be pursued.[235] However, it seems as though a claimant does not have to exhaust domestic remedies if there are insufficient funds to do so.[236] (See the discussion that follows on why the case has not been brought in Namibia or Germany.)

Another critical issue is that the ICCPR does not apply retrospectively. In *Somers v. Hungary*,[237] the HRC held that a state takes on the responsibilities of the ICCPR only after it has ratified the Covenant.[238] Yet the HRC has examined and found in favor of claimants in cases where the events happened before the ICCPR came into force or was ratified by a state. The HRC has decided many cases focusing on deprivation of property rights and on the questions of compensation where dispossession has occurred even before the ICCPR or its Optional Protocol was ratified by the country in question. Thus, the HRC in the *Lubicon Lake* communication in 1990 found that Canada had breached Article 27 of the ICCPR when it permitted land expropriation from an indigenous group.[239] The decision in *Diergaardt of Rehoboth Baster Community et al. v. Namibia* showed, *prima facie*, unjustifiable interference with property rights.

An example relating to loss of property before the date of ratification of the ICCPR is the case of *Simvnek v. The Czech Republic*.[240] In this case the applicants lost their property in 1987—four years before the Czech Republic ratified the Optional Protocol in June 1991. However, the state enacted legislation in April 1991 to provide compensation to those who lost property if they retained Czech nationality and were permanent residents elsewhere. Although the applicant did not meet these conditions, and even though the legislation was enacted before the Czech Republic ratified the Optional Protocol, the HRC held that it constituted a violation as a "continuing violation is to be interrupted as an affirmation after the entry into force of the Optional Protocol, by act or by clear implication of the previous violations of the State Party."[241] The Human Rights Committee in *Brok v. Czech Republic* held that the Czech restitution process violated the guarantee of equality contained in the International Covenant on Civil and Political Rights by excluding some from that process.[242]

These decisions are not limited to questions of property rights, as can be seen in the *Somers* ruling, which notes that "there is no right, as such, to have (expropriated or nationalized) property restituted."[243] However, the HRC does examine historical issues under Article 26 of the Covenant, which provides that "[a]ll persons are equal before the law and are entitled without any discrimination to the equal protection of the law"; additionally, it prohibits any discrimination and guarantees "to all persons equal and effective protection against discrimination on any ground such as race, color, sex, language, religion, political or other opinion, national or social origin, property, birth, or other status." Thus, in the *Somers* case, the HRC held that compensation schemes for confiscated property must be "applied equally and without discrimination."[244] The question of retroactivity is dealt with by examining whether the violations have continued to occur after the entry into force of the Optional Protocol. If the violation has continued in some way after ratification, then the earlier events can be incorporated as part of the issues under review. Thus, in *E. and A.K.*, the HRC held that violations committed before the ICCPR came into force can be brought if there has been "an affirmation, after the entry into force of the Optional Protocol, by act or by clear affirmation, of the previous violations" by the state.[245] In *Brok v. Czech Republic*, the HRC found that the legislation in the Czech Republic with respect to providing restitution denied the complainant equal protection of the law guaranteed by Article 26 of the Covenant and that the statute arbitrarily distinguished between various property owners.[246]

In *Drobek v. Czech Republic*[247] and *Malik v. Czech Republic*,[248] the Human Rights Committee examined property confiscation in Czechoslovakia shortly after World War II and assessed whether the restitution process for property confiscation which discriminated against Sudeten German property constituted equality discrimination. In *Malik*, the HRC held that that policy did not appear to be "prima facie discriminatory … merely because … it does not compensate the victims of injustices committed in the period before the communist regime."[249] It reasoned that differentiation in treatment is not discriminatory "if the criteria for such differentiation are reasonable and objective and if the aim is to achieve a purpose which is legitimate under the Covenant."[250] So, based on the cases the HRC has decided, it is unclear what they regard as constituting fair discrimination.

For a complaint to be filed under the CERD, the relevant state must recognize the Committee's competence to hear such a complaint by making a declaration in terms of Article 14. Both Namibia and Germany have adopted the Article 14 Declaration which provides for individual complaints to the CERD. If a state has undertaken adoption, anyone can file a complaint claiming that their rights have been violated. While there is no specific time period within which the claim must be filed, it is regarded as necessary to do so soon after all domestic remedies have been exhausted. The principle of non-discrimination and equal treatment is found in Article 1(1) of the CERD. In March 2005, the CERD held that New Zealand's Foreshore and Seabed Act 2004 violated Maori rights. Thus, the CERD has examined issues relating to land claimed by or belonging to an indigenous group. As Charters states, treaty bodies have examined land rights through a wide variety of interpretations of rights to property and cultural non-discrimination.[251]

In summary, although individuals can submit complaints regarding restitution to both the Human Rights Committee and the CERD, it is not necessarily easy to overcome the obstacles of the jurisprudence of these bodies concerning historic human rights violations.

APPROACHING REGIONAL HUMAN RIGHTS INSTITUTIONS

The mechanisms addressed here are the African Commission, the African Court of Human Rights, and the European Court of Human Rights, as the Herero claim could, in theory, be brought there. There are other regional mechanisms, such as the inter-American system, which might avail themselves to other groups.

The African Commission and the African Court of Human Rights

Article 21(2) of the African Charter on Human and Peoples' Rights refers to adequate compensation for spoliation of resources. Yet, generally speaking, the African Commission (unlike many other human rights supervisory and enforcement organs) has been reluctant to award damages or reparations, even in cases where it determined that the Charter has been violated.

In *Henry Kalenga v. Zambia*,[252] the detained person was held without a trial by order of the President. Despite this violation, the Commission closed the file on this matter after the person was released, claiming his release and the fact that they received no further correspondence on the case were sufficient. In the case of *Louis Mega Mekongo v. Cameroon*,[253] the Commission found that the complainant was entitled to reparations for the prejudice he had suffered, but that the valuation of the amount of such reparations should be determined in accordance with the laws of Cameroon.[254] In the *Malawi Africa Association and Others v. Mauritania* case, the Commission made an elaborate recommendation ordering remedies against the respondent, the State of Mauritania.[255] Along with other stipulations, the Commission ordered the Mauritanian government to take appropriate measures to ensure payment of compensatory benefits to widows and beneficiaries of the victims of the alleged violations.[256] The latter two cases are, however, exceptions to the norm, as the African Commission has not awarded reparations in the majority of cases. Hence, it is generally not seen as effective in achieving redress for victims. The absence of a regional court limits the avenues open to victims for achieving reparations.

The African Court of Human Rights[257] came into being on February 25, 2004. It took five years to get the requisite fifteen countries to ratify the Protocol.[258] As its name indicates, this court will be important for human rights cases, as it will be able to issue binding and enforceable decisions. Apprehensions about having two courts, the African Court of Human Rights and the African Court of Justice, delayed the process of getting the court off the ground. In July 2004, the African Union agreed to merge the two courts to circumvent this problem. The combined court will take human rights cases referred to it by the African Commission on Human and Peoples' Rights and by states that are parties to the Protocol. Unfortunately, it will not allow individuals or NGOs to initiate cases unless the state against which the case is being brought consents to such jurisdiction. However, Article 27 authorizes the Court to order appropriate remedies when it finds a violation of any rights.

Judges of the court were elected in January 2006 at the African Heads of State and Government summit in Khartoum, Sudan. The court should begin its work in the near future. It remains to be seen whether historic human rights violations can be brought before the court. However, the real question is who the defendant will be: a multinational, a former colonial power, or a present African government.

The European Court of Human Rights

The European Court of Human Rights is another institution to which the Herero may want to bring their historic human rights violations case. In fact, this option is available to many groups or individuals. A case could be brought by way of a contentious action, or by approaching the Committee of Ministers to ask the Court for an advisory opinion. Article 47 permits the court to hear even matters outside the scope of the European Convention.

Before the creation of this court, a reservation Germany made to the Convention in 1952 could have influenced any case against Germany for historic human rights violations:

> In conformity with Article 57 of the Convention the German Federal Republic makes the reservation that it will only apply the provisions of Article 7, paragraph 2, of the

> Convention within the limits of Article 103, clause 2, of the Basic Law of the German Federal Republic. This provides that "*any act is only punishable if it was so by law before the offence was committed.*"[259]

However, because Germany withdrew this reservation in 2001, it should no longer have any bearing on the case.

Article 13 of the European Convention on Human Rights provides that individuals whose rights are protected in the Convention shall have "an effective remedy before a national authority." Article 50 of the Convention permits the European Court of Human Rights to provide just satisfaction to victims. For the European Court to hear a matter, Articles 34 and 35 require that the human rights violation in question is covered in the Convention or in a Protocol ratified by the state whose conduct is the subject of the complaint.

The European Convention has different types of complaint procedures, including inter-state and individual complaints. No special authorization is necessary if one state party complains about the conduct of another state party. While in many treaties inter-state complaints are rare, in the European system states have used this complaint system multiple times. One example is the case of *Denmark v. Turkey*.[260] The individual complaint mechanism provides that the Court may receive applications from any person, non-governmental organization, or group of individuals claiming to be the victim by one of the High Contracting Parties of the rights set forth in the Convention or the protocols thereto.[261]

Under Protocol 11 of the Convention, this mechanism is compulsory for all states party to the Convention. A group of individuals or a non-governmental organization are also permitted to file a complaint. According to Article 35(1), domestic remedies must first be exhausted. This article further requires that the complaint is filed within six months of the last domestic jurisdictional decision.

The European Court of Human Rights has awarded compensation for interference with property rights in cases like *Chassagnou v. France*.[262] The case of *Yagci and Sargin v. Turkey*[263] examined Turkey's contention that its acceptance of the Court's jurisdiction was for matters that occurred subsequent "to the date of accepting jurisdiction."[264] The Court, however, held that "from the critical date onwards all the State's acts and omissions not only must conform to the Convention but are also undoubtedly subject to review by the Convention institutions."[265]

The principle of non-discrimination and equal treatment is found in Article 14 of the European Convention. In the case of *Gratzinger and Gratzingerova v. Czech Republic*, the Court examined these issues with respect to the Convention's equality provision and found no violation. It held that "a 'long-extinguished' property right could not be revived."[266]

The court stipulates that the violation under review must be committed after the "critical date" of ratification and the implementation of the Convention by the state in question. However, while the Court will not look at matters retrospectively, if a violation is a "continuing situation" it does not matter whether the violation happened before ratification, as long as the violation continues beyond the "critical date." This has been an accepted principle from at least 1962, following the case of *De Becker v. Belgium*.[267] It "extends jurisdiction to cases that originated before the entry into force of the declaration of acceptance, but that produced legal effects after that date."[268] This principle is also helpful in circumventing the rule that the application must be filed within six months, as the Court has allowed cases beyond six months in which the situation is ongoing, even if the violation occurred a long time ago. However, *McDaid & Others v. United Kingdom* demonstrates that it can be difficult to "fit into" the rule.[269] In this case, it was argued that the Bloody Sunday killings in Northern Ireland in 1972 were improperly investigated and that the state did not fulfill its duty to protect its citizens. Yet the Court ruled that

> the concept of a "continuing situation" refers to a state of affairs which operates by continuous activities by or on the part of the State to render the applicants victims. Since the applicants' complaints have as their source specific events which occurred on identifiable dates, they cannot be construed as a continuing situation for the purposes of the six months rule.... The fact that an event has significant consequences over time does not itself constitute a continuing situation.[270]

On the other hand, in *Cyprus v. Turkey*[271] (2002), the Court found that as there had been no investigation by the Turkish authorities and because these authorities refused to allow Cypriots to return to their homes, this constituted a "continuing situation." For those wishing to bring historic claims, Pauwelyn usefully argues that this Court focuses on the ongoing effects of the violation on the victim, and not on evidence of continuing violations by the perpetrator. Other institutions often examine the same type of issues but rather look at whether persisting acts by the perpetrator constitute a "continuing situation."[272]

Although the Court demands that domestic remedies must be exhausted, it overlooks this stipulation when such attempts would be ineffectual.[273] This (as is discussed below) offers another means by which historic human rights violations can be brought before the Court.

Even if the violations were committed outside Europe, the Court can still adjudicate on the matter, as long as those who carried out the acts were agents of the state. Thus, in *Loizidou v. Turkey*,[274] the court held:

> The concept of "jurisdiction" under Article 1 of the Convention is not restricted to the national territory of the Contracting States. Accordingly, the responsibility of Contracting States can be involved by acts and omissions of their authorities which produce effects outside their own territory.[275]

A very recent case which addresses historic violations is *Broniowski v. Poland*.[276] In this case the applicant's family, among more than a million people, had to abandon their property because they were repatriated from territory that fell outside Poland after World War II. According to the Polish Government the anticipated total number of people that fell into the affected class is about 80,000 people, and there were 167 applications before the European Court on these matters. In its judgment in 2004, the Court held that there had been a violation of the applicant's rights, finding that the "crux of the applicant's Convention claim lay in the State's failure to satisfy his entitlement to compensatory property, which had been continuously vested in him under Polish law."[277] The Court found that because the Polish government adopted the 1985 and 1997 Land Administration Acts it reaffirmed its obligation to compensate the claimants and to maintain and incorporate its international obligations into domestic law. The applicant was awarded 12,000 euros for costs and expenses, less 2,409 euros received in legal aid from the Council of Europe.

This case has various implications, including the fact that the Court, as Drzewicki has pointed out, is now expanding its rulings to apply to a whole class of people where appropriate:

> The Court has required the Polish State to fulfill an obligation by addressing a "systemic dysfunction" impacting on an entire class of individuals.... The Court is thus extending its ruling beyond the individual directly affected, to include an entire class of "Bug River claimants" in a similar position to the applicant.[278]

In summary, the European system does offer avenues and possibilities of success, although it may be difficult to prove that a "continuing situation" exists. The potential for this system to assist claimants for historical violations may shift in the future, as the Court has a huge backlog of tens of thousands of cases, many relating to continuing violations. As a result, it may want to prevent a new wave of cases involving historic human rights violations that occurred outside of Europe from being brought before it.

APPROACHING DOMESTIC COURTS

Approaching the Courts in Germany

The Herero claims have not been brought forward in Germany because the chance of success in a civil liability lawsuit are remote, as the claims are beyond the statute of limitations of 30 years.[279] If criminal prosecution were relevant to the case, it is important to note that Germany only enacted the German Code of Crimes against International Law (*Völkerstrafgesetzbuch*, CCIL)[280] in June 2002. This law, for the first time, establishes war crimes and crimes against humanity as crimes for which people can be held accountable in the legislation of the Federal Republic of Germany. While crimes against humanity were prosecuted under the Nuremberg laws,[281] they were never incorporated into the laws of the Federal Republic—they were incorporated into the laws of the German Democratic Republic.[282] Hence, these types of crimes were impossible or extremely difficult to prosecute before 2002. In addition, the will to prosecute was not present.

However, as a result of Germany's obligations under the Genocide Convention, section 220a of the Criminal Code from 1954 provided for the crime of genocide. Yet, as German law academics Gerhard Werle and Florian Jessberger have pointed out, "German criminal law prior to the enactment of the CCIL reflected the traditionally skeptical attitude toward international criminal justice."[283] Hence, before 2003, cases of crimes against humanity and war crimes not linked to World War II could have been brought in the German Democratic Republic, but not in the Federal Republic of Germany. Nonetheless, the courts could hear criminal cases concerning genocide, as there was legislation permitting this. Critically, under section 6 of the German Criminal Code universal jurisdiction applied to the crime of genocide in terms of the old law. However, that legislation was weak as it did not define the specific violation in the law, and many aspects of the international criminal law regarding specific crimes were not found in the domestic legislation.[284] The amended law (CCIL) sorted out the anomalies and omissions and provides that crimes against humanity, war crimes, genocide, and various other international crimes are punishable in Germany "even when the offence was committed abroad and bears no relation to Germany."[285]

Various claims could be made if a civil action is brought in Germany concerning the Herero genocide. These include claims that the GSWA events were in violation of German law, in violation of Germany's international obligations at the time, or in violation of the protection treaties between the German government and the indigenous groups in GSWA. Yet the chances of such a case succeeding in Germany are probably slim (for various reasons), but could nonetheless be brought for publicity value and to "exhaust local remedies."

Approaching the Courts in Namibia

The Herero could even sue the present Namibian state as a successor state for atrocities committed against them, and also for land claims. Yet this too might be problematic, as Berat points out that Namibia in 1990 began as a new state, "a tabula rasa in international relations" and would therefore not be responsible for actions of prior states in the country.[286] A case could then be brought against individuals in Namibia, for example, claiming that they illegally obtained the land they occupy and that those who have benefited from that land were unlawfully enriched.

In the United States cases, questions have arisen as to why the Herero did not bring their case in Namibia years ago. However, it must be remembered that in 1946 Paramount Chief Frederick Maharero attempted to place claims against Germany before the United Nations.[287] In Namibia itself, as Dinah Shelton has noted, "the [Herero] claim was effectively blocked until Namibian independence in 1990."[288] According to Sidney Harring, the "claim is not justiciable in Namibian courts."[289] Rachel Anderson also supports this view.[290] However, the justiciability of the case in Namibia remains to be seen. Although many of the Namibian judges are sympathetic to the ruling party, Namibia appears to be ready to test such a case in its courts.

In the past, the Herero could not bring their case in Namibia for many reasons. Before independence apartheid was in full force in Namibia. Judges at the time were white, and were from and appointed by South Africa, through a racially biased system. The first Chief Justice of independent Namibia, H.J. Berker (who was the Judge-President, before Namibian independence, of the South West Africa division of the Supreme Court of South Africa), stated that before independence the whole system of justice was under South African control, including the appointment of judges.[291] The Namibian Ministry of Justice in 2006 on its website maintained that pre-independence Namibia had an apartheid system of justice in which "it was inconceivable for a black magistrate or judge to preside over a case where the defendant or the accused person was white.... [N]o black person was appointed to the bench of the High Court.[292] There was concomitantly great distrust of the courts. Stefan Schulz and Marthinus Hamutenya have described the mindset at the time, including mistrust of the courts, and have argued that it took a lot of time after independence for the courts to gain legitimacy as Namibian courts.[293]

Thus, even in Namibia, race was the essence of the apartheid system. That South Africa was hostile to any assertion of indigenous claims against former colonial powers is self-evident. While Sam Amoo and others have argued that the "record of the Namibian Judiciary indicates that from 1985 to date, it has demonstrated the will-power and integrity not to compromise its independence and to interpret and apply the laws of Namibia to uphold and protect the rights of the individual as provided in the Bill of Rights,"[294] the reality is that South African judges were applying these supposedly libertarian concepts. Some of these South African judges were trying to show they were less conservative than people assumed, and were already vying to keep their jobs after Namibian independence. They would not have, at that stage, ruled favorably in such a case against South Africa or Germany. This was apparent even in 1991, when the chief coordinator of the governing SWAPO party noted that the Namibian judiciary was "an exclusive mutual admiration and private club of the white minority.... Is it not the best of times for a drastic change from old bones to new ones in our judicial system?[295]

Thus, even after Namibian independence, the claims could not have been brought before domestic courts. Namibia was a nation in transition with all the uncertainties that come with such a status. South Africa's presence was still felt in most areas of the society. The reasons for not bringing a case soon after independence include doubt that such a case was possible, lack of funding to do so, unwillingness of the courts to hear such cases, a dearth of attorneys willing to take them on, the continued presence of South African judges on the bench in

Namibia unsympathetic to such cases, the new Namibian government's opposition to these cases, and the resultant fear that those involved would be harassed or worse. Regarding the Herero complaint, it is argued that even after independence the courts were effectively closed because of the domination of South African judges, the presence of the SA Defense Force, and the threat of reprisal.[296] The opposition of the new ruling party, SWAPO, to the aims and objectives of the case may have exacerbated this fear, as well as the potential impact the case (and its possible success) could have on development aid from Germany.

Approaching the Courts in South Africa

It is also possible for complainants to file similar claims against the South African state, possibly in South Africa. As has been noted, "The African inhabitants of South West Africa have experienced both the harshness of German rule and the severity of the South African administration's segregation policies."[297] Yet, as Freda Troup points out, South Africa's role was not only its own implementation of a discriminatory system. She notes that when South Africa took over control of South West Africa the farmers of German origin were not

> dispossessed and repatriated as were enemy subjects in Tanganyika and the Cameroons, they remained in possession of their farms. This might have been most praiseworthy treatment of the Union's late enemies, had it not been at the expense of her late native allies, whose lands the Germans had appropriated. Not only were the Germans allowed to remain on their lands, but there was no barrier to the entry into the country of others; nor were they subject to any political or other disabilities. In 1924 the Naturalization of Aliens Act automatically gave union nationality to all German adult males unless they objected. The following year the Legislative Assembly was set up. In the election the Germans gained seven out of twelve elective seats and had a majority of one after the nominated seats had been filled.[298]

Later, during World War II, South Africa interned those of German origin in South West Africa and removed the rights to citizenship of thousands of them. After the war, the National Party came to power in South Africa in 1948. A number of its own members were themselves interned due to their German sympathies during the war. South Africa then gave the German settlers their citizenship back and had very good relations with them, at the expense of the indigenous groups.

Some may argue that South Africa is liable for events that occurred during its rule of the territory, especially after it contravened international law. South Africa can certainly be held accountable for its human rights violations in a range of African countries during the apartheid years, yet it is unlikely that any of these countries will try to hold the new democratic dispensation in South Africa liable for what the minority apartheid regime did before the advent of democracy in 1994. Whether the Herero would attempt to hold South Africa accountable for what happened to them during German colonial times remains to be seen. Certainly the Foreign States Immunities Act, 1981 (Act 87 of 1981) and the Diplomatic Immunities and Privileges Act, 2001 (Act 37 of 2001) may obstruct attempts to sue Germany or Namibia or obtain execution of judgment before the South African courts.

LENGTH OF TIME

The post-World War II era defined the movement toward granting individuals reparations for violations of human rights. Before that time, victims would have struggled to claim their rights, let alone (in most cases) sue for suffering. However, as noted above, occasionally victims could bring their cases. An example of an unsuccessful and lengthy attempt to gain reparations is the reparations movement for slavery in the United States. According to Verdun, there have been five major "waves of political activism" to attain reparations for African Americans from the mid-nineteenth century.[299] It would be fair to say that their claim is time-barred, despite the length of time they have devoted to achieving redress. A recent attempt to revive a claim for slavery was undertaken in September 2006, when the United States Federal Appeals Court for the 7th Circuit was asked to permit the review of a case. This claim is against seventeen corporations, including JP Morgan Chase & Co., Aetna Inc., Bank of America, Lehman Brothers, and others for owning, insuring, and transporting slaves as well as giving loans to owners of slaves. Thus, in the United States claimants have employed various strategies over the last 150 years to attain reparations, all of which have been unsuccessful.

The Herero have also been struggling to gain redress for years. As mentioned, because there was no route to pursue claims in South West Africa at least until independence in 1990, Paramount Chief Maharero attempted to place claims against Germany before the United Nations in 1946.[300] However, the arguments utilized against the case of African-American slaves cannot be used against the Herero. For example, in the United States a significant argument is that the perpetrators of the deeds are not identifiable, as the slave owners died a long time ago, and their descendants cannot be traced and held accountable.[301] This amounts to an absence of "correlativity" between victim and perpetrator.[302] The Herero case is vastly different, and these arguments are not appropriate in the Namibian context. German settlers who lived in the territory participated directly and indirectly in the Herero genocide, and many of the soldiers who conducted the war stayed on in GSWA after the conclusion of their service period and received appropriated Herero land. German settlement patterns grew exponentially after the war because soldiers were given 5,000 hectares of land at well below the market rate of thirty pfennigs per hectare as an incentive to remain and farm in the territory.[303] Much of the land allocated to settlers, German soldiers, and other groups belonged once to the Herero, and to this day remain in the hands of the descendants of these groups. Thus, unlike in the U.S. case, connections between the individual perpetrators and their descendants can be identified. These land appropriation violations are in addition to the violations of companies who aided, participated, and funded the genocide and used Herero slave labor without compensating them.

The responsibility of the German government, and potentially the government of South Africa as a successor regime, remains valid through principles of state succession. As far as the individuals are concerned, their descendants are identifiable in Namibia, and where they are in possession of land they have inherited from their ancestors who obtained this land from the Herero at greatly reduced prices, their profits can be precisely measured in today's terms.

The argument often raised against reparations is that those who suffered are no longer alive. Yet this reasoning does not account for the current lasting effects of those killings and dispossessions. It also ignores the fact that the attempts to attain redress in the past have been frustrated by those who caused the harm, so that the victims were unable to bring such claims in a timely manner. If this is the case, it provides an incentive for perpetrators to continue to frustrate claims, hoping that time bars will eventually work in their favor. Many now question the notion that only those directly harmed ought to benefit. Additionally, group reparations, in addition to individual reparations, are now widely recognized.

One early example of group reparations occurred in 1865 when General Sherman proclaimed that land in the Sea Islands and around Charleston, South Carolina would be available for the exclusive use of former slaves. This order was later codified in Section 4 of the Freedmen's Bureau Act of 1865.[304] Another example, also in the United States, dates from 1946 when $800 million was paid to Native American tribes[305] for land that had been appropriated from them without payment. In 1997 the United States offered an apology and gave about $9 million to African Americans who had been refused syphilis treatment in a government-sponsored trial from the 1930s.[306] Further, when the United States compensated the Aleut Indians, thousands of whom were relocated from southeast Alaska during the same period as the internment of Japanese Americans, the Aleuts obtained damages for the children of survivors as well as for the villages that were affected by the relocations, even though it took almost fifty years for this to happen. In this case, the court recognized that the problems caused by the relocation not only affected the communities at the time but were still having ill effects four or five decades later, and would continue to do so for the foreseeable future. Another important example occurred in the United States, when the government paid reparations as a result of the internment of Japanese Americans during World War II.

An example with great relevance to the Herero case is the case of *Aloeboetoe v. Suriname*, decided by the Inter-American Court of Human Rights.[307] There, the Court recognized that the Saramaca tribe as a group was entitled to reparations. This reinforces the acceptance that not only individuals and their direct descendents are entitled to reparations, but groups as well.

This being said, there have been unsuccessful claims for damages dating back fifty years or more in other courts. The U.S. courts have been most sympathetic to this type of litigation. Many ex-comfort women from Korea and other countries have filed suit against the Japanese government in Japanese courts. Of those cases only one was successful, but it too was later overturned by the High Court.

A case that dates further back is one in which descendants of Armenians (mostly U.S. citizens) who died in the Armenian genocide around World War I, who had purchased insurance policies from European and American insurance companies, sued the New York Life Insurance Company.[67] In *Marootian v. New York Life Insurance Company* the defendants argued that time barred the proceedings and that the policies contained clauses stating that French or English courts had jurisdiction in the event of litigation. California enacted a statute permitting suits relating to Armenian genocide-era policies and extended the time limit to 2010. The case was then settled. This case is important because it extended the time limit for claims by almost 100 years. In addition, the beneficiaries were not those who had taken out the policies.[68]

How far back in time the courts are willing to examine issues remains a major concern. However, this is not an insurmountable obstacle, as has been illustrated by several cases where equitable tolling to periods of prescription was permitted. A number of cases of reparations owed from World War II abuses have been documented, some of which were only paid out in the 1990s; in fact, a few payments were granted in the last year or two. More recently, in 2006 a court in France levied a fine on the state-owned railway for deporting Jews during World War II. As a result, Jewish individuals have already lodged more than 1200 claims for compensation.

Other examples exist even before World War II. Another recent case is the agreement by Canada in 2006 to apologize to Chinese immigrants upon whom a head tax was imposed between 1885 and 1923. Those Canadian-Chinese still alive would be given $20,000 in compensation. In another Canadian case, Ukrainians are seeking damages for the detention of about 5,000 Ukrainian-Canadians during World War I in Canada. Additionally, the descendants of persons expelled from Nova Scotia want reparations from the British government,[308] and descendants of people from India aboard the ship *Komagata Maru* denied entry in Vancouver in 1914 also seek relief.[309]

Another recent example of claims for reparations stretching back many years was settled in Australia. In 2006 the government of Tasmania agreed to compensate Aboriginal children who were forcibly removed from their families by the Australian government between 1900 and 1972. The amount of compensation is believed to be about $100,000 per person.

In South Africa, a process of land restitution has been instituted to find ways of compensating or giving back land to black individuals or communities whose land was confiscated from 1913 onward (about ten years after the Herero confiscations). Under the Restitution of Land Rights Act of 1994, restitution of rights in land can occur for persons or communities who were dispossessed through any "racially based discriminatory law."[310] The affected communities or individuals must prove that they had individual or communal land rights or that their ancestors had land rights which were removed after June 19, 1913, the date when legislation was enacted to remove certain black people from their land. This process has recognized the complexities of making restitution for events dating so far back (as would apply to the Herero). At the time, there was no written title and land was often held communally, and thus historians, lawyers, and others employed by the Commission of the Restitution of Land Rights (CRLR) to substantiate claims have undertaken significant research. By the end of 1998, 65,000 claims had been lodged with the CRLR. This number is higher than what Namibia would have to deal with in a similar process.

A recent European example of reparations granted for historical events occurred when in 2004 the Geneva appeals court in Switzerland permitted Gypsies to sue IBM over allegations that the computer company's punch-card machines helped the Nazis commit mass murder more efficiently. The Court overruled a lower court's decision to refuse to hear the case on the basis that it lacked jurisdiction.

This is not an isolated example. A recent U.K. legal process, which will presumably have far-reaching implications, entailed the success of 228 Samburu and Maasai farmers in Kenya who received £4.5M in damages from the U.K.'s Ministry of Defense, after their family members has been killed or maimed over the past fifty years by British Army explosives left behind on military ranges in that country. The claim, launched in 2000 before the High Court, accused the U.K. Ministry of Defense of failing to remove all potentially dangerous devices from their bases in Kenya with the same thoroughness as in their bases in Cyprus and Canada. While this claim was settled, another claim is still pending, after a second group of 1,044 claimants was offered about half a million pounds in November 2003, which they turned down. The settlement in the first case resulted in a number of other cases, including charges of rape against British army soldiers. About 650 Kenyan women will receive British legal aid to pursue the case. This claim against the British Ministry of Defense (MoD) is for acts of rape allegedly committed by British soldiers in Kenya between 1972 and 2002. The MoD is being sued for negligence in that it failed to take steps to prevent the rapes.[311]

The Maasai community is bringing a case that is very significant as a potential precedent, as it pertains to colonial (mal-)practices. The case challenges a 1913 British court decision to force some 10,000 Maasai off their land in Laikipia and into a new area on the Tanzanian border, where they were afflicted by malaria.[312] If this claim is successful, it will have major implications for land dispossession issues, particularly during colonialism. Such claims have been dealt with in Australia, New Zealand, South Africa, and the United States, but have not been very successful when the claims were against other countries. The exception is Britain, who provided some compensation to Zimbabwe in the 1990s for land in possession of white farmers.

The Nandi people of Uganda are apparently preparing to sue Britain for killing their prophet Koitalel arap Samoei in 1905 during a military campaign to suppress Nandi resistance. Allied to this is a request to the Kenyan government by the Pan-African Reparations Movement to set up a Commission to investigate how many Kenyans were "killed and maimed" during the colonial rule. The group argued that the "British should compensate our freedom fighters, particularly the Mau Mau, who gallantly resisted colonial oppression and exploitation."[313]

Britain was also sued together with the Kabaka of Buganda, Ronald Muwenda Mutebi, the Ugandan government, the Electoral Commission (EC), the Uganda Land Board, and 366 absentee landlords in Buyaga and Bugangaizi counties in Kibaale for plundering resources and killing people in the Bunyoro-Kitara Kingdom in Uganda in the 1890s. The plaintiffs sought compensation in the amount $250 million for genocide and dispossessing Bunyoro's indigenous people. However, in August 2005 the Ugandan High Court cleared Britain of plundering resources and killing people in the Bunyoro-Kitara Kingdom and ordered that the case be sent to the land division of the High Court.[314]

There are a few examples in the United States where reparations were paid about 70 years after the events occurred, and not only to direct victims but also to their descendants. In 1923 the small black town of Rosewood was destroyed, and many of its residents were murdered. In 1995 the State of Florida agreed to pay each of the nine survivors of the Rosewood Massacre $150,000,[315] and each of the 145 descendants received amounts of up to $22,535.[316] Another example pertains to the 1921 Tulsa race riot, in which 300 black people were killed and many black businesses destroyed. In 1997 the Oklahoma state legislature decided to compensate those who survived and even descendents of the victims.[317] For past abuses against Native Americans, reparation payments were made to the Klamaths of Oregon, the Sioux of South Dakota, the Seminoles of Florida, the Chippewas of Wisconsin, and the Ottowas of Michigan.[318]

Finally, reparations for violations that occurred in the nineteenth century have also been paid recently. One example is payment by the New Zealand government according to the Waikatu Raupatu Claims Settlement Act of 1995. This Act provided for substantial payment to the Maoris for land seized from them.[319] New Zealand established the Waitangi Tribunal in 1975, permitting Maoris to bring claims dating from 1840.

CONCLUSION

Achieving reparation for harm that occurred in the context of gross human rights violations has seen major developments internationally, regionally, and locally for victims in the recent past. These developments have occurred at an institutional level, with the formation of bodies such as the International Criminal Court as well as the war crimes tribunals for Yugoslavia and Rwanda. There has also been development in the jurisprudence and standards relating to when reparations are due. These developments and advances, however, have not often translated into specific reparations for victims, especially in Africa where gross human rights abuses have been part of the landscape in pre-colonial, colonial, and post-colonial societies and countries. Any discussion of reparations due for those who have suffered gross human rights abuses in Africa has to begin in the nineteenth century when the European powers carved up Africa into areas for their exploitation. This is not to say that no abuses occurred before then, but reparations for those abuses would be practicably impossible to achieve because identifying specific perpetrators would be extraordinarily difficult.

Claims against colonial powers, while difficult, can be brought, although numerous legal difficulties would have to be surmounted. A useful dividing line before which claims are even less likely to be successful is around 1885, as it was then when the scramble for Africa culminated and saw the colonial powers meeting at the Berlin Conference and drafting a Treaty to determine which state would get which area in Africa. That same Treaty provided that the local population would be well treated by the colonizers.

Conclusion

For more than a century, the genocide of the Herero of Namibia between the years 1904 and 1908 at the hands of Germany has been relatively ignored amid the development of international criminal, humanitarian, and human rights law prohibiting such acts. The decimation of their population and dispossession of their land continues to marginalize the Herero on the Namibian political stage and, as a result, they remain one of the nation's most impoverished ethnic groups.

This book has illustrated the political and legal significance of the Herero claims for reparations from Germany as a result of the 1904 genocide. In the process of exploring the historical and legal legitimacy of this claim, several themes have emerged.

First, it is crucial to appreciate the enduring legacy that the genocide has played upon Herero identity to the present day.

The lasting effects of population decimation, land dispossession, and political marginalization continue to haunt the Herero and impede their economic, social, and political progress in modern-day Namibia. Second, as the historical legal analysis set forth here has illustrated, Germany's actions at the turn of the last century clearly violated not only present-day prohibitions against genocide, slave labor, and crimes against humanity but also existing customary and treaty norms of the time. Third, it is equally clear that international law in the 1900s not only proscribed crimes against humanity and genocide but also provided reparations to survivors of such atrocities as well, reparations that form the basis of civil damages cases today. Fourth and finally, the success or failure of the Herero's claims for reparations as a result of the 1904 genocide will have profound effects upon historically victimized peoples and individuals as well as their aggressors. In sum, the Herero case is not merely an isolated attempt to

Herero men in German uniforms from 100 years ago and women in Victorian dress, as occurs at special events today. Courtesy of Casper Erichsen.

capitalize upon a recent heightened interest in international atrocities; rather, it is a sound legal claim grounded in horrific facts that, once acknowledged by Germany or a court of law, could pave the way for future historical reparations claims.

THE DEFINING ROLE OF THE 1904 GENOCIDE UPON THE HERERO

As Chapter One illustrated, an understanding of the 1904 Herero genocide is crucial in order to fully appreciate the political climate of present-day Namibia, Herero claims of reparations, and reaction thereto. Land is the common denominator amongst these issues given that it both motivated German colonial policy toward German South West Africa (GSWA) and continues to unsettle relations among Namibia's ethnic groups today.

Present-day Namibia's political and ethnic dynamics are rooted in the colonial legacy known to much of Africa. The arbitrary delineation of Southern Africa's national borders in the late nineteenth century fostered the conditions for political unrest that persists today. For example, Germany's intent to ensure access to its East African colonies resulted in GSWA's acquisition of the

Caprivi strip, a geographical and demographic anomaly that continues to destabilize the politics of Namibia, as evidenced by an attempted regional, political, and ethnic coup in 1999, as well as relations with its neighbors.

In this context, the history of the Herero warrants closer examination not only because they were singled out (along with the Nama and Damara peoples) for extinction by the German colonial powers but also because that isolated abuse continues to marginalize the Herero in Namibia today. Due to their historical sovereignty over arable land and unwillingness to fully submit to German settler dominance, the Herero were targeted with systematic killing, eviction, deprivation of land, and other atrocities. The stagnated economic and political position of the Herero today indicates that the tribe has not recovered from this abuse.

Present-day Namibia remains embroiled in a simmering land conflict that—as in colonial times—is exacerbated by the nation's dry and arid climate, which subjects the little crop-suitable land available to great conflict. However, the economic marginalization of the Herero and other minorities today stems from more than merely climatic conditions. Current income data presented in Chapter One reveals that the colonial and current dispossession of Herero land has continued to affect the tribe's socio-economic status.

Germany's colonial occupation of GSWA has had and continues to have profound effects on the identity and memory of the Herero and their relations with other groups in modern-day Namibia. German customs have influenced the tribe's dress and religious practices, a vivid reminder of their past. The decimation of more than half the tribe's population has reduced the Herero to a mere minority in independent Namibia. The dispossession of land and cattle amongst the Herero left them economically disabled, even to this day.

The South West People's Organization's (SWAPO) moral capitalization of the Herero genocide during Namibia's struggle for independence has enflamed inter-ethnic and political tensions. While SWAPO representatives at home and in exile were quick to deploy the murder and dispossession of the Herero as a catalyst for international support, the tribe's plight was quickly forgotten once the party assumed power in post-independence elections. In its rush to independent rule, the SWAPO government opted not to confront the nation's past through any of the well-worn transitional justice mechanisms, such as prosecutions, truth commissions, or lustration. This absence of remembrance has only amplified the traumatic experience of groups such as the Herero and fostered ethnic and political tension. As a result, Herero leaders still use the 1904 genocide as a rallying cry when pressing for the recognition of their leaders, martyrs, and land claims. Still, the historical abuse of the Herero, which has had devastating political, economic, and social consequences, continues to fester unaddressed and may continue to disrupt intra-Namibian relations.

Given the above context therefore, it is important to understand that the current case for reparations is about more than restitution; it is about the preservation of ethnic memory and identity for a group that has been denied official recognition and land by its post-independent government. The same is likely true for other African tribes mentioned in Chapter Three, such as the Maasai of Kenya and the ancestors of those who lived in Uganda's Bunyoro-Kitara Kingdom. When examining historical reparations cases, it is thus vital to carefully consider the current political, economic, and social conditions of the party claiming them to discern its motivations for and stake in the award of restitution.

THE ILLEGALITY OF GERMANY'S ACTIONS UNDER EARLY 20TH CENTURY INTERNATIONAL LAW

As stated at the outset of this book, a threshold question that must be answered when analyzing the Herero's claim for reparations as a result of the 1904 genocide—as well as historical reparations claims elsewhere—concerns the group's legal status at the time. If Germany had not obtained sovereignty over Herero territory prior to 1904, then its conduct is governed by the law regulating international armed conflict. If, however, sovereignty had been obtained, then its conduct must be judged by customary law regarding intrastate uprising. As the ensuing historical and legal analysis illustrated, however, Germany lacked such control over Herero areas in the early twentieth century.

Despite the proliferation of treaties signed between German colonial officials and various Herero leaders, none of these documents surrendered Herero sovereignty to the settler administration. On the contrary, the form and substance of these agreements, which were negotiated on parity between German officials and tribal chiefs, often for purposes of protection from other tribes or foreign policy, only served to reinforce Herero control over their own territory, a fact recognized by both tribal and settler leaders in their correspondence at the time. It was not until Germany's military defeat of the Herero at the beginning of the twentieth century that it gained control over Herero territory and began to clear the tribe from its land. As a result, Germany's actions against the Herero were governed by the law of international armed conflict—both treaty and customary—in force at the time.

Chapter Two outlined the crucial legal history behind the development of relevant international humanitarian, criminal, and human rights norms—both treaty and customary—as well as civil laws that might apply to Germany's treatment of the Herero at the outset of the twentieth century. The Martens Clause, contained in the 1899 and 1907 Hague Conventions, plays a significant role in the applicable legal framework because it extended the protections of international law to groups and individuals. This gives the Herero standing to claim reparations for violations of international law in 1904. Therefore, as evidenced in Chapter Two, a familiarity with the historical backdrop to the development of relevant international legal norms is essential to understanding the basis upon which the current reparations case is predicated.

Contrary to conventional wisdom, Chapter Two argued that the regimes of international humanitarian and international human rights law did not materialize at the end of World War II but instead surfaced much earlier. For example, doctrines such as "humanitarian intervention" were developed at least as far back as the nineteenth century. Most importantly, concepts such as crimes against humanity, slavery, and genocide amounted to illegal activity under customary international law well before 1904. As a result, Germany was obligated not to violate them during its tenure in GSWA.

While international law is generally believed to have developed from norms and customs of conduct governing relations between states, this does not preclude the discipline's application to individual rights. This has been evidenced by international humanitarian law's attention to the protection of civilians, a customary international legal norm that predates the drafting of the Hague and Geneva Conventions. This body of law applied to the Herero genocide in 1904 because Germany was engaged in an international armed conflict with the Herero, given that the tribe enjoyed an international legal personality as a result of its sovereign control over its own territory. Moreover, humanitarian law—contained in treaties and customary international law—did not require reciprocity; states were bound by the protective norms contained in the 1899 Hague Convention, which prohibited many of Germany's actions, regardless of whether their enemies—the Herero—had signed the treaty.

Germany's behavior—detailed in Chapter One—constituted clear violations of the international legal norms set forth in Chapter Two. For example, the 1899 Hague Convention (to which Germany was a signatory at the time) as well as customary law prohibited the use of poison, murder, giving of quarter, and destruction of property, all of which are examples of German conduct in 1904 GSWA.

Beyond the confines of humanitarian law, Germany's conduct amounted to illegalities under other branches of international law. The concept of crimes against humanity, for instance, applies in times of peace and as well as war. Rooted in the teachings of Socrates and Aristotle, crimes against humanity have been the subject of national and international prosecutions since the early 1300s. Moreover, the Martens Clause of the 1899 Hague Convention signaled the norm's rise to codification in international humanitarian law. As a reflection of the norm's acceptance in international law at the time of the Herero genocide, many of the world's leaders referred to Germany's actions in GSWA as crimes against humanity. These statements are further historical evidence of the norms' status in international law and form the basis of the tribe's claim today.

Additionally, international human rights law in 1904 prohibited Germany's abuse of the Herero. While the individual's standing in human rights law has been long disputed, historical research presented in this book indicates that individuals had standing before international and national courts prior to World War II. Those who argue that individuals were not historically protected by international human rights law place too much emphasis on the lack of enforcement mechanisms available prior to Nuremburg. Lack of enforcement is not to be confused with lack of legal protection, and the international community's shortcoming in providing institutional teeth to the human rights regime prior to the International Military Tribunals should not be read as *carte blanche* for abusive states. Given that the Herero had standing in 1904, they certainly have standing now upon the same grounds and can exercise that position to claim reparations from Germany today on the basis of its actions in the past.

In addition to customary norms present at the turn of the twentieth century, Germany had signed numerous treaties during the late nineteenth century that prohibited its extermination campaign in GSWA. In particular, the Berlin Act of 1885 and the Anti-Slavery Convention of 1890 both charged Germany with protecting local populations within its colonies. Needless to say, these obligations were grossly violated during Germany's vicious campaign against the Herero in 1904.

Likewise, there can be little doubt that Germany's systematic killing, enslavement, and dispossession of the Herero constituted genocide, not only under the formal legal definition adopted in the 1948 Genocide Convention but under the customary international legal norms of the early 1900s. The *travaux preparatoires* to the Genocide Convention, as well as international case law interpreting its provisions, clearly indicate that the intentional extermination of an entire ethnic group was already banned under customary international law prior to the adoption of the convention. Even if it were not, the Convention

Kaiser Wilhelm II. Courtesy of Klaus Dierks.

Mass executions carried out on the Herero. Courtesy of National Archives of Namibia.

itself applies retroactively. Thus, the German settler administration's targeting of the Herero as a group with the intention of destroying the entire tribe was a clear violation of the international law proscribing genocide.

In addition, German officials were responsible for violating international treaty and customary norms prohibiting the use of slavery. Both treaties and practice throughout the 1800s evinced a belief among states that international law proscribed the use of slave labor and required states to care for civilians who fell into their hands during conflict. At the same time, states also agreed by treaty that minority groups deserved special protections and that, if minorities were being persecuted, states had a duty to intervene and protect them, regardless of notions of sovereignty. As detailed in Chapter One, to the extent that German settlers spared the Herero from death, it was only for the purposes of extracting free labor.

As a result, these actions simply constituted another category of international norms that Germany violated in 1904 and for which the Herero now seek restitution.

In summary, Chapter Two made clear that international law had developed—by treaty, jurisprudence, and practice—to such a point that German officials surely possessed the requisite *scienter* to render them culpable for violations of human rights and humanitarian and criminal law. Historical research into media reports and official statements both within and without Germany reveal that the Fatherland's citizens and leaders knew of the atrocities being committed in GSWA. More importantly, denialist statements from the chancellor and the colonial director indicate that they were well aware of their obligations under the Martens Clause and other international legal instruments; they simply refused to acknowledge that their troops' conduct in the colony amounted to illegal behavior. However, Germany's historical position—that their settlers and troops were not committing such acts—merely confirms the fact that the government was well aware of existing legal norms at the time. Thus, any defense that argues that international law at the time did not proscribe Germany's actions in Namibia should fail, given the state's recognition of the applicable norms.

Finally, it is important to remember throughout this discussion that the focus of the Herero's current suit is not criminal prosecution but rather civil damages. Thus, the analysis of Germany's acts in 1904 against a backdrop of the applicable international law at the time is only significant to the current reparations litigation insofar as it helps determine responsibility—as opposed to criminal liability—for the abuse of the Herero population at the turn of the last century.

BOTH EXISTING AND HISTORICAL INTERNATIONAL LAWS ENTITLE THE HERERO TO REPARATIONS

Chapter Three outlined the developing international legal norms of reparations and apologies for historical claims. For what good are international norms prohibiting genocide, slavery, and dispossession if they do not yield tangible compensation and recognition for those who have suffered? While the current trend toward international prosecutions may serve present-day victims, in a case such as the Herero genocide—where the perpetrators have long since died and the effects still linger among the victims' ancestors—reparations hold the best hope for addressing historical injustices.

The final chapter began with the acknowledgement that, while claims for reparations have been notoriously difficult to obtain, some success has been achieved at the national level through domestic legislation that awards damages for injuries sustained as a result of violations of international law. An understanding of the Herero's possible avenues to achieving reparations is important for forecasting potential future claims by former colonies against Western powers.

Careful historical and legal analysis offered in Chapter Three revealed that reparations were in fact a longstanding norm of customary international law before they enjoyed codification status in international humanitarian law. United States jurisprudence from as far back as 1796 indicates that individuals were awarded compensation in domestic courts for rights violations during wartime. Also important are national, regional, and international cases that have recognized the standing of the individual under international law. This standing has enabled the progress of reparations claims on a variety of levels. As a result, it is conceivable that the Herero could bring a suit for reparations before a tribunal at any level, though the practical considerations favoring the U.S. venue were also discussed and will be addressed again below.

In addition to national case law, international humanitarian law—in both treaty and customary form—has allowed for reparations for nearly as long as domestic case law. Beginning with the 1907 Hague Convention IV respecting the Laws and Customs of War through to the statute of the International Criminal Court (ICC), international instruments have provided for the restitution of property and compensation for suffering as a result of international crimes and violations. These treaties advanced the position of the individual in international law, allowing them to claim reparations for injuries sustained during times of conflict. As a result, arguments that the Herero lack standing for offenses committed by the Germans at the turn of the century are inaccurate.

Chapter Three also highlighted the painful irony of Germany's involvement in establishing this norm of individual standing for reparations. German representatives pushed at international conferences for this recognition both during and after its abominations in GSWA. Moreover, Germany received and doled out compensation to dispossessed populations in its colonies as early as 1904, indicating that it accepted the international legal norms of restitution. Today, the German government seeks to escape liability under the very norms it championed decades ago. The Herero's suit intends to prevent such a gross evasion of international obligation.

Arguments that the Hereros' reparation claims are barred by the passage of a century also fail on account of Germany's own state practice. The German government compensated individuals for injuries sustained in World War II well into the 1990s. These very reparations were granted in response to similar violations—such as slave labor—as those visited upon the Herero at the turn of the century.

Lastly, several model cases, such as those in the United States regarding slavery reparations and those in Canada with respect to its 1885 head tax against the Chinese, indicate that claims for reparations are not as readily time barred as skeptics would believe.

Herero women prisoners. Courtesy of National Archives of Namibia.

As described in Chapter Three, restitution and compensation are not the only reparations groups and individuals who have been injured under international law seek. Official apologies can provide victims with a sense of closure or jumpstart more comprehensive reparations schemes. Statements by the heads of state in the United Kingdom and Czechoslovakia are but two examples of such apologies. Frustratingly, the Herero genocide is unique in history in that it has not received so much as an adequate—let alone official—apology, perhaps a manifestation of the West's persistent racial discrimination against Africa. As the statements and visits by German officials to Namibia presented in Chapter Three demonstrate, Germany remains virtually intractable on the issue of apologies to the Herero. Time and again, German officials have claimed that any calls for an apology for the genocide are time barred, not legally required, or mooted by German development aid to Namibia. They certainly did not admit that Germany had waged a genocide against the Herero or label its development assistance to its former colony anything other than "aid." As a result, the Herero community has rejected these purported apologies. Unfortunately, their acceptance by the Namibian government has foreclosed Herero avenues to achieving reparations via its own state—either within Namibian courts or international tribunals—as Namibia remains unwilling to press the apology issue (to say nothing of reparations) with a major development partner.

Chapter Three also traced the development of the international legal norm of reparations from the 1989 draft basic principles by Professor Theo van Boven to the follow-up conducted by Professor Cherif Bassiouni. International criminal courts, including the newly established ICC, and national courts have also recognized the right to reparation under international law. Several of the most significant cases have emerged from federal courts in the United States under the Alien Tort Claims Act (ATCA) and the Inter-American and European regional human rights system. Awards to victims of the Holocaust and other human rights abuses have fueled the Herero's claim for reparations, filed in U.S. courts in 2001.

As discussed in Chapter Three, the Herero's choice of venue was guided more by political, rather than legal, concerns. First, Namibia's unwillingness to file a claim against its development partner, Germany, in international court (an avenue also precluded by the lack of retroactivity in the Rome Statute) or in the courts of its trading partner, South Africa, make U.S. courts a more viable alternative. While the African Court of Human Rights is not fully operational, the European Court of Human Rights presents a temporal jurisdictional challenge as well as a nearly insurmountable backlog of cases.

Instead, the Herero have sued several corporations, including Deutsche Bank, Woermann Line, and Otavi Mines and Railway Company in U.S. Federal Court for subjecting them to forced and slave labor. Unfortunately, a number of filing errors and interpretive irregularities by the federal district courts have resulted in the dismissal of the claims. Regardless of the case's ultimate disposition, its symbolism lies in bringing attention to the conduct and inaction of Germany and its multinational corporate co-defendants.

THE EFFECT OF THE HERERO'S REPARATIONS CASE UPON SIMILAR CLAIMS

As discussed in Chapter Three, one of the fears ignited by the Herero litigation is that a successful outcome will open the floodgates to similar cases from many former European colonies. Given the horrors perpetrated throughout Africa by the United Kingdom, Germany, Belgium, and others, many more cases could emerge from the historical pipeline should the Herero win. While several former colonial powers have attempted to escape criminal and civil liability for their colonial abuses through development grants, aid is not a substitute for reparations because it lacks the recognition of wrongdoing, the apologetic sentiment, and the ability to target injured communities and individuals with specificity.

Doubts have also been raised regarding claims for reparations against states, as some argue that only individuals are liable under the Genocide Convention. However, as demonstrated here, both the convention and international case law have proved the contrary. Moreover, evidence amassed against the Kaiser and General von Trotha provides the basis for state liability via state actors. Similarly, arguments that modern-day Germany did not succeed colonial Germany are unfounded as a matter of law and fact. As a result, Germany is liable for its 1904 acts of genocide, either as a state or via its agents. Should a court of law or other tribunal reach this conclusion in the case of the Herero, the results threaten exorbitant payouts by former colonial powers and corporations to historically oppressed people throughout the developing world.

CONCLUSION

This book has illustrated the theoretical and legal viability of the Herero's claims for reparations against Germany as a result of its genocidal behavior at the turn of the twentieth century. It has also illuminated several themes that hold significance for historical reparations claims elsewhere. First, the legacy of violations of international law upon aggrieved parties should not be underestimated. With good reason, the Herero see the 1904 genocide as a cultural and historical marker, having defined their identity as a political, ethnic, and economic bloc within Namibia. That marginalization—begun over a century ago—persists today and should give former colonies and current courts pause. Such marginalization should not go uncompensated or unacknowledged.

Second, while the post-World War II era has seen a wealth of development in the areas of international criminal, human rights, and humanitarian law, that progress should not obfuscate the existence of relevant legal norms at the turn of the last century. While there may not have been an International Criminal Court or a widely ratified Geneva Convention in existence in 1904, there were certainly customary legal prohibitions on forced labor, slavery, and genocide. As a result, reparations exist for such abuses today.

Third and similarly, the recent surge in successful ATCA cases in the United States and remedial awards from regional human rights tribunals should not leave historically abused people and their advocates with the impression that reparations for violations of international law are a twenty-first century phenomenon. Rather, case law and early twentieth century treaties illustrate that restitution for crimes committed during war was a customary norm. Given that Germany was locked in an international armed conflict with the sovereign Herero at the turn of the twentieth century, the tribe is entitled to compensation for Germany's illegal conduct at the time.

Finally, while the Herero are legally entitled to, as well as in economic, social, and political need of, restitution, official state apologies are a key component of any comprehensive reparations package. The German government must pave the way to the repair and empowerment of the Herero by acknowledging what its ancestors tacitly acknowledged over a century ago: that the administration of GSWA and the state of Germany violated international law in their abuse of the Herero.

In the absence of an acceptable German response to Herero calls for justice, the tribe's search for legal recourse continues. While political and procedural hurdles abound at the national, regional, and international levels, such challenges should not stymie the litigation effort or preclude a just result. The indignity and injustice visited upon the Herero continue to identify the indigenous community, as well as national Namibian politics. Only a proper apology and adequate remedy—including land compensation—will rectify the past and restore hope for the future.

Despite various initiatives, Herero unity remains an unattainable goal at present. As mentioned, the divisions and the conflict they have engendered stem from the election and role of the paramount chief, which chiefs the state accepts, differences between the various Herero communities, and the continuing struggle of several committees to deal with questions concerning the genocide. A new grouping, The Ovaherero/Ovambanderu Council for Dialogue on 1904 Genocide Technical Committee, aims to bridge the divide and achieve a unified position on what is sought. While the paramount chief has delegated his chieftainship duties to someone else, it continues to be a source of tension that he holds two offices, and ongoing attempts are made to persuade him to relinquish one of these positions. Until a resolution is found, these issues remain obstacles to Herero unity, which in turn impede an effective reparations campaign.

One positive development that occurred in 2006 was Germany's invitation to the government of Namibia to establish a German-Namibian Special Initiative Concept. Part of this initiative is to create targeted development, and Germany acknowledges the special need for such developments as a result of its

Herero Day 2003 at Otjozondjupa-Okahandja. Courtesy of Jeremy Sarkin.

historical, political, and moral responsibilities. While this initiative came about as a result of discussions between Germany and Namibia, it also occurred because of direct discussions between the Herero and Germany. Regardless of whether these initiatives result in a better allocation of the development aid pie, the Herero are committed to pursuing their claims in different forums. It is probable that other cases will arise from similarly marginalized groups in former colonized countries who also seek redress for historical wrongs.

While many former colonizing states argue that development aid is a form of reparations, it is highly problematic that aid often does not reach those deprived and dispossessed in the past who ought to be receiving it. There is no doubt that Africa needs assistance to deal with its problems. Certainly debt relief is one way of providing this assistance and is currently being pursued. Some argue that debt relief ought to become a viable means of reparations for what was done in Africa and to Africans during the colonial period. The legacy of colonialism has left African countries with debts totaling U.S. $330 billion. African countries spend U.S. $15 billion each year simply servicing this debt load.

To assist poor African countries, Ibrahima Fall, the UN secretary general's representative in the Great Lakes region, called on the international community to create "a second Marshall Plan" to salvage countries in the region. This is not the first time a Marshall Plan has been proposed. In January 2005, for example, the British Chancellor of the Exchequer, Gordon Brown, offered debt relief but stated that the days of the United Kingdom's apologizing for colonialism were over. While technically not equivalent to reparations, this endeavor could result in various compensation packages, depending on which states support it. However, many Africans are unlikely to accept these initiatives as a substitute for reparations, and the call for reparations is likely to intensify.

COMMEMORATION - OHAMAKARI BATTLE
(11 AUGUST 1904)

"Ohamakari Place of Brutal Mayhem, Last Bastion of Early Colonial Resistance and the Cradle of the Liberation Struggle, Democracy, Reconciliation, Peace and Stability"

OKAKARARA, 14 AUGUST 2004
(Okakarara Community Cultural and Tourist Center)

OHAMAKARI PROGRAMME

Directors of Ceremony: Dr.R. Ndjoze-Ojo, Mr.I.Kanguatjivi and Mr M.T. Omeb
Translators: Hijonganda Kamburona and Mbeuta ua Ndjarakana

06H00-07H00: Battle Cries and Brass Band
07H00-08H45 Arrival of Public
08H45-09H00: Arrival of Dignitaries
09H00-09h05: Namibia National Anthem and AU Anthem
09H05-09H20: Opening Prayer/Devotion: Rev N. Kathindi/Bish Dr Z. Kameeta
09H20-09H25: Opening Remarks: Dr Becky Ndjoze-Ojo
09H25-09H30: Welcoming Remarks: Hon Theophellus Eiseb, Governor of Otjozondjupa Region
09H30-09H40: Ongumbiro ya Katjikururume Jackson M. Kaujeua
09H40-09H45: Supreme Traditional Leader Tuvahi D. Kambazembi II: Destruction and Restoration of our Dignity
09H45-09H50: King Elifas Kauluma: Battle of Namutoni
09H50-10H05: Guest Speaker: Professor Jeremy Sarkin, Faculty of Law, University of the Western Cape - Definition of Ovaherero/Ovambanderu Genocide in International Law
10H05-10H10: Supreme Traditional Leader Munjuku Nguvauva II: Causes and Effects of the Genocide of 1904
10H10-10H15: Mr Raimar von Hase – The need for reconciliation
10H15-10H25: Interlude
10H25-10H30: Supreme Traditional Leader, Captain Christiaan Rooi: The resistance against German imperial war in the South
10H30-10H35: Supreme Traditional Leader Joel Tjikuirire: How did we end up in the Southern part of Namibia?
10H35-10H40: Chief Johannes Kaumo Maharero: How did we end up in the Diaspora in Botswana?
10H40-10H45: Snr Traditional Councilor, Mika Muhenje: How did we end up in Angola?
10H45-10H50: Ms Johana Kahatjipara: Role of women during the German-Herero War.

10H50-11H00: Interlude
11H00-11H15: Dr. Zed Ngavirue (The Ohamakari Battle unplugged)
11H15-11H20: Senior Chief John Tjikuua: The Importance of Ongweru
11H20-11H25: A representative of the traditional flags (Omarapi)
11H25-11H30: Paramount Chief Kuaima Riruako – The impact of Genocide on the descendants of the past adversaries (German imperial wars)
11H30-11H35: Supreme Traditional Leader Kaihepovazandu Aphons Maharero:
Unwavering Stand of Kamaharero on the Land Issue
11H35-11H40: H.E Norman S. Moleboge, the Botswana High Commissioner to Namibia.
11H40-11H55: Minister of Economic Cooperation and Development of the Federal Republic of Germany, Hon. Heidemarie Wieczorec-Zeul
11H55-12H10: Keynote Address: Hourable Hifikepunye Pohamba,
Minister of Lands, Resettlement and Rehabilitation
12H10-12H15: Vote of thanks: Ranongouje Tjihuiko
12H15-12H20: Closing Remarks:
His Worship Kandukira, the Major of Okakarara
12H20-12H25: AU Anthem and Namibia National Anthem
12H25-12H35 Laying of Wreath:
Supreme Traditional Leader Tezee Kaihepovazandu Maharero
12H35-12H45: Short presentation of the Okakarara Community Cultural Centre by the Project Director Penson Mootu followed by revealing of the plaque for the inauguration of the Okakarara Community Cultural and Tourist Centre by the Minister of Lands, Resettlement and Rehabilitation, Hon Hifikepunye Pohamba, and the Minister of Economic Cooperation and Development of the Federal Republic of Germany, Hon. Heidemarie Wieczorek-Zeul
13H00: Lunch - Cultural Programs Continue

NOTE: Please consult the Technical Committee for any wishes regarding this Programme (Mr Honga, Mr Hongoze, Mr Tjihuiko and Mr Tjikuua)

Notes

INTRODUCTION

1. Barkan, E. (2003). Genocide of indigenous peoples: Rhetoric of human rights. In Gellately, R. & Kiernan, B. (eds.), *The specter of genocide mass murder in historical perspective*. Cambridge: Cambridge University Press, 117.

2. Du Plessis, M. (2003). Historical injustice and international law: An exploratory discussion of reparation for slavery. *Human Rights Quarterly*, *25*, 624–659.

3. Anderson, R. (2005). Redressing colonial genocide under international law: The Hereros' cause of action against Germany. *California Law Review*, 1155.

4. Faulkner, W. Quoted in Ogden, T.H. (1994). *Subjects of analysis*. New Jersey/London: Jason Aronson, 39.

5. Diamond, J. (1997). *Guns, germs and steel: the fates of human societies*. New York: W.W. Norton Publishers, 376–377.

6. See Africa Watch. (1992). *Accountability in Namibia: Human rights and transition to democracy*. New York: Human Rights Watch; Dobell, L. (1997). Silence in context: Truth and/or reconciliation in Namibia. *Journal of Southern African Studies*, *23*, 2; Tapscott, C. (1993). National reconciliation, social equity and class formation in independent Namibia. *Journal of Southern African Studies*, *19*, 29–39.

7. One of the most important studies is Africa Watch (1992). *Accountability in Namibia: Human rights and the transition to democracy*. New York: Human Rights Watch.

8. Conway, P. (2003). Truth and reconciliation: The road not taken in Namibia. *The Online Journal of Peace and Conflict Resolution*, 66–76, available at http://www.trinstitute.org/ojpcr/5_1conway.htm.

9. *The Namibian* editorial, October 11, 1996. Quoted in Conway, P. (2003). Truth and reconciliation: The road not taken in Namibia. *The Online Journal of Peace and Conflict Resolution*, 66–76, available at http://www.trinstitute.org/ojpcr/5_1conway.htm.

10. Melber, H. (1991). *Krieg und Kriegsbewältigung in Namibia: Wir können vergeben, aber nicht vergessen.* Freiburg: Arnold-Bergstraesser-Institut, 38. Cited in Hunter, J. (ed.), *Who should own the land? Analyses and views on land reform and the land question in Namibia and southern Africa.* Windhoek: Namibia Institute for Democracy, 4.

11. Zimmerman has called the events in GSWA perhaps the first explicitly genocidal policy ever. Zimmerman, A. (2003). Adventures in the skin trade: German anthropology and colonial corporeality. In Penny, H.G. & Bunzl, M. (eds.), *Worldly provincialism: German anthropology in the Age of Empire.* Ann Arbor: University of Michigan Press, 157.

12. Fraenkel, P. & Murry, R. (1985). *The Namibian Report, No. 19.* London: Minority Rights Group International, 6.

13. Woermann lines involved even earlier: In early 1904 Hereros working in Swakopmund were interned on two Woermann line ships anchored off the coast of the town for use as labor. See Erichsen, C.W. (2004). *The Angel of Death has descended violently among them: A study of Namibia's concentration camps and prisoners-of-war, 1904–08.* MA thesis (History), University of Namibia, chapter 2, 57. Arthur Koppel Company was involved in railway construction and used Herero slave labor for that purpose. This will be dealt with further when the Herero court cases are examined.

14. Bley, H. (1971). *South-West Africa under German rule 1894–1914.* London: Heinemann; Drechsler, H. (1980). *Let us die fighting: The struggle of the Herero and Nama against the German imperialism (1894–1915).* (Bernd Zöllner transl.) London: Zed Press; Bridgman, J.M. (1981). *The revolt of the Hereros.* Los Angeles: University of California Press; Gewald, J.-B. (1996). *Towards redemption: A socio-political history of the Herero of Namibia between 1890 and 1923.* Leiden: CNWS Publications; Gewald, J-B. (1999). *Herero heroes: A socio-political history of the Herero of Namibia 1890–1923.* Oxford: James Currey.

15. Cornevin, R. (1969). The Germans in Africa before 1918. In Gann, L.H. & Duigan, P. *Colonialism in Africa 1870–1960.* Cambridge: Cambridge University Press, chapter 12, 223. Also cited in Jonassohn, K. & Bjornson, S.K. (1998). *Genocide and gross human rights violations.* New Brunswick: Transaction, 73. Gann also observes the biases of the various stages. Gann, L.H. (1973). South West Africa under German Rule 1894–1914. *The International Journal of African Historical Studies, 6,* 121–126, 121.

16. Alvarez, A. (2001). *Governments, citizens, and genocide: A comparative and interdisciplinary approach.* Bloomington: Indiana University Press, 3.

17. Moses, A.D. (2002). Conceptual blockages and definitional dilemmas in the 'racial century': Genocides of indigenous peoples and the Holocaust. *Patterns of Prejudice, 36,* 7–36, 9.

18. Bley, H. (1971). *South-West Africa under German rule 1894–1914.* London: Heinemann. Introduction (no page number).

19. See generally Boahen, A. (1989). *African perspectives on colonialism.* Baltimore: Johns Hopkins University Press.

20. See for example Bedoukian, K. (1978). *Some of us survived: The story of an Armenian boy.* New York: Farrar, Straus & Giroux.

21. Administrator's Office Windhuk [sic], 9th ed. (1918). *Report on the natives of South-West Africa and their treatment by Germany.* London: His Majesty's Stationery Office.

22. Report by Captain H.S.P. Simon, Report on German South West Africa, April 6, 1909, FO 367/136. Quoted in Louis, W.M.R. (1967). Great Britain and German

expansion in Africa 1884–1919. In Gifford, P. & Louis, W.M.R. (eds.), *Britain and Germany in Africa: Imperial rivalry and colonial rule*. New Haven: Yale University, 3–46, 33–34.

23. Quoted in Louis, W.M.R (1967). Great Britain and German expansion in Africa 1884–1919. In Gifford, P. & Louis, W.M.R. (eds.), *Britain and Germany in Africa: Imperial rivalry and colonial rule*. New Haven: Yale University, 3–46, 38.

24. Pienaar, H. A massacre no one seems to want to remember. *Weekend Argus*, August 27, 2005.

25. Kooijmans, P.H. (1991). In the shadowland between civil war and civil state: Some reflections on the standard-setting process. In Delissen, A.J. M. & Tanja, G.J. (eds.), *Humanitarian law of armed conflict: Challenge ahead*. Dordrecht: Martinus Nijhoff Publishers, 225–247, 225.

26. In Seventh Annual Activity Report of the African Commission on Human and Peoples' Rights, 1993–94, ACHPR/RPT17th at Annex XI. Quoted in Zegveld, L. (2003). Remedies for victims of violations of international humanitarian law. *International Review of the Red Cross*, *85*, 497, 519 fn 76.

27. Mazzeschi, R.P. (2003). Reparation claims by individuals for state breaches of humanitarian law and human rights: An overview. *Journal of International Criminal Justice*, *1*, 339.

28. Hofmann, R. & Riemann, F. (2004). *Compensation for victims of war—background report*. International Law Association Committee on Compensation for Victims of War, 7.

29. Dolzer, R. (2002). The settlement of war-related claims: Does international law recognize a victim's private right of action? Lessons after 1945. *Berkeley Journal of International Law*, *20*, 296.

30. Du Plessis, M. (2003). Historical injustice and international law: An exploratory discussion of reparation for slavery. *Human Rights Quarterly*, *25*, 624–659.

31. Jochnick, C. & Normand, R. (1994). The legitimation of violence: A critical history of the laws of war. *Harvard International Law Journal*, *49*, 62.

32. Detter De Lupis, I. (1987). *The law of war*. New York: Cambridge University Press, 167.

33. Caron, D.D. (2000). War and international adjudication: Reflections on the 1899 Peace Conference. *American Journal of International Law*, *94*, 13.

34. Lauterpacht, H. (1952). The problem of the revision of the law of war. *British Year Book of International Law*, *29*, 360, 363–364.

35. Kunz, J.L. (1956). The laws of war. *American Journal of International Law*, *50*, 313, 322. Both quoted in Jochnick, C. & Normand, R. (1994). The legitimation of violence: A critical history of the laws of war. *Harvard International Law Journal*, 49, 55 and fn 17.

36. See Solf, W.A. (1983). The status of combatants in non-international armed conflicts under domestic law and transnational practice. *American University Law Review*, 33.

37. Bley, H. (1967). Social discord in South West Africa 1894–1904. In Gifford, P. & Louis, W.M.R. (eds), *Britain and Germany in Africa: Imperial rivalry and colonial rule*. New Haven: Yale University, 607–630, 612.

38. De Guzman, M.M. (2000). The road from Rome: The developing law of crime against humanity. *Human Rights Quarterly*, *22*, 335–403, 355.

39. Fenrick, W.J. (1999). Should crimes against humanity replace war crimes? *Columbia Journal of Transnational Law*, *37*, 767, 781.

40. Alexander, N. (1983). *The Namibian war of anti-colonial resistance 1904–1907.* Windhoek: Namibian Review Publications, 27.

41. Gewald, J-B. (1999). *Herero heroes: A socio-political history of the Herero of Namibia 1890–1923.* Oxford: James Currey, 141.

42. Melber, H. (1985). Namibia: The German roots of Apartheid. *Race and Class, 27*, 63–77, 73.

43. Lundtofte, H. (2003). Radicalization of the German suppression of the Herero rising in 1904. In Jensen, S.L.B. (ed.). *Genocide: Cases, comparisons and contemporary debates.* Copenhagen: Danish Center for Holocaust and Genocide Studies, 27.

44. Gewald, J-B. (1999). *Herero heroes: A socio-political history of the Herero of Namibia 1890–1923.* Oxford: James Currey.

45. Shelton, D. (2004). The world of atonement reparations for historical injustices. *Miskolc Journal of International Law, 1*, 259–289, 290.

46. See Werner, W. (1997). From colonial pastures to enclosures: The development of land tenure in Herero reserves. Windhoek: *NEPRU Working Paper no. 60.*

47. Bley, H. (1967). Social discord in South West Africa 1894–1904. In Gifford, P. & Louis, W.M.R. (eds), *Britain and Germany in Africa: Imperial rivalry and colonial rule* New Haven: Yale University, 607–630, 628.

48. Pakendorf, G. (1987). The literature of expropriation: Peter Moor's journey to South-West and the conquest of Namibia. In Totemeyer, G., Kandetu, V. & Werner, W. (eds), *Namibia in perspective.* Windhoek: Council of Churches in Namibia, 172–183, 174.

49. Wellington, J. (1967). *South West Africa and its human issues.* Oxford: Clarendon Press, 207.

50. Melber, H. (1985). Namibia's the German roots of Apartheid. *Race and Class, 27*, 63–77, 73.

51. Alexander, N. (1983). *The Namibian war of anti-colonial resistance 1904–1907.* Windhoek: Namibian Review Publications, fn 1.

52. Alexander, N. (1983). *The Namibian war of anti-colonial resistance 1904–1907.* Windhoek: Namibian Review Publications, 24.

53. Schrank, G.I. (1974). *German South West Africa: Social and economic aspects of its history 1884–1915.* PhD thesis (History), New York University, 162.

54. Ritter-Petersen, H.G. (1991). *The Herrenvolk mentality in German South West Africa 1884–1914.* D. Litt. (History). Pretoria: University of South Africa, 200.

55. Africanus (1917). *The Prussian lash in Africa.* London: Hodder and Stoughton, 21.

56. The manuscript is 52 pages long and deals with a number of rebellions and the manner in which they were dealt with in German-occupied territories in Africa. It is to be found at the Jacob Rader Marcus Center of the American Jewish Archives, Cincinnati, the Raphael Lemkin papers, Box 6, Folder 9.

57. Lemkin, R. (undated). *The Germans in Africa*, found at the Jacob Rader Marcus Center of the American Jewish Archives, Cincinnati, the Raphael Lemkin papers, Box 6, Folder 9 page 46.

58. 1906 is used by Manfred M. Deckert in Deckert, M.E. (1966). The causes of the Herero uprising of 1904–1906 in South West Africa in Cordier, A.W. (ed.). *Columbia Essays in International Affairs* New York: Columbia University Press, 255.

59. Prein, P. (1994). Guns and top hats: African resistance in German South West Africa 1907–1915. *Journal of African Studies, 20*, 99–121.

60. Drechsler, H. (1980). *Let us die fighting: The struggle of the Herero and Nama against the German Imperialism (1894–1915)*. London: Zed Press, 1980 (Bernd Zöllner transl.), 260. Cited in Prein, P. (1994). Guns and top hats: African resistance in German South West Africa 1907–1915. *Journal of African Studies, 20*, 99–121.

61. Gewald, J-B. (1999). *Herero heroes: A socio-political history of the Herero of Namibia 1890–1923* Oxford: James Currey, 221.

62. The rebellion of the Nama was recognized as an anti-colonial resistance movement. In this regard Tecklenburg, then deputy governor of GSWA, reported to the Colonial Department in January 1905 that "[t]he one and only reason for the rebellion is the desire to end German colonial rule." Stoecker, H. (ed). (1986). *German imperialism in Africa: From the beginnings until the Second World War*. London: C. Hurst & Co., 59. This continued resistance to German rule was provoked by their losses of land and cattle. Had the local population not been treated unfairly and had German rule not been as brutal, the rebellion might not have occurred.

63. Du Pisani, A. (1986). *South West African/Namibia: The politics of continuity and change*. Johannesburg: Jonathan Ball, 23.

64. The Mbanjeru was a Herero tribe, the Bondelswartz a Nama tribe. More about these tribes in the next chapter. However, there are three different spellings of Bondelswartz that are used—Bondelswarts/Bondelzwarts/Bondelswartz. Bondelswartz seems to be the correct spelling and will be used throughout.

65. Stoecker, H. (ed.) (1986). *German imperialism in Africa: From the beginnings until the Second World War*. London: C. Hurst & Co., 47–60.

66. Sole, T.E. (1968). The Südwestafrika Denkmünze and the South West African campaigns of 1903–1908. *Military History Journal, 1*, 19–23.

67. Sole, T.E. (1968). The Südwestafrika Denkmünze and the South West African campaigns of 1903–1908. *Military History Journal, 1*, 19–23.

68. Stoecker, H. (ed.) (1986). *German imperialism in Africa: From the beginnings until the Second World War*. London: C. Hurst & Co., 61.

69. Stoecker, H. (ed.) (1986). *German imperialism in Africa: From the beginnings until the Second World War*. London: C. Hurst & Co., 61. Morenga and Kooper were both Namas.

70. Masson, J.R. (1995). A fragment of colonial history: The killing of Jakob Marengo. *Journal of South African Studies, 21*, 247–256.

71. Various texts give different spellings of his name, e.g. Kooper, Kopper, Koper.

72. Gewald, J-B. (1999). *Herero heroes: A socio-political history of the Herero of Namibia 1890–1923*. Oxford: James Currey, 141. See also Gewald, J-B. & Silvester, J. (2003). *Words cannot be found. German colonial rule in Namibia: An annotated reprint of the 1918 Blue Book*. Leiden: Brill, 162 fn 146.

73. Stoecker, H. (ed.) (1986). *German imperialism in Africa: From the beginnings until the Second World War*. London: C. Hurst & Co., 140–1.

74. Gewald, J-B. (1999). *Herero heroes: A socio-political history of the Herero of Namibia 1890–1923*. Oxford: James Currey, 141 fn 1.

75. Hintze, H. (May 27, 2005). Germany To Pay N$160 Million For Reconciliation. *The Namibian*.

76. The Declaration was adopted with 144 states in favor and 4 against (Australia, Canada, New Zealand, and the United States). Eleven countries abstained (Azerbaijan, Bangladesh, Bhutan, Burundi, Colombia, Georgia, Kenya, Nigeria, Russian Federation, Samoa, and Ukraine).

77. Keal, P. (2003). *The European conquest and the rights of indigenous peoples: The moral backwardness of international society*. Cambridge: Cambridge University Press, 8.

78. Anaya, S.J. (2004). *Indigenous people in international law* (2nd ed.). Oxford: Oxford University Press, 4.

79. McCormack, T.L.H. (1977). Selective reaction to atrocity: War crimes and the development of international criminal law. *Albany Law Review 60*, 681, 697.

80. See generally Sarkin, J. & Binchy, W. (eds.) (2001). *Human rights, the citizen and the state*. Dublin: Round Hall, Sweet & Maxwell.

81. See further Sarkin, J. Van de Lanotte, J. & Haeck, Y. (eds.) (2001). *Resolving the tensions between crime and human rights: European and South African perspectives*. Antwerpen: Maklu. See also Ambos, K. & Othman, M. (2003). Introduction. In Ambos, K. & Othman, M. (eds.), *New approaches in international justice: Kosovo, East Timor, Sierra Leone and Cambodia*. Freiburg im Breisgau: Iuscrim, 4.

82. The UN Security Council established the International Criminal Tribunal for Yugoslavia by Security Council Resolution 827 in 1993.

83. The UN Security Council established the ICTR by Security Council Resolution 955 in November 1994.

84. The Rome Statute was drawn up in 1998 and the Court came into operation on 1 July 2002 after the 60 necessary state ratifications were achieved.

85. The African Court of Human Rights was established in terms of the *Protocol to the African Charter on Human and Peoples' Rights Establishing an African Court on Human and Peoples' Rights*. The Protocol stated that the Court shall come into force thirty days after fifteen instruments of ratification or accession have been deposited. It took five years to get the requisite fifteen country ratifications and the Court came into being on February 25, 2004. The ratification of the Protocol by the Comoros on January 25, 2004 paved the way for this to happen. Judges were elected in 2006. The Court will make a significant difference on the African continent, as it will be able to issue binding and enforceable decisions. When it starts operating, the Court will hear human rights cases referred to it by the African Commission on Human and Peoples' Rights and by states that are party to the Protocol. Regrettably it will not allow individuals or NGOs to institute cases, unless the state in question has consented to such jurisdiction.

86. See Sarkin, J. (2002). Finding a solution for the problems created by the politics of identity in the Democratic Republic of Congo (DRC): Designing a constitutional framework for peaceful co-operation. In Konrad Adenauer Foundation (eds), *The politics of identity*. Pretoria: Konrad Adenauer Foundation.

87. The declaration of the World Conference against Racism held in 2001 recognized in Article 158 "that these historical injustices have undeniably contributed to the poverty, underdevelopment, marginalization, social exclusion, economic disparities, instability, and insecurity that affect many people in different parts of the world, in particular developing countries. The Conference recognizes the need to develop programmes for the social and economic development of these societies and the Diaspora, within the framework of a new partnership based on the spirit of solidarity and mutual respect." United Nations A, General Assembly Distr., General, A/Conf. 189/ September 24, 2001, Original: English, World Conference against Racism, Racial Discrimination, Xenophobia and Related Intolerance Durban, August 31 to September 8, 2001. Adopted on September 8, 2001 in Durban, South Africa (final version released on December 31, 2001). The Durban Declaration was signed by 168 nations.

88. See Sebok, A.J. (2001). Slavery, reparations, and potential legal liability: The hidden legal issue behind the U.N. racism conference. In http://writ.news.findlaw.com/sebok/20010910.html (last visited on May 23, 2002).

89. See Bennett, T.W. & Powell, C.H. (1999). Aboriginal title in South Africa revisited. *South African Journal on Human Rights, 15*, 449–485.

CHAPTER 1

1. Kelly, M.J. (2002). Can sovereigns be brought to justice? The crime of genocide's evolution and the meaning of the Milosevic trial. *Saint John's Law Review, 76*, 257, 331.

2. Anderson, R. (2005). Redressing colonial genocide under international law: The Hereros' cause of action against Germany. *California Law Review*, 1155, 1174.

3. Different sources give different explanations of the meaning of "Namib": some say it is a Nama word meaning "vast"; others explain that it is a Nama/Damara word meaning "shield" or "enclosure," as it protects the interior from access by sea and had shielded the indigenous people from colonial settlement until well into the nineteenth century.

4. General Assembly Resolution 2372 (XXII) June 12, 1968. See Dale, R. (1976). Colonial rulers and ruled in South West Africa and the Bechuanaland Protectorate 1884–1966: A framework for comparative study. *Journal of Southern African Affairs, 1*, 95–110.

5. This will be discussed further below.

6. Du Pisani, A. (1986). *South West Africa/Namibia: The politics of continuity and change*. Johannesburg: Jonathan Ball, 6.

7. Du Pisani, A. (1986). *South West Africa/Namibia: The politics of continuity and change*. Johannesburg: Jonathan Ball, 6.

8. Rotberg, R.I. (1983). Political and economic realities in a time of settlement. In Rotberg, R.I. (ed.), *Namibia: Political and economic prospects*. Cape Town: David Phillip, 29–40.

9. Diebold, E., Engelhardt, S. & Iskenius, D. (2004). Facing the past to liberate the future: Colonial Africa in the German mind. *Humanity in Action: Reports of the 2004 Fellows in Denmark, Germany and the Netherlands*. New York, *6*, 53–57, 53.

10. Bauer, G. (1999). Challenges to democratic consolidation in Namibia. In Joseph, R. (ed.) *State conflict and democracy in Africa*. Boulder: Lynne Rienner, 437–438.

11. Packenham, T. (1992). *The scramble for Africa: White man's conquest of the Dark Continent from 1875–1912*. New York: Avon Books.

12. Omer-Cooper, J. (1994). *History of Southern Africa* (2 ed.). London: James Currey, 78.

13. Du Pisani, A. (1986). *South West Africa/Namibia: The politics of continuity and change*. Johannesburg: Jonathan Ball, 23.

14. Matua, M. (1995). Why redraw the map of Africa: A moral and legal inquiry. *Michigan Journal of International Law, 16*, 1113.

15. Fisch, M. (1999). *The secessionist movement in the Caprivi: A historical perspective*. Windhoek: Namibia Scientific Society, 7.

16. Amnesty International AI Index: AFR 42/001/2003, August 4, 2003, Namibia: Justice delayed is justice denied: The Caprivi treason trial.

17. Pankhurst, D. (1995). Towards reconciliation of the land issue in Namibia: Identifying the possible, assessing the probable. *Development and Change, 26*, 551–585, 553.

18. Hishongwa, N. (1997). *The contract labour system and its effects on family and social life in Namibia: A historical perspective*. Windhoek: Gamsberg MacMillan, 17.

19. Bauer, G. (2000). Namibia in the first decade of independence: How democratic? *Journal of Southern African Studies*, *27*, 52.

20. Gretschel, H-V. (2001). Education in Namibia. In Diener, I. & Graefe, O. (eds.). *Contemporary Namibia: The first landmarks of a post-apartheid society*. Windhoek: Gamsberg MacMillan, 111–128, 111.

21. During German rule the Nama were often called "Hottentots," a derogatory label originally meaning "stammerer." Stoecker, H. (ed.) (1986). *German imperialism in Africa: From the beginnings until the Second World War*. London: C. Hurst & Co., 39 fn 2.

22. A figure of just under two percent is given in Suzman, J. (2001). *Regional assessment of the status of the San in southern Africa*. Windhoek: Legal Assistance Centre (LAC).

23. Malan, J.S. (1995). *Peoples of Namibia*. Pretoria: Rhino Publishers, 4.

24. Suzman, J. (2002). *Minorities in imperial Namibia*. London: Minority Rights Group International, 5.

25. United Nations Development Programme (1998). *Human development report*. Cited in Suzman, J. (2002). *Minorities in imperial Namibia*. London: Minority Rights Group International, 6.

26. United Nations Development Programme (1998). *Human development report*. Cited in Suzman, J. (2002). *Minorities in imperial Namibia*. London: Minority Rights Group International, 38.

27. Suzman, J. (2002). *Minorities in imperial Namibia*. London: Minority Rights Group International, 5.

28. Pankhurst, D. (1995). Towards reconciliation of the land issue in Namibia: Identifying the possible, assessing the probable. *Development and Change*, *26*, 551–585, 552 fn 1.

29. Harring, S.L. (2002). German reparations to the Herero nation: An assertion of Herero nationhood in the path of Namibian development? *West Virginia Law Review*, *104*, 393.

30. Malan, J.S. (1995). *Peoples of Namibia*. Pretoria: Rhino Publishers, 67.

31. See further Bratton, M. & Van de Walle, N. (1997). *Democratic experiments in Africa: Regime transitions in comparative perspective*. Cambridge: Cambridge University Press; Du Toit, P. (1999). Bridge or bridgeheads: Comparing the party systems of Botswana, Namibia, Zimbabwe, Zambia and Malawi. In Giliomee, H. & Simkins, C. (eds.), *The awkward embrace: One-party domination and democracy*. Cape Town: Tafelberg.

32. Du Pisani, A. (1986). *South West Africa/Namibia: The politics of continuity and change*. Johannesburg: Jonathan Ball, 22.

33. Wallenkampf, A.V. (1969). *The Herero rebellion in South West Africa: A study in German colonialism*. PhD thesis. Los Angeles: UCLA, 69.

34. Stoecker, H. (ed.). (1986). *German imperialism in Africa: From the beginnings until the Second World War*. London: C. Hurst & Co., 18.

35. Stoecker, H. (ed.). (1986). *German imperialism in Africa: From the beginnings until the Second World War*. London: C. Hurst & Co., 21.

36. Ritter-Petersen, H.G. (1991). *The Herrenvolk mentality in German South West Africa 1884–1914*. DLitt. (History). Pretoria: University of South Africa, 21.

37. See Dugard, J. (ed.) (1973). *The South West Africa/ Namibia dispute*. Berkeley, Los Angeles/London: University of California Press.

38. Advisory Opinion of the International Court of Justice (ICJ), June 21, 1971.

39. Soggot, D. (1986). *Namibia: The violent heritage*. London: Rex Collings, ix.

40. Madley, B. (2004). Patterns of frontier genocide 1803–1910: The aboriginal Tasmanians, the Yuki of California, and the Herero of Namibia. *Journal of Genocide Research, 6*, 167–192, 168.

41. Suzman, J. (2002). *Minorities in imperial Namibia*. London: Minority Rights Group International, 7.

42. Hellberg, C-J. (1997). *Mission, colonialism, and liberation: The Lutheran Church in Namibia 1840–1966*. Windhoek: New Namibia Books, 13.

43. See generally Thompson, L. (ed.). (1969). *African societies in Southern Africa*. London: Heinemann.

44. Cohrssen, F.K. (1994). *A critical evaluation of the juridical status of Walvis Bay in colonial and post-colonial international law and practice, 1868–1993*. PhD, University of Natal, 21.

45. Berat. L. (1990). *Walvis Bay: The last frontier*. New Haven, CT: Yale University Press, 29.

46. Cohrssen, F.K. (1994). *A critical evaluation of the juridical status of Walvis Bay in colonial and post-colonial international law and practice, 1868–1993*. PhD University of Natal, 270.

47. Korman, S. (1996). *The right of conquest: The acquisition of territory by force in international law and practices*. Oxford: Clarendon Press, 109.

48. O'Connell, D.P. (1970). *International Law* (2nd ed.) London: Stevens, 435. Cited in Korman, S. (1996). *The right of conquest: The acquisition of territory by force in international law and practices*. Oxford: Clarendon Press, 109.

49. Detter, I. (1966). The problem of unequal treaties. *International and Comparative Law Quarterly*, 1069–1089, 1070.

50. Mugambwa, J. (1987). Treaties or scraps of paper? A second look at the legal character of the nineteenth century. British/African colonial agreements. *Comparative and International Law Journal of Southern Africa, 20*, 79–93, 80.

51. Westlake, J. (1904). *International Law: Part 1: Peace*. Cambridge: Cambridge University Press, 40. Cited in Shaw, M. (1986). *Title to territory: African international legal issues*. Oxford: Clarendon Press, 43.

52. Shaw, M. (1986). *Title to territory: African international legal issues*. Oxford: Clarendon Press, 44.

53. Keal, P. (2003). *European conquest and the rights of indigenous peoples: The moral backwardness of international society*. Cambridge: Cambridge University Press, 29.

54. Wallace-Bruce, N.I. (1985). Africa and international law—the emergence to statehood. *Journal of Modern African Studies, 23*, 575–602.

55. Wallace-Bruce, N.I. (1985). Africa and international law—the emergence to statehood. *Journal of Modern African Studies, 23*, 575–602. Cited in Flint, J. (ed.) (1976). *The Cambridge history of Africa, Volume 5*. Cambridge: Cambridge University Press, 4.

56. Lindley, M.F. (1926). *The acquisition and government of backward territory in international law*. London: Longmans, Green & Co, 22 & 33.

57. Berman, H. (1985). Are indigenous populations entitled to international juridical personality? *American Society International Law Proceedings, 79*, 189, 190. Cited in

Marks, G.C. (1992), Indigenous peoples in international law: The significance of Francisco de Vitoria and Bartolome de las Casas. *Australian Year Book of International Law*, *13*, 1–51, 3.

58. Korman, S. (1996). *The right of conquest: The acquisition of territory by force in international law and practices*. Oxford: Clarendon Press, 41; Shaw, M. (1986). *Title to territory: African international legal issues*. Oxford: Clarendon Press, 43.

59. Mugambwa, J. (1987). Treaties or scraps of paper? A second look at the legal character of the nineteenth century. British/African colonial agreements. *Comparative and International Law Journal of Southern Africa*, *20*, 79–93, 87.

60. 1926 53 HCTLR 10, 26 cited in Mugambwa, J. (1987). Treaties or scraps of paper? A second look at the legal character of the nineteenth century. British/African colonial agreements. *Comparative and International Law Journal of Southern Africa*, *20*, 79–93, 87.

61. Alexandrowicz, C.H. (1973). *The European-African confrontation*, 7 fn 36. Cited in Shaw, M. (1986). *Title to territory: African international legal issues*. Oxford: Clarendon Press, 38–39.

62. Western Sahara Advisory Option, I.C.J. Reports 1975, para. 80. Cited in Huaraka, T. (1978). Walvis Bay and international law. *Indian Journal of International Law*, 160–174, 164.

63. Shaw, M. (1986). *Title to territory: African international legal issues*. Oxford: Clarendon Press, 38.

64. Wallace-Bruce, N.I. (1985). Africa and international law—the emergence to statehood. *Journal of Modern African Studies*, *23*, 575–602, 578, 579, 581.

65. Wallace-Bruce, N.I. (1985). Africa and international law—the emergence to statehood. *Journal of Modern African Studies*, *23*, 575–602, 583.

66. Wallace-Bruce, N.I. (1985). Africa and international law—the emergence to statehood. *Journal of Modern African Studies*, *23*, 575–602, 581–583.

67. Permanent Court of International Justice Reports (The Hague, 1931), Series A/B, No. 41, 57–8. Cited in Wallace-Bruce, N.I. (1985). Africa and international law—the emergence to statehood. *Journal of Modern African Studies*, *23*, 575–602.

68. Wallace-Bruce, N.I. (1985). Africa and international law—the emergence to statehood. *Journal of Modern African Studies*, *23*, 575–602.

69. Wallace-Bruce, N.I. (1985). Africa and international law—the emergence to statehood. *Journal of Modern African Studies*, *23*, 575–602.

70. Shaw, M. (1986). *Title to territory: African international legal issues*. Oxford: Clarendon Press, 11–16.

71. Shaw, M. (1986). *Title to territory: African international legal issues*. Oxford: Clarendon Press, 17.

72. Crawford, J. (1979). *The creation of states in international law*. Oxford: Clarendon Press, 176. Cited in Wallace-Bruce, N.I. (1985). Africa and international law—the emergence to statehood. *Journal of Modern African Studies*, *23*, 583.

73. ICJ Reports 1975, 43.

74. Shaw, M. (1986). *Title to territory: African international legal issues*. Oxford: Clarendon Press, 45.

75. Shaw, M. (1986). *Title to territory: African international legal issues*. Oxford: Clarendon Press, 45.

76. Shaw, M. (1986). *Title to territory: African international legal issues*. Oxford: Clarendon Press, 45.

77. Goldblatt, I. (1971). *History of South West Africa, from the beginning of the nineteenth century*. Cape Town: Juta & Co., 111.

78. Pendleton, W.C. (1976). Herero reactions: The pre-colonial period, the German period and the South African period. In Chanaiwa, D. *Profiles of self-determination: African responses to European colonialism in southern Africa*. Present, Northridge: California State University Foundation, 167–194, 167.

79. Huaraka, T. (1978). Walvis Bay and international law. *Indian Journal of International Law* 160–174, 162.

80. Shelton, D. (2003). The world of atonement: Reparations for historical injustices. *Netherlands International Law Review*, 289–325.

81. Mugambwa, J. (1987). Treaties or scraps of paper? A second look at the legal character of the nineteenth century. British/African colonial agreements. *Comparative and International Law Journal of Southern Africa*, *20*, 79–93.

82. Ritter-Petersen, H.G. (1991). *The Herrenvolk mentality in German South West Africa 1884–1914*. DLitt. (History). Pretoria: University of South Africa, 22–24.

83. Pendleton, W.C. (1976). Herero reactions: The pre-colonial period, the German period and the South African period. In Chanaiwa, D. *Profiles of self-determination: African responses to European colonialism in southern Africa*. Present, Northridge: California State University Foundation, 167–194, 175 and in Bley, H. (1971). *South-West Africa under German rule 1894–1914*. London: Heinemann, 3.

84. At times Hendrik Witbooi was able to unite the Nama during times of war (as happened with the Herero too). While the Witboois were often in conflict with the Herero, Hendrik was able to conclude a peace agreement between the Witboois and the Herero, which then saw a united African front against the Germans. Bley, H. (1971). *South-West Africa under German rule 1894–1914*. London: Heinemann, 3.

85. Captain Curt von Francois, the Imperial Commissioner in charge of German interests in GSWA.

86. Cited in Ritter-Petersen, H.G. (1991). *The Herrenvolk mentality in German South West Africa 1884–1914*. DLitt (History). Pretoria: University of South Africa, 36.

87. Baty, T. (1900). *International law in South Africa*. London: Stevens & Haynes, 79.

88. Schwabe, K. (1904). *Mit Schwert und Pflug in Deutsch-südwestafrika: Vier Kriegs- und Wanderjahre*, Berlin, 244. Cited in Ritter-Petersen, H.G. (1991). *The Herrenvolk mentality in German South West Africa 1884–1914*. DLitt (History). Pretoria: University of South Africa, 38–39.

89. Cohrssen, F.K. (1994). *A critical evaluation of the juridical status of Walvis Bay in colonial and post-colonial international law and practice, 1868–1993*. PhD thesis. University of Natal, 235.

90. Wellington, J. H. (1967). *South West Africa and its human issues*. Oxford: Clarendon Press, 201.

91. Cohrssen, F K. (1994). *A critical evaluation of the juridical status of Walvis Bay in colonial and post-colonial international law and practice, 1868–1993*. PhD thesis, University of Natal, 235 fn 3.

92. Ritter-Petersen, H.G. (1991). *The Herrenvolk mentality in German South West Africa 1884–1914*. DLitt (History). Pretoria: University of South Africa, 29.

93. Swan, J. (1991). The final solution in South West Africa. *Military History Quarterly*, *3*, 36–55, 38.

94. Cooper, A.D. (2001). *Owambo politics in the twentieth century*. Lanham: University Press of America, 56.

95. Goldblatt, I. (1971). *History of South West Africa, from the beginning of the nineteenth century*. Cape Town: Juta & Co., 111.

96. Stoecker, H. (ed.). (1986). *German imperialism in Africa: From the beginnings until the Second World War*. London: C Hurst & Co., 48.

97. Goldblatt, I. (1971). *History of South West Africa, from the beginning of the nineteenth century* Cape Town: Juta & Co., 112.

98. Hendrik Witbooi's role is controversial. His status as a hero of anti-racial resistance has been questioned since he supplied troops to the Germans to assist in their operations over a ten-year period. See Appulus, E. Hendrik Witbooi: SWAPO's phoney hero. *Windhoek Observer*, December 20, 1997; Gewald, J-B. & Silvester, J. (2003). *Words cannot be found. German colonial rule in Namibia: An annotated reprint of the 1918 Blue Book*. Leiden: Brill, 166 fn 155.

99. Goldblatt, I. (1971). *History of South West Africa, from the beginning of the nineteenth century*. Cape Town: Juta & Co., 112.

100. Du Pisani, A. (1986). *South West Africa/Namibia: The politics of continuity and change*. Johannesburg: Jonathan Ball, 26.

101. There seems to be disagreement about the number.

102. Ngavirue, Z. (1972). *Political parties and interest groups in South West Africa: A study of a plural society*. PhD thesis. Oxford University, 8.

103. Ngavirue, Z. (1972). *Political parties and interest groups in South West Africa: A study of a plural society*. PhD thesis. Oxford University, 13.

104. Ngavirue, Z. (1972). *Political parties and interest groups in South West Africa: A study of a plural society*. PhD thesis. Oxford University, 7.

105. Ngavirue, Z. (1972). *Political parties and interest groups in South West Africa: A study of a plural society*. PhD thesis. Oxford University, 8–10.

106. Shaw, M. (1986). *Title to territory: African international legal issues*. Oxford: Clarendon Press, 40.

107. Shaw, M. (1986). *Title to territory: African international legal issues*. Oxford: Clarendon Press, 40.

108. Malan, J.S. (1995). *Peoples of Namibia*. Pretoria: Rhino Publishers, 78.

109. Pendleton, W.C. (1976). Herero reactions: The pre-colonial period, the German period and the South African period. In Chanaiwa, D. *Profiles of self-determination: African responses to European colonialism in southern Africa*. Present, Northridge: California State University Foundation, 167–194, 169.

110. Gewald J.-B. (1999). *Herero heroes: A socio-political history of the Herero of Namibia 1890–1923*. Oxford: James Currey, 31 fn 9.

111. Deckert, M.E. (1966). The causes of the Herero uprising of 1904–1906 in South West Africa. In Cordier, A.W. (ed.). *Columbia essays in international affairs*. New York: Columbia University Press 255, 258.

112. Deckert, M.E. (1966). The causes of the Herero uprising of 1904–1906 in South West Africa. In Cordier, A.W. (ed.). *Columbia essays in international affairs*. New York: Columbia University Press 255, 258.

113. Soggot, D. (1986). *Namibia: The violent heritage*. London: Rex Collings, 4.

114. Packenham, T. (1992). *The scramble for Africa: White man's conquest of the dark continent from 1876 to 1912*. New York: Avon Books, 605.

115. Wallenkampf, A.V. (1969). *The Herero Rebellion in South West Africa: A study in German colonialism*. PhD thesis, Los Angeles: UCLA, 83.

116. Lindley, M.F. (1926). *The acquisition and government of backward territory in international law*. London: Longmans, Green & Co., 166.

117. Detter, I. (1966). The problem of unequal treaties. *International and Comparative Law Quarterly*, 1069–1089, 1070.

118. Ngavirue, Z. (1972). *Political parties and interest groups in South West Africa: A study of a plural society*. PhD thesis. Oxford University, 76.

119. Ngavirue, Z. (1972). *Political parties and interest groups in South West Africa: A study of a plural society*. PhD thesis. Oxford University, 76.

120. Ngavirue, Z. (1972). *Political parties and interest groups in South West Africa: A study of a plural society*. PhD thesis. Oxford University ,76–78.

121. Lindley, M.F. (1926). *The acquisition and government of backward territory in international law*. London: Longmans, Green & Co., 184–185.

122. Anghie, A. (2004). *Imperialism, sovereignty and the making of international law*. Cambridge: Cambridge University Press, 87.

123. Keal. P. (2003). *European conquest and the rights of indigenous peoples: The moral backwardness of international society*. Cambridge: Cambridge University Press, 51.

124. Lindley, M.F. (1926). *The acquisition and government of backward territory in international law*. London: Longmans, Green & Co., 182.

125. Ngavirue, Z. (1972). *Political parties and interest groups in South West Africa: A study of a plural society*. PhD thesis. Oxford University, 77.

126. Lugard, F.D. (1922). *Dual mandate in British tropical Africa*. London/Edinburgh: William Blackwood & Sons, 17. Cited in Cohrssen, F.K. (1994). *A critical evaluation of the juridical status of Walvis Bay in colonial and post-colonial international law and practice, 1868–1993*. PhD thesis, University of Natal, 23.

127. Uzoigwe, G.N. (1976). Spheres of influence and the doctrine of the hinterland in the partition of Africa. *Journal of African Studies, 3*, 183–203. Cited in Cohrssen, F.K. (1994). *A critical evaluation of the juridical status of Walvis Bay in colonial and post-colonial international law and practice, 1868–1993*. PhD thesis, University of Natal, 23 fn 3.

128. Lindley, M.F. (1926). *The acquisition and government of backward territory in international law*. London: Longmans, Green & Co., 181.

129. Lindley, M.F. (1926). *The acquisition and government of backward territory in international law*. London: Longmans, Green & Co.,185.

130. Lindley, M.F. (1926). *The acquisition and government of backward territory in international law*. London: Longmans, Green & Co., 184–185.

131. Ritter-Petersen, H.G. (1991). *The Herrenvolk mentality in German South West Africa 1884–1914*. DLitt (History). Pretoria: University of South Africa, 38–39.

132. Ritter-Petersen, H.G. (1991). *The Herrenvolk mentality in German South West Africa 1884–1914*. DLitt (History). Pretoria: University of South Africa, 41.

133. Gewald J-B. (1999). *Herero heroes: A socio-political history of the Herero of Namibia 1890–1923*. Oxford: James Currey, 55.

134. Packenham, T. (1992) . *The scramble for Africa: White man's conquest of the dark continent from 1876 to 1912*. New York: Avon Books, 608.

135. Heywood, A. & Maasdorp, E. (transl.) (1989). *The Hendrik Witbooi papers*. Windhoek: National Archives of Namibia, 176.

136. Gewald J-B. (1999). *Herero heroes: A socio-political history of the Herero of Namibia 1890–1923*. Oxford: James Currey, 81.

137. Gewald J-B. (1999). *Herero heroes: A socio-political history of the Herero of Namibia 1890–1923*. Oxford: James Currey, 81.

138. Gewald J-B. (1999). *Herero heroes: A socio-political history of the Herero of Namibia 1890–1923*. Oxford: James Currey, 83.

139. Gewald J-B. (1999). *Herero heroes: A socio-political history of the Herero of Namibia 1890–1923*. Oxford: James Currey, 92.

140. Ritter-Petersen, H.G. (1991). *The Herrenvolk mentality in German South West Africa 1884–1914*. DLitt (History). Pretoria: University of South Africa, 42.

141. Ritter-Petersen, H.G. (1991). *The Herrenvolk mentality in German South West Africa 1884–1914*. DLitt (History). Pretoria: University of South Africa, 43.

142. Leutwein, T.G. (1906). *Elf Jahre Gouverneur in Deutsch-Südwestafrika*, Berlin: Mittler, 95. Cited in Ritter-Petersen, H.G. (1991). *The Herrenvolk mentality in German South West Africa 1884–1914*. DLitt (History). Pretoria: University of South Africa, 44.

143. Ritter-Petersen, H.G. (1991). *The Herrenvolk mentality in German South West Africa 1884–1914*. DLitt (History). Pretoria: University of South Africa, 157.

144. Ritter-Petersen, H.G. (1991). *The Herrenvolk mentality in German South West Africa 1884–1914*. DLitt (History). Pretoria: University of South Africa, 153.

145. Ritter-Petersen, H.G. (1991). *The Herrenvolk mentality in German South West Africa 1884–1914*. DLitt (History). Pretoria: University of South Africa, 212.

146. Gewald, J-B. (2003). Herero genocide in the twentieth century: Politics and memory. In Abbink, J., De Bruijn, M. & Van Walraven, K. *Rethinking resistance: Revolt and violence in African history*. Leiden: Brill, 279–304, 303.

147. Wiesel, E., cited in Stannard, D.E. (1996). Uniqueness as denial: The politics of genocide scholarship. In Rosenbaum, A.S. (ed.), *Is the Holocaust unique? Perspectives on comparative genocide*. Boulder, CO: Westview Press, 163–208, 163.

148. Gewald, J-B. (2003). Herero genocide in the twentieth century: Politics and memory. In Abbink, J., De Bruijn, M. & Van Walraven, K. *Rethinking resistance: Revolt and violence in African history*. Leiden: Brill, 279–304.

149. Hendrickson, H. (1994). The long dress and the construction of Herero identities in southern Africa. *African Studies*, *53*, 25–54.

150. First, R. (1967). *South West Africa*. Baltimore: Penguin Books 27.

151. Hendrickson, H. (1994). The long dress and the construction of Herero identities in southern Africa. *African Studies*, *53*, 25–54, 26–27.

152. Pendleton, W.C. (1976). Herero reactions: The pre-colonial period, the German period and the South African period. In Chanaiwa, D. *Profiles of self-determination: African responses to European colonialism in southern Africa*. Present, Northridge: California State University Foundation, 167–194, 184.

153. Werner, W. (1998). *No-one will become rich: Economy and society in the Herero reserves in Namibia 1913–1946*. Basel: P. Schlettwein, 79.

154. Malan, J.S. (1995). *Peoples of Namibia*. Pretoria: Rhino Publishers, 83.

155. Pendleton, W.C. (1976). Herero reactions: The pre-colonial period, the German period and the South African period. In Chanaiwa, D. *Profiles of self-determination: African responses to European colonialism in southern Africa*. Present, Northridge: California State University Foundation, 167–194, 186.

156. Nora, P. in Macklem, P. (2005). Rybná 9, Praha 1: Restitution and memory in international human rights law. *European Journal of International Law, 16*, 1–25.

157. Barkan, E. (2001). Symposium. Holocaust restitution: Reconciling moral imperatives with legal initiatives and diplomacy. Between restitution and international morality. *Fordham International Law Journal*, 46, 47. See further Barkan, E. (2000). *The guilt of nations: Restitution and negotiating historical injustices*. New York: W.W. Norton.

158. Wilets, J.D. (2001): Introduction: The building blocks to recognition of human rights and democracy: Reconciliation, rule of law and domestic and international peace. *ILSA Journal of International and Comparative Law*, *7*, 597, 598.

159. On the choices available to newly democratic states, see Huyse, L. (1995). Justice after transitions: On the choices successor elites make in dealing with the past. In Kritz, N. (ed.), *Transitional Justice: How emerging democracies reckon with former regimes*. Washington, D.C.: United States Institute of Peace, 104–115.

160. Sarkin, J. (1999). The necessity and challenges of establishing a truth and reconciliation commission in Rwanda. *Human Rights Quarterly, 21*, 767, 799.

161. Gewald, J-B. (1999). The road of the man called Love and the sack of Sero: The Herero-German War and the export of the Herero labor to the South African Rand. *Journal of African History*, *40*, 21–40, 29.

162. Kuteeve, P. (October 6, 2004). Herero leader's remains returned, reburied. *Africa News Service*.

163. Luttig, H.G. (1933). *The religious system and social organization of the Herero: A study in Bantu culture*. Utrecht: Kemink & Zoon, 3.

164. Luttig, H.G. (1933). *The religious system and social organization of the Herero: A study in Bantu culture*. Utrecht: Kemink & Zoon, 3.

165. Vedder, H. (1966). *South West Africa in early times*. New York: Barnes & Noble, 47.

166. Vedder, H. (1966). *South West Africa in early times*. New York: Barnes & Noble, 162.

167. Hellberg, C-J. (1997). *Mission, colonialism, and liberation: The Lutheran Church in Namibia 1840–1966*. Windhoek: New Namibia Books, 13.

168. On the way in which history is used in the political process, see Afreds, J. (2000). History and nation-building. The political uses of history in post-colonial Namibia. *MFS-Reports: 2*. Uppsala: Department of Economic History.

169. Dentlinger, L. DTA Slams Govt over Recognition of Herero Chiefs. *Africa News Service*, August 20, 2004.

170. Suzman, J. (2002). *Minorities in imperial Namibia*. London: Minority Rights Group International, 13.

171. See generally the concentration of power, Bauer, G. (2000). Namibia in the first decade of independence: How democratic? *Journal of Southern African Studies*, *27*, 33–55.

172. Mumbuna, M. (September 16, 2004). Academics Dissect Herero Genocide. *Africa News Service*.

173. Mumbuna, M. (September 16, 2004). Academics Dissect Herero Genocide. *Africa News Service*.

174. Hunter, J. (2004). Who should own the land? An introduction. In Hunter, J. (ed.), *Who should own the land? Analyses and views on land reform and the land question in Namibia and southern Africa*. Windhoek: Namibia Institute for Democracy, 1.

175. See Harring, S.L. (1996). The constitution of Namibia and the 'rights and freedoms' guaranteed communal land holders: Resolving the inconsistency between article 16, article 100 and schedule 5. *South African Journal on Human Rights, 12*, 467–484.

176. Daniels, C. (2003). The struggle for indigenous people's rights. In Melber, H. (ed.), *Re-examining liberation in Namibia: Political culture since independence*. Uppsala: Nordic Africa Institute, 47–48.

177. Hunter, J. (2004). Who should own the land? An introduction. In Hunter, J. (ed.), *Who should own the land? Analyses and views on land reform and the land question in Namibia and southern Africa*. Windhoek: Namibia Institute for Democracy, 1.

178. See further Botha, C. (2000). The politics of land settlement in Namibia, 1890–1960. *South African Historical Journal, 42*, 232–276.

179. De Villiers, B. (2003). *Land reform: Issues and challenges. A comparative overview of experiences in Zimbabwe, Namibia, South Africa and Australia*. Johannesburg: Konrad Adenauer Foundation Occasional papers, 38.

180. De Villiers, B. (2003). *Land reform: Issues and challenges. A comparative overview of experiences in Zimbabwe, Namibia, South Africa and Australia*. Johannesburg: Konrad Adenauer Foundation Occasional Papers, 35.

181. Breytenbach, W. (2004). Land reform in southern Africa. In Hunter, J. (ed.), *Who should own the land? Analyses and views on land reform and the land question in Namibia and southern Africa*. Windhoek: Namibia Institute for Democracy, 46, 50.

182. Schuring, E. (2004). *History obliges: The real motivations behind German aid flows in the case of Namibia*. MA thesis (Law & Diplomacy), Fletcher School of Law and Diplomacy, Tufts University, 51.

183. Breytenbach, W. (2004). Land reform in southern Africa. In Hunter, J. (ed.), *Who should own the land? Analyses and views on land reform and the land question in Namibia and southern Africa*. Windhoek: Namibia Institute for Democracy, 46, 50.

184. Hunter, J. (2004). Who should own the land? An introduction. In Hunter, J. (ed.), *Who should own the land? Analyses and views on land reform and the land question in Namibia and southern Africa*. Windhoek: Namibia Institute for Democracy, 3. See also De Villiers, B. (2003). *Land reform: Issues and challenges. A comparative overview of experiences in Zimbabwe, Namibia, South Africa and Australia*. Johannesburg: Konrad Adenauer Foundation Occasional Papers, 35.

185. In 1989, SWAPO gained 57 percent of the votes, in 1994 it increased to 73 percent, and in 1999 its share of electoral support was 76 percent.

186. Pitswane, J. (1992). Namibia: Challenges of the first decade. In Benjamin, L. & Gregory, C. (eds.), *Southern Africa at the crossroads*? Rivonia: Justified Press, 114.

187. Werner, W. (2000). Agriculture and land. In Melber, H. (ed.), *Namibia: A decade of independence 1990–2000*. Windhoek: Namibian Economic Policy Research Unit (publication no. 7), 29–48.

188. Moyo, S. (2004). Socio-economic dominance of ethnic and racial groups—the African experience. *Human development Report, Occasional Paper 8*. United Nations Development Programme, 41. See also De Villiers, B. (2003). *Land reform: Issues and challenges. A comparative overview of experiences in Zimbabwe, Namibia, South Africa and Australia*. Johannesburg: Konrad Adenauer Foundation Occasional Papers, 33.

189. Human Sciences Research Council (2003). *Seeking ways out of the impasse on land reform in southern Africa*, 21.

190. IRIN Africa English reports, Namibia: *Threat of fine, prison sparks response from land owners*, October 5 2005.

191. Statement by United Democratic Front leader Justus Garoeb, cited in De Villiers, B. (2003). *Land reform: Issues and challenges. A comparative overview of experiences in Zimbabwe, Namibia, South Africa and Australia.* Johannesburg: Konrad Adenauer Foundation Occasional Papers, 36.

192. Rotberg, R.I. (1983). Political and economic realities in a time of settlement. In Rotberg, R.I. (ed.), *Namibia: Political and economic prospects*. Cape Town: David Phillip, 29–40, 37.

193. Katjavivi, P. (1989). *A history of resistance in Namibia*. Paris, London & Addis Ababa: UNESCO, 51.

194. Suzman, J. (2002). *Minorities in imperial Namibia*. London: Minority Rights Group International, 15.

195. Soggot, D. (1986). *Namibia: The violent heritage*. London: Rex Collings, 189.

196. Soggot, D. (1986). *Namibia: The violent heritage*. London: Rex Collings, 190.

197. Werner, W. (1998). *No-one will become rich: Economy and society in the Herero reserves in Namibia 1913–1946*. Basel: P. Schlettwein, 21.

198. Gewald J-B. (1999). *Herero heroes: A socio-political history of the Herero of Namibia 1890–1923*. Oxford: James Currey, 29.

199. Deckert, M.E. (1966). The causes of the Herero uprising of 1904–1906 in South West Africa. In Cordier, A.W. (ed.). *Columbia Essays in International Affairs*. New York: Columbia University Press 255, 260.

200. Resolution at the National Conference on Land Reform and the Land Question. (1991). Conference Brief, Windhoek. Cited in De Villiers, B. (2003). *Land reform: Issues and challenges. A comparative overview of experiences in Zimbabwe, Namibia, South Africa and Australia.* Johannesburg: Konrad Adenauer Foundation Occasional Papers, 33.

201. Hunter, J. (2004). Who should own the land? An introduction. In Hunter, J. (ed.), *Who should own the land? Analyses and views on land reform and the land question in Namibia and southern Africa*. Windhoek: Namibia Institute for Democracy, 3.

202. Malan, J.S. (1995). *Peoples of Namibia*. Pretoria: Rhino Publishers, 8.

203. Suzman, J. (2002). *Minorities in imperial Namibia*. London: Minority Rights Group International, 19.

204. Suzman, J. (2002). *Minorities in imperial Namibia*. London: Minority Rights Group International.

205. Maletsky, C. (March 31, 2005). Govt Ups the Pressure on 'Reluctant' Farmers. *The Namibian*.

206. Reparations Not on the Table. *The Namibian*, August 31, 2000.

207. Reparations Not on the Table. *The Namibian*, August 31, 2000.

208. Bensman, T. (March 18, 1999). Tribe Demands Holocaust Reparations; Germany's Genocidal War against Namibia's Herero Was Rehearsal for World War II Atrocities. *The Salt Lake Tribune*.

209. Bensman, T. (March 18, 1999). Tribe Demands Holocaust Reparations; Germany's Genocidal War against Namibia's Herero Was Rehearsal for World War II Atrocities. *The Salt Lake Tribune*.

210. Gewald, J-B. (2003). Herero genocide in the twentieth century: Politics and memory. In Abbink, J., De Bruijn, M. & Van Walraven, K. *Rethinking resistance: Revolt and violence in African history*. Leiden: Brill, 279–304.

211. Gewald, J-B. (2003). Herero genocide in the twentieth century: Politics and memory. In Abbink, J., De Bruijn, M. & Van Walraven, K. *Rethinking resistance: Revolt and violence in African history*. Leiden: Brill, 279–304.

212. Nujoma, S. (1986). Preface. In Dreschler, H. (1986). *Let us die fighting*. Berlin: Akademie-Verlag, vii.

213. See generally Bauer, G. (2001). Namibia in the first decade of independence: How democratic? *Journal of Southern African Studies*, *27*, 33–55.

214. Gewald, J-B. (2003). Herero genocide in the twentieth century: Politics and memory. In Abbink, J., De Bruijn, M. & Van Walraven, K. *Rethinking resistance: Revolt and violence in African history*. Leiden: Brill, 279–304.

215. Gewald, J-B. (2003). Herero genocide in the twentieth century: Politics and memory. In Abbink, J., De Bruijn, M. & Van Walraven, K. *Rethinking resistance: Revolt and violence in African history*. Leiden: Brill, 279–304.

216. The other Committee is the National Preparatory Committee for the Commemoration of 1904.

217. Dentlinger, L. (August 20, 2004). DTA Slams Govt over Recognition of Herero Chiefs. *Africa News Service*.

218. See generally Nujoma, S. (2001). *Where others wavered: The autobiography of Sam Nujoma*. London: Panaf Books. See also Saunders, C. (2003). Liberation and democracy: A critical reading of Sam Nujoma's 'autobiography', in Melber, H. (ed.), *Re-examining liberation in Namibia: Political cultures since independence*. Uppsala: Nordic Africa Institute, 87.

219. Amupadhi, T. (August 11, 2003). German Scouts Cancel Herero War Remembrance following Nujoma's Threat. *Africa News Service*.

220. Mumbuna, M. (September 16, 2004). Academics Dissect Herero Genocide. *Africa News Service*.

221. Riruako, K. Statement at the International Conference on the German-Herero War—one hundred years after Bremen. Germany (November 18–21).

222. Riruako, K. Statement at the International Conference on the German-Herero War—one hundred years after Bremen. Germany (November 18–21).

223. Riruako, K. Statement at the International Conference on the German-Herero War—one hundred years after Bremen. Germany (November 18–21).

224. Haelbich, E. (November 23, 2004). Herero Reconciliation in the Spotlight at Bremen Summit. *Africa News Service*.

225. A letter that appeared in the Namibian German newspaper *Allegemeine Zeitung* on February 11, 2005, (discussed below) read: Only a few selected people, who by even the most conservative definition of representativity could be said to have been a representative sample of the Ovaherero-Ovambanderu, were invited. Some who have been at the forefront of the centenary commemorations were for the most part ignored and only invited at the eleventh hour. Matundu-Tjiparuro, K. (February 11, 2005). An open letter to Professor Hinz and fellow verkrampte academics. *Allegemeine Zeitung*.

226. Gewald, J-B. & Silvester, J. (2003). *Words cannot be found. German colonial rule in Namibia: An annotated reprint of the 1918 Blue Book*. Leiden: Brill, xxxv.

227. Gewald, J-B. & Silvester, J. (2003). *Words cannot be found. German colonial rule in Namibia: An annotated reprint of the 1918 Blue Book*. Leiden: Brill, 101 fn 106.

228. See Botha, C. (2000). The politics of land settlement in Namibia, 1890–1960. *South African Historical Journal*, *42*, 232–276.

229. Pienaar, H. (August 27, 2005). A massacre no one seems to want to remember. *Weekend Argus.*

230. Pienaar, H. (August 27, 2005). A massacre no one seems to want to remember. *Weekend Argus.*

231. Becker, H. in Schuring, E. (2004). *History obliges: The real motivations behind German aid flows in the case of Namibia.* MA thesis (Law & Diplomacy), Fletcher School of Law and Diplomacy, Tufts University, 45.

232. See generally Collier, P. (1999). Aid dependency: A critique. *Journal of African Economies*, *8*, 528–545; and De Renzio, P. (2005). Can more aid be spent in Africa? *Opinions.* London: Overseas Development Institute, 30.

233. This was the official figure for 2003. United Nations Development Programme (2005). *Human Development Report*, 278.

234. United Nations Development Programme (2005). *Human Development Report*, 94.

235. United Nations Development Programme (2005). *Human Development Report*, 94.

236. Schuring, E. (2004). *History obliges: The real motivations behind German aid flows in the case of Namibia.* MA thesis (Law & Diplomacy), Fletcher School of Law and Diplomacy, Tufts University, 58.

237. 1) Egypt, 2) Zambia, 3) Tanzania, 4) Ethiopia, 5) Kenya, 6) Mozambique, 7) Cameroon, 8) Ghana, 9) Congo, 10) Morocco, 11) Mali, 12) Burkina Faso, 13) Zimbabwe, 14) Sudan, 15) Malawi, 16) South Africa, 17) Rwanda, 18) Benin, 19) Ivory Coast, 20) Uganda, 21) Senegal, 22) Niger, 23) Namibia, 24) Madagascar, 25) Guinea, 26) Togo, 27) Chad, 28) Somalia, 29) Burundi, 30) Mauritania. Schüring E. (2004). *History obliges: The real motivations behind German aid flows in the case of Namibia.* MA thesis (Law & Diplomacy), Fletcher School of Law and Diplomacy, Tufts University, 22.

238. 1) Egypt, 2) Zambia, 3) Ethiopia, 4) Mozambique, 5) Tanzania, 6) Kenya, 7) Ghana, 8) Cameroon, 9) Mali, 10) Congo, 11) Burkina Faso, 12) Malawi, 13) Uganda, 14) Zimbabwe, 15) Ivory Coast, 16) Rwanda, 17) South Africa, 18) Benin, 19) Morocco, 20) Namibia, 21) Senegal, 22) Niger, 23) Sudan, 24) Madagascar, 25) Chad, 26) Guinea, 27) Togo, 28) Burundi, 29) Nigeria, 30) Angola.

239. Schuring, E. (2004). *History obliges: The real motivations behind German aid flows in the case of Namibia.* MA thesis (Law & Diplomacy), Fletcher School of Law and Diplomacy, Tufts University, 22.

240. Schuring, E. (2004). *History obliges: The real motivations behind German aid flows in the case of Namibia.* MA thesis (Law & Diplomacy), Fletcher School of Law and Diplomacy, Tufts University, 23.

241. Schuring, E. (2004). *History obliges: The real motivations behind German aid flows in the case of Namibia.* MA thesis (Law & Diplomacy), Fletcher School of Law and Diplomacy, Tufts University, 62.

242. In the aforementioned letter to the Namibian *Allegemeine Zeitung*, Kae Matundu-Tjiparuro pointed out that "the millions of Euros to Namibia by no means blind some of us, as the German Federal Republic government would often sing, chorus-trumpeted by its envoys at every opportunity. These Euros are first in the best interest of Namibians of German descent. The country must remain peaceful and tranquil for their sake. Otherwise Germany may be faced with massive evacuations. Such peacefulness and tranquillity is only in the best interest of the landed. And there is no denying who are the most landed of the ill-gotten land. In the meantime the landless, among them my

people, must be pacified with aid crumbs." Matundu-Tjiparuro, K. (*Allegemeine Zeitung*, February 11, 2005). An open letter to Professor Hinz and fellow verkrampte academics.

CHAPTER 2

1. Shelton, D. (2004). The world of atonement reparations for historical injustices. *Miskolc Journal of International Law*, *1*, 259–289, 290.

2. Gasser, H-P. (2002). International humanitarian law and human rights law in non-international armed conflict: Joint venture or mutual exclusion. *German Yearbook of International Law*, *45*, 149–162, 155.

3. Marks, G.C. (1992). Indigenous peoples in international law: The significance of Francisco de Vitoria and Bartolome de las Casas. *Australian Year Book of International Law*, *13*, 1–51.

4. Scott, M. (1958). The international status of South West Africa, *International Affairs*, *34*, 318–329.

5. Gifford, A. (1993). The legal basis of the claim for reparations. Cited in Du Plessis, M. (2003). Historical injustice and international law: An exploratory discussion of reparation for slavery. *Human Rights Quarterly*, *25*, 624–659.

6. Van Bueren, G. It's Britain's guilty secret, *Guardian*, May 25, 2001. Cited in Du Plessis, M. (2003). Historical injustice and international law: An exploratory discussion of reparation for slavery. *Human Rights Quarterly*, *25*, 624–659.

7. Dinstein, Y. (1996). Crimes against humanity. In Makarczyk, J. (ed.), *Theory of international law at the threshold of the 21st century*. The Hague/Boston: Kluwer Law International, 891, 908. Cited in De Guzman, M.M. (2000). The road from Rome: The developing law of crimes against humanity. *Human Rights Quarterly*, *22*, 335–403, 337 fn 21.

8. See http://www.yale.edu/lawweb/avalon/lawofwar/hague02.htm.

9. Romano, C.P.R. (2002). International justice and developing countries: A quantitative analysis. *The Law and Practice of International Courts and Tribunals*, *1*, 367–399.

10. See Weeramantry, C.G. (2004). *Universalising international law*. Dordrecht: Martinus Nijhoff, 256.

11. Weeramantry, C.G. (2004). *Universalising international law*. Dordrecht: Martinus Nijhoff, 256. Judge Weeramantry also notes that "The Martens Clause has thus become an established and integral part of the corpus of customary international law [under any definition, no matter how narrow]. International law has long passed the stage when it could be debated whether such principles had crystallized into customary international law. No State would today repudiate any one of these principles."

12. Cassese, A. (2000). The Martens Clause: Half a loaf or simply pie in the sky? *European Journal of International Law*, *11*, 187–216.

13. Bassiouni, M.C. (1999). *Crimes against humanity in International Criminal Law* (2nd rev. ed.). Cambridge, MA: Kluwer Law International, 60–61.

14. Nelayeva, G. Development of treaties concerning punishment of individuals for unlawful acts of war committed by individuals in international law. Found at http://www.idebate.org/magazines/vol2issue3/058icc.pdf.

15. Pictet, J. (1985). *Development and principles of international humanitarian law*. Dordrecht/Geneva: Martinus Nijhoff & Henry Dunant Institute, 62. Cited in Ticehurst,

R. (1997). The Martens Clause and the laws of armed conflict. *International Review of the Red Cross, 317*, 125, 127.

16. Ticehurst, R. (1997). The Martens Clause and the laws of armed conflict. *International Review of the Red Cross, 317*, 125, 127.

17. Hague Convention No. II of 1899; *Convention [No. II] with respect to the laws and customs of war on land, with annex of regulations*, July 29, 1899, 32 Stat. 1803, 1 Bevans, C. (1968). *Treaties and other international agreements of the United States of America, 1776–1949*, 247.

18. See Weeramantry, C.G. (2004). *Universalising international law*. Dordrecht: Martinus Nijhoff, 16.

19. Weeramantry, C.G. (2004). *Universalising international law*. Dordrecht: Martinus Nijhoff, 18.

20. Weeramantry, C.G. (2004). *Universalising international law*. Dordrecht: Martinus Nijhoff, 18.

21. See definition of international law in Black's legal dictionary: Black, H.C. & Garner, B.A. (eds.) (2000). *Black's law dictionary* (abridged). St. Paul, MN: West Publishing.

22. ICJ Statute Art. 38.

23. See Harris, D. (2004). *Cases and materials in international law* (6th ed.). London: Sweet & Maxwell. See also Cassese, A. (2001). *International law*. Oxford: Oxford University Press.

24. Pustogarov, V. (1996). Fyodor Fyodorovich Martens (1845–1909): A humanist of modern times. *International Review of the Red Cross, 312*, 300–314.

25. ICJ Statute Art. 38 (1)(b); this definition has also been articulated as "constant and uniform usage, accepted as law." ICJ Asylum Case—*Columbia v Peru, ICJ Reports* 1950, 266.

26. See Simma, B. & Alston, P. (1988–1989). The sources of human rights law: Custom, *jus cogens*, and general principles. *Australian Year Book of International Law, 12*, 82.

27. Simma, B. & Alston, P. (1988–1989). The sources of human rights law: Custom, *jus cogens*, and general principles. *Australian Year Book of International Law, 12*, 83.

28. See Harris, D. (2004). *Cases and materials in international law* (6th ed.). London: Sweet & Maxwell, 12. See also Janis, M. (1988). *An introduction to international law*. Boston: Little Brown, 31–34.

29. See Roberts, A. (2001). Traditional and modern approaches to customary international law: A reconciliation. *American Journal of International Law, 95*, 757.

30. *Opinio juris* includes statements of state representatives, legal manuals such as military manuals, declarations made by states in the United Nations and in response to apparent breaches of international law by other states, and other types of written or uttered illustrations of a state government's attitude towards a legal principle of international law.

31. Roberts, A. (2001).Traditional and modern approaches to customary international law: A reconciliation. *American Journal of International Law, 95*, 757.

32. Brierly, J.L. (1944). *The outlook for international law*. Oxford: Clarendon Press, 5.

33. Schindler, D. (1982). Human rights and humanitarian law: Interrelationship of the laws. *American University Law Review, 31*, 935.

34. Allen, R.G., Cherniack, M. & Andreopoulos, G.J. (1996). Refining war: Civil wars and humanitarian controls. *Human Rights Quarterly, 18*, 747–781.

35. See Rodley, N.S. (1999). *The treatment of prisoners under international law* (2nd ed.). Oxford: Clarendon Press, 57.

36. Kastenberg, J. (2003–2004). The customary international law of war and combatant status: Does the current executive branch policy determination on unlawful combatant status for terrorists run afoul of international law, or is it just poor public relations? *Gonzaga Law Review*, 495, 508.

37. Best, G. (1980). *Humanity in warfare: The modern history of the international law of armed conflict*. New York: Columbia University Press, 60.

38. Dugard, J. (1998). Bridging the gap between human rights and humanitarian law: The punishment of offenders. *International Review of the Red Cross, 324*, 445–453.

39. Dugard, J. (1998). Bridging the gap between human rights and humanitarian law: The punishment of offenders. *International Review of the Red Cross, 324*, 445–453.

40. Dugard, J. (1998). Bridging the gap between human rights and humanitarian law: The punishment of offenders. *International Review of the Red Cross, 324*, 445–453.

41. Dugard, J. (1998). Bridging the gap between human rights and humanitarian law: The punishment of offenders. *International Review of the Red Cross, 324*, 445–453.

42. 1st Geneva Convention—*Amelioration of the condition of the wounded and sick members of Armed Forces in the field*; 2nd Geneva Convention—*Amelioration of the condition of the wounded and sick members of Armed Forces at sea*; 3rd Geneva Convention—*Treatment of prisoners of war*; 4th Geneva Convention—*Protection of civilian persons in time of war*.

43. 1st additional protocol—*Protection of victims of international armed conflicts*; 2nd additional protocol—*Protection of victims of non-international armed conflicts*.

44. German crimes in South West Africa: Official records revealing cruelties inflicted on natives under German colonial rule, vol xxvii. *New York Times current history: The European war*. New York: New York Times, 1920, 322.

45. Detter Delupis, I. (1988). *The law of war*. Cambridge: Cambridge University Press, 259.

46. Article 23 (b).

47. The *si omnes* provisions state that a treaty only applies to those who are party to it.

48. See Bassiouni, M. C (1999). Crimes against humanity. In Bassiouni, M.C. (ed.), *International criminal law, vol.1, crimes of war* (2nd ed.). Ardsley, New York: Transnational Publishers, 43.

49. See Sunga, L.S. (1992). *Individual responsibility in international law for serious human rights violations*. Dordrecht: Martinus Nijhoff. See also Menon, P.K. (1992). The international personality of individuals in international law: A broadening of the traditional doctrine. *Journal of Transnational Law and Policy, 1*, 151.

50. Dugard, J. (2000). *International law: A South African perspective*. Kenwyn: Juta, 1.

51. Cassese, A. (2001). *International law*. Oxford: Oxford University Press, 46.

52. Cassese, A. (2001). *International law*. Oxford: Oxford University Press, 67.

53. Cassese, A. (2001). *International law*. Oxford: Oxford University Press, 67.

54. See Plattner, D. (1992). Assistance to the civilian population: The development and present state of international humanitarian law. *International Review of the Red Cross, 288*, 246–263.

55. See Plattner, D. (1992). Assistance to the civilian population: The development and present state of international humanitarian law. *International Review of the Red Cross, 288*, 246–263.

56. See Plattner, D. (1992). Assistance to the civilian population: The development and present state of international humanitarian law. *International Review of the Red Cross, 288*, 246–263.

57. See generally Abplanalp, P. (1995). The international conferences of the Red Cross as a factor for the development of international humanitarian law and the cohesion of the International Red Cross and Red Crescent Movement. *International Review of the Red Cross, 308*, 520–549.

58. 1868 Declaration of St. Petersburg (prohibiting the use of certain projectiles in wartime).

59. Levie, H.S. (ed.) (1987). *The law of non-international armed conflict, protocol II to the 1949 Geneva Conventions*. Dordrecht: Martinus Nijhoff.

60. Green, L. (1999). International regulations of armed conflicts. In Bassiouni, M.C. (ed.), *International criminal law, Vol. 1, crimes of war* (2nd ed.). Ardsley, New York: Transnational Publishers, 355.

61. Van Dongen, Y. (1991). *The protection of civilian populations in time of armed conflict*. Groningen: Rijksuniversiteit Groningen, 22.

62. Bugnion, F. (2004).The role of the Red Cross in the development of international humanitarian law: The International Committee of the Red Cross and the development of international humanitarian law. *Chicago Journal of International Law, 5*, 191, 200.

63. The first Geneva Convention was signed by Baden, Belgium, Denmark, France, Hesse, Italy, Netherlands, Portugal, Prussia, Switzerland, and Wurtemberg. By 1906 it was signed and ratified by 48 states. Best, G. (1980). *Humanity in warfare: The modern history of the international law of armed conflict*. New York: Columbia University Press, 345, fns 34, 36. See Schindler, D. & Toman, J. (2004). *The laws of armed conflicts: A collection of conventions, resolutions, and other documents* (4th ed.). Leiden/Boston: Martinus Nijhoff, 205–206.

64. The Corfu Channel Case (Merits) 1949. *ICJ Reports* 4, 22.

65. The Corfu Channel Case (Merits) 1949. *ICJ Reports* 4, 22.

66. *Prosecutor v. Tadic*, No. IT-94-1-AR72, Appeal on jurisdiction at paragraph 141 (Oct. 2, 1995), 35 ILM 32.

67. Dugard, J. (1991). The treatment of rebels in conflicts of a disputed character: The Anglo-Boer War and the ANC-Boer War compared. In Delissen, A.J.M. & Tanja, G.J. (eds.). *Humanitarian law of armed conflict: Challenges ahead*. Dordrecht: Martinus Nijhoff, 447, 448.

68. Dugard, J. (1991). The treatment of rebels in conflicts of a disputed character: The Anglo-Boer War and the ANC-Boer War compared. In Delissen, A.J.M. & Tanja, G.J. (eds.). *Humanitarian law of armed conflict: Challenges ahead*. Dordrecht: Martinus Nijhoff, 447, 448.

69. Abi-Saab, G. (1984). The specificities of humanitarian law. In Swinarski, C. (ed.) *Studies and essays on international humanitarian law and Red Cross principles*. Dordrecht: Martinus Nijhoff, 265–280.

70. Provost, R. (2002). *International human rights and humanitarian law*. Cambridge: Cambridge University Press, 121.

71. Eide, A. (1984).The laws of war and human rights—differences and convergences. In Swinarski, C. (ed.) *Studies and essays on international humanitarian law and Red Cross principles*. Dordrecht: Martinus Nijhoff, 675–697.

72. Provost, R. (2002). *International human rights and humanitarian law*. Cambridge: Cambridge University Press, 137.

73. Shelton, D. (2005). *Remedies in international human rights law*. Oxford: Oxford University Press (2nd ed.), 97.

74. Baty, T. (1900). *International law in South Africa*. London: Stevens & Haynes, 79.

75. Von Glahn, G. (1992). *Law among nations: An introduction to public international law* (6th rev. ed.). New York: Macmillan, 696.

76. Baty, T. (1900). *International law in South Africa*. London: Stevens & Haynes, 79.

77. Hinz referring to Ipsen, K. (1999). *Völkerrecht: Ein Studienbuch* (4th ed.). München: C.H. Becksche Verlag, 1071.

78. Hinz, M. (2003). One hundred years later: Germany on trial in the USA—the Herero reparations claim for genocide. *Namibian Human Rights Online Journal, 1*. http://www.hrdc.unam.na/journal/V1_N1_Dec2003/Docs/Herero_case.doc.

79. Meron, T. (2000). The humanization of humanitarian law. *American Journal of International Law*, 239, 248.

80. McCoubrey, H. (1998). *International humanitarian law* (2nd ed.). Burlington, VT: Ashgate, 26.

81. Van Dongen, Y. (1991). *The protection of civilian populations in time of armed conflict*. Groningen: Rijksuniversiteit Groningen, 1.

82. Van Dongen, Y. (1991). *The protection of civilian populations in time of armed conflict*. Groningen: Rijksuniversiteit Groningen, fn 9, paragraph 2.3.

83. Doswald-Beck, L. & Vite, S. (1993). International humanitarian law and human rights law. *International Review of the Red Cross, 293*, 94–119.

84. Article 27 & 58.

85. Article 4. The word "humanity" is mentioned a few other times in the Code, but rather to signify humane conduct.

86. Goodman, D.P. (1985). The need for fundamental change in the law of belligerent occupation. *Stanford Law Review, 37*, 1573, 1577.

87. Kalshoven, F. (1987). *Constraints on the waging of war*. Dordrecht: Martinus Nijhoff, 19–20.

88. Van Dongen, Y. (1991). *The protection of civilian populations in time of armed conflict*. Groningen: Rijksuniversiteit Groningen, 21.

89. Green, L.C. (1996). Enforcement of the law in international and non-international conflicts: The way ahead. *Denver Journal of International Law and Policy*, 285, 297.

90. Bantekas, I. (2002). *Principles of direct and superior responsibility in international humanitarian law*. Manchester: Manchester University Press, 6. This conclusion is shared by Green: Green, L.C. (1998/1999). Cicero and Clausewitz or Quincy Wright: The interplay of law and war. *United States Air Force Academy Journal of Legal Studies, 9*, 12.

91. Green, L.C. (2000). *Contemporary law of armed conflict*. Manchester: Manchester University Press, 30.

92. Friedman, L. & Tiefenbrun, S. (eds.) (1999). *War crimes and war crimes tribunals: Past, present, and future*. Hempstead, NY: Hofstra University School of Law, 799–801.

93. Green, L.C. (1998/1999). Cicero and Clausewitz or Quincy Wright: The interplay of law and war. *United States Air Force Academy Journal of Legal Studies*, *9*, 12.

94. Van Dongen, Y. (1991). *The protection of civilian populations in time of armed conflict*. Groningen: Rijksuniversiteit Groningen, fn 9, paragraph 2.3.

95. Cited in Green, L.C. (1998/1999). Cicero and Clausewitz or Quincy Wright: The interplay of law and war. *United States Air Force Academy Journal of Legal Studies*, *9*, text following fn 125. See further on the humanity aspect, Roberge, M-C. (1997). Jurisdiction of the ad hoc tribunals for the former Yugoslavia and Rwanda over crimes against humanity and genocide. *International Review of the Red Cross*, *321*, 651–664.

96. Meron, T. (1997). Francis Lieber's code and principles of humanity. *Columbia Journal of Transnational Law*, *36*, 269, 279.

97. Cassese, A. (2000). The Martens Clause: Half a loaf or simply pie in the sky? *European Journal of International Law*, *11*, 187–216, 193.

98. Howard, M.E. (1967). The armed forces. In *The new Cambridge modern history XI: Material progress and worldwide problems 1870–1898*. Cambridge: Cambridge University Press, 204–242.

99. Found in Green, L.C. (1998/1999). Cicero and Clausewitz or Quincy Wright: The interplay of law and war. *United States Air Force Academy Journal of Legal Studies*, *9*, text following fn 126.

100. Green, L.C. (1998/1999). Cicero and Clausewitz or Quincy Wright: The interplay of law and war. *United States Air Force Academy Journal of Legal Studies*, *9*, 12.

101. Green, L.C. (1998/1999). Cicero and Clausewitz or Quincy Wright: The interplay of law and war. *United States Air Force Academy Journal of Legal Studies*, *9*, 12. Quoting from Schindler, D. & Toman, J. (1988). *The laws of armed conflict*. Boston: Martinus Nijhoff, 36.

102. See Stephens, D. (2001). Human rights and armed conflict—the advisory opinion of the International Court of Justice in the Nuclear Weapons Case. *Yale Human Rights and Development Law Journal*, *4*, 8.

103. Legality of the threat or use of nuclear weapons. Advisory opinion of July 8, 1996. *ICJ Reports*, paragraph 75.

104. Doty, G. (1998). The US and the development of the laws of land warfare. *Military Law Review*, *156*, 224, 241. Quoting the US Department of State (1998). *Papers Relating to the Foreign Relations of the US*.

105. Davis, G. (1907). Lieber's instructions for the government of armies in the field. *American Journal of International Law*, *1*, 13.

106. See Scott, J.B. (1909). *The Hague Peace Conferences of 1899 and 1907*. Baltimore, MD: Johns Hopkins, 525–527. See also Baxter, R.R. (1963). The first modern codification of the law of war—Francis Lieber and general orders no. 100 (II). *International Review of the Red Cross*, *3*, 234.

107. Paust, J.J. (2001). Dr. Francis Lieber and the Lieber Code. *American Society International Law Proceedings*, April 4–7, *95*, 112, 113.

108. Paust, J.J. (2001). Dr. Francis Lieber and the Lieber Code. *American Society International Law Proceedings*, April 4–7, *95*, 112, 113.

109. *Law and customs of war on land* (Hague, II), July 29, 1899, 32 Stat. 1803, T.S. No. 403. Reprinted in 1 Bevans, C. (1968). *Treaties and other international agreements of the United States of America 1776–1949*, 247.

110. Pustogarov, V. (1996). Fyodor Fyodorovich Martens (1845–1909): A humanist of modern times. *International Review of the Red Cross*, *312*, 300, 310.

111. Security Council Resolution 1483, paragraph 5 (May 22, 2003).

112. Lieber Code, Article 22.

113. Lieber Code, Article 23.

114. Lieber Code, Article 25.

115. *Convention (II) with respect to the laws and customs of war on land and its annex: Regulations concerning the laws and customs of war on land.* The Hague, July 29, 1899.

116. Hinz, M. (2003). One hundred years later: Germany on trial in the USA—the Herero reparations claim for genocide. *Namibian Human Rights Online Journal*, *1*, 1, 4. http://www.hrdc.unam.na/journal/V1_N1_Dec2003/Docs/Herero_case.doc.

117. See further Schindler D. & Toman, J. (1981). *The laws of armed conflicts: A collection of conventions, resolutions and other documents.* Alphen aan den Rijn: Sijthoff & Noordhoff.

118. Shelton, D. (2004). The world of atonement reparations for historical injustices. *Miskolc Journal of International Law*, *1*, 259–289.

119. Harring. S.L. (2002). German reparations to the Herero nation: An assertion of Herero nationhood in the path of Namibian development? *West Virginia Law Review*, 393, 407.

120. Doswald-Beck, L. & Vite, S. (1993). International humanitarian law and human rights law. *International Review of the Red Cross*, *293*, 94–119.

121. Draper, G.I.A.D. (1971). The relationship between the human rights regime and the law of the armed conflicts. *Israel Yearbook on Human Rights*, 191–207.

122. Farer, T.J. (1971). The laws of war 25 years after Nuremberg. *International Conciliation*. Carnegie Endowment for International Peace, *585*, 9.

123. Goldstone, R.J. (2004). International human rights and criminal justice in the first decade of the 21st century. *Human Rights Brief*, *11*, 3.

124. See Chapter 3.

125. Drost, P.N. (1965). *Human rights as legal rights*. Leiden: A.W. Sijthoff, 17.

126. Greppi, E. (1999).The evolution of individual criminal responsibility under international law. *International Review of the Red Cross*, *835*, 531–553.

127. See Fleck, D. (ed.) (1995). *The handbook of humanitarian law in armed conflicts*. New York: Oxford University Press.

128. Shaw, M.N. (2003). *International law* (5th ed.). Cambridge: Cambridge University Press, 234.

129. Farer, T.J. (1971). The laws of war 25 years after Nuremberg. *International Conciliation*. Carnegie Endowment for International Peace, *585*, 10.

130. Farer, T.J. (1971). The laws of war 25 years after Nuremberg. *International Conciliation*. Carnegie Endowment for International Peace, *585*, 10.

131. Draper, G.I.A.D. (1971). The relationship between the human rights regime and the law of the armed conflicts. *Israel Yearbook on Human Rights*, 191–207.

132. Anderson, R. (2005). Redressing colonial genocide under international law: The Hereros' cause of action against Germany. *California Law Review*, 1155, 1169.

133. General Act of the Conference of Berlin, February 26, 1885.

134. General Act of the Brussels Conference, July 2, 1890.

135. Anderson, R. (2005). Redressing colonial genocide under international law: The Hereros' cause of action against Germany. *California Law Review*, 1155, 1174.

136. Jackson, R.H. (1945). Report to the President by Mr. Justice Jackson, June 6, 1945 (released to the public June 7, 1945), *Department State Bulletin*, *12*, 1071, 1076. Reprinted in the report of Robert H. Jackson, United States Representative to the International Conference on Military Trials, London, 1945, at 42, 50 (reprint 1971) (1949). Cited in Farer, T.J. (2000). Restraining the barbarians: Can international criminal law help? *Human Rights Quarterly*, *22*, 90–117.

137. Paust, J. (1995). Threats to accountability after Nuremberg: Crimes against humanity, leader responsibility and national fora. *New York Law School Journal of Human Rights*, *12*, 545.

138. *Prosecutor v. Jean-Paul Akayesu*, Case No. ICTR-96-4-T, Judgment, Trial Chamber 1, Sept. 2, (1998), paragraph 565.

139. Swaak-Goldman, O. (2000). Crimes against humanity. In McDonald, G.K. & Swaak-Goldman, O. (eds.). *Substantive and procedural aspects of international criminal law: The experience of international and national courts*, *Vol. I*. The Hague/London/Boston: Kluwer Law International, 143–168.

140. Sieghart, P. (1983). *The international law of human rights*. Oxford: Clarendon Press, 13.

141. Many others concur that the roots of human rights and humanitarian law are much older indeed. Judge Weermantry, for example, in his dissent in the ICJ *Nuclear Weapons* case finds that "It greatly strengthens the concept of humanitarian laws of war to note that this is not a recent invention, nor the product of any one culture. The concept is of ancient origin, with a lineage stretching back at least three millennia.... It is against such a varied cultural background that these questions must be considered and not merely as though they are a new sentiment invented in the 19th century and so slenderly rooted in universal tradition that they may be lightly overridden." Dissenting Opinion, Judge Weeramantry, in Legality of the Threat or Use of Nuclear Weapons, Advisory Opinion, July 8, 1996, *ICJ Reports*, *226*.

142. Jorgensen, N.H.B. (2000). *The responsibility of the states for international crime*. Oxford: Oxford University Press, 123. See further Gross, L. (1948). The peace of Westphalia, 1648–1948. *American Journal of International Law*, *42*, 20.

143. Scott, J.B. (1934). *The Spanish origin of international law—Francisco de Vitoria and his law of nations*. London: Humphrey Milford, App. F, cxxiv. Cited in Green, L.C. (1998/1999). Cicero and Clausewitz or Quincy Wright: The interplay of law and war. *United States Air Force Academy Journal of Legal Studies, 9*, 59, 60. Green cites many examples indicating the origins and situations in which these norms were stated and upheld.

144. Schwarzenberger, G. (1947). The judgment of Nuremberg, *Tulane Law Review*, *21*, 329, 330. Also in McCormack, T.L.H. (1997). Selective reaction to atrocity: War crimes and the development of international criminal law. *Albany Law Review*, *60*, 681.

145. Neier, A. (1998). War crimes: Brutality, genocide, terror and the struggle for justice. *New York Times Books*, 12. See further Bassiouni, M.C. (1991). The time has come for an international criminal court. *Indiana International & Comparative Law Review*, *1*, 1. See also Schwarzenberger, G. (1968). *International law as applied by international courts and tribunals*, *Vol. II: The law of armed conflict*. London: Stevens, 15.

146. Greppi, E. (1999). The evolution of individual criminal responsibility under international law. *International Review of the Red Cross*, *835*, 531–553.

147. Dugard, J. (1998). Bridging the gap between human rights and humanitarian law: The punishment of offenders. *International Review of the Red Cross*, *324*, 445–453.

148. Ögren, K. (1996). Humanitarian law in the articles of war decreed in 1621 by King Gustavus II Adolphus of Sweden. *International Review of the Red Cross, 313*, 438.

149. Glauner, L. (2002). The need for accountability and reparation: 1830–1976. The United States Government's role in the promotion, implementation, and execution of the crime of genocide against Native Americans. *Depaul Law Review, 51*, 911, 919. See Also Gross, L. (1948). The Peace of Westphalia, 1648–1948. *American Journal of International Law, 42*, 20.

150. Drost, P. N. (1951). *Human rights as legal rights*. Leiden: A.W. Sijthoff, 16.

151. 1868 Declaration of St. Petersburg (prohibiting the use of certain projectiles in wartime).

152. 1868 Declaration of St. Petersburg (prohibiting the use of certain projectiles in wartime).

153. Journals of the Continental Congress—Declaration by the Representative of the United Colonies of North America, Now Meeting in General Congress at Philadelphia, Setting Forth the Causes and Necessity of Their Taking Up Arms (July 6, 1775).

154. Orentlicher, D. (1998). The law of universal conscience: Genocide and crimes against humanity. Paper presented at the Committee on Conscience conference *Genocide and crimes against humanity: Early warning and prevention*, at the United States Holocaust Memorial Museum. http://www.ushmm.org/conscience/events/conference_98/orentlicher.pdf. Cited in Olusanya, O. (2004). *Double jeopardy: Without parameters*. Antwerp: Intersentia, 44.

155. Lauren, P.G. (1998). *The evolution of international human rights*. Philadelphia: University of Pennsylvania Press, 66.

156. Jones, J.R.W.D. (1998). *The practise of the international criminal tribunals for the former Yugoslavia and Rwanda*. Irvington-on-Hudson, NY: Transnational Publishers, 49.

157. Lauren, P.G. (1998). *The evolution of international human rights*. Philadelphia: University of Pennsylvania Press, 66.

158. Lauren, P.G. (1998). *The evolution of international human rights*. Philadelphia: University of Pennsylvania Press, 66.

159. Gladstone, W. (1877). *Lessons of the massacre*. London: Murray, 77–79. Cited in Lauren, P.G. (1998). *The evolution of international human rights*. Philadelphia: University of Pennsylvania Press, 67.

160. Lauren, P.G. (1998). *The evolution of international human rights*. Philadelphia: University of Pennsylvania Press, 75.

161. Cassese, A. (2000). The Martens Clause: Half a loaf or simply pie in the sky? *European Journal of International Law, 11*, 187–216, 188.

162. Meron, T. (2000). The Martens Clause, principles of humanity, and dictates of public conscience. *American Journal of International Law, 94*, 78, 79.

163. Kwakwa, E. (1992). *The international law of armed conflict: Personal and material fields of application*. Dordrecht: Kluwer Academic, 36.

164. De Guzman, M.M. (2000). The road from Rome: The developing law of crime against humanity. *Human Rights Quarterly, 22*, 335–403, 344.

165. Ticehurst, R. (1997). The Martens Clause and the laws of armed conflict. *International Review of the Red Cross, 317*, 125, 127.

166. Orentlicher, D. (1998). The law of universal conscience: Genocide and crimes against humanity. Paper presented at the Committee on Conscience conference *Genocide and crimes against humanity: Early warning and prevention*, at the United States

Holocaust Memorial Museum. http://www.ushmm.org/conscience/events/conference_98/orentlicher.pdf. Cited in Olusanya, O. (2004). *Double jeopardy: Without parameters.* Antwerp: Intersentia, 45.

167. Cassese, A. (2000). The Martens Clause: Half a loaf or simply pie in the sky? *European Journal of International Law, 11*, 187–216.

168. Cassese, A. (2000). The Martens Clause: Half a loaf or simply pie in the sky? *European Journal of International Law, 11*, 187–216.

169. Ticehurst, R. (1997). The Martens Clause and the laws of armed conflict. *International Review of the Red Cross, 317*, 125, 127.

170. Shamsey, J. (2002). Comment: 80 years too late: The international criminal court and the 20th century's first genocide. *Journal of Transnational Law & Policy, 11*, 327, 369.

171. Cooper, B. (ed.) (1999). *War crimes: The legacy of Nuremberg.* New York: TV Books, 57.

172. Cited in Schwelb, E. (1946). Crimes against humanity. *British Yearbook of International Law, 23*, 178, 180.

173. Glauner, L. (2002). The need for accountability and reparation: 1830–1976. The United States Government's role in the promotion, implementation, and execution of the crime of genocide against Native Americans. *Depaul Law Review, 51*, 911, 920.

174. Hill, D.J. (1917). The rights of the civil population in territory occupied by a belligerent. *American Journal of International Law, 11*, 133–137.

175. Van Dongen, Y. (1991). *The protection of civilian populations in time of armed conflict.* Groningen: Rijksuniversiteit Groningen, paragraph 3.3.

176. Dadrian, V.N. (1998). The Armenian genocide and the legal and political issues in the failure to prevent or to punish the crime. *University of West Los Angeles Law Review, 29*, 43, 57. Also cited in Shamsey, J. (2002). Comment: 80 years too late: The international criminal court and the 20th century's first genocide. *Journal of Transnational Law & Policy, 11*, 327, 370.

177. Allen, C.A. (1989). Civilian starvation and relief during armed conflict: The modern humanitarian law. *Georgia Journal of International and Comparative Law, 1*, 16.

178. See Cassese, A. (2000). The Martens Clause: Half a loaf or simply pie in the sky? *European Journal of International Law, 11*, 187–216.

179. Dissenting Opinion of Judge Weeramantry. Legality of the threat or use of nuclear weapons. Advisory opinion of July 8, 1996. *ICJ Reports*, 41.

180. Cassese, A. (2000). The Martens Clause: Half a loaf or simply pie in the sky? *European Journal of International Law, 11*, 187–216.

181. Ticehurst, R. (1997). The Martens Clause and the laws of armed conflict. *International Review of the Red Cross, 317*, 125, 130.

182. Another citation is the *United States of America v. Alfred Krupp von Bohlen und Halbach* (The Krupp Trial), *Law Reports of the War Commission, 10*, 69, 1949.

183. Paragraphs 78, 84, and 87.

184. Paragraph 84.

185. Cassese, A. (2000). The Martens Clause: Half a loaf or simply pie in the sky? *European Journal of International Law, 11*, 187–216, 206.

186. Legality of the threat or use of nuclear weapons. Advisory opinion of July 8, 1996. *ICJ Reports* 226, 406. (Shahabuddeen, J., dissenting).

187. Meron, T. (2000). The Martens Clause, principles of humanity, and dictates of public conscience. *American Journal of International Law*, *94*, 78.

188. Ticehurst, R. (1997). The Martens Clause and the laws of armed conflict. *International Review of the Red Cross*, *317*, 125, 126.

189. Ticehurst, R. (1997). The Martens Clause and the laws of armed conflict. *International Review of the Red Cross*, *317*, 125, 126.

190. Paragraph 525.

191. Paragraph 527.

192. Case IT-95-11-R61 Case IT-95-11-R61, *Prosecutor v. Milan Martic*, March 8, 1996. The tribunal consisted of Judges Jorda (presiding), Odio-Benito and Fouad Riad.

193. Allen, C.A. (1989). Civilian starvation and relief during armed conflict: The modern humanitarian law. *Georgia Journal of International and Comparative Law*, *1*, 19.

194. In *United States of America v. Alfred Krupp von Bohlen und Halbach* (The Krupp Trial), *Law Reports of the War Commission*, *10*, 69, 1949.

195. The Corfu Channel case (Merits) 1949. *ICJ Reports* 4, 22.

196. The Corfu Channel case (Merits) 1949. *ICJ Reports* 4, 22.

197. Bassiouni, M.C. (1999). *Crimes against humanity in International Criminal Law* (2nd rev ed.). Cambridge, MA: Kluwer Law International, 48.

198. Woolsey, T.S. (1891). *Introduction to the study of international law* (6th edition). New York: Charles Scribner's sons, 23.

199. Shelton, D. (2004). The world of atonement reparations for historical injustices. *Miskolc Journal of International Law*, *1*, 259–289, 270 fn 78.

200. Roosevelt, T. (1904). State of the Union Message, December 6. http://www.theodore-roosevelt.com/sotu4.html.

201. Kuper, L. (1981). *Genocide: Its political use in the twentieth century*. New Haven, CT: Yale University Press, 20. Cited in Churchill, W. (2000). Defining the unthinkable: Towards a viable understanding of genocide. *Oregon Review of International Law* 3, 8–9.

202. Stoecker, H. & Sebald, P. (1987). Enemies of the colonial idea. In Knoll, A.J. & Gann, L.H. (eds.), *Germans in the tropics: Essays in German colonial history* (2nd ed.). New York/London: Greenwood Press, 59–72, 64.

203. Cited in Hempenstall, P. (1987). The neglected empire: The superstructure of the colonial state in the German Melanesia. In Knoll, A.J. & Gann, L.H. (eds.), *Germans in the tropics: Essays in German colonial history* (2nd ed.). New York/London: Greenwood Press, 93.

204. Fenrick, W.J. (1999). Should crimes against humanity replace war crimes? *Columbia Journal of Transnational Law*, *37*, 767.

205. Report of the International Commission to Inquire into the Causes and Conduct of the Balkan Wars, Washington 1914.

206. Shamsey, J. (2002). Comment: 80 years too late: The international criminal court and the 20th century's first genocide. *Journal of Transnational Law & Policy*, *11*, 327, 369.

207. Bassiouni, M.C. (1991). The time has come for an international criminal court. *Indiana International and Comparative Law Review*, *1*, 1.

208. Howard, M.E. (1967). The armed forces. In Hinsley, F. (ed.). *The new Cambridge modern history XI: Material progress and worldwide problems 1870–1898*. Cambridge: Cambridge University Press, 204–242.

209. Bassiouni, M.C. (1999). Crimes against humanity. In Bassiouni, M.C. (ed.), *International criminal law, Vol. 1, crimes of war* (2nd ed.). Ardsley, New York: Transnational Publishers, 48.

210. *Control Council Law No. 10* of 1945. Punishment of persons guilty of war crimes, crimes against peace and against humanity, December 20, 1945. *Official Gazette Control Council for Germany*, *3*, 50–55 (1946).

211. Swaak-Goldman, O. (2000). Crimes against humanity. In McDonald, G.K. & Swaak-Goldman, O. (eds.). *Substantive and procedural aspects of international criminal law: The experience of international and national courts, Vol. I*. The Hague/London/Boston: Kluwer Law International, 152.

212. On what constitutes a civilian population, see Fenrick, W.J. (1997). Attacking the enemy civilian as a punishable offence. *Duke Journal of Comparative & International Law*, *7*, 539–570.

213. Bridgman, J. (1981). *The revolt of the Hereros*. Los Angeles: University of California Press, 115.

214. *Prosecutor v. Mskic, Radic and Sljivancanin*, Review of the Indictment Pursuant to Rule 61 of the Rules of Procedure and Evidence, ICTY Case No. IT-95-13-R61, Trial Chamber 1, April 3, 1996, paragraph 29.

215. *Prosecutor v. Dusko Tadic a.k.a. Dule* Case No. IT-94-1-T, May 7, 1997 (ICTY Trial Chamber), paragraph 638.

216. *Prosecutor v. Tadic* Case No. IT-94-1, April 26, 2000, paragraph 15.

217. Decision on the Defence Motion for Interlocutory Appeal on Jurisdiction, *Prosecutor v. Tadic*, Case No. IT-94-1-T, App. Ch., paragraph 141 (ICTY October 2, 1995).

218. Dugard, J. (1998). Bridging the gap between human rights and humanitarian law: The punishment of offenders. *International Review of the Red Cross*, *324*, 445–453.

219. See for example Chigas, G. (2000). The politics of defining justice after the Cambodian genocide. *Journal of Genocide Research*, *2*, 245–265.

220. Churchill, W. (2000). Defining the unthinkable: Towards a viable understanding of genocide. *Oregon Review of International Law*, 3, 3.

221. See the decision of the International Court of Justice *Application of the Convention on the Prevention and Punishment of the Crime of Genocide* (*Bosnia and Herzegovina v. Yugoslavia* (Serbia and Montenegro), Further Requests for the Indication of Provisional Measures, September 13, 1993. *ICJ Reports*, 325. See also Cassese, A. (2003). *International criminal law*. Oxford: Oxford University Press, 98.

222. Rome Statute of the International Criminal Court, UN Diplomatic Conference of Plenipotentiaries on the Establishment of an International Criminal Court, UN Doc. A/CONF. 183/9 (1998).

223. See, for example, Knoops, G-J. (2003). *An introduction to the law of international criminal tribunals*. Ardsley: Transnational Publishers, 24.

224. Schabas, W. (2000). Groups protected by the Genocide Convention: Conflicting interpretations from the International Criminal Tribunal for Rwanda. *ILSA Journal of International & Comparative Law*, *6*, 375, 386.

225. See, for example, Van Schaack, B. (1997). The crime of political genocide: Repairing the Genocide Convention's blind spot. *Yale Law Journal*, *106*, 2259–2291.

226. Drost, P.N. (1959). *Crime of State Book II: Genocide*. Leiden: A.W. Sijthoff, 52.

227. United Nations Economic and Social Council Commission on Human Rights Sub-Commission on Prevention of Discrimination and Protection of Minorities,

Thirty-Eighth Session, Item 4 of the Provisional Agenda, E/Cn.4/Sub.2/1985/6, July 2, 1985. Review of Further Developments in Fields with which the Sub-Commission has Been Concerned. Revised and Updated Report on the Question of the Prevention and Punishment of the Crime of Genocide Prepared by Mr. B. Whitaker. (E/CN.4/Sub.2/416), paragraph 24.

228. *Prosecutor v Jean-Paul Akayesu*, Case No. ICTR-96-4-T (ICTR Trial Chamber Sep. 2, 1998), paragraph 513.

229. *Prosecutor v Jean-Paul Akayesu*, Case No. ICTR-96-4-T (ICTR Trial Chamber Sep. 2, 1998), paragraph 515.

230. *Prosecutor v Jean-Paul Akayesu*, Case No. ICTR-96-4-T (ICTR Trial Chamber Sep. 2, 1998), paragraph 512.

231. *Prosecutor v Jean-Paul Akayesu*, Case No. ICTR-96-4-T (ICTR Trial Chamber Sep. 2, 1998), paragraph 514.

232. Article 2.

233. Article 4.

234. Article 6.

235. Greenawalt, A.K.A. (1999). Rethinking genocidal intent: The case for a knowledge-based interpretation. *Columbia Law Review*, *99*, 2259.

236. *Prosecutor v Jean-Paul Akayesu*, Case No. ICTR-96-4-T, Judgment, Trial Chamber 1 (Sep. 2, 1998), paragraph 498.

237. Boyajian, L.Z. & Grigorian, H.M. (1998). Reflections on the denial of the Armenian genocide. *The Psychoanalytic Review*, *85*, 505.

238. See Amann, D.M. (1999). *Prosecutor v Akayesu*—Judgment by International Criminal Tribunal for Rwanda on charges of genocide and international crimes of sexual violence. *American Journal of International Law*, *93*, 195.

239. *Prosecutor v Jean-Paul Akayesu*, Case No. ICTR-96-4-T, Judgement, September 2, 1998, paragraph 521.

240. Paragraph 172.

241. Report of the International Law Commission on the Work of Its Forty-Eighth Session, May 6 to 26 July 26, 1996, G.A.O.R., 51st session, Supplement No. 10 (A/51/10) 89.

242. *Prosecutor v Jelisic*, Case No. IT-95-10A, Judgement, paragraph 82.

243. *Prosecutor v Jean-Paul Akayesu*, Case No. ICTR-96-4-T, Judgement, September 2, 1998, paragraph 497.

244. Simon, T.W. (1996). Defining genocide. *Wisconsin Law Journal*, *15*, 243, 247.

245. Fein, H. (1994). Genocide, terror, life integrity, and war crimes: The case for discrimination. In Andreopoulos, G.J. (ed.), *Genocide: Conceptual and historical dimensions*. Philadelphia: University of Pennsylvania Press, 97.

246. International Criminal Tribunal for the former Yugoslavia, Decision of Trial Chamber 1, *Radovan Karadzic*, *Ratko Mladic* case (Cases Nos. IT-95-5-R61 and IT-95-18-R61); Consideration of the Indictment within the Framework of Rule 61 of the Rules of Procedure and Evidence, paragraph 94–95.

247. Steinmetz, G. (2005). From 'Native Policy' to exterminationism: German Southwest Africa, 1904. In *Comparative Perspective, Theory and Research in Comparative Social Analysis, Paper 30*, 4–5. Los Angeles: Department of Sociology, UCLA, 1. http://repositories.cdlib.org/cgi/viewcontent.cgi?article=1036&context=uclasoc.

248. *Sikirica* Judgement on Defence Motions to Acquit, paragraph 65.

249. *Prosecutor v Radislav Krstić*, Case No. IT-98-33-T (ICTY Appeal Chambers, April 19, 2004), paragraph 8.

250. Schabas, W.A. (2000). *Genocide in international law*. Cambridge: Cambridge University Press, 444.

251. ICTY Appeals Chamber: *Prosecutor v. Dusko Tadic*, Case No. IT-94-1-A (July 15, 1999), paragraph 145 (emphasis in original).

252. Case IT-94-1, (1999) ILM, Vol. 38, 1518; See paragraph 117.

253. *Legality of Use of Force (Yugoslavia v Belgium et al.)*. Request for the Indication of Provisional Measures, Order, June 2, 1999, paragraph 39.

254. Schabas, W.A. (2000). *Genocide in international law*. Cambridge: Cambridge University Press, 444.

255. Application of the Convention on the Prevention and Punishment of the Crime of Genocide (Bosnia and Herzegovina v. Serbia and Montenegro), ICJ, 26 February 2007.

256. Paragraph 173.

257. Paragraph 401.

258. Smith, R.W. (1999). State power and genocidal intent: On the uses of genocide in the twentieth century. In Chorbajian, L. & Shirinian, G. (eds.). *Studies in comparative genocide*. New York: St Martin's Press, 3–14, 4.

259. *Prosecutor v Jelisic*, Case No IT-95-10A, Judgement (Appeals Chamber), July 5, 2001, paragraph 47.

260. *Prosecutor v Akayesu*, Case No. ICTR-96-4-T (1998).

261. *Prosecutor v Kayishema and Ruzindana*, Case No. ICTR-95-1, ICTR T. Ch. II, May 21, 1999, paragraph 175, quoting *Prosecutor v Alfred Musema*, Case No. ICTR-96-13-T, paragraph 631.

262. *Akayesu*, Case No. ICTR-96-4-T.

263. See further Baade, H. (1961). 'The Eichmann Case': Some procedural legal aspects. *Duke Law Journal*, 400, 418.

264. *Attorney General of the Government of Israel v Eichmann*, 36 *Israel Law Reports*, 5. Cited in Ratner, S. & Abrams, J. (1997). *Accountability for human rights atrocities in international law*. Oxford: Oxford University Press, 28.

265. Berat, L. (1993). Genocide: The Namibian case against Germany. *Pace International Law Review*, *5*, 165, 210.

266. Hochschild, A. (1999). *King Leopold's ghost—a story of greed, terror and heroism in colonial Africa*. New York: Houghton Mifflin, 281.

267. Weitz, E.D. (2003). *A century of genocide: Utopias of race and nation*. Princeton, NJ: Princeton University Press.

268. Smith, R.W. (1999). State power and genocidal intent: On the uses of genocide in the twentieth century. In Chorbajian, L. & Shirinian, G. (eds.), *Studies in comparative genocide*. New York: St. Martin's Press, 3–14.

269. Berat, L. (1993). Genocide: The Namibian case against Germany. *Pace International Law Review*, *5*, 165, 202.

270. Schaller, D. J. (2005). Raphael Lemkin's view of European colonial rule in Africa: Between condemnation and admiration. *Journal of Genocide Research*, *7*, 531–538.

271. Lemkin, R. (undated). Untitled and unpublished manuscript dealing with the Herero, found at the Jacob Rader Marcus Center of the American Jewish archives Cincinnati; the Raphael Lemkin Papers, Box 6, Folder 12.

272. Lemkin, R. (1944). *Axis rule in occupied Europe: Laws of occupation—analysis of government—proposals for redress*. Washington D.C.: Carnegie Endowment for International Peace, 90.

273. Lemkin, R. (undated). Untitled and unpublished manuscript dealing with the Herero found at the Jacob Rader Marcus Center of the American Jewish archives Cincinnati; the Raphael Lemkin Papers, Box 6, Folder 12, p. 16.

274. Greenawalt, A.K.A. (1999). Rethinking genocidal intent: The case for a knowledge-based interpretation. *Columbia Law Review*, *99*, 2259, 2293.

275. Kriangsak, K. (2001). *International criminal law*. New York: Oxford University Press, 68.

276. Lippman, M. (1994). The 1948 Convention on the Prevention and Punishment of the Crime of Genocide: Forty-five years later. *Temple International & Comparative Law Journal, 8*, 1, 11–13. See also Gellately and Kiernan who consider genocide an "aggravated crime against humanity." Gellately, R. & Kiernan, B. (2003). The study of mass murder and genocide. In Gellately, R. & Kiernan, B. (eds.), The specter of genocide mass murder in historical perspective. Cambridge: Cambridge University Press, 14.

277. Stoett, P. (2004). Shades of complicity: Towards a typology of transnational crimes against humanity. In Jones, A. (ed.), *Genocide, war crimes, and the West*. London: Zed Books, 31–55.

278. Schabas, W. A. (2003). National courts finally begin to prosecute genocide, the 'crime of crimes'. *Journal of International Criminal Justice*, *1*, 39–63, fn 73.

279. Meron, T. (1995). International criminalization of internal atrocities. *American Journal of International Law*, *89*, 554, 558.

280. *Prosecutor v Kayishema*, Case No. ICTR-95-1-T, Judgement, (International Criminal Tribunal Rwanda, Trial Chamber II, May 21, 1999), paragraph 89.

281. Schabas, W.A. (2003). National courts finally begin to prosecute genocide, the 'crime of crimes.' *Journal of International Criminal Justice*, *1*, 39–63.

282. Schabas, W.A. (2001). *Problems of international codification—were the atrocities in Cambodia and Kosovo genocide? New England Law Review*, *35*, 287–320, 299.

283. *Prosecutor v. Zoran Kupreskic and Others*, Case No. IT-95-16-A, January 14, 2000 (ICTY Trial Chamber 11), paragraph 636.

284. *Prosecutor v Dusko Tadic a.k.a. Dule*, Case No. IT-94-1-T, May 7, 1997 (ICTY Trial Chamber), paragraph 8.

285. *Prosecutor v Dusko Sikirica, Damir Dosen and Dragan Kolundzija* It-95-8 Keraterm Camp September 3, 2001; Judgement on Defence Motions to Acquit, paragraph 58.

286. Frulli, M. (2001). Are crimes against humanity more serious than war crimes? *European Journal of International Law*, *12*, 329.

287. Green, L.C. (1997–1998). 'Grave breaches' or crimes against humanity? *U.S.A.F. Academic Journal of Legal Studies*, *8*, 19, 29. Cited in Schabas, W.A. (2003). National courts finally begin to prosecute genocide, the 'crime of crimes'. *Journal of International Criminal Justice*, *1*, 39–63, fn 73.

288. Sartre, J-P., in Schabas, W.A. (2000). *Genocide in international law*. Cambridge: Cambridge University Press, 1.

289. Kelly, M. J. (2002). Can sovereigns be brought to justice? The crime of genocide's evolution and the meaning of the Milosevic trial. *Saint John's Law Review*, 257, 263. See also Meron, T. (1992). Shakespeare's Henry the Fifth and the Hundred Years War. *American Journal of International Law*, *86*, 1.

290. United Nations Economic and Social Council Commission on Human Rights Sub-Commission on Prevention of Discrimination and Protection of Minorities Thirty-Eighth Session, Item 4 of the Provisional Agenda, E/Cn.4/Sub.2/1985/6, July 2, 1985. Review of Further Developments in Fields with Which the Sub-Commission Has Been Concerned. Revised and Updated Report on the Question of the Prevention and Punishment of the Crime of Genocide Prepared by Mr. B. Whitaker. (E/CN.4/Sub.2/416).

291. Lemkin, R. (1945). Genocide—a modern crime. *Free World*, April 4, 39. Cited in Cribb, R. Genocide in the non-Western world: Implications for Holocaust studies. In Jensen, S.L.B. (2003). *Genocide: Cases, comparisons and contemporary debates*. Copenhagen: Danish Center for Holocaust and Genocide Studies, 123. See further on Lemkin Jacobs, S.L. (1999). The papers of Raphael Lemkin: A first look. *Journal of Genocide Research*, *1*, 105–114.

292. Smith, R.W. (1999). State power and genocidal intent: On the uses of genocide in the twentieth century. In Chorbajian, L. & Shirinian, G. (eds.), *Studies in comparative genocide*. New York: St. Martin's Press, 3–14.

293. Smith, R.W. (1999). State power and genocidal intent: On the uses of genocide in the twentieth century. In Chorbajian, L. & Shirinian, G. (eds.), *Studies in comparative genocide*. New York: St Martin's Press, 3–14, 9–10.

294. Kelly, M.J. (2002). Can sovereigns be brought to justice? The crime of genocide's evolution and the meaning of the Milosevic trial. *Saint John's Law Review*, 257, 264. See also Keen, M.H. (1965). *The laws of war in the late Middle Ages*. London: Routledge & Kegan Paul.

295. See Chalk, F. & Jonassohn, K. (1990). *The history and sociology of genocide: Analyses and case studies*. New Haven: Yale University Press. See also Chalk, F. & Jonassohn, K. (1988). The history and sociology of genocidal killings. In Charney, I.W. (ed.), *Genocide: A critical bibliographic review*. London: Mansell, 39.

296. Ratner, S. & Abrahams, J. (1997). *Accountability for human rights atrocities in international law*. Oxford: Oxford University Press, 44.

297. Ratner, S. & Abrahams, J. (1997). *Accountability for human rights atrocities in international law*. Oxford: Oxford University Press, 24–44.

298. Nagan, W.P. & Rodin, V.F. (2003–2004). Racism, genocide, and mass murder: Toward a legal theory about group deprivations. *National Black Law Journal*, 133, 183.

299. Although the convictions were not based on findings of genocide, various indictments used the term. See Schabas, W.A. (2003). National courts finally begin to prosecute genocide, the 'crime of crimes'. *Journal of International Criminal Justice*, *1*, 39–63, fn 2.

300. See further Davidson, E. (1966). *The trial of the Germans: An account of the twenty-two defendants before the International Military Tribunal at Nuremberg*. New York: Macmillan. See further Breitman, R. (1991). *The architect of genocide: Himmler and the Final Solution*. New York: Alfred Knopf.

301. Trials of War Criminals before the Nuremberg Military Tribunals under Control Council Law No. 10, IV (Washington, D.C., 1949), II, 773, 797.

302. Schabas, W.A. (1997). Conceptualizing violence: Present and future developments in international law. *Albany Law Review*, *60*, 733, 741.

303. Churchill, W. in Kuper, L. (1981). *Genocide: Its political use in the twentieth century*. New Haven, CT: Yale University Press, 12.

304. Nersessian, D.L. (2002). The contours of genocide intent: Troubling jurisprudence from the international criminal tribunals, *Texas International Law Journal*, *37*,

231, 236; and Schabas W.A. (1999). 'The Genocide Convention at fifty.' *United States Institute for Peace Report*. http://63.104.169.22/pubs/Specialreports/sr990107.pdf.

305. Nersessian, D.L. (2002). The contours of genocide intent: Troubling jurisprudence from the international criminal tribunals. *Texas International Law Journal*, *37*, 254.

306. Schabas, W. A. (2003). National courts finally begin to prosecute genocide, the 'crime of crimes'. *Journal of International Criminal Justice*, *1*, 39–63, fn 2.

307. See Lemkin, R. (1944). *Axis rule in occupied Europe: Laws of occupation—analysis of government—proposals for redress*. Washington D.C.: Carnegie Endowment for International Peace.

308. See further Jacobs, S.L. (1999). The papers of Raphael Lemkin: A first look. *Journal of Genocide Research*, *1*, 105–114.

309. Cesaire, A. (1996). *Discourse on colonialism*. New York: New York University Press. See further Mamdani, M. (2002). Making sense of political violence in postcolonial Africa. *Identity, Culture and Politics*, *3*, 1–24.

310. Howard-Hassman, R.E. (2005). The second great transformation: Human rights leapfrogging in the era of globalisation. *Human Rights Quarterly*, *27*, 1–40, 33.

311. Morgenthau, H. (1918). *Ambassador Morgenthau's story*. New York: Doubleday.

312. The French word for killing in genocide cases is *meurte*. Kittichaisaree, K. (2002). *International criminal law*. Oxford: Oxford University Press, 17.

313. Smith, H.W. (1998). The talk of genocide, the rhetoric of miscegenation: Notes on the debates in the German Reichstag concerning Southwest Africa, 1904–14. In Friedrichsmeyer, S., Lennox, S., & Zantop, S. (eds.), *The imperialist imagination: German colonialism and its legacy*. Ann Arbor: University of Michigan Press, 217.

314. Jonassohn, K. & Bjornson, S.K. (1998). *Genocide and gross human rights violations*. New Brunswick: Transaction, 140.

315. Papini, R. (1994). The stepped diamond of mid-century beadfabric: Aesthetic assimilation beyond the second Izwekufa. In Seinaert, E., Bell, N. and Lewis, M. (eds.). *Oral tradition and its transmission*. Durban: University of Natal Press.

316. Mahoney, M.R. (2003). The Zulu Kingdom as a genocidal and post-genocidal society, c. 1810 to the present. *Journal of Genocide Research*, *5*, 263, 255.

317. Markusen, E. (1987) in Wallimann, I. & Dobkowski, M.N. (eds.), *Genocide and the modern age: Etiology and case studies of mass death*. New York: Greenwood Press, 100.

318. Dufour, F.G. (2001). Toward a socio-historical theory of persecution and an analytical concept of genocide. Occasional paper no 67. Toronto: York University Centre for German & European Studies, 2.

319. Gellately, R. & Kiernan, B. (2003). The study of mass murder and genocide. In Gellately, R. & Kiernan, B. (eds.), *The specter of genocide mass murder in historical perspective*. Cambridge: Cambridge University Press, 3.

320. On the drafting process, see Lippman, M. (1985). The drafting of the 1948 Convention on the Prevention and Punishment of the Crime of Genocide. *Boston University Journal of International Law*, *3*, 62.

321. General Assembly Resolution 96 (I), U.N. Doc. A/64/Add.1 (1946). See further Jessup, P.C. (1947). The crime of aggression and the future of international Law. *Political Science Quarterly*, *62*, 1–10.

322. Schabas, W. A. (2003). National courts finally begin to prosecute genocide, the 'crime of crimes'. *Journal of International Criminal Justice*, *1*, 39–63, fn 73.

323. Freeman, M. (1995). Genocide, civilization and modernity. *British Journal of Sociology*, *46*, 207–225.

324. *ICJ Reports*, 1951, 23.

325. *Polyukhovich v Commonwealth* (1991) 172, CLR 501.

326. *R v Finta* (1989) 61 DLR (4th) 85.

327. Clarke, R. (2002). Retrospectivity and the constitutional validity of the Bali bombing and East Timor trials, *Australian Journal of Asian Law*, *5*, 128, 140–141.

328. De Zayas, A. Memorandum on the genocide against the Armenians 1915–1923 and the application of the 1948 Genocide Convention. European Armenian Federation for Justice & Democracy (EAFJD) (ed.), at http://www16.brinkster.com/eafjd/en/bulletins/dezayas_report.pdf.

329. De Zayas, A. Memorandum on the genocide against the Armenians 1915–1923 and the application of the 1948 Genocide Convention. European Armenian Federation for Justice & Democracy (EAFJD) (ed.), at http://www16.brinkster.com/eafjd/en/bulletins/dezayas_report.pdf.

330. ICTJ Legal Analysis on Applicability of UN Convention on Genocides prior to January 12, 1951.

331. Berat, L. (1993). Genocide: The Namibian case against Germany. *Pace International Law Review*, *5*, 165, 207.

332. Lauterpacht, H. in Oppenheim, H. (1955). *International law: A treatise*, *Vol. 1: Peace* (8th ed.). New York: David Mackay, 751.

333. Report of the ad hoc working group of experts established under Resolution 2(XXIII) and 2(XXIV) of the Commission on Human Rights, Doc.E/CN.4/984/Add.18.

334. Steinmetz, G. (2005). From 'Native Policy' to exterminationism: German Southwest Africa, 1904. In *Comparative Perspective, Theory and Research in Comparative Social Analysis*, *Paper 30*, 4–5. Los Angeles: Department of Sociology, UCLA, 1. Found at: http://repositories.cdlib.org/cgi/viewcontent.cgi?article=1036&context=uclasoc.

335. Vienna Convention on the Law of Treaties, May 23, 1969, UN Doc. A/CONF. 39/27 (1969), Article 28.

336. *Ambatielos* case (*Greece v U.K.*). Preliminary objections, 1952, ICJ, 27, 40 (July 1). Cited in ICTJ Legal Analysis on Applicability of UN Convention on Genocides prior to January 12, 1951.

337. Schabas, W. A. (2003). National courts finally begin to prosecute genocide, the 'crime of crimes'. *Journal of International Criminal Justice*, *1*, 39–63.

338. *Prosecutor v Jean-Paul Akayesu*, Case No. Ictr-96-4, Judgement of September 2, 1998, paragraph 495.

339. Secretary-General's Report pursuant to paragraph 2 of Resolution 808 (1993) of the Security Council, May 3, 1993, S/25704.

340. Adopted November 26, 1968, and entered in force on November 11, 1970.

341. Hinz, M. (2003). One hundred years later: Germany on trial in the USA—the Herero reparations claim for genocide. *Namibian Human Rights Online Journal*, *1*, 17. http://www.hrdc.unam.na/journal/V1_N1_Dec2003/Docs/Herero_case.doc.

342. *Attorney-General v Eichmann*, 36 *International Law Report*, 277 (Sup.Ct. Israel 1962). Cited in Berat, L. (1993). Genocide: The Namibian case against Germany. *Pace International Law Review*, *5*, 165, 206–207.

343. The Whitaker report notes: "In the wake of the Nazi atrocities, the Genocide Convention provided a permanent definition for part of the concept of 'crimes against

humanity' contained in the Nuremberg principles, which themselves were an extension of international criminal jurisdiction regarding war crimes. The convention, which sought to codify a fundamental principle of civilization, in addition extended liability for such crimes to times of peace and not only to wartime." United Nations Economic and Social Council Commission on Human Rights Sub-Commission on Prevention of Discrimination and Protection of Minorities Thirty-eighth session, Item 4 of the provisional agenda, E/CN.4/Sub.2/ 1985/6, July 2, 1985. Review of further developments in fields with which the sub-commission has been concerned. Revised and updated report on the question of the prevention and punishment of the crime of genocide, prepared by Mr. B. Whitaker, paragraph 25.

344. It is for this reason that scholars are interested in the re-characterization process in terms of which the same facts are characterized under different crimes or the same facts give rise to cumulative charges. As was noted by Judge Robinson at the ICTY in the *Tadic* decision: "It is a fair comment that the Tribunal's approach to cumulative charging is relatively flexible and liberal. Trial Chambers have on several occasions dismissed preliminary objections to the form of an indictment on the ground of cumulative charging by holding that such objections would only be relevant at the sentencing stage. One way of dealing with this issue is by imposing concurrent sentences; but another way is to impose the same sentence for two crimes when they are constituted by the same acts. The Tribunal, in the future, may yet have to confront at a preliminary stage, more squarely than it has in the past, the issue of cumulative charges." Cited in Olusanya, O. (2004). *Double jeopardy: Without parameters*. Antwerp: Intersentia, 177.

345. Du Plessis, M. (2003). Historical injustice and international law: An exploratory discussion of reparation for slavery. *Human Rights Quarterly*, *25*, 624–659, 635.

346. Robertson, G. (2000). *Crimes against humanity: The struggle for global justice*. New York: New Press, 209.

347. Stoecker, H. (1987). The position of Africans in the German colonies. In Knoll, A.J. & Gann, L.H. (eds.), *Germans in the tropics: Essays in German colonial history* (2nd ed.). New York/London: Greenwood Press, 119–129, 119.

348. Stoecker, H. (1987). The position of Africans in the German colonies. In Knoll, A.J. & Gann, L.H. (eds.), *Germans in the tropics: Essays in German colonial history* (2nd ed.). New York/London: Greenwood Press, 119–129, 119.

349. Stoecker, H. (1987). The position of Africans in the German colonies. In Knoll, A.J. & Gann, L.H. (eds.), *Germans in the tropics: Essays in German colonial history* (2nd ed.). New York/London: Greenwood Press, 119–129, 128 fn 1.

350. Bassiouni, M.C. (1991). Enslavement as an international crime, *New York University Journal of International Law and Politics*, *23*, 445, 445–446.

351. Section I: On belligerents, in Chapter 1, Article 6: Employment at labour.

352. Bassiouni, M.C. (1991). Enslavement as an international crime, *New York University Journal of International Law and Politics*, *23*, 445, 446.

353. Bassiouni, M.C (1986). *International criminal law, Vol. 1: Crimes of war*. New York: Dobbs Ferry, 419.

354. Bassiouni, M.C (ed.). (1986). *International criminal law, Vol. 1: Crimes of war*. New York: Dobbs Ferry, 419.

355. Breaking the Silence: Learning about the Transatlantic Slave Trade. http://www.antislavery.org/breakingthesilence.

356. Du Plessis, M. (2003). Historical injustice and international law: An exploratory discussion of reparation for slavery. *Human Rights Quarterly*, *25*, 624–659, 628 fn 14.

357. Cited in Du Plessis, M. (2003). Historical injustice and international law: An exploratory discussion of reparation for slavery. *Human Rights Quarterly*, *25*, 624–659, 634 fn 45.

358. Eide, A. (1984).The laws of war and human rights—differences and convergences. In Swinarski, C. (ed.) *Studies and essays on international humanitarian law and Red Cross principles*. Dordrecht: Martinus Nijhoff, 675–697.

359. Sieghart, P. (1983). *The international law of human rights*. Oxford: Clarendon Press, 13.

360. Lauren, P.G. (1998). *The evolution of international human rights*. Philadelphia: University of Pennsylvania Press, 65.

361. Lauren, P.G. (1998). *The evolution of international human rights*. Philadelphia: University of Pennsylvania Press, 314, fn 95.

362. Lauren, P.G. (1998). *The evolution of international human rights*. Philadelphia: University of Pennsylvania Press, 65.

363. The London Treaty for the Pacification of Greece (1827).

364. However, Gibney, Tomaševski and Vedsted-Hansen see this principle no longer being in place after World War II, but do not specify that it had broken down before that. They argue that "the notion of sovereignty still serves to protect against some forms of state responsibility, only now it is far more likely that countries will invoke the sovereignty of another state in order to remove themselves from any and all responsibility in assisting an outlaw state." Gibney, M., Tomaševski, K. & Vedsted-Hansen, J. (1999). Transnational state responsibility for violations of human rights. *Harvard Human Rights Journal*, *12*, 267.

365. Lauren, P.G. (1998). *The evolution of international human rights*. Philadelphia: University of Pennsylvania Press, 66.

366. Van Bueren, G. (2004). Slavery as piracy—the legal case for reparations for slavery. In Walden, R. (ed.). *Racism and human rights*. Leidein: Brill, 41–53.

367. Bargar, B.D. (1968). Review. XL. *Journal of Modern History*, 597.

368. Mackenzie, K. (1974). Some British reactions to German colonial methods 1885–1907. *The Historical Journal*, *17*, 165–175, 166.

369. Report of the British Consul, Roger Casement, on the Administration of the Congo Free State—British Parliamentary Papers, 1904, LXII, Cd. 1933.

370. See Hochschild, A. (1999). *King Leopold's ghost- A story of greed, terror and heroism in colonial Africa*. New York: Houghton Mifflin, 200.

371. Rees, W.L. (1888). German conduct in Samoa. XXIV. *Nineteenth Century*, 734–752.

372. Mackenzie, K. (1974). Some British reactions to German colonial methods 1885–1907. *The Historical Journal*, *17*, 165–175.

373. Mackenzie, K. (1974). Some British reactions to German colonial methods 1885–1907. *The Historical Journal*, *17*, 165–175.

374. Mackenzie, K. (1974). Some British reactions to German colonial methods 1885–1907. *The Historical Journal*, *17*, 165–175.

375. Mackenzie, K. (1974). Some British reactions to German colonial methods 1885–1907. *The Historical Journal*, *17*, 165–175.

376. Mackenzie, K. (1974). Some British reactions to German colonial methods 1885–1907. *The Historical Journal*, *17*, 165–175.

377. Cameron, V.L. (1890). England and Germany in Africa: III. XLVIII *Fortnightly Review*, 144–163. Cited in Mackenzie, K. (1974). Some British reactions to German colonial methods 1885–1907. *The Historical Journal*, *17*, 165–175, 167.

378. Beckett, E.W. (1980). England and Germany in Africa. XLVIII. *Fortnightly Review*, 128–143. Cited in Mackenzie, K. (1974). Some British reactions to German colonial methods 1885– 1907. *The Historical Journal, 17*, 165–175.

379. Louis, W.R. (1967). *Britain and Germany's lost colonies 1914–1919*. Oxford: Clarendon Press, 16.

380. Louis, W.R. (1967). *Britain and Germany's lost colonies 1914–1919*. Oxford: Clarendon Press, 35.

381. Eltzbacher, O. (1905). The German danger to South Africa. *The nineteenth century and after, 58*, 524–538. Cited in Mackenzie, K. (1974). Some British reactions to German colonial methods 1885–1907. *The Historical Journal, 17*, 165–175.

382. Mackenzie, K. (1974). Some British reactions to German colonial methods 1885–1907. *The Historical Journal, 17*, 165–175.

383. Hull, I.V. (2005). *Absolute destruction: Military culture and practices of war in Imperial Germany*. Ithaca: Cornell University Press, 146.

384. Stated by Stubel in the *Reichstag* on March 17, 1904 and cited in Hull, I.V. (2005). *Absolute destruction: Military culture and practices of war in Imperial Germany*. Ithaca: Cornell University Press, 14.

385. Cited in Hull, I.V. (2005). *Absolute destruction: Military culture and practices of war in Imperial Germany*. Ithaca: Cornell University Press, 17.

386. Hull, I.V. (2005). *Absolute destruction: Military culture and practices of war in Imperial Germany*. Ithaca: Cornell University Press, 17.

387. Dedering, T. (1999). The prophet's 'War against Whites': Shepherd Stuurman in Namibia and South Africa 1904–1907. *Journal of African History, 40*, 1–19.

388. See further Illife, J. (1969). *Tanganyika under German rule, 1905–1912*. Cambridge: Cambridge University Press.

389. See generally Knoll, A.J. & Gann, L.H. (eds.). (1987). *Germans in the tropics: Essays in German colonial history* (2nd ed.). New York/London: Greenwood Press.

390. See further Smith, H.W. (1998). The talk of genocide, the rhetoric of miscegenation: Notes on the debates in the German Reichstag concerning Southwest Africa, 1904–14. In Friedrichsmeyer, S., Lennox, S. & Zantop, S. (eds.), *The imperialist imagination: German colonialism and its legacy*. Ann Arbor: University of Michigan Press.

391. Babing, A. (2004). The role of the German Democratic Republic (GDR) in the international struggle against racism, apartheid and colonialism. Paper presented at A Decade of Freedom Conference, Durban, South Africa, October 10–13, 2004.

392. This was even remarked about at the time. In this regard see Kindt, L. (1905). Vom Aufstand in Ostafrika. *Koloniale Zeitschrift, XI* (25), 435–437.

393. See Blackshire-Belay, C.A. (1992). German imperialism in Africa: The distorted images of Cameroon, Namibia, Tanzania and Togo. *Journal of Black Studies, 23*, 235–246, 241.

394. Wieczorek-Zeul, H. (2004). Speech delivered at the commemoration ceremony for the centenary of the battle at the Waterberg, August 14, 2004. Found at www.bmz.de/de/presse/reden/ministerin/rede20040814.html.

395. Bridgman, J. (1981). *The revolt of the Hereros*. Los Angeles: University of California Press, 46.

396. Bridgman, J. (1981). *The revolt of the Hereros*. Los Angeles: University of California Press, 127.

397. Hull, I.V. (2005). *Absolute destruction: Military culture and practices of war in Imperial Germany*. Ithaca: Cornell University Press, 129.

398. Hull, I.V. (2005). *Absolute destruction: Military culture and practices of war in Imperial Germany*. Ithaca: Cornell University Press, 129.

399. Rahn, W. (1997). Sanitätsdienst der Schutztruppe für Südwestafrika während der Aufstände 1904–1907 und der Kalahari-Expedition 1908. *Beiträge zur deutschen Kolonialgeschichte*, 83. Cited in Nordbruch, C. (2004). Atrocities committed on the Herero people during the suppression of their uprising in German South West Africa 1904–1907? An analysis of the latest accusations against Germany and an investigation on the credibility and justification of the demands for reparation. Paper delivered to the European American Culture Council, Sacramento, April 25, 2004. http://www.nordbruch.org/artikel/sacramento.pdf.

400. Steinmetz, G. (2005). From 'Native Policy' to exterminationism: German Southwest Africa, 1904. In *Comparative Perspective, Theory and Research in Comparative Social Analysis, Paper 30*, 6–7. Los Angeles: Department of Sociology, UCLA, 1. http://repositories.cdlib.org/cgi/viewcontent.cgi?article=1036&context=uclasoc.

401. Hull, I.V. (2005). *Absolute destruction: Military culture and practices of war in Imperial Germany*. Ithaca: Cornell University Press, 33.

402. Nordbruch, C. (2004). Atrocities committed on the Herero people during the suppression of their uprising in German South West Africa 1904–1907? An analysis of the latest accusations against Germany and an investigation on the credibility and justification of the demands for reparation. Paper delivered to the European American Culture Council, Sacramento, April 25, 2004. http://www.nordbruch.org/artikel/sacramento.pdf.

403. O'Connor, R. (1973). *The Boxer Rebellion*. London: Robert Hale, 182.

404. Letter from Bulow to Kaiser Wilhelm, November 24, 1904. Drechsler, H. (1980). *Let us die fighting: The struggle of the Herero and Nama against the German imperialism (1894–1915)*. London: Zed Press (Bernd Zöllner, transl.), 164.

405. Hull, I.V. (2005). *Absolute destruction: Military culture and practices of war in Imperial Germany*. Ithaca: Cornell University Press, 64.

406. Hull, I.V. (2005). *Absolute destruction: Military culture and practices of war in Imperial Germany*. Ithaca: Cornell University Press, 119–120.

407. Great General Staff of the Imperial Germany (1915). *The war book of the German General Staff*, (J.H. Morgan, transl.). New York: McBride, Nast & Co., 72; Jochnick, C. & Normand, R. (1994). The legitimation of violence: A critical history of the laws of war. *Harvard International Law Journal*, *35*, fn 55.

408. Best, G. (1983). *Humanity in warfare: The modern history of the international law of armed conflicts*. London: Methuen, 145.

409. Jochnick, C. & Normand, R. (1994). The legitimation of violence: A critical history of the laws of war. *Harvard International Law Journal, 35*, fn 55. See O'Brien, W.V. (1957). The meaning of 'Military Necessity' in international law. *World Polity*, *1*, 109, 121; Best, G. (1983). *Humanity in warfare: The modern history of the international law of armed conflicts*. London: Methuen, 145.

410. Jochnick, C. & Normand, R. (1994). The legitimation of violence: A critical history of the laws of war. *Harvard International Law Journal*, *35*, fn 58.

411. Best, G. (1983). *Humanity in warfare: The modern history of the international law of armed conflicts*. London: Methuen, 64.

412. Cited in Best, G. (1983). *Humanity in warfare: The modern history of the international law of armed conflicts*. London: Methuen, 147.

413. Helmut Bley translates the words as "contradictory to all Christian and humane principles." Bley, H. (1971). *South West Africa under German rule 1894–1914*. London: Heinemann, 163. See also Helbig, H. (1983). *Mythos-Deutsch-Südwest: Namibia und die Deutschen*. Weinheim/Basel: Beltz Verlag, 158.

414. Berat, L. (1993). Genocide: The Namibian case against Germany. *Pace International Law Review*, *5*, 207.

415. Wellington, J.H. (1967). *South West Africa and its human issues*. Oxford: Clarendon Press, 208.

416. Goldblatt, I. (1971). *History of South West Africa: From the beginning of the nineteenth century*. Cape Town: Juta, 148.

417. Wellington, J.H. (1967). *South West Africa and its human issues*. Oxford: Clarendon Press, 208.

CHAPTER 3

1. Gewald, J-B. & Silvester, J. (2003). *Words cannot be found. German colonial rule in Namibia: An annotated reprint of the 1918 Blue Book*. Leiden: Brill, xxxvi–xxxvii.

2. Aukerman, M.J. (2002). Extraordinary evil, ordinary crime: A framework for understanding transitional justice. *Harvard Human Rights Journal*, *15*, 40, 55.

3. See Sohn, L. (1982). The new international law: Protection of the rights of individuals rather than states. *American University International Law Review*, *32*, 1.

4. Dolzer, R. (2002). The settlement of war-related claims: Does international law recognize a victim's private right of action? Lessons after 1945. *Berkeley Journal of International Law*, *20*, 296, 302.

5. Junk, J. & Miner, J.M. (2004). Compensating historical injustice: More than just money. *Humanity in action. Reports of the 2004 Fellows in Denmark, Germany and the Netherlands*. New York, *6*, 43–47, 43.

6. One interesting exception occurred in October 2006, in a move first proposed by the Green Party in 2003, when Munich, the capital of Bavaria in Germany, agreed to change the name of Von Trotha Street (which crosses another street called Waterberg Street) to Herero Street. While the councillors of the Social Democratic Party (SPD) and the Green Party supported the move, those from the conservative Christian Social Union (CSU) and the Liberal Party (FDP) did not. See Almut Hielscher (2006). Notorious street name to be changed. *New Era, 11*.

7. Sarkin, J. (2004). The coming of age of claims for reparations for human rights abuses committed in the South. *Sur International Human Rights Journal*, *1*, 67–125.

8. *Ware v. Hylton*, 3 U.S. (3 Dall.) 199, 279 (1796). The court reports Dall are named for court reporter Alexander J. Dallas.

9. Woolsey, T.S. (1891). *Introduction to the study of international law* (6th ed.). New York: Charles Scribner's Sons, 17–18.

10. Woolsey, T.S. (1891). *Introduction to the study of international law* (6th ed.). New York: Charles Scribner's Sons, 17–18.

11. Kalshoven, F. (1991). State responsibility for warlike acts of the armed forces: From Article 3 of the Hague Convention IV of 1907 to Article 91 of Additional Protocol I and beyond. *International and Comparative Quarterly, 40*, 830.

12. Kalshoven, F. (1991). State responsibility for warlike acts of the armed forces: From Article 3 of the Hague Convention IV of 1907 to Article 91 of Additional Protocol I and beyond. *International and Comparative Quarterly, 40*, 831.

13. Kalshoven, F. (1991). State responsibility for warlike acts of the armed forces: From Article 3 of the Hague Convention IV of 1907 to Article 91 of Additional Protocol I and beyond. *International and Comparative Quarterly, 40*, 831.

14. Randelzhofer, A. (1999). The legal position of the individual under present international law. In Randelzhofer, A. & Tomuschat, C. (eds.), *State responsibility and the individual: Reparations in instances of grave violations of human rights.* The Hague: Martinus Nijhoff, 231, 238–239.

15. P.C.I.J. (1928) Series B, No. 15, at 16–24.

16. Sohn, L.B. & Buergenthal, T. (1973). *International protection of human rights.* Indianapolis: Bobbs-Merrill, 10.

17. Sohn, L.B. & Buergenthal, T. (1973). *International protection of human rights.* Indianapolis: Bobbs-Merrill, 9.

18. Sohn, L.B. & Buergenthal, T. (1973). *International protection of human rights.* Indianapolis: Bobbs-Merrill, 9.

19. Forsythe, D.P. (1991). *The internalization of human rights.* Lexington, MA: Lexington Books, 36.

20. Forsythe, D.P. (1991). *The internalization of human rights.* Lexington, MA: Lexington Books, 38.

21. Mazzeschi, R.P. (2003). Reparation claims by individuals for state breaches of humanitarian law and human rights: An overview. *Journal of International Criminal Justice, 1*, 339, 341–342.

22. Expert opinions by F. Kalshoven, E. David & C. Greenwood (1999). In Fujita, H., Suzuki, I. & Nagano, K. (eds.), *War and rights of individuals: Renaissance of individual compensation.* Tokyo: Nippon Hyoron-sha, 39 et sequitur.

23. Expert opinions by F. Kalshoven, E. David & C. Greenwood (1999). In Fujita, H., Suzuki, I. & Nagano, K. (eds.), *War and rights of individuals: Renaissance of individual compensation.* Tokyo: Nippon Hyoron-sha, et sequitur.

24. Frulli, M. (2003). When are states liable towards individuals for serious violations of humanitarian law? The *Markovic* Case. *Journal of International Criminal Justice, 1*, 406, 417.

25. Kalshoven, F. (1991). State responsibility for warlike acts of the armed forces: From Article 3 of the Hague Convention IV of 1907 to Article 91 of Additional Protocol I and beyond. *International and Comparative Quarterly, 40*, 833.

26. Hofmann, R. & Riemann, F. (2004). *International Law Association Committee on Compensation for Victims of War: Compensation for victims of war—background report*, March 17, 2004, 7.

27. Hofmann, R. & Riemann, F. (2004). *International Law Association Committee on Compensation for Victims of War: Compensation for victims of war—background report*, March 17, 2004, 7.

28. Gillard, E-C. (2003). Reparation for violations of international humanitarian law. *International Review of the Red Cross, 85*, 529, 532.

29. ICRC, Geneva (1958). The ICRC Commentary to the 1949 Geneva Conventions, Vol. IV, at 211 & 603, cited in the *International Law Association Report*, 15 fn 62.

30. *Barcelona Traction, Light and Power Company, Limited (Belgium v. Spain)*, Judgment of February 5, 1970, *ICJ Reports* (1970), 46.

31. Hofmann, R. & Riemann, F. (2004). *International Law Association Committee on Compensation for Victims of War: Compensation for victims of war—background report*, March 17, 2004, 7.

32. Mazzeschi, R.P. (2003). Reparation claims by individuals for state breaches of humanitarian law and human rights: An overview. *Journal of International Criminal Justice, 1*, 339. See various authors on this in Fujita, H., Suzuki, I., & Nagano, K. (eds.). (1999). *War and rights of individuals: Renaissance of individual compensation*. Tokyo: Nippon Hyoron-sha.

33. Abi-Saab, G. (1984). The specificities of humanitarian law. In Swinarski, C. (ed.). *Studies and essays of international humanitarian law and Red Cross principles in honour of Jean Pictet*. Geneva/The Hague: ICRC, 269. Cited in Zegveld, L. (2003). Remedies for victims of violations of international humanitarian law. *International Review of the Red Cross, 85*, 497, 498 fn 1.

34. Gillard, E-C. (2003). Reparation for violations of international humanitarian law. *International Review of the Red Cross, 85*, 529, 532.

35. Treaty of Peace between the Allied and Associated Powers and Germany, June 28, 1919.

36. See further Diebold, E., Engelhardt, S. & Iskenius, D. (2004). Facing the past to liberate the future: Colonial Africa in the German mind. *Humanity in action. Reports of the 2004 Fellows in Denmark, Germany and the Netherlands*. New York, 6.

37. Culver, J. (Jr). (December 2004). Berlin Anti-Colonial Conference: 120 years of African resistance. *The Black Commentator, 116*, 2. http://www.blackcommentator.com/116/116_berlin_conference.html.

38. Posner, E.A. & Vermeule A. (2003). Reparations for slavery and other historical injustices. *Columbia Law Review, 103*, 689, 694.

39. Tavuchis, N. (1991). *Mea Culpa: A sociology of apology and reconciliation*. Stanford, CA: Stanford University Press, 20.

40. Tavuchis, N. (1991). *Mea Culpa: A sociology of apology and reconciliation*. Stanford, CA: Stanford University Press, 20.

41. Gardner Feldman, L. (1999). The principle and practice of "Reconciliation" in German foreign policy: Relations with France, Israel, Poland and the Czech Republic. *International Affairs, 75*, 334–337.

42. See Boraine, A. Toward reconciliation: War criminal's remorse could help Bosnia heal. *International Herald Tribune*, December 18, 2002. http://www.iht.com/articles/80569.html.

43. Nobles, M. Official apologies and their effects on political membership in democracies. Paper prepared for presentation at the American Political Science Association Meeting, Philadelphia, PA, August 28–31, 2003. Available at http://web.mit.edu/polisci/research/mnobles/official_apologies_in_democracies.pdf.

44. Barkan, E. (2000). *The guilt of nations: Restitution and negotiating historical injustices*. Baltimore: Johns Hopkins University Press, 264.

45. Barkan, E. (2000). *The guilt of nations: Restitution and negotiating historical injustices*. Baltimore: Johns Hopkins University Press, 264.

46. See Macklem, P. (2005). Rybná 9, Praha 1: Restitution and memory in international human rights law. *European Journal of International Law*, *16*, 1–25, 17.

47. Reparations Not on the Table. *The Namibian*, August 31, 2000.

48. On apologies generally see Brooks, R.L. (ed.). (1999). *When sorry isn't enough: The controversy over apologies and reparations for human injustice*. New York: New York University Press.

49. Maletsky, C. Hereros Temporarily Drop Claim in $2 bn Suit. *Business Day*, September 20, 2001.

50. Reparations Not on the Table. *The Namibian*, August 31, 2000.

51. Tavuchis, N. (1991). *Mea Culpa: A sociology of apology and reconciliation*. Stanford, CA: Stanford University Press, 88.

52. Orenstein, A. (1999). Apology expected: Incorporating a feminist analysis into evidence policy where you would least expect it. *Southwestern University Law Review*, *28*, 221, 239.

53. Tavuchis, N. (1991). *Mea Culpa: A sociology of apology and reconciliation*. Stanford, CA: Stanford University Press, 15.

54. McGregor, L. (2001). Individual accountability in South Africa: Cultural optimum or political facade? *American Journal of International Law*, *95*, 32, 38. See also O'Hara, E.A. & Yarn, D. (2002). On apology and consilience. *Washington Law Review*, *77*, 1121–1192.

55. Cited in Kandetu, V. (2005). Namibia: Cold discourse upon chronic pain. *New African*, *436*, 64–66.

56. See further Diebold, E., Engelhardt, S., & Iskenius, D. (2004). Facing the past to liberate the future: Colonial Africa in the German mind. *Humanity in action. Reports of the 2004 Fellows in Denmark, Germany and the Netherlands*. New York, *6*. On the legal consequences of an apology see Rehm, P.H. & Beatty, D.R. (1996). Legal consequences of apologising. *Journal of Dispute Resolution*, *1*, 115–130. On apologies generally see Gibney, M. & Roxstrom, E. (2001). The status of state apologies. *Human Rights Quarterly*, *23*, 911; Cunningham, M. (1999). Saying sorry: The politics of apology. *The Political Quarterly*, *70*, 285; Alter, S. (1999). *Apologising for serious wrongdoing: Social, psychological and legal considerations*. Report for the Law Commission of Canada. Available at: http://www.lcc.gc.ca/en/themes/mr/ica/2000/html/apology.asp; Brooks, R. (ed.). (1999). *When sorry isn't enough: The controversy over apologies and reparations for human injustice*. New York: New York University Press; Govier, T. & Verwoerd, W. (2002). The promise and pitfalls of apologies. *Journal of Social Philosophy*, *33*, 67–82. See also Tavuchis, N. (1991). *Mea Culpa: A sociology of apology and reconciliation*. Stanford, CA: Stanford University Press; and Daly, E. & Sarkin, J. (2006). *Reconciliation in divided societies: Searching for common ground*. Philadelphia: University of Pennsylvania Press.

57. Matundu-Tjiparuro, K. Presumed Apology. *New Era*, August 16, 2004.

58. Lazare, A. (1995). Go ahead, say you're sorry. *Psychology Today*, *28*, 40, 42.

59. Hintze, H. (2005). Germany to Pay N$160 Million for Reconciliation. *The Namibian*, May 27, 2005.

60. Barkan, E. Restitution and amending historical injustices in international morality. Available at http://www.eucenter.scrippscol.edu/publications/papers/barkan.pdf.

61. Paramount Chief Kuaima Riruako at the Centenary Commemoration of the Extermination Order of General Lothar von Trotha at the Ozombu Zovindimba, Otjinene Constituency on October 30, 2004.

62. Maletsky, C. Germany Denies Herero Negotiations. *Africa News Service*, December 9, 2004.

63. Maletsky, C. Germany Denies Herero Negotiations. *Africa News Service*, December 9, 2004.

64. Hintze, H. (2005). Germany to Pay N$160 Million for Reconciliation. *The Namibian*, May 27, 2005.

65. Hintze, H. (2005). Germany to Pay N$160 Million for Reconciliation. *The Namibian*, May 27, 2005.

66. Namibia: Germany's Herero reconciliation efforts rebuffed. United Nations Office for the Coordination of Humanitarian Affairs Integrated Regional Information Network (IRIN), December 2, 2005.

67. Cited in Gewald, J-B. and Silvester, J. (2003). *Words cannot be found. German colonial rule in Namibia: An annotated reprint of the 1918 Blue Book*. Leiden: Brill, 172.

68. Hamta, M. Von Trotha Family Backs Herero Compensation. *Africa News Service*, September 13, 2004.

69. Ritter-Petersen, H.G. (1991). *The Herrenvolk mentality in German South West Africa 1884–1914*. D. Litt. (History). Pretoria: University of South Africa, 242.

70. Rohrbach, P. (1907). *Deutsche Kolonialwirtschaft, Vol. I: Südwestafrika*. Berlin/Schöneberg: Buchverlag der Hilfe.

71. See Von Falkenhausen, H. (1906). *Ansiedlerschicksale: Elf Jahre in Deutsch-Südwestafrika 1894–1904*. Berlin: Reimer.

72. Ritter-Petersen, H.G. (1991). *The Herrenvolk mentality in German South West Africa 1884–1914*. D. Litt. (History). Pretoria: University of South Africa, 218–219.

73. Bullock, A.L.C. (1939). *German's colonial demands*. London: Oxford University Press, 196.

74. The Potsdam Agreement of 1945 and The Paris Agreement of 1946.

75. See Schwerin, K. (1972). German compensation for victims of Nazi persecution. *Northwestern University Law Review*, *67*, 479, 515–518; Schwerin, K. (1995). German compensation for victims of Nazi persecution. In Kritz, N. (ed.), *Transitional Justice, Vol. II*. Washington, D.C.: United States Institute for Peace, 51; Balabkins, N. (1993). *West German reparations to Israel*. Piscataway, NJ: Rutgers University Press; and Zweig, R.W. (1987). *German reparations and the Jewish world: A history of the claims conference*. Boulder, CO: Westview Press.

76. Zweig, R. (2001). *German reparations and the Jewish world*. London: Frank Cass.

77. Another such agreement was signed between France and Germany.

78. Norway-Federal Republic of Germany, Art.1 (1). Signed on August 7, 1959, entered into force on April 23, 1960. *United Nations Treaty System*, *358*, 185.

79. Statement by Chief Kuaima Riruako on file with the author.

80. Statement by Chief Kuaima Riruako on file with the author.

81. UN Commission on Human Rights, *Study concerning the right to restitution, compensation and rehabilitation for victims of gross violations of human rights and fundamental freedoms* (Van Boven Report), paragraph 107, UN Doc. E/CN.4/Sub.2/1993/8, July 2, 1993, 50.

82. Barkan, E. Restitution and amending historical injustices in international morality. Available at http://www.eucenter.scrippscol.edu/publications/papers/barkan.pdf.

83. See generally Eizenstat, S. (1997). *U.S. and Allied efforts to recover and restore gold and other assets stolen or hidden by Germany during World War II—preliminary study*. Available at http://www.ushmm.org/assets/nazigold.htm.

84. See Pross, C. (1998). *Paying for the past: The struggle over reparations for surviving victims of the Nazi terror*. Baltimore: Johns Hopkins University Press.

85. Junk, J. & Miner, J.M. (2004). Compensating historical injustice: More than just money. *Humanity in action. Reports of the 2004 Fellows in Denmark, Germany and the Netherlands*. New York, *6*, 43–47, 44.

86. U.S. Department of State Office of the Spokesman, March 8, 2005. Statement by Richard Boucher (Spokesman). German foundation boosts payments to victims of Nazi medical experiments.

87. U.S. Department of State Office of the Spokesman, March 8, 2005. Statement by Richard Boucher (Spokesman). German foundation boosts payments to victims of Nazi medical experiments.

88. Junk, J. & Miner, J.M. (2004). Compensating historical injustice: More than just money. *Humanity in action. Reports of the 2004 Fellows in Denmark, Germany and the Netherlands*. New York, *6*, 43–47.

89. *Otavi Mines Minerals 100th anniversary commemorative publication (1900–2000)*.

90. Bravenboer, B. & Rusch, W. (1997). *The first 100 years of state railways in Namibia*. Windhoek: Trans-Namibian Museum, 64.

91. Bravenboer, B. & Rusch, W. (1997). *The first 100 years of state railways in Namibia*. Windhoek: Trans-Namibian Museum, 95.

92. Bravenboer, B. & Rusch, W. (1997). *The first 100 years of state railways in Namibia*. Windhoek: Trans-Namibian Museum, 65.

93. Junk, J. & Miner, J.M. (2004). Compensating historical injustice: More than just money. *Humanity in action. Reports of the 2004 Fellows in Denmark, Germany and the Netherlands*. New York, *6*, 43–47.

94. Kamali, M. (2001). Accountability for human rights violations: A comparison of transitional justice in East Germany and South Africa. *Columbia Journal of Transnational Law*, *40*, 89, 111.

95. Kamali, M. (2001). Accountability for human rights violations: A comparison of transitional justice in East Germany and South Africa. *Columbia Journal of Transnational Law*, *40*, 89, 104.

96. See further Rosenberg, T. (1999). *The haunted land—facing Europe's ghosts after communism*. New York: Random House.

97. Markovits, I. (2001). Selective memory: How the law affects what we remember and forget about the past. *Law and Society Review*, *35*, 513, 516.

98. Kamali, M. (2001). Accountability for human rights violations: A comparison of transitional justice in East Germany and South Africa. *Columbia Journal of Transnational Law*, *40*, 89, 116–117.

99. Müller, K. January 26, 2004. http://www.manskligarattigheter.gov.se/stockholmforum/2004/page1423.html.

100. Müller, K. January 26, 2004. http://www.manskligarattigheter.gov.se/stockholmforum/2004/page1423.html.

101. Declaration by the Stockholm International Forum 2004. http://www.manskligarattigheter.gov.se/stockholmforum/2004/page1617.html.

102. Paramount Chief Riruako's Press Conference: Response of the Herero nation to the official apology of the Federal Republic of Germany, August 19, 2004. Speech on file with author.

103. Van Boven, T. (1993). *Study concerning the right to restitution, compensation and rehabilitation for victims of gross violations of human rights and fundamental freedoms*, UN GAOR 4th Comm., 45th Session, Provisional Agenda Item 4, paragraph 57, UN Doc. E/CN.4/Sub.2/1993/8.

104. Horowitz, D. Advert found on *FrontPage Magazine* website in March 2001. Available at Frontpagemag.comhorowitzsnotepad/2001/hn01-03-01.htm.

105. See *Universal Declaration of Human Rights* Article 8; International Covenant on Civil and Political Rights, Article 2(3) (a), and the Convention against Torture and Other Cruel, Inhuman, or Degrading Treatment or Punishment, Article 14 (1).

106. See the *Chozrow Factory* case, *Publications of the Permanent Court of International Justice*, Collection of Judgments, Series A, No. 9, 21; Series A, No. 17, 29 (June 27, 1928). This case was cited with approval in the February 14, 2002 judgment, *Democratic Republic of the Congo v. Belgium*, in which the court held that "reparation must, as far as possible, wipe out all the consequences of the illegal act and re-establish the situation which would, in all probability, have existed if that act had not been committed."

107. An example is the finding of the Inter-American Court of Human Rights in the *Velásquez Rodriguez* case. See Inter-American Court of Human Rights, *Velásquez Rodriguez v. Honduras*, Serie C, nr. 7, Judgment of July 21, 1989 (Compensatory Damages), paragraph 71. See further Tomuschat, C. (2002). Reparation for victims of grave human rights violations. *Tulane Journal of International and Comparative Law*, *10*, 157–184.

108. See, for example, Fernandez, L. (1996). Possibilities and limitations of reparations for the victims of human rights violations in South Africa. In Rwelamira, M. & Werle, G. (eds.), *Confronting past injustices: Approaches to amnesty, reparation and restitution in South Africa and Germany*. Durban: Community Law Centre, University of the Western Cape, 65–78.

109. For a claim to succeed against a country, plaintiffs would have to surmount certain obstacles. In the United States, the Foreign Sovereign Immunities Act often operates to insulate state actors from liability. See further Saunders, L. (2001). Rich and rare are the gems they wear: Holding De Beers accountable for trading conflict diamonds. *Fordham International Law Journal*, *24*, 1402–1476. The Supreme Court in *Argentine Republic v. Almerada Hess Shipping Corporation* held that the Act of 1976 established a general immunity of foreign states from suits before American courts. See *Argentine Republic v. Almerada Hess Shipping Corp.*, 488 U.S. 428 (1989).

110. See Penrose, M. (2000). It's good to be the king! Prosecuting heads of state and former heads of state under international law. *Columbia Journal of Transnational Law*, *39*, 193; Perez, A. (2000). The perils of Pinochet: Problems for transitional justice and a supranational governance solution. *Denver Journal of International Law and Policy*, *28*, 175; Pierson, C. (2000). Pinochet and the end of immunity. *Temple International and Comparative Law Journal*, *14*, 263; and Hasson, A. (2002). Extraterritorial jurisdiction and sovereign immunity on trial: Noriega, Pinochet and Milosevic: Trends in political accountability and trans-national criminal law. *Boston College International & Comparative Law Review*, *25*, 125.

111. Ellinikos, M. (2001). American MNCs continue to profit from the use of forced and slave labor: Begging the question: Should America take a cue from Germany? *Columbia Journal of Law and Social Problems*, *35*, 1, 26.

112. In the decision *Prosecutor v. Tadic* IT-94-1-A (July 15, 1999) the tribunal considered international principles for attributing actions of private actors to state actors. The tribunal held that a state can be held responsible because of its request to a private individual to discharge tasks on its behalf. *Judgment of the Appeals Chamber*, at paragraph 119.

113. See Bazyler, M.J. (2002). The Holocaust restitution movement in comparative perspective. *Berkeley Journal of International Law*, *20*, 11.

114. See Bazyler, M.J. (2002). The Holocaust restitution movement in comparative perspective. *Berkeley Journal of International Law*, *20*, 11.

115. 630 F.2d 876, 880 (2d Cir. 1980).

116. 630 F.2d 876, 890 (2d Cir. 1980).

117. *Velásquez Rodriguez* Case, Judgment of July 29, 1988, Inter-Am.Ct.H.R. (Ser. C) No. 4 (1988) paragraph 170.

118. Stevens, B. (2002). Translating Filartiga: A comparative and international law analysis of domestic remedies for international human rights violations. *Yale Journal of International Law*, *27*, 1, 24.

119. Court of First Instance of Leivadia, October 30, 1997. (1997). *American Journal of International Law*, *92*, 765; Case No. 11/2000, Hellenic Supreme Court, May 4, 2000.

120. Gillard, E.C. (2003). Reparations for violations of international humanitarian law. *International Review of the Red Cross*, *85*, 529, 538.

121. In *Abebe-Jira v. Negewo*, 72 F.3d 844 (11th Cir. 1996), Ethiopians filed suit against a former official of the government in that country charging torture. Each plaintiff was awarded $200,000 in compensatory damages and $300,000 in punitive damages. See also *Alejandre v. Republic of Cuba*, 996 F. Supp. 1239 (S.D. Fla. 1997).

122. Redress (2000). *Challenging impunity for torture: A manual for bringing criminal and civil proceedings in England and Wales for torture committed abroad.* London, 36.

123. Reydams, L. (2003). *Universal jurisdiction: International and municipal legal perspective.* Oxford: Oxford University Press.

124. Bassiouni, M.C. (1998). *The statute of the International Criminal Court: A documentary history.* Ardsley, NY: Transnational Publishers.

125. On the obligations of states see further Nina, H.B.J. (2000). *The responsibility of states for international crimes.* Oxford: Oxford University Press.

126. Redress (2003). *Reparation for torture: A survey of law and practice in thirty selected countries.* London, 48.

127. Redress (2003). *Reparation for torture: A survey of law and practice in thirty selected countries.* London, 48.

128. Redress (2003). *Reparation for torture: A survey of law and practice in thirty selected countries.* London, 3.

129. Hakata, M. (2001). Hereros Sue Germany for Reparations. *New African*, 12–14. See also Shigwedha, A. (2001). *Hereros v. Germany. New African*, 14.

130. The Herero People's Reparation Corporation, the Herero tribe through its Paramount Chief Kuaima Riruako, 199 individuals and the Chief Hosea Kutako Foundation filed in the Superior Court of the District of Columbia a case captioned *The Herero People's Reparation Corporation, et al. v. Deutsche Bank AG, et al.*, 01 CA 4447.

131. The Terex claim was later dropped—at least temporarily. See *UN Integrated Regional Information Network*, September 21, 2001.

132. Various strategies have been attempted to claim reparations for the atrocities committed against the Herero. Speaking at the commemoration of Herero Day at Okahandja in 1999, Chief Riruako stated: "On the threshold of the new millennium the Hereros, as a nation, have decided to take Germany to the International Court for a decision regarding reparations. We also warn the Namibian Government not to stand in our way as we explore this avenue to justice." Each year in August the Hereros come together in memory of their fallen heroes who died during the 1904–1907 Herero-German war. See Maletsky, C. International Court Dashes Hereros' Reparation Hopes. *The Namibian*, September 8, 1999.

133. Bridgland, F. Germany's Genocide Rehearsal. *The Scotsman*, September 26, 2001. See also Wellington, J.H. (1967). *South West Africa and its human issues.* Oxford: Clarendon Press.

134. Maletsky, C. Hereros Temporarily Drop Claim in $2 bn Suit. *Business Day*, September 20, 2001.

135. On September 19, 2001 plaintiffs filed against the Federal Republic of Germany. See *The Herero Peoples' Reparation Corporation, et al. v. Federal Republic of Germany*, 1:01CV01987CKK. See also Maletsky C. & Mokopanele, T. SA Refuses to Consider Reparation for Hereros. *Business Day*, September 28, 2001.

136. Bridgland, F. Germany's Genocide Rehearsal. *The Scotsman*, September 26, 2001.

137. The role of Woermann Lines in GSWA is controversial. They had the shipping monopoly to the colony and controlled all landings in the ports, but by 1907 their domination was regarded as being against the public interest. It was alleged in the *Reichstag* that, compared to other companies, Woermann Lines charged the government exorbitant prices and made huge profits as a result. Epstein, K. (1959). Erzberger and the German colonial scandals, 1905–1910. *English Historical Review*, *74*, 637–663, 643–644.

138. Stoecker, H. (ed.). (1986). *German imperialism in Africa: From the beginnings until the Second World War*. London: C. Hurst, 24.

139. Herero complaint in the Washington, D.C. case. Gewald notes that the exodus of people after the concentration camps were closed caused Woermann Lines to be short of labour for loading their ships. Gewald, J-B. (1999). The road of the man called Love and the sack of Sero: The Herero-German War and the export of the Herero labour to the South African Rand. *Journal of African History*, *40*, 21–40, 29.

140. For more on the mining companies see Goldblatt, I. (1971). *History of South West Africa, from the beginning of the nineteenth century*. Cape Town: Juta.

141. Stoecker, H. (ed.) (1986). *German imperialism in Africa: From the beginnings until the Second World War*. London: C. Hurst, 52.

142. *Herero People's Reparations Corporation v. Deutsche Bank*, 370 F.3d 1192, 361 U.S. App. D.C. 468, (2004).

143. DC Circuit and other federal courts "clearly counsel against recognizing a cause of action for violations of international law in the absence of a federal statute." *The Herero People's Reparations Corporation v. Deutsche Bank AG*, No. 01-1868, mem. op. at 16 (D.D.C. July 31, 2003); and "[T]he Restatement of Foreign Relations Law fails to support such a proposition, the Court is left to conclude that Plaintiffs have failed to present a valid cause of action. Accordingly, Plaintiffs have failed to state a claim upon

which relief can be granted, and the Court will dismiss their Amended complaint pursuant to Federal Rule of Civil Procedure 12(b)(6)." At 21.

144. *Herero People's Reparations Corporation v. Deutsche Bank*, 370 F.3d 1192, 361 U.S. App. D.C. 468, (2004).

145. 2006 WL 182078.

146. 2006 WL 182078.

147. *See Halio v. Marcos*, 103 F.3d 767, 772–773.

148. 334 F. Supp. at 366.

149. 2006 WL 182078, at 9.

150. 2006 WL 182078, at 9.

151. 2006 WL 182078, at 9.

152. 672 F. Supp. at 1550.

153. 963 F. Supp. at 897.

154. 103 F.3d 767.

155. 542 U.S. 692, 124 S.Ct. 2739, 159 L.Ed.2d 718 (2004).

156. At 738.

157. 542 U.S. 692, 124 S. Ct. 2739, 159 L.Ed.2d 718 (2004)

158. See Sebok, A.J. (2001). Slavery, reparations, and potential legal liability: The hidden legal issue behind the U.N. racism conference. http://writ.news.findlaw.com/sebok/20010910.html (last visited on May 23, 2002).

159. Regarding the Herero's claim, Harring argues that they "are aware that reparations regimes operant in the world today are political and not legal. But, these political actions have a common history of being moved by extensive legal posturing, creating a powerful moral climate supporting reparations, and shaping public opinion." Harring, S.L. (2002). German reparations to the Herero nation: An assertion of Herero nationhood in the path of Namibian development? *West Virginia Law Review*, *104*, 393, 410.

160. Zia-Zarifi, S. (1999). Suing multinational corporations in the U.S. for violating international law. *University of California Los Angeles Journal of International Law and Foreign Affairs*, *4*, 81, 85. See further Frey, B. (1997). The legal and ethical responsibilities of transnational corporations in the protection of human rights. *Minnesota Journal of Global Trade*, *6*, 153.

161. For the relevance of colonial issues today see generally Steinmetz, G. (2003). The implications of colonial and postcolonial studies for the study of Europe. *European Studies Newsletter (Council for European Studies)*, *32*, 1–3.

162. Steinmetz has noted that: "Colonial massacre marks a third boundary condition to native policy, along with the limit conditions of full-scale assimilation and incommensurable difference. Colonialism, as Sartre noted, was always a contradictory system, one that 'wills simultaneously the death and the multiplication of its victims.' The governor of Southwest Africa, Theodor Leutwein, insisted that colonialism without the colonized was a contradiction in terms. Leutwein's protest came in response to General von Trotha's infamous Proclamation to the Herero on October 2, 1904, which declared that all Herero had to leave the colony or face death. Like the Herero, Leutwein lost that battle.... The colonizers's treatment of the Southwest African Herero illustrates a degraded, negative, objectifying form of assimilation. Rather than accepting the Herero as equals, the central aim of Governor Leutwein before 1904 and of the post-war Governors vis-à-vis the survivors of the 1904 massacre was to transform the Herero from something fundamentally incomprehensible into a degraded version of the German

colonizer. This program of negative assimilation sought to align Herero subjectivities and material practices with the culture of the colonizers, making them similar enough to the Germans be easily manageable as a labor force, but without ever suggesting the possibility of complete identity or legal equality. The surviving Herero were to be turned into a deracinated, atomized proletariat, and their traditional social and political structures were outlawed and crushed." Steinmetz, G. (2003). The devil's handwriting: Precolonial discourse, ethnographic acuity and cross-identification in German colonialism. *Comparative Studies in Society and History, 45*, 41–95. See also Krüger, G. (1999), *Kriegsbewältigung und Geschichtsbewusstsein: Realität, Deutung und Verarbeitung des deutschen Kolonialkrieges in Namibia, 1904 bis 1907.* Göttingen: Vandenhoek & Ruprecht.

163. Lovejoy, P. (2000). *Transformation in slavery: A history of slavery in Africa* (2nd ed.). Cambridge: Cambridge University Press, 65–66, 142.

164. Blaut, J.M. (1993). *The colonizer's model of the world: Geographical diffusionism and Eurocentric history.* New York: Guilford Press, 184.

165. In this regard Adam Hochschild notes that it is difficult to comprehend how the European reform movement focused its attention exclusively on Leopold's Congo when "if you reckon [the] mass murder by the percentage of the population killed," the Germans did as much in Namibia, if not worse, than Leopold in Congo. "By these standards," Hochschild argues, "the toll was even worse among the Hereros in German South West Africa, today's Namibia." Cited in Ankomah, B. (1999). The butcher of Congo. *New African, 387*, 14–18.

166. Gutto, S. (1993). *Human and peoples' rights for the oppressed: Critical essays on theory and practice from sociology of law perspective.* Lund: Lund University Press, 58–59.

167. See Cook, S. & Borah, W. (1971). *Essays in population history: Mexico and the Caribbean.* Berkeley, CA: University of California Press.

168. Miller, M.S. (ed.). (1993). Cultural *survival, state of the peoples: A global human rights report on societies in danger.* Boston: Beacon Press, 74.

169. Mande, M. & Edwin, E. Justice for Maji Maji. *The East African* (Nairobi), February 28, 2006.

170. Kenya: Ex-Mau Mau Set Date to File Case Against UK. *The Nation* (Nairobi) May 6, 2006.

171. See examples of these opinions in Chapter Three.

172. Howard, R.E. (1986). *Human rights in Commonwealth Africa.* Totowa, NJ: Rowman & Littlefield, 9.

173. In this regard the Herero Chief has argued: "We are taking our case to America because it's easier and fairer and we can get support from the public there. Jews could not take their case to Germany, what chance then do we have of succeeding [in Germany]?" *The Independent*, London, September 9, 2001.

174. Goldstone, R. Ethnic Reconciliation Needs the Help of a Truth Commission. *International Herald Tribune*, October 24, 1998.

175. Harring, S.L. (2002). German reparations to the Herero nation: An assertion of Herero nationhood in the path of Namibian development? *West Virginia Law Review, 104*, 393, 414–415.

176. Fröschle, H. Ein normaler Kolonialkrieg, kein Genozid. 262 *FAZ*, November 11, 2002, 11. Cited in Schuring, E. (2004). *History obliges: The real motivations behind*

German aid flows in the case of Namibia. MA thesis (Law & Diplomacy), Fletcher School of Law and Diplomacy, Tufts University, 34.

177. *Business Day*, July 19, 2004.

178. Human Rights Watch, An approach to reparations, July 19, 2001. Available at http://hrw.org/english/docs/2001/07/19/global285_txt.htm.

179. Human Rights Watch, An approach to reparations, July 19, 2001. Available at http://hrw.org/english/docs/2001/07/19/global285_txt.htm.

180. Sautman, B. (2001). Is Tibet China's colony? The claim of demographic catastrophe. *Columbia Journal of Asian Law*, *15*, 81, 85.

181. Waldron, J. (1992). Superseding historic injustice. *Ethics*, *103*, 4–28, 7.

182. Jere-malanda, R. (2000). Massacre in the desert. *You*, 34–40, 40.

183. Feagin, J.R. & O'Brien, E. (1999). The long-overdue reparations for African Americans. In Brooks, R.L. (ed.), *When sorry isn't enough: The controversy over apologies and reparations for human injustice*. New York: New York University Press, 418, 420.

184. Waldron, J. (1992). Superseding historic injustice. *Ethics*, *103*, 4–28, 7.

185. See Harring, S.L. (1996). The constitution of Namibia and the 'rights and freedoms' guaranteed communal land holders: Resolving the inconsistency between article 16, Article 100 and Schedule 5. *South African Journal on Human Rights, 12*, 467–484; and Harring, S.L. (2002). Stolen lands under the constitution of Namibia: Land reform under the rule of law. In Hinz, M., Amoo, S. & Van Wyk, D. (eds.), *The constitution at work: 10 years of Namibian nationhood*. Windhoek: University of Namibia Press, 145.

186. *Eddie Mabo and Others versus The State of Queensland*, decision of the High Court of Australia No. 2 (1992) 175 CLR 1 F.C. See Horn, N. (2005). Eddie Mabo and Namibia: Land Reform and Pre-Colonial Land Rights. *Sur Human Rights Journal*, *3*, 81–93.

187. Article 4.

188. Shaw, M.N. (1989). Genocide and international law. In Dinstein, Y. (ed.), *International law at a time of perplexity (Essays in honour of Shabtai Rosenne)*. Dordrecht: Martinus Nijhoff, 797, 814.

189. Report of the International Law Commission on the Work of its Fiftieth Session, April 20–June 12, 1998, July 27–August 14, 1998, UN Doc. A/53/10 and Corr. 1, paragraph 249.

190. See Schabas, W.A. (2000). *Genocide in international law*. Cambridge: Cambridge University Press, 436.

191. *Whitaker Report*, paragraph 54.

192. *Kayishema & Ruzindana*, Judgement, ICTR-95-1-T decision of May 21, 1999, paragraph 94.

193. *Application of the Convention on the Prevention and Punishment of the Crime of Genocide* (*Bosnia and Herzegovina v. Yugoslavia (Serbia and Montenegro)*), Preliminary Objections, [1996] *ICJ Reports*, 595.

194. *Application of the Convention on the Prevention and Punishment of the Crime of Genocide* (*Bosnia and Herzegovina v. Yugoslavia (Serbia and Montenegro)*), Preliminary Objections, [1996] *ICJ Reports*, paragraph 32.

195. First Report on State Responsibility by Mr James Crawford, Special Rapporteur, UN Doc. A/CN.4/490/Add.2, paragraph 63.

196. See Schabas, W.A. (2000). *Genocide in international law*. Cambridge: Cambridge University Press, 436 et seq.

197. Shaw, M.N. (1986). *International Law* (2nd ed.). Cambridge: Grotius Publications, 407.

198. Murphy, J.F. (1999). Civil liability for the commission of international crimes as an alternative to criminal prosecution. *Harvard Human Rights Journal*, *12*, 1, 32.

199. Murphy, J.F. (1999). Civil liability for the commission of international crimes as an alternative to criminal prosecution. *Harvard Human Rights Journal*, *12*, 1, 32.

200. *Alejandre v. Republic of Cuba*, 996 F. Supp. 1239 (S.D. Fla. 1997).

201. See *Flatow v. Republic of Iran*, 999 F. Supp. 1 (D.D.C. 1998); *Cicippio v. Republic of Iran*, 18 F. Supp. 2d 62 (D.D.C. 1998).

202. See *Rein v. Socialist People's Libyan Arab Jamahiriya*, 995 F. Supp. 325 (E.D.N.Y. 1998).

203. Nollkaemper, A. (2003). Concurrence between individual responsibility and state responsibility in international law. *International and Comparative Law Quarterly*, *52*, 615.

204. Application of the Genocide Convention case, Preliminary Objections, paragraph 32. The ICC Statute also notes in Article 25(4) that "No provision in this Statute relating to individual criminal responsibility shall affect the responsibility of States under international law."

205. See Dupuy, P.M. (2002). International criminal responsibility of the individual and international responsibility of the state. In Cassese, A., Gaeta, P. & Jones, J.R.W.D. (eds.), The *Rome Statute of the International Criminal Court: A commentary*. Oxford: Oxford University Press, 1085; Triffterer, O. (1996). Prosecution of states for crimes of state. *Revue Internationale de Droit Penal*, *67*, 341.

206. *Attorney General of the Government of Israel v. Eichmann* (1968) 36 ILR, 277.

207. See further Yablonka, H. (2004). *The state of Israel vs. Adolf Eichmann* (translated from Hebrew by O. Cummings with D. Herman). New York: Schocken Books.

208. Nollkaemper, A. (2003). Concurrence between individual responsibility and state responsibility in international law. *International and Comparative Law Quarterly*, 615.

209. Case of Certain questions relating to settlers of German origin in the territory ceded by Germany to Poland, Advisory opinion. PCIJ, Series B, No 6, 22, September 10, 1923. Cited in Nollkaemper, A. (2003). Concurrence between individual responsibility and state responsibility in international law. *International and Comparative Law*, *52*, 615.

210. On whether acts of individuals would see state liability, see Spinedi, M. (2002). State responsibility v. individual responsibility for international crimes: *Tertium non Datu*. *European Journal of International Law*, *13*, 895.

211. Paragraph 527, fn 105.

212. Du Plessis, M. (2003). Historical injustice and international law: An exploratory discussion of reparation for slavery. *Human Rights Quarterly*, *25*, 624–659, 632 fn 37.

213. Rasulov, A. (2003). Revisiting state succession to humanitarian treaties: Is there a case for automaticity? *European Journal of International Law*, *14*, 141.

214. Rasulov notes: "The concept of 'continuity' as used in the context of succession to treaties should be distinguished from the concept of 'continuity' as used in the context of describing the change in the legal identity of a state. The state that continues the personality of its predecessor is a continuator state, whereas the state that only continues its predecessor's treaties is a successor state." Rasulov, A. (2003). Revisiting state succession to humanitarian treaties: Is there a case for automaticity? *European Journal of International Law*, *14*, 141.

215. The 1978 *Vienna Convention on Succession of States in Respect of Treaties* only entered into force in 1996 and thus would not influence this question unless deemed to be retrospective. Besides, neither Germany nor Namibia is party to the Convention.

216. Gewald, J-B. (2003). Imperial Germany and the Herero of southern Africa: Genocide and the quest for recompense. In Jones, A. (ed.), *Genocide, war crimes, and the West: Ending the culture of impunity*. London: Zed Press, 59–77.

217. Berat, L. (1993). Genocide: The Namibian case against Germany. *Pace International Law Review*, *5*, 165, 201.

218. Junk, J. & Miner, J.M. (2004). Compensating historical injustice: More than just money. *Humanity in action. Reports of the 2004 Fellows in Denmark, Germany and the Netherlands*. New York, 43–47, 44.

219. Rasulov, A. (2003). Revisiting state succession to humanitarian treaties: Is there a case for automaticity? *European Journal of International Law*, *14*, 141.

220. Kamminga, M. (1996). State succession in respect of human rights treaties. *European Journal of International Law*, *7*, 469, 482.

221. Shelton, D. (1999). *Remedies in international human rights law*. Oxford: Oxford University Press, 147. This is stated in the context of the European system, but equally valid generally. The European position is now different and thousands of individual claims are permitted in that regional system each year.

222. Shelton, D. (2003). The world of atonement: Reparations for historical injustices. *Netherlands International law Review*, *60*, 289–325, 319.

223. Interpretation of Peace Treaties with Bulgaria, Hungary and Romania, First Phase, Advisory Opinion, *ICJ Reports* 1950, 71 and cited with approval in the ICJ Palestinian Wall case, paragraph 47.

224. Application for Review of Judgement No. 273 of the United Nations Administrative Tribunal, Advisory Opinion, *ICJ Reports* 1982, 333–334, paragraph 21.

225. International Court of Justice, July 9, 2004. *Legal Consequences of the Construction of a Wall in the Occupied Palestinian Territory*, paragraph 17.

226. Western Sahara, *ICJ Reports* 1975, 25, paragraphs 32–33.

227. See further MacEdo, S. (ed.). (2004). *Universal jurisdiction: National courts and the prosecution of serious crimes under international law*. Philadelphia: University of Pennsylvania Press.

228. Hanski, R. & Scheinin, M. (2003). *Leading cases of the Human Rights Committee*. Turku/Abo (Finland): Institute for Human Rights Abo Akademi University, 11.

229. O'Sullivan, M. (2005). Past violations under international human rights law: The indigenous 'Stolen Generation' in Australia. *Netherlands Quarterly of Human Rights*, *23*, 243–272, 255.

230. Established in terms of UN GA Resolution 2200 A (XXI) of December 16, 1966 and entered into force March 23, 1976. By July 2004, 152 states were parties to the Convention.

231. Hanski, R. & Scheinin, M. (2003). *Leading cases of the Human Rights Committee*. Turku/Abo (Finland): Institute for Human Rights Abo Akademi University, 14–17.

232. HRC General Comment 18, paragraph 10.

233. O'Sullivan, M. (2005). Past violations under international human rights law: The indigenous 'Stolen Generation' in Australia. *Netherlands Quarterly of Human Rights*, *23*, 243–272.

234. *Tk v. France*, Comm. No. 220/1987, December 8, 1989. UN Doc. CCPR/c/37/D/220/1987.

235. O'Sullivan, M. (2005). Past violations under international human rights law: The indigenous 'Stolen Generation' in Australia. *Netherlands Quarterly of Human Rights*, *23*, 243–272.

236. *Hylton v. Jamaica*, Comm. No. 407/1990, July 15, 1994. UN Doc. CCPR/51/D/407/1990, paragraph 79.

237. CCPR/C/57/D/566/1993. Decision of July 29, 1996, paragraph 2.3.

238. This was also the case in *E. and A. K. v. Hungary*, Decision of May 5, 1992. CCPR/C/50/D/520/1992.

239. Charters, C. (2005). Developments in indigenous peoples' rights under international law and their domestic implications. *New Zealand Universities Law Review*, *21*, 511–553.

240. No 516/1992 views adopted July 31, 1995, 54th Session of the Human Rights Committee. Cited in Higgins, R. (1997). Time and the law: International perspectives on an old problem. *International and Comparative Law Quarterly*, *46*, 501, 505.

241. Cited in Higgins, R. (1997). Time and the law: International perspectives on an old problem. *International and Comparative Law Quarterly 46*, 501, 505.

242. Macklem, P. (2005). Rybná 9, Praha 1: Restitution and memory in international human rights law. *European Journal of International Law*, *16*, 1–25.

243. *Somers*, CCPR/C/57/D/566/1993. Decision of July 29, 1996, paragraph 9.6.

244. *Somers*, CCPR/C/57/D/566/1993. Decision of July 29, 1996, paragraph 9.4. Cited in Macklem, P. (2005). Rybná 9, Praha 1: Restitution and memory in international human rights law. *European Journal of International Law*, *16*, 1–25, 3.

245. *E. and A.K.*, paragraph 6.4. Cited in Macklem, P. (2005). Rybná 9, Praha 1: Restitution and memory in international human rights law. *European Journal of International Law*, *16*, 1–25.

246. Macklem, P. (2005). Rybná 9, Praha 1: Restitution and memory in international human rights law. *European Journal of International Law*, *16*, 1–25.

247. CCPR/C/D 643/1995, Decision of July 14, 1997.

248. *Malik v. Czech Republic*, CCPR/C/D 669/1995, Decision of October 21, 1998.

249. *Malik v. Czech Republic*, CCPR/C/D 669/1995, Decision of October 21, 1998, paragraph 6.5.

250. UN Human Rights Committee, General Comment no. 18 (37th session, 1989). UN Doc. HRI/GEN/1/Rev.3, paragraph 13. Cited in Macklem, P. (2005). Rybná 9, Praha 1: Restitution and memory in international human rights law. *European Journal of International Law*, *16*, 1–25.

251. Charters, C. (2005). Developments in indigenous peoples' rights under international law and their domestic implications. *New Zealand Universities Law Review*, *21*, 511–553, 518.

252. *Henry Kalenga v. Zambia*, African Commission on Human and Peoples' Rights, Comm. No. 11/88, 1994.

253. *Embga Mekongo Louis v. Cameroon*, African Commission on Human and Peoples' Rights, Comm. No. 59/91, 1995.

254. *Embga Mekongo Louis v. Cameroon*, African Commission on Human and Peoples' Rights, Comm. No. 59/91, 1995.

255. *Malawi Africa Association and Others v. Mauritania*, African Commission on Human and Peoples' Rights, Comm. Nos. 54/91, 61/91, 98/93, 164/97 to 196/97, and 210/98, 2000. Gumedze, S. (2005). Bringing communications before the African Commission on Human Rights and People's Rights. *African Human Rights Law Journal, 3*, 118–148.

256. *Organisation Mondiale Contre La Torture v. Rwanda*, African Commission on Human and Peoples' Rights, Comm. Nos. 27/89, 46/91, 49/91, 99/93, 1996.

257. *The Protocol to the African Charter on Human and Peoples' Rights Establishing an African Court on Human and Peoples' Rights.*

258. The protocol was adopted by the Assembly of Heads of State and Government of the Organization of African Unity (OAU), at its 34th Ordinary Session, June 1998, in Ouagadougou, Burkina Faso. The 15 countries are: Algeria, Burkina Faso, Burundi, Gambia, Libya, Lesotho, Mali, Mauritania, Rwanda, South Africa, Senegal, Togo, Uganda, Ivory Coast, and the Comoros.

259. The European Court of Human Rights: *Notes for the guidance of persons wishing to apply to the European Court of Human Rights*, 17. Available at http://www.echr.coe.int/NR/rdonlyres/23F65B04-5BB6-48DB-AFED-C47A906F092E/0/NoticeENG.pdf.

260. [2000] ECHR 150 (April 5, 2000).

261. Article 34.

262. [1999] ECHR 22 (April 29, 1999).

263. (1995) 20 EHRR, 505.

264. Higgins, R. (1997). Time and the law: International perspectives on an old problem. *International and Comparative Law Quarterly, 46*, 501, 506.

265. 524, cited in Higgins, R. (1997). Time and the law: International perspectives on an old problem. *International and Comparative Law Quarterly, 46*, 501, 506.

266. [1999] ECHR 22 (April 29, 1999).

267. *De Becker v. Belgium* [1962] ECHR 1.

268. Rudolf, B. (1997). *Loizidou v. Turkey. American Journal of International Law, 91*, 532.

269. (1996) 22 EHRR, 197.

270. (1996) 22 EHRR, 197, 203.

271. (2002) 35 EHRR, 30.

272. Pauwelyn, J. (1995). The concept of a 'continuing violation' of an international obligation: Selected problems. *British Year Book of International Law, 66*, 415–450.

273. Harris, D.J., O'Boyle, M. & Warbrick, C. (1995). *Law of the European Convention on Human Rights*. London: Butterworths, 616.

274. (1997) 23 EHRR, 513.

275. (1997) 23 EHRR, 513 at 515.

276. (2004) ECHR, 274 (June 22, 2004).

277. (2004) ECHR 274 (June 22, 2004).

278. Drzewicki, K. (2004). Case commentary, *Broniowski v. Poland. European Human Rights Law Review, 5*, 580.

279. Paech, N. (2004). Der juristische Weg der Wiedergutmachung: Schadenersatz für Völkermord? In Böhlke-Itzen, J. (ed.), *Kolonialschuld und Entschädigung: der deutsche Völkermord an den Herero (1904–1907)*. Frankfurt am Main: Brandes & Apsel, 16.

280. *Federal Gazette* I (2002), 2254.

281. Defined in Principle VI (c) of the Nuremberg Charter as "murder, extermination, enslavement, deportation and other inhumane acts done against any civilian population, before or during the war, or persecutions on political, racial or religious grounds, when such acts are done or such persecutions are carried on in execution of or in connexion with any crime against peace or any war crime." Principle VI (c) provided that crimes against humanity were punishable as crimes under international law.

282. Werle, G. & Jessberger, F. (2002). International criminal justice is coming home: The new German code of crimes against international law. *Criminal Law Forum, 13*, 191–223, 192.

283. Werle, G. & Jessberger, F. (2002). International criminal justice is coming home: The new German code of crimes against international law. *Criminal Law Forum, 13*, 191–223, 198.

284. Werle, G. (2000). Völkerstrafrecht und geltendes deutsches Strafrecht. *Juristenzeitung, 55*, 755; Werle, G. (1997). Menschenrechtsschutz durch Völkerstrafrecht. *Zeitschrift für die Gesamte Strafrechtswissenschaft, 109*, 808–829.

285. Section 1, CCIL.

286. Berat, L. (1993). Genocide: The Namibian case against Germany. *Pace International Law Review, 5*, 165, 200. See also Berat, L. (1990). Namibia: The road to independence and the problem of succession of states. *Journal of Political Science, 18*, 33.

287. Herero legal claims against Germany in SW Africa. http://www.marcusgarveylibrary.org.uk/hererofarmlands.htm.

288. Shelton, D. (2004). The world of atonement reparations for historical injustices. *Miskolc Journal of International Law, 1*, 259–289.

289. Harring, S.L. (2002). German reparations to the Herero nation: An assertion of Herero nationhood in the path of Namibian development? *West Virginia Law Review, 104*, 393, 410.

290. Anderson, R. (2005). Redressing colonial genocide under international law: The Hereros' cause of action against Germany. *California Law Review, 93*, 1155–1189.

291. Konrad-Adenauer-Stiftung/Namibia Institute for Democracy (1994). *Namibia: Views and perspectives since independence.* Windhoek: Konrad-Adenauer-Stiftung/Namibia Institute for Democracy, 46.

292. http://www.op.gov.na/Decade_peace/moj.htm.

293. Schulz, S. & Hamutenya, M. (2003). Juvenile justice in Namibia: Law reform towards reconciliation and restorative justice? Polytechnic of Namibia. http://www.restorativejustice.org/resources/docs/namibia.

294. Amoo, S.K. (1985). The jurisprudence and the constitutional paradigm of the Namibian courts from 1985 to present times. *Namibian Human Rights On-Line Journal*, 2. http://www.unam.na/centres/hrdc/journal/edition2/docs/SKAmoo_1_2004.pdf.

295. *The Namibian*, October 18, 1991.

296. Herero complaint in the appeal to the Third Circuit.

297. Scott, M. (1958). The international status of South West Africa. *International Affairs, 34*, 318–329, 321.

298. Troup, F. (1950). *In face of fear: Michael Scott's challenge to South Africa.* London: Faber & Faber, 63.

299. Verdun, V. (1993). If the shoe fits, wear it: An analysis of reparations to African Americans, *Tulane Law Review, 67*, 597, 602.

300. Herero legal claims against Germany in SW Africa. http://www.marcusgarveylibrary.org.uk/hererofarmlands.htm.

301. Horowitz, D. (2002). *Uncivil wars: The controversy over reparations for slavery*. San Francisco: Encounter Books.

302. Coleman Jordan, E. (2003). A history lesson: Reparations for what? *New York University Annual Survey of American Law*, *58*, 557, 558.

303. Weigend, G.G. (1985). German settlement patterns in Namibia. *Geographical Review*, *75*, 156–169, 162.

304. Hall, D. (2004). The spirit of reparation. *Boston College Third World Law Journal*, *24*, 1, 3–4 fn 8.

305. On the genocide perpetrated on the indigenous population in today's USA, see Brantlinger P. (1998). Forgetting genocide: Or, the last of *The Last of the Mohicans*. *Cultural Studies*, *12*, 15–30.

306. Levmore, S. (1999). Privatizing reparations: Changes, anticipations, and reparations. *Columbia Law Review*, *99*, 1657.

307. *Aloeboetoe y otros v. Suriname*, Series C No. 15, September 10, 1993.

308. See further Perrin, W.A. (1999). The petition to obtain an apology for the Acadian deportation. *Southern University Law Review*, *27*, 1.

309. Shelton, D. (2003). The world of atonement: Reparations for historical injustices. *Netherlands International law Review*, *60*, 289–325, 293.

310. Preamble to Restitution of Land Rights Act 22 of 1994.

311. United Nations Office for the Coordination of Humanitarian Affairs Integrated Regional Information Network IRIN Africa English reports, 7/2/2003.

312. Redfern, P. Colonialism: Britain Faces Lawsuits. *The East African* (Nairobi), January 26, 2004.

313. Amadi Mugasia Group Seeks Probe on Colonialists. *The East African Standard*, November 24, 2003.

314. Mukisa, L. Court Clears UK on Bunyoro Killings. *The Monitor*, August 24, 2005.

315. Lyons, M.E. (2002). World Conference against Racism: New avenues for slavery reparations. *Vanderbilt Journal of Transitional Law*, *35*, 1235.

316. Lyons, M.E. (2002). World Conference against Racism: New avenues for slavery reparations. *Vanderbilt Journal of Transitional Law*, *35*, 1235, 1241.

317. Hall, D. (2004). The spirit of reparation. *Boston College Third World Law Journal*, *24*, 1, 6.

318. Lyons, M.E. (2002). World Conference against Racism: New avenues for slavery reparations. *Vanderbilt Journal of Transitional Law*, *35*, 1235, 1246.

319. Van Bueren, G. (2004). Slavery as piracy: The legal case for reparations for slavery. In Walden, R. (ed.), *Racism and Human Rights*. Leiden: Brill, 41–53, 45.

Bibliography

Abi-Saab, G. (1984). The specificities of humanitarian law. In Swinarski, C. (ed.) *Studies and essays on international humanitarian law and Red Cross principles.* Dordrecht: Martinus Nijhoff, 265–280.

Abplanalp, P. (1995). The international conferences of the Red Cross as a factor for the development of international humanitarian law and the cohesion of the International Red Cross and Red Crescent Movement. *International Review of the Red Cross, 308*, 520–549.

Abrams, J. (2001). The atrocities in Cambodia and Kosovo: Observations on the codification of genocide. *New England Law Review*, *35*, 303–310.

ACHPR. (1994). *Henry Kalenga v. Zambia*, African Commission on Human and Peoples' Rights, Comm. No. 11/88.

ACHPR. (1995). *Embga Mekongo Louis v. Cameroon*, African Commission on Human and Peoples' Rights, Comm. No. 59/91.

ACHPR. (1996). *Organisation Mondiale Contre La Torture v. Rwanda*, African Commission on Human and Peoples' Rights, Comm. Nos. 27/89, 46/91, 49/91, 99/93.

ACHPR. (2000). *Malawi Africa Association and Others v. Mauritania*, African Commission on Human and Peoples' Rights, Comm. Nos. 54/91, 61/91, 98/93, 164/97 to 196/97, and 210/98.

Adalian, R.P (1997). The Armenian genocide. In Totten, S., Parsons, W.S. & Charny, I.W. (eds.), *Century of genocide: Eyewitness accounts and critical views.* New York/London: Garland.

Adams, F., Werner, W., & Vale, P. (1990). *The land issue in Namibia: An inquiry.* Windhoek: Namibian Institute for Social and Economic Research, University of Namibia.

Adams, W. (1923). The American Peace Commission and the punishment of crimes committed during war. *Law Quarterly Review*, *39*, 245.

Administrator's Office Windhuk [sic] (ed.). (1918). *Report on the natives of South-West Africa and their treatment by Germany.* London: His Majesty's Stationery Office.

Afreds, J. (2000). History and nation-building. The political uses of history in post-colonial Namibia. *MFS-Reports: 2*. Uppsala: Department of Economic History.

Africa Watch. (1992). *Accountability in Namibia: Human rights and transition to democracy*. New York: Human Rights Watch.

Akhavan, P. (1995). Enforcement of the Genocide Convention: A challenge to civilization. *Harvard Human Rights Journal, 8*, 229–258.

Alexander, N. (1983). *The Namibian war of anti-colonial resistance 1904–1907*. Windhoek: Namibian Review Publications.

Alexander, N.E. (1981). Jakob Marengo and Namibian History. *Social Dynamics, 7*, 1–8.

Alexandrowicz , C.H. (1973). *The European-African confrontation*. Leiden: Sijtoff.

Allen, C.A. (1989). Civilian starvation and relief during armed conflict: The modern humanitarian law. *Georgia Journal of International and Comparative Law*, 1.

Allen, R.G., Cherniack, M. & Andreopoulos, G. J. (1996). Refining war: Civil wars and humanitarian controls. *Human Rights Quarterly, 18*, 747–781.

Alnaes, K. (1989). History of trauma. *Journal of African History, s* (1), 179.

Alvarez, A. (2001). *Governments, citizens, and genocide: A comparative and interdisciplinary approach*. Bloomington: Indiana University Press.

Amann, D.M. (1999). *Prosecutor v. Akayesu*: Judgment by International Criminal Tribunal for Rwanda on charges of genocide and international crimes of sexual violence. *American Journal of International Law, 93*, 195.

Ambos, K. & Othman, M. (2003). Introduction. In Ambos, K. & Othman, M. (eds.), *New approaches in international justice: Kosovo, East Timor, Sierra Leone and Cambodia*. Freiburg im Breisgau: Iuscrim.

Amnesty International AI Index: AFR 42/001/2003, August 4, 2003, Namibia: Justice delayed is justice denied: The Caprivi treason trial.

Amoo, S.K. (1985). The jurisprudence and the constitutional paradigm of the Namibian courts from 1985 to present times. *Namibian Human Rights On-Line Journal, 2*. Available at http://www.unam.na/centres/hrdc/journal/edition2/docs/SKAmoo_1_2004.pdf.

Amupadhi, T. German Scouts cancel Herero War Remembrance following Nujoma's Threat. *Africa News Service*, August 11, 2003.

Anaya, S.J. (2004). *Indigenous people in international law* (2nd ed.). Oxford: Oxford University Press.

Anderson, R. (2005). Redressing colonial genocide under international law: The Hereros' cause of action against Germany. *California Law Review*, 1155.

Anghie, A. (2004). *Imperialism, sovereignty and the making of international law*. Cambridge: Cambridge University Press

Ankomah, B. (1999). The butcher of Congo. *New African, 387*, 14–18.

Appulus, E. Hendrik Witbooi: SWAPO's Phoney Hero. *Windhoek Observer*, December 20, 1997.

Arendt, H. (1951). *The origins of totalitarianism*. New York: Harcourt Brace & Jovanovich.

Arendt, H. (1963). *Eichmann in Jerusalem. A report on the banality of evil*. New York: Viking Press.

Aronson, T. (1971). *The Kaisers*. London: Corgi Books.

Attorney General of the Government of Israel v. Eichmann. Israel Law Reports, 36, 5.

Aukerman, M.J. (2002). Extraordinary evil, ordinary crime: A framework for understanding transitional justice. *Harvard Human Rights Journal, 15*, 39.

Aydelotte, W.O. (1970). *Bismarck and British colonial policy: The problems of South West Africa 1883–1885* (2nd ed.). New York: Russell & Russell.

Baade, H. (1961). The Eichmann case: Some procedural legal aspects. *Duke Law Journal*, 400.

Babing, A. (2004). The role of the German Democratic Republic (GDR) in the international struggle against racism, apartheid and colonialism. Paper presented at A Decade of Freedom Conference, Durban, South Africa, October 10–13, 2004.

Baehr, P. (ed.). (2003). The portable Hannah Arendt New York: Penguin.

Balabkins, N. (1993). *West German reparations to Israel*. Piscataway, NJ: Rutgers University Press.

Balakian, P. (2003). *The burning Tigris: The Armenian genocide and America's response*. New York: Harper Collins.

Balfour, M. (1964). *The Kaiser and his times*. Boston: Houghton Mifflin.

Ball, H. (1999). *Prosecuting war crimes and genocide: The twentieth-century experience*. Lawrence: University Press of Kansas.

Bantekas, I. (2003). *Principles of direct and superior responsibility in international humanitarian law*. Manchester: Manchester University Press.

Barkan, E. (2000). *The guilt of nations: Restitution and negotiating historical injustices*. Baltimore: Johns Hopkins University Press.

Barkan, E. Restitution and amending historical injustices in international morality. Available at http://www.eucenter.scrippscol.edu/publications/papers/barkan.pdf.

Barkan, E. (2001). Symposium. Holocaust restitution: Reconciling moral imperatives with legal initiatives and diplomacy. Between restitution and international morality. *Fordham International Law Journal*, 46.

Barkan, E. (2003). Genocide of indigenous peoples: Rhetoric of human rights. In Gellately, R. & Kiernan, B. (eds.), *The specter of genocide mass murder in historical perspective*. Cambridge: Cambridge University Press, 117.

Bass, G.J. (2000). *Stay the hand of vengeance*. Princeton, NJ: Princeton University Press.

Bassiouni, M.C. Crimes against humanity. Crimes of war project. http://www.crimesofwar.org/thebook/crimes-against-humanity.html.

Bassiouni, M.C (ed.). (1986). *International criminal law, Vol. 1: Crimes of war*. New York: Dobbs Ferry.

Bassiouni, M.C. (1991). The time has come for an international criminal court. *Indiana International & Comparative Law Review*, *1*, 1.

Bassiouni, M.C. (1991). Enslavement as an international crime. *New York University Journal of International Law and Politics*, *23*, 445.

Bassiouni, M.C. (1998). *The statute of the International Criminal Court: A documentary history*. Ardsley, NY: Transnational Publishers.

Bassiouni, M.C. (1999). Crimes against humanity. In Bassiouni, M.C. (ed.). *International criminal law, Vol. 1, Crimes of War* (2nd ed.). Ardsley, NY: Transnational Publishers, 43.

Bassiouni, M.C. (1999). Crimes against humanity. In *International Criminal Law* (2nd rev. ed.). Cambridge, MA: Kluwer Law International.

Bassiouni, M.C. (1999). The normative framework of international humanitarian law: Overlaps, gaps and ambiguities. In Bassiouni, M.C. (ed.), *International criminal law, Vol. 1, Crimes of war* (2nd ed.). Ardsley, NY: Transnational Publishers, 617.

Bassiouni, M.C. & Nanda, V.P. (1973). *A treatise in international criminal law, Volume 1—Crimes and punishment*: Springfield, IL: Charles C Thomas.

Baty, T. (1900). *International law in South Africa*. London: Stevens & Haynes.

Bauer, G. (1999). Challenges to democratic consolidation in Namibia. In Joseph, R. (ed.) *State conflict and democracy in Africa*. Boulder, CO: Lynne Rienner.

Bauer, G. (2000). Namibia in the first decade of independence: How democratic? *Journal of Southern African Studies*, *27*, 33–55.

Bauman, Z. (1989). *Modernity and the holocaust*. Cambridge: Polity.

Baumgart, W. (1987). German imperialism in historical perspective. In Knoll, A.J. & Gann, L.H. (eds.), *Germans in the tropics: Essays in German colonial history*. New York/London: Greenwood Press.

Baxter, R.R. (1963). The first modern codification of the law of war—Francis Lieber and general orders no. 100 (II). *International Review of the Red Cross*, *3*, 234.

Bazyler, M.J. (2002). The Holocaust restitution movement in comparative perspective. *Berkeley Journal of International Law*, *20*, 11.

Becker, H. (1989). Namibia und die Deutschen. *Blätter des iz3w*, *156*.

Beckett, E.W. (1980). England and Germany in Africa. XLVIII. *Fortnightly Review*, 128–143.

Bedoukian, K. (1978). *Some of us survived: The story of an Armenian boy*. New York: Farrar, Straus & Giroux.

Bedszent, G. Terror und Enteignung, In *Junge Welt*, March 13, 1998.

Bennett, T.W. & Powell, C.H. (1999). Aboriginal title in South Africa revisited. *South African Journal on Human Rights*, *15*, 449–485.

Bensman, T. Tribe demands Holocaust reparations; Germany's Genocidal War against Namibia's Herero was Rehearsal for World War II Atrocities. *The Salt Lake Tribune*, March 18, 1999.

Bensman, T. *Forgotten victims: African tribe wants apology*. Available at http://www.pewfellowships.org/stories/namibia/forgotten-victims.html.

Berat, L. (1990). *Walvis Bay: The last frontier*. New Haven: Yale University Press.

Berat, L. (1990). Namibia: The road to independence and the problem of succession of states. *Journal of Political Science*, *18*, 33.

Berat, L. (1993). Genocide: The Namibian case against Germany. *Pace International Law Review*, *5*, 165.

Beris, A.P.J. (1996). *From mission to local church: One hundred years of mission by the Catholic Church in Namibia*. Windhoek: Roman Catholic Church.

Berman, H. (1985). Are indigenous populations entitled to international juridical personality? *American Society International Law Proceedings*, *79*, 189.

Best, G. (1980). *Humanity in warfare: The modern history of the international law of armed conflict*. New York: Columbia University Press.

Best, G. (1983). *Humanity in warfare: The modern history of the international law of armed conflicts*. London: Methuen.

Best, G. (1991). The restraint of war in historical and philosophical perspectives. In Delissen, A. & Tanja, G. (eds.). *Humanitarian law of armed conflict: Challenges ahead*. Dordrecht/Boston/London: Martinus Nijhoff.

Bischoping, K. & Fingerhut, N. (1996). Border lines: Indigenous peoples in genocide studies. *Canadian Review of Sociology and Anthropology*, *33*, 481–506.

Blackshire-Belay, C.A. (1992).German imperialism in Africa: The distorted images of Cameroon, Namibia, Tanzania and Togo. *Journal of Black Studies*, *23*, 235–246.

Blaut, J.M. (1993). *The colonizer's model of the world: Geographical diffusionism and Eurocentric history*. New York: Guilford Press.

Bley, H. (1967). Social discord in South West Africa 1894–1904. In Gifford, P. & Louis, W.M.R. (eds.), *Britain and Germany in Africa: Imperial rivalry and colonial rule* New Haven: Yale University.

Bley, H. (1967). German South West Africa after the conquest 1904–1914. In Segal, R. & First, R. *South West Africa: Travesty of trust*. London: Andre Deutsch, 35–53.

Bley, H. (1968). *Kolonialherrschaft und Sozialstruktur in Deutsch-Südwestafrika 1894–1914*. Hamburg, Leibniz.

Bley, H. (1971). *South West Africa under German rule 1894–1914*. London: Heinemann.

Blue, G. (1999). Gobineau on China; Race theory, the "Yellow Peril," and the critique of modernity. *Journal of World History*, *10*, 93–139.

Boahen, A. (1989). *African perspectives on colonialism*. Baltimore: Johns Hopkins University Press.

Boesche, R. (1995). *Theories of tyranny from Plato to Arendt*. University Park, PA: Pennsylvania State University Press.

Boehmer, E. (1995). *Colonial and postcolonial literature: Migrant metaphors*. Oxford: Oxford University Press.

Bogdan, A. (2002). Cumulative charges, convictions and sentencing at the ad hoc International Tribunals for the Former Yugoslavia and Rwanda. *Melbourne Journal of International Law*, *3*, 1–32.

Böhlke-Itzen, J. (2004). *Kolonialschuld und Entschädigung: Der deutsche Völkermord an den Herero (1904–1907)*. Frankfurt am Main: Brandes & Apsel.

Bollig, M. & Gewald, J-B. (2000). People, cattle and land: An introduction. In Bollig, M. & Gewald, J-B. (eds.), *People, cattle and land: Transformations of a pastoral society in South Western Africa*. Köln: Rudiger Koppe Verlag.

Bollig, M. & Gewald, J-B. (eds.), *People, cattle and land: Transformations of a pastoral society in South Western Africa*. Köln: Rudiger Koppe Verlag.

Bölsche, J. Die Peitsche des Bändigers, *Der Spiegel* 3, January 12, 2004.

Boraine, A. (2000). *A country unmasked*. Cape Town: Oxford University Press.

Boraine, A. Toward reconciliation: War criminal's remorse could help Bosnia heal. *International Herald Tribune*, December 18, 2002. Available at http://www.iht.-com/articles/80569.html.

Botha, C. (2000). The politics of land settlement in Namibia, 1890–1960. *South African Historical Journal, 42*, 232–276.

Boyajian, L.Z. & Grigorian, H.M. (1998). Reflections on the denial of the Armenian genocide. *The Psychoanalytic Review*, *85*, 505.

Brantlinger P. (1998). Forgetting genocide: Or, the last of *The Last of the Mohicans*. *Cultural Studies, 12*, 15–30.

Brath, E. African Liberation Day Rally for Reparations, *New York Amsterdam News*, May 20, 2004.

Bratton, M. & Van de Walle, N. (1997). *Democratic experiments in Africa: Regime transitions in comparative perspective*. Cambridge: Cambridge University Press.

Bravenboer, B. & Rusch, W. (1997). *The first 100 years of state railways in Namibia*. Windhoek: Trans-Namibian Museum.

Breitman, R. (1991). *The architect of genocide: Himmler and the Final Solution.* New York: Alfred Knopf.

Bridgland, F. Germany's Genocide Rehearsal. *The Scotsman*, September 26, 2001.

Bridgman, J. (1981). *The revolt of the Hereros.* Los Angeles: University of California Press.

Brierly, J.L. (1944). *The outlook for international law.* Oxford: Clarendon Press.

Brooks, R.L. (ed.), (1999). *When sorry isn't enough: The controversy over apologies and reparations for human injustice.* New York: New York University Press.

The Bryce Report into German atrocities in Belgium: Report of the Committee on Alleged German Outrages Appointed by His Britannic Majesty's Government and Presided Over by the Right Hon. Viscount Bryce, O.M., May 12, 1915

Buford, W. & Van der Merwe, H. (2004). Reparations in southern Africa. *Cahiers d'études africaines, 44.* Found at http://www.csvr.org.za/papers/papwbhv.htm.

Bugnion, F. (2004). The role of the Red Cross in the development of international humanitarian law: The International Committee of the Red Cross and the development of international humanitarian law. *Chicago Journal of International Law, 5,* 191.

Bullock, A.L.C. (1939). *German's colonial demands.* London: Oxford University Press.

Caldwell, P. (1994). National Socialism and constitutional law: Carl Schmitt, Otto Koellreutter, and the debate over the nature of the Nazi state, 1933–1937. *Cardozo Law Review, 16*, 399.

Calvert, A.F. (1915). *South West Africa: During the German occupation 1884–1914.* London: T. Werner Laurie.

Calvert, A.F. (1969). *South-West Africa during the German occupation 1884–1914.* New York: Negro University Press.

Cameron, V.L. (1890). England and Germany in Africa: III. *Fortnightly Review, XLVIII,* 144–163.

Caron, D.D. (2000). War and international adjudication: Reflections on the 1899 Peace Conference. *American Journal of International Law, 94*, 13.

Carstens, P., Klinghardt, G., & West, M. (eds.). (1987). *Trails in the thirstland: The anthropological field diaries of Winifred Hoernle.* Cape Town: Centre for African Studies, University of Cape Town.

Cassese, A. (2000). The Martens Clause: Half a loaf or simply pie in the sky? *European Journal of International Law, 11*, 187–216.

Cassese, A. (2001). *International law.* Oxford: Oxford University Press.

Cassese, A. (2003). *International criminal* law. Oxford: Oxford University Press.

Cecil, L. (1996). *Wilhelm II. Vol. II: Emperor and exile, 1900–1941.* Chapel Hill: University of North Carolina Press.

Cesaire, A. (1996). *Discourse on colonialism.* New York: New York University Press.

Chalk, F. (1994). Redefining genocide. In Andreopoulos, G.J. (ed.). *Genocide: Conceptual and historical dimensions.* Philadelphia: University of Pennsylvania Press.

Chalk, F. & Jonassohn, K. (1988). The history and sociology of genocidal killings. In Charney, I.W. (ed.), *Genocide: A critical bibliographic review.* London: Mansell, 39.

Chalk, F. & Jonassohn, K. (1990). *The history and sociology of genocide: Analyses and case studies.* New Haven: Yale University Press.

Charny, I.W. (1992). *How can we commit the unthinkable? Genocide: The human cancer.* Boulder, CO: Westview Press.

Charny, I.W. (1994). Toward a generic definition of genocide In Andreopoulos, G.J. (ed.), *Genocide: Conceptual and historical dimensions*. Philadelphia: University of Pennsylvania Press, 73–74.

Charny, I.W. (2000). Innocent denials of known genocides: A further contribution to a psychology of denial of genocide. *Human Rights Review*, *1*, 15–39.

Charny, I.W. (2003). A classification of denials of the Holocaust and other genocides. *Journal of Genocide Research*, *5*, 11–34.

Charters, C. (2005). Developments in indigenous peoples' rights under international law and their domestic implications. *New Zealand Universities Law Review*, *21*, 511–553.

Chesterman, S. (2000). An altogether different order: Defining the elements of crimes against humanity. *Duke Journal of Comparative & International Law*, *10*, 307.

Chigas, G. (2000). The politics of defining justice after the Cambodian genocide. *Journal of Genocide Research*, *2*, 245–265.

Chirot, D. Are ethnic genocides, cleansings, and other such massacres normal? Found at http://www.yale.edu/ccr/chirot.doc.

Churchill, W. (2000). Defining the unthinkable: Towards a viable understanding of genocide. *Oregon Review of International Law*, 3.

Cigar, N. (1995). *Genocide in Bosnia: The policy of ethnic cleansing*. College Station, Texas: Texas A&M University Press.

Clark, C. (2000). *Kaiser Wilhelm II. Profiles in power*. Essex: Pearson Education.

Clark, R. & Sann, M. (eds.). (1996). *The prosecution of international crimes*. Somerset, NJ: Transaction.

Clarke, R. (2002). Retrospectivity and the constitutional validity of the Bali bombing and East Timor trials. *Australian Journal of Asian Law*, *5*, 128.

Clemente, S. E. (1992). *For King and Kaiser: The making of the Prussian army officer, 1860–1914*. New York: Greenwood Press.

Cocker, M. (1998). *Rivers of blood, rivers of gold: Europe's conflict with tribal peoples*. London: Jonathan Cape.

Cohen, S. (1993). Human rights and crimes of the state: The culture of denial. *Australia and New Zealand Journal of Criminology*, *26*, 97–115.

Cohrssen, F.K. (1994). *A critical evaluation of the juridical status of Walvis Bay in colonial and post-colonial international law and practice, 1868–1993*. PhD, University of Natal.

Coleman Jordan, E. (2003). A history lesson: Reparations for what? *New York University Annual Survey of American Law*, *58*, 557.

Colijn, G.J. (2003). Carnage before our time: Nineteenth century colonial genocide. *Journal of Genocide Research*, *5*, 617–625.

Collier, P. (1999). Aid dependency: A critique. *Journal of African Economies*, *8*, 528–545.

Control Council Law No. 10 of 1945. (1946). Punishment of Persons Guilty of War Crimes, Crimes against Peace and against Humanity, December 20, 1945. *Official Gazette Control Council for Germany*, *3*, 50–55.

Convention (II) with Respect to the Laws and Customs of War on Land and its annex: *Regulations Concerning the Laws and Customs of War on Land*. The Hague, July 29, 1899.

Conway, P. (2003). Truth and reconciliation: The road not taken in Namibia. *The Online Journal of Peace and Conflict Resolution*, 66–76. http://www.trinstitute.org/ojpcr/5_1conway.htm.

Cook, S. & Borah, W. (1971). *Essays in population history: Mexico and the Caribbean.* Berkeley, CA: University of California Press.

Cooper, A.D. (2001). *Ovambo politics in the twentieth century.* Lanham: University Press of America.

Cooper, B. (ed.) (1999). *War crimes: The legacy of Nuremberg.* New York: TV Books.

Cornevin, R. (1969). The Germans in Africa before 1918. In Gann, L.H. & Duigan, P. *Colonialism in Africa 1870–1960.* Cambridge: Cambridge University Press, 223.

Court of First Instance of Leivadia, October 30, 1997. (1997). *American Journal of International Law, 92,* 765; Case No.11/2000, Hellenic Supreme Court, May 4, 2000.

Craig, G. (1955). *The politics of the Prussian army 1640–1945.* London: Oxford University Press.

Crawford, J. (1979). *The creation of states in international law.* Oxford: Clarendon Press.

Cribb, R. Genocide in the non-Western world: Implications for Holocaust studies. In Jensen, S.L.B. (2003). *Genocide: Cases, comparisons and contemporary debates.* Copenhagen: Danish Center for Holocaust and Genocide Studies, 123.

Crothers, G.D. (1968). *The German elections of 1907.* New York: Columbia University Press.

Culver, J., Jr. Berlin Anti-Colonial Conference: 120 years of African resistance. *The Black Commentator, 116,* December 2, 2004. http://www.blackcommentator.com/116/116_berlin_conference.html.

Cunningham, M. (1999). Saying sorry: The politics of apology. *The Political Quarterly, 70,* 285. Alter, S. (1999). *Apologising for serious wrongdoing: Social, psychological and legal considerations.* Report for the Law Commission of Canada. Available at http://www.lcc.gc.ca/en/themes/mr/ica/2000/html/apology.asp.

Dadrian, V.N. (1998). The Armenian genocide and the legal and political issues in the failure to prevent or to punish the crime. *University of West Los Angeles Law Review, 29,* 43.

Dadrian, V.N. (1999). The determinants of the Armenian genocide. *Journal of Genocide Research, 1,* 65–80.

Dale, R. (1976). Colonial rulers and ruled in South West Africa and the Bechuanaland Protectorate 1884–1966: A framework for comparative study. *Journal of Southern African Affairs, 1,* 95–110.

Daly, E. & Sarkin, J. (2007). *Reconciliation in divided societies: Searching for common ground.* Philadelphia: University of Pennsylvania Press.

Daniels, C. (2003). The struggle for indigenous people's rights. In Melber, H. (ed.), *Re-examining liberation in Namibia: Political culture since independence.* Uppsala: Nordic Africa Institute.

Davidson, E. (1966). *The trial of the Germans: An account of the twenty-two defendants before the International Military Tribunal at Nuremberg.* New York: Macmillan.

Davis, A.N. (1918). *The Kaiser as I know him.* New York: Harper & Brothers.

Davis, G. (1907). Lieber's instructions for the government of armies in the field. *American Journal of International Law, 1,* 13.

Deacon, H. (2004). Marion Wallace, health, power and politics in Windhoek, Namibia 1915–1945 (Review). *Bulletin of the History of Medicine, 78,* 916–917.

Deckert, M.E. (1966). The causes of the Herero uprising of 1904–1906 in South West Africa. In Cordier, A. W. (ed). *Columbia essays in international affairs*. New York: Columbia University Press, 255.

Declaration by the Stockholm International Forum (2004). http://www.manskligarattigheter.gov.se/stockholmforum/2004/page1617.html.

Declaration Renouncing the Use, in Time of War, of Explosive Projectiles Under 400 Grammes Weight (St. Petersburg Declaration), reprinted in *American Journal of International Law*, *1*, 95 (1907).

Dedering, T. (1993). The German-Herero War of 1904: Revisionism of genocide or imaginary historiography. *Journal of Southern African Studies*, *19*, 80.

Dedering, T. (1999). A certain rigorous treatment of all parts of the nation: The annihilation of the Herero in German South West Africa, 1904. In Levine, M. & Roberts, P. (eds.), *The massacre in history*. New York: Oxford: Berghahn Books.

Dedering, T. (1999). The prophet's "War against Whites": Shepherd Stuurman in Namibia and South Africa 1904–1907. *Journal of African History*, *40*, 1–19.

De Guzman, M.M. (2000). The road from Rome: The developing law of crime against humanity. *Human Rights Quarterly*, *22*, 335–403.

Dentlinger, L. (2004) DTA Slams Govt over Recognition of Herero Chiefs. *Africa News Service*, August 20, 2004.

Dentlinger, L. (2005) Hereros Back Pohamba's Decision Not to Endorse German Reparation Deal. *The Namibian*, December 2, 2005.

De Renzio, P. (2005). Can more aid be spent in Africa? *Opinions* 30. London: Overseas Development Institute.

Destexhe, A. (1995). *Rwanda and genocide in the twentieth century* (Alison Marschner, transl.). New York: New York University Press.

Detter, I. (1966). The problem of unequal treaties. *International and Comparative Law Quarterly*, 1069–1089.

Detter Delupis, I. (1987). *The law of war*. New York: Cambridge University Press.

De Villiers, B. (2003). *Land reform: Issues and challenges. A comparative overview of experiences in Zimbabwe, Namibia, South Africa and Australia*. Johannesburg: Konrad Adenauer Foundation

De Zayas, A. Memorandum on the genocide against the Armenians 1915–1923 and the application of the 1948 Genocide Convention. European Armenian Federation for Justice & Democracy (EAFJD) (ed.). Available at http://www16.brinkster.com/eafjd/en/bulletins/dezayas_report.pdf.

Diamond, Jared. (1997). *Guns, germs and steel: The fates of human societies*. New York: W.W. Norton Publishers.

Diebold, E., Engelhardt, S. & Iskenius, D. (2004). Facing the past to liberate the future: Colonial Africa in the German mind. *Humanity in action. Reports of the 2004 Fellows in Denmark, Germany and the Netherlands*, *6*. New York.

Dienst, W. (1982). Kaiser Wilhelm II in the context of his military and naval entourage. In Röhl, J.C.G. & Sombart, N. (eds.), *Kaiser Wilhelm II: New interpretations. The Corfu Papers*. Cambridge: Cambridge University Press, 169.

Dinstein, Y. (1996). Crimes against humanity. In Makarczyk, J. (ed.), *Theory of international law at the threshold of the 21st century*. The Hague/Boston: Kluwer Law International, 891.

Dobell, L. (1997). Silence in context: Truth and/or reconciliation in Namibia. *Journal of Southern African Studies*, *23*, 2.

Dolzer, R. (2002). The settlement of war-related claims: Does international law recognize a victim's private right of action? Lessons after 1945. *Berkeley Journal of International Law*, 296.

Dorpalen, A. (1952). Empress Auguste Victoria and the fall of the German monarchy. *American Historical Review*, *58*, 17–38.

Doswald-Beck, L. & Vite, S. (1993). International humanitarian law and human rights law. *International Review of the Red Cross*, *293*, 94–119.

Doty, G. (1998). The US and the development of the laws of land warfare. *Military Law Review*, *156*, 224.

Draper, G.I.A.D. (1971). The relationship between the human rights regime and the law of the armed conflicts. *Israel Yearbook on Human Rights*, 191–207.

Drechsler, H. (1966). *Südwestafrika unter deutscher Kolonialherrschaft: Der Kampf der Herero und Nama gegen den deutschen Imperialismus (1884–1915)*. Berlin: Akademie-Verlag.

Drechsler, H. (1980). *Let us die fighting: The struggle of the Herero and Nama against the German imperialism (1894–1915)* (Bernd Zöllner, transl.). London: Zed Press.

Drechsler, H. (1986). *Let us die fighting*. Berlin: Akademie-Verlag.

Dreyer, R.F. (1987). *The mind of official imperialism: British and Cape government perceptions of German rule in Namibia from the Heligoland-Zanzibar Treaty to the Kruger telegram, 1890–1896*. Essen: Reimar Hobbing.

Drost, P. N. (1951). *Human rights as legal rights*. Leiden: A.W. Sijthoff

Drost, P.N. (1959). *Crime of state Book II: Genocide*. Leiden: A.W. Sijthoff.

Drost, P.N. (1965). *Human rights as legal rights*. Leiden: A.W. Sijthoff.

Drumbl, M. (2005). Collective violence and individual punishment: The criminality of mass atrocity. *Northwestern University Law Review*, *99*, 539.

Drzewicki, K. (2004). Case commentary, *Broniowski v. Poland*. *European Human Rights Law Review*, *5*, 580.

Dufour, F.G. (2001). Toward a socio-historical theory of persecution and an analytical concept of genocide. Occasional paper no. 67. Toronto: York University Centre for German & European Studies.

Dugard, J. (ed.). (1973). *The South West Africa/Namibia dispute: Documents and scholarly writings on the controversy between South Africa and the United Nations*. Berkeley: University of California Press.

Dugard, J. (1991). The treatment of rebels in conflicts of a disputed character: The Anglo-Boer War and the ANC-Boer War compared. In Delissen, A.J.M. & Tanja, G.J. (eds.), *Humanitarian law of armed conflict: Challenges ahead*. Dordrecht: Martinus Nijhoff, 447.

Dugard, J. (1998). Bridging the gap between human rights and humanitarian law: The punishment of offenders. *International Review of the Red Cross*, *324*, 445–453.

Dugard, J. (2000). *International law: A South African perspective*. Kenwyn: Juta.

Duigan, P. (1969). Review of John Wellington's *South West Africa and its human issues*. *American Historical Review*, *74*, 1333–1334.

Du Pisani, A. (1987). Namibia: The historical legacy. In Totemeyer, G. Kandetu, V., & Werner, W. (eds.), *Namibia in perspective*. Windhoek: Council of Churches.

Du Pisani, A. (1986). *SWA/Namibia: The politics of continuity and change*. Johannesburg: Jonathan Ball.

Du Plessis, M. (2003). Historical injustice and international law: An exploratory discussion of reparation for slavery. *Human Rights Quarterly*, *25*, 624–659.

Du Preez, P. (1994). *Genocide. The psychology of mass murder*. London: Boyars/Bowerdean.

Dupuy, P.M. (2002). International criminal responsibility of the individual and international responsibility of the state. In Cassese, A., Gaeta, P., & Jones, J.R.W.D. (eds.), The *Rome Statute of the International Criminal Court: A commentary*. Oxford: Oxford University Press, 1085.

Du Toit, P. (1999). Bridge or bridgeheads: Comparing the party systems of Botswana, Namibia, Zimbabwe, Zambia and Malawi. In Giliomee H. & Simkins, C. (eds.), *The awkward embrace: One-party domination and democracy*. Cape Town: Tafelberg.

Eckert, A. (1997). Theories of colonial rule. *Journal of African History*, *38*, 325.

Eddie Mabo and Others versus The State of Queensland, decision of the High Court of Australia No. 2 (1992) 175 CLR 1 F.C. (Australia)

Eide, A. (1984). The laws of war and human rights: Differences and convergences. In Swinarski, C. (ed.). *Studies and essays on international humanitarian law and Red Cross principles*. Dordrecht: Martinus Nijhoff, 675–697.

Eizenstat, S. (1997). *U.S. and Allied efforts to recover and restore gold and other assets stolen or hidden by Germany during World War II: Preliminary study*. Available at http://www.ushmm.org/assets/nazigold.htm.

Ellinikos, M. (2001). American MNCs continue to profit from the use of forced and slave labor: Begging the question: Should America take a cue from Germany? *Columbia Journal of Law and Social Problems*, *35*, 1.

Elsea, Z. (2004). Facing genocide: The humanitarian crisis in Sudan. *Harvard International Review*, *26*, 11.

Eltzbacher, O. (1905). The German danger to South Africa. *The nineteenth century and after*, *58*, 524–538.

Encyclopaedia Americana, Vol. 14 (1971). New York.

Encyclopaedia Britannica Vol. VII (1911).

Epstein, K. (1959). Erzberger and the German colonial scandals, 1905–1910. *English Historical Review*, *74*, 637–663.

Erichsen, C.W. (2003 August/September). Namibia's Island of Death. *New African*, 46.

Erichsen, C.W. (2004). *The Angel of Death has descended violently among them: A study of Namibia's concentration camps and prisoners-of-war, 1904–08*. MA thesis (History), University of Namibia.

Esterhuyse, J.H. (1968). *South West Africa: The establishment of German authority in South West Africa*. Cape Town: C. Struik.

The European Court of Human Rights (2006). *Notes for the guidance of persons wishing to apply to the European Court of Human Rights*, 17. Available at http://www.echr.coe.int/NR/rdonlyres/23F65B04-5BB6-48DB-AFED-C47A906F092E/0/NoticeENG.pdf.

The European Court of Human Rights. *De Becker v. Belgium* [1962] ECHR 1.

Eveleigh, W. (1915). *South-West Africa*. Cape Town: Maskew Miller.

Expert opinions by F. Kalshoven, E. David & C. Greenwood (1999). In Fujita, H., Suzuki, I. & Nagano, K. (eds.), *War and rights of individuals: Renaissance of individual compensation*. Tokyo: Nippon Hyoron-sha.

Farer, T.J. (1971). The laws of war 25 years after Nuremberg. *International Conciliation, 585*. Carnegie Endowment for International Peace, 9.

Farer, T.J. (2000). Restraining the barbarians: Can international criminal law help? *Human Rights Quarterly, 22*, 90–117.

Feagin, J.R. & O'Brien, E. (1999). The long-overdue reparations for African Americans. In Brooks, R.L. (ed.), *When sorry isn't enough: The controversy over apologies and reparations for human injustice*. New York: New York University Press, 418.

Fein, H. (1992). *Genocide watch*. New Haven, CT: Yale University Press.

Fein, H. (1994). Genocide, terror, life integrity, and war crimes: The case for discrimination. In Andreopoulos, G.J. (ed.), *Genocide: Conceptual and historical dimensions*. Philadelphia: University of Pennsylvania Press, 97.

Fein, H. (1999). Genocide and gender: The uses of women and group destiny. *Journal of Genocide Research, 1*, 59.

Fenrick, W.J. (1999). Should crimes against humanity replace war crimes? *Columbia Journal of Transnational Law, 37*, 767.

Fernandez, L. (1996). Possibilities and limitations of reparations for the victims of human rights violations in South Africa. In Rwelamira, M. & Werle, G. (eds.), *Confronting past injustices: Approaches to amnesty, reparation and restitution in South Africa and Germany*. Durban: Community Law Centre, University of the Western Cape, 65–78.

First, R. (1967). *South West Africa*. Baltimore: Penguin Books.

Fisch, M. (1999). *The secessionist movement in the Caprivi: A historical perspective*. Windhoek: Namibia Scientific Society.

Fleck, D. (ed.). (1995). *The handbook of humanitarian law in armed conflicts*. New York: Oxford University Press.

Flint, J. (ed.). (1976). *The Cambridge history of Africa, Vol. 5*. Cambridge: Cambridge University Press.

Flynn, M. (2000). Genocide: It's a crime everywhere but not in Australia. *Western Australian Law Review, 29*, 59.

Forsythe, D.P. (1991). *The internalization of human rights*. Lexington, MA: Lexington Books.

Foster, D. (2000). Entitlement as explanation for perpetrators' actions. *South African Journal of Psychology, 30*, 10.

Foster, D. (2000). The Truth and Reconciliation Commission and understanding perpetrators. *South African Journal of Psychology, 30*, 2–10.

Fraenkel, P. & Murry, R. (1985). *The Namibian Report, No. 19*. London: Minority Rights Group International.

Freeman, M. (1995). Genocide, civilization and modernity. *British Journal of Sociology, 46*, 207–225.

Frey, B. (1997). The legal and ethical responsibilities of transnational corporations in the protection of human rights. *Minnesota Journal of Global Trade, 6*, 153.

Friedman, L. & Tiefenbrun, S. (eds.) (1999). *War crimes and war crimes tribunals: past, present, and future*. Hempstead, NY: Hofstra University School of Law, 799–801.

Fröschle, H. Ein normaler Kolonialkrieg, kein Genozid. 262 *FAZ*, November 11, 2002.

Frulli, M. (2001). Are crimes against humanity more serious than war crimes? *European Journal of International Law, 12*, 329.

Frulli, M. (2003). When are states liable towards individuals for serious violations of humanitarian law? The *Markovic* case. *Journal of International Criminal Justice*, *1*, 406.

Gage, R.H. & Waters, A.J. (1917). *Imperial German Criminal Code* (English translation). Johannesburg: W.E. Horton & Co.

Gambari, I.A. (1971). Review of H. Bley. *South West Africa under German Rule, 1894–1914*; South-West Africa (Namibia): Proposals for Action. *The Journal of Modern African Studies*, *9*, 484–486.

Gann, L.H. (1987). Marginal colonialism: The German case, 1–17. In Knoll, A.J. & Gann, L.H. (eds.), *Germans in the tropics: Essays in German colonial history*. New York/London: Greenwood Press.

Gann, L.H. (1973). South West Africa under German rule, 1894–1914. *The International Journal of African Historical Studies, 6*, 121–126.

Gann, L.H. & Duigan, P. (1977). *The rulers of German Africa 1884–1914*. Quoted in Jonassohn, K. (1996), Before the Holocaust deniers. *Culture and Society*, 31.

Gann, L.H. & Duigan, P. (1977). *The rulers of German Africa 1884–1914*. Stanford, CA: Stanford University Press.

Gardner Feldman, L. (1999). The principle and practice of Reconciliation in German foreign policy: Relations with France, Israel, Poland and the Czech Republic. *International Affairs*, *75*, 334–337.

Gasser, H-P. (2002). International humanitarian law and human rights law in non-international armed conflict: Joint venture or mutual exclusion. *German Yearbook of International Law*, *45*, 149–162.

Gellately, R. & Kiernan, B. (2003). The study of mass murder and genocide. In Gellately, R. & Kiernan, B. (eds.), *The specter of genocide mass murder in historical perspective*. Cambridge: Cambridge University Press.

Gellately, R. & Kiernan, B. (eds.), (2003). *The specter of genocide mass murder in historical perspective*. Cambridge: Cambridge University Press.

General Act of the Brussels Conference, July 2, 1890.

General Act of the Conference of Berlin, February 26, 1885.

General Assembly Resolution 96 (I), U.N. Doc. A/64/Add.1 (1946).

Gewald, J-B. (1994). The great general of the Kaiser. *Botswana Notes and Records*, *26*, 67–76.

Gewald, J-B. (1996). *Towards redemption: A socio-political history of the Herero of Namibia between 1890 and 1923*. Leiden: CNWS Publications;

Gewald, J-B. (1999). The road of the man called Love and the sack of Sero: The Herero-German War and the export of the Herero labour to the South African Rand. *Journal of African History*, *40*, 21–40.

Gewald, J-B. (1999). *Herero heroes: A socio-political history of the Herero of Namibia 1890–1923*. Oxford: James Currey.

Gewald, J-B. (2000). Colonization, genocide and resurgence: The Herero of Namibia, 1890–1933. In Bollig, M. & Gewald, J-B. (eds.), *People, cattle and land: Transformations of a pastoral society in South Western Africa*. Köln: Rudiger Koppe Verlag.

Gewald, J-B. (2002). Missionaries, Hereros, and motorcars: Mobility and the impact of motor vehicles in Namibia before 1940. *International Journal of African Historical Studies*, *35*, 257–285.

Gewald, J-B. (2002). Flags, funerals and fanfares: Herero and missionary contestations of the acceptable, 1900–1940. *Journal of African Cultural Studies*, *15*, 105.

Gewald, J-B. (2003). Herero genocide in the twentieth century: Politics and memory. In Abbink, J., De Bruijn, M., & Van Walraven, K. (eds.), *Rethinking resistance: Revolt and violence in African history*. Leiden: Brill.

Gewald, J-B. (2003). Imperial Germany and the Herero of Southern Africa: Genocide and the quest for recompense. In Jones, A. (ed.), *Genocide, war crimes, and the West: Ending the culture of impunity*. London: Zed Press, 59–77.

Gewald, J-B. & Silvester, J. (2003). *Words cannot be found. German colonial rule in Namibia: An annotated reprint of the 1918 Blue Book*. Leiden: Brill.

Gewald, J-B. (2003). The Herero genocide: German unity, settlers, soldiers, and ideas. In Bechhaus-Gerst, M. & Klein-Arendt, R. (eds.), *Die (koloniale) Begegnung: AfrikanerInnen in Deutschland 1880–1945, Deutsche in Afrika 1880–1918*. Frankfurt am Main: Peter Lang, 109–127.

Gibney, M. & Roxstrom, E. (2001). The status of state apologies. *Human Rights Quarterly*, *23*, 911.

Gibney, M., Tomaševski, K., & Vedsted-Hansen, J. (1999). Transnational state responsibility for violations of human rights. *Harvard Human Rights Journal*, *12*, 267.

Gibson, G.D. (1956). Double descent and its correlates among the Herero of Ngamiland. *American Anthropologist* New Series, *58*, 109–139.

Gillard, E-C. (2003). Reparation for violations of international humanitarian law. *International Review of the Red Cross*, *85*, 529.

Gilroy, P. (1998). Afterword: Not being inhuman. In Cheyette, B. & Marcus, L. (eds.), *Modernity, culture and the Jew*. Cambridge: Polity Press.

Gladstone, W. (1877). *Lessons of the massacre*. London: Murray.

Glauner, L. (2002). The need for accountability and reparation: 1830–1976. The United States Government's role in the promotion, implementation, and execution of the crime of genocide against Native Americans. *De Paul Law Review*, *51*, 911.

Goldblatt, I. (1971). *History of South West Africa, from the beginning of the nineteenth century*. Cape Town: Juta & Co.

Goldhagen, D. (1996). *Hitler's willing executioners: Ordinary Germans and the Holocaust*. New York. Vintage Books.

Goldstone, R. (1998). Ethnic reconciliation needs the help of a truth commission. *International Herald Tribune*, October 24, 1998.

Goldstone, R.J. (2004). International human rights and criminal justice in the first decade of the 21st century. *Human Rights Brief*, *11*, 3.

Goodman, D.P. (1985). The need for fundamental change in the law of belligerent occupation. *Stanford Law Review*, *37*, 1573.

Government of South Africa (1928). *The native tribes of South West Africa*. Cape Town: Cape Times Limited.

Govier, T. & Verwoerd, W. (2002). The promise and pitfalls of apologies. *Journal of Social Philosophy*, *33*, 67–82.

Great General Staff of the Imperial Germany (1915). *The war book of the German General Staff*, (J.H. Morgan, transl.). New York: McBride, Nast & Co.

Green, L. (1999). International regulations of armed conflicts. In Bassiouni, M.C. (ed.), *International criminal law, Vol. 1, Crimes of war* (2nd ed.). Ardsley, NY: Transnational Publishers, 355.

Green, L.C. (1998/1999). Cicero and Clausewitz or Quincy Wright: The interplay of law and war. *United States Air Force Academy Journal of Legal Studies*, *9*, 12.

Green, L.C. (1997–1998). "Grave breaches" or crimes against humanity? *U.S.A.F. Academic Journal of Legal Studies*, *8*, 19.

Green, L.C. (2000). *Contemporary law of armed conflict*. Manchester: Manchester University Press.

Green, L.C. (1996). Enforcement of the law in international and non-international conflicts: The way ahead. *Denver Journal of International Law and Policy*, 285.

Greenawalt, A.K.A. (1999). Rethinking genocidal intent: The case for a knowledge-based interpretation. *Columbia Law Review*, *99*, 2259.

Greppi, E. (1999). The evolution of individual criminal responsibility under international law. *International Review of the Red Cross*, *835*, 531–533.

Gretschel, H-V. (2001). Education in Namibia. In Diener, I. & Graefe, O. (eds.). *Contemporary Namibia: The first landmarks of a post-apartheid society*. Windhoek: Gamsberg MacMillan.

Gross, L. (1948). The Peace of Westphalia, 1648–1948. *American Journal of International Law*, *42*, 20.

Großer Generalstab (ed.). (1906). *Die Kämpfe der deutschen Truppen in Südwestafrika. Auf Grund amtlichen Materials bearbeitet von der Kriegsgeschichtlichen, Abteilung I des Großen Generalstabes. Band I. Der Feldzug gegen die Hereros*. Berlin: Ernst Siegfried Mittler & Sohn.

Gruenwald, O. (2000). The other Holocaust: Twentieth-century communist genocide. *Journal of Interdisciplinary Studies*, *12*, 85.

Gründer, H. (1998). Genozid oder Zwangsmodernisierung? Der moderne Kolonialismus in universalgeschichtlicher Perspektive. In Dabag, M. & Platt, K. (eds.), *Genozid und Moderne. Bd 1. Strukturen kollektiver Gewalt im 20. Jahrhundert*. Opladen: Leske & Buderich, 135.

Gründer, H. (2004). *Geschichte der deutschen Kolonien*. Paderborn: Ferdinand Schöningh Verlag.

Gumedze, S. (2005). Bringing communications before the African Commission on Human Rights and People's Rights. *African Human Rights Law Journal*, *3*, 118–148.

Gutto, S. (1993). *Human and peoples' rights for the oppressed: Critical essays on theory and practice from sociology of law perspective*. Lund: Lund University Press.

Haarhoff, D. (1991). *The wild South-West: Frontier myths and metaphors in literature set in Namibia, 1760–1988*. Johannesburg: Witwatersrand University Press.

Haelbich, E. Herero Reconciliation in the Spotlight at Bremen Summit. *Africa News Service*, November 23, 2004.

Hague Convention No. II of 1899; *Convention [No. II] with Respect to the Laws and Customs of War on Land, with Annex of Regulations*, July 29, 1899, 32 Stat. 1803, 1; Bevans, C. (1968). *Treaties and other international agreements of the United States of America, 1776–1949*, 247.

Hall, D. (2004). The spirit of reparation. *Boston College Third World Law Journal*, *24*, 1.

Hakata, M. (2001). Hereros Sue Germany for Reparations. *New African*, 12–14.

Hamta, M. (2004). Von Trotha Family Backs Herero Compensation. *Africa News Service*, September 13.

Hannum, H. (1989). International law and Cambodian genocide: The sounds of silence. *Human Rights Quarterly*, *11*, 82.

Hansen, A.B. (2002). *Partition and genocide. Manifestation of violence in Punjab 1937–1947*. New Delhi: India Research Press.

Hanski, R. & Scheinin, M. (2003). *Leading cases of the Human Rights Committee*. Turku/Abo (Finland): Institute for Human Rights Abo Akademi University.

Harring, S.L. (1996). The constitution of Namibia and the "rights and freedoms" guaranteed communal land holders: Resolving the inconsistency between article 16, article 100 and schedule 5. *South African Journal on Human Rights*, *12*, 467–484.

Harring, S.L. (2002). German reparations to the Herero nation: An assertion of Herero nationhood in the path of Namibian development? *West Virginia Law Review*, *104*, 393.

Harring, S.L. (2002). Stolen lands under the constitution of Namibia: Land reform under the rule of law. In Hinz, M., Amoo, S., & Van Wyk, D. (eds.), *The constitution at work: 10 years of Namibian nationhood*. Windhoek: University of Namibia Press, 145.

Harris, D. (2004). *Cases and materials in international law* (6th ed.). London: Sweet & Maxwell.

Harris, D.J., O'Boyle, M., & Warbrick, C. (1995). *Law of the European Convention on Human Rights*. London: Butterworths.

Harrland, P. Zwei Wochen aus dem Tagebuche eines Gefreiten bei der Kolonne, in *Deutsche Reiter*, 288.

Hasson, A. (2002). Extraterritorial jurisdiction and sovereign immunity on trial: Noriega, Pinochet and Milosevic: Trends in political accountability and trans-national criminal law. *Boston College International & Comparative Law Review*, *25*, 125.

Hayes, P., Silvester, J., Wallace, M. & Hartman, W. (1998). *Namibia under South African rule: Mobility and containment 1915–1946*. Oxford: James Currey.

Helbig, H. (1983). *Mythos-Deutsch-Südwest: Namibia und die Deutschen*. Weinheim/Basel: Beltz Verlag.

Hellberg, C-J. (1997). *Mission, colonialism, and liberation: The Lutheran Church in Namibia 1840–1966*. Windhoek: New Namibia Books.

Hempenstall, P.J. (1978). *Pacific islanders under German rule. A study in the meaning of colonial resistance*. Canberra: Australian National University Press.

Hempenstall, P. (1987). The neglected empire: The superstructure of the colonial state in the German Melanesia. In Knoll, A.J. & Gann, L.H. (eds.), *Germans in the tropics: Essays in German colonial history* (2nd ed.). New York/London: Greenwood Press, 93.

Hendersen, W.O. (1938). Germany's trade with her colonies, 1884–1914. *Economic History Review*, *9*, 1–19, 2.

Hendrickson, H. (1994). The long dress and the construction of Herero identities in southern Africa. *African Studies*, *53*, 25–54.

Herero People's Reparations Corporation v. Deutsche Bank, 370 F.3d 1192, 361 U.S. App. D.C. 468, (2004). (USA)

Herero legal claims against Germany in SW Africa. Found at http://www.marcusgarvey-library.org.uk/hererofarmlands.htm.

Hereros oppose Waterberg celebrations: *Alter Kamerad* Denies "Extermination." *Windhoek Advertiser*, July 29, 1964.

Herz, R.L. (2000 Winter). Litigating environmental abuses under the Alien Tort Claims Act: A practical assessment. *Virginia Journal of International Law*, *40*, 545.

Heywood, A., Lau, B., & Ohly R. (eds.). (1992). *Warriors, leaders, sages and outcasts in the Namibian past*. Windhoek: Michael Scott Oral Records Project.

Heywood, A. & Maasdorp, E. (transl.) (1989). *The Hendrik Witbooi papers.* Windhoek: National Archives of Namibia.

Heywood, A. & Maasdorp, E. (transl.) (1995). *The Hendrik Witbooi papers* (2nd ed.). Windhoek: National Archives of Namibia.

Higgins, R. (1997). Time and the law: International perspectives on an old problem. *International and Comparative Law Quarterly, 46*, 501.

Hill, D.J. (1917). The rights of the civil population in territory occupied by a belligerent. *American Journal of International Law, 11*, 133–137.

Hintrager, O. (1955). *Suedwestafrika in der deutschen Zeit.* Munchen: Kommissionsverlag.

Hintze, H. (2005). Germany to Pay N$160 Million for Reconciliation. *The Namibian*, May 27, 2005.

Hinz, M.O. (2003). One hundred years later: Germany on trial in the USA: The Herero reparations claim for genocide. *Namibian Human Rights Online Journal, 1.*

Hishongwa, N. (1997). *The contract labour system and its effects on family and social life in Namibia: A historical perspective.* Windhoek: Gamsberg MacMillan.

Hochschild, A. (1999). *King Leopold's ghost—a story of greed, terror and heroism in colonial Africa.* New York: Houghton Mifflin.

Hofmann, R. & Riemann, F. (2004). *Compensation for victims of war: Background report.* International Law Association Committee on Compensation for Victims of War.

Horne, J. & Kramer, A. (2001). *German atrocities 1914: A history of denial.* New Haven: Yale University Press.

Howard, M.E. (1967). The armed forces. In Hinsley, F. (ed.). *The new Cambridge modern history XI: Material progress and worldwide problems 1870–1898.* Cambridge: Cambridge University Press, 204–242.

Howard, R.E. (1986). *Human rights in Commonwealth Africa.* Totowa, NJ: Rowman & Littlefield.

Howard-Hassmann, R.E. (2005). The second great transformation: Human rights leapfrogging in the era of globalization. *Human Rights Quarterly, 27*, 1–40.

Huaraka, T. (1978).Walvis Bay and international law. *Indian Journal of International Law*, 160–174.

Hull, I.V. (1982). *The entourage of Kaiser Wilhelm II, 1888–1918.* New York: Cambridge University Press.

Hull, I.V. (2003). Military culture and the production of final solutions in the colonies: The example of Wilhelminian Germany. In Gellately, R. & Kiernan, B. (eds.), *The specter of genocide mass murder in historical perspective.* Cambridge: Cambridge University Press.

Hull, I.V. (2005). *Absolute destruction: Military culture and practices of war in Imperial Germany.* Ithaca: Cornell University Press.

Humphrey, M. (2000). From terror to trauma: Commissioning truth for national reconciliation. *Social Identities, 6*, 7–28.

Humphrey, M. (2003). From victim to victimhood: Truth commissions and trials as rituals of political transition and individual healing. *Australian Journal of Anthropology, 14*, 171.

Hunter, J. (2004). Who should own the land? An introduction. In Hunter, J. (ed.), *Who should own the land? Analyses and views on land reform and the land question in Namibia and southern Africa.* Windhoek: Namibia Institute for Democracy.

Huttenbach, H.R. (1988). Locating the Holocaust on the genocide spectrum: Towards a methodology of definition and categorization. *Holocaust and Genocide Studies, 3*, 289–303.

Huttenbach, H.R. (1999). The psychology and politics of genocide denial: A comparison of four case studies. In Chorbajian, L. & Shirinian, G. (eds.), *Studies in comparative genocide*. New York: St. Martin's Press, 217.

Huyse, L. (1995). Justice after transitions: On the choices successor elites make in dealing with the past. In Kritz, N. (ed.), *Transitional justice: How emerging democracies reckon with former regimes*. Washington, D.C.: United States Institute of Peace.

ICJ Ambatielos Case (Greece v. U.K.), Preliminary Objections, 1952 I.C.J. 27, 40 (July 1).

ICJ Application of the Convention on the Prevention and Punishment of the Crime of Genocide (Bosnia and Herzegovina v. Yugoslavia (Serbia and Montenegro)), Preliminary Objections [1996], *ICJ Reports*, 595.

ICJ Application of the Convention on the Prevention and Punishment of the Crime of Genocide (Bosnia and Herzegovina v. Yugoslavia (Serbia and Montenegro), Further Requests for the Indication of Provisional Measures, September 13, 1993. *ICJ Reports*, 325.

ICJ Asylum Case: *Columbia v. Peru, ICJ Reports* 1950, 266.

ICJ Barcelona Traction, Light and Power Company, Limited (*Belgium v. Spain*), Judgement of February 5, 1970, *ICJ Reports* (1970).

ICJ The Corfu Channel Case (Merits), 1949. *ICJ Reports*, 4.

ICJ Legality of the Threat or Use of Nuclear Weapons, Advisory Opinion of July 8, 1996. *ICJ Reports*, 75.

ICJ Legality of the Threat or Use of Nuclear Weapons, Advisory Opinion of July 8, 1996. *ICJ Reports* 226.

ICJ Legality of Use of Force (Yugoslavia v. Belgium et al.), Request for the Indication of Provisional Measures, Order, June 2, 1999.

ICJ Western Sahara, *ICJ Reports* 1975.

ICTJ Legal Analysis on Applicability of UN Convention on Genocides prior to January 12, 1951.

ICTR Prosecutor v. Akayesu, No. ICTR-96-4-T (ICTR Trial Chamber Sept. 2, 1998).

ICTR Prosecutor v. Alfred Musema, No. ICTR-96-13-T.

ICTR Prosecutor v. Jean-Paul Akayesu, No. ICTR-96-4-T, Judgement, Trial Chamber 1, Sept. 2, (1998).

ICTR Prosecutor v. Kayishema, No. ICTR-95-1-T, Judgement, (International Criminal Tribunal Rwanda, Trial Chamber II, May 21, 1999).

ICTR Prosecutor v. Kayishema and Ruzindana, No. ICTR-95-1, ICTR T. Ch. II, May 21, 1999.

ICTR Prosecutor v. Jean Kambanda, ICTR 97-23-S. Sep. 4, 1998.

ICTY Decision of Trial Chamber 1, *Radovan Karadzic, Ratko Mladic* case (Cases Nos. IT-95-5-R61 and IT-95-18-R61); Consideration of the Indictment within the framework of Rule 61 of the Rules of Procedure and Evidence.

ICTY Appeals Chamber: *Prosecutor v. Dusko Tadic*, No. IT-94-1-A (July 15, 1999).

ICTY Decision on the Defence Motion for Interlocutory Appeal on Jurisdiction, *Prosecutor v. Tadic*, Case No. IT-94-1-T, App. Ch. (ICTY October 2, 1995).

ICTY Prosecutor v. Dusko Sikirica, Damir Dosen and Dragan Kolundzija It-95-8 Keraterm Camp September 3, 2001; Judgement on Defence Motions to Acquit.

ICTY Prosecutor v. Dusko Tadic a.k.a. Dule, No. IT-94-1-T, May 7, 1997 (ICTY Trial Chamber).
ICTY Prosecutor v. Jelisic, No. IT-95-10A, Judgement.
ICTY Prosecutor v. Milan Martic, March 8, 1996
ICTY Prosecutor v. Mskic, Radic and Sljivancanin, Review of the Indictment Pursuant to Rule 61 of the Rules of Procedure and Evidence, ICTY No. IT-95-13-R61, Trial Chamber 1, April 3, 1996.
ICTY Prosecutor v. Radislav Krstić, No. IT-98-33-T (ICTY Appeal Chambers, April 19, 2004).
ICTY Prosecutor v. Jelisic, No. IT-95-10A, Judgement (Appeals Chamber), July 5, 2001.
ICTY Prosecutor v. Tadic, No. IT-94-1, April 26, 2000.
ICTY Prosecutor v. Tadic, No. IT-94-1-AR72, Appeal on Jurisdiction, 35 ILM 32, Oct. 2, 1995.
ICTY Prosecutor v. Zoran Kupreskic and Others, No. IT-95-16-A, January 14, 2000 (ICTY Trial Chamber 11).
ICTY Sikirica, Judgement on Defence Motions to Acquit.
Illife, J. (1969). *Tanganyika under German rule, 1905–1912*. Cambridge: Cambridge University Press.
International Committee of the Red Cross (1958). The ICRC Commentary to the 1949 Geneva Conventions, Vol. I–IV.
International Court of Justice, July 9, 2004. *Legal consequences of the construction of a wall in the occupied Palestinian territory*.
Inter-American Court of Human Rights, *Velásquez Rodriguez v. Honduras*, Serie C, nr. 7, Judgment of July 21, 1989 (Compensatory Damages).
Inter-American Court of Human Rights *Velásquez Rodriguez*, Judgement of July 29, 1988, Inter-Am.Ct.H.R. (Ser. C) No. 4 (1988).
Inter-American Court of Human Rights *Aloeboetoe y otros v. Suriname*, Series C No 15, September 10, 1993.
Ipsen, K.(1999). *Völkerrecht: Ein Studienbuch*, (4th ed.). München: C.H. Becksche Verlag.
Jackson, R.H. (1945). Report to the President by Mr. Justice Jackson, June 6, 1945 (released to the public June 7, 1945), *Department State Bulletin, 12*, 1071, 1076. Reprinted in Report of Robert H. Jackson, United States Representative to the International Conference on Military Trials, London, 1945, at 42, 50 (reprint 1971) (1949).
Jacobs, S.L. (1999). The papers of Raphael Lemkin: A first look. *Journal of Genocide Research, 1*, 105–114.
Janis, M. (1988). *An introduction to international law*. Boston: Little Brown.
JanMohamed, A.R. (1986). The economy of Manichean allegory: The function of racial difference in colonialist literature. In Gates, H.L. (ed.), *Race, Writing and Difference*. Chicago: University of Illinois Press.
Jaspers, K. (2001). *The question of German guilt*. New York: Fordham University Press
Jere-malanda, R. (2000). Massacre in the Desert. *You*, 34–40.
Jessup, P.C. (1947). The crime of aggression and the future of international Law. *Political Science Quarterly, 62*, 1–10.
Jochnick, C. & Normand, R. (1994). The legitimation of violence: A critical history of the laws of war. *Harvard International Law Journal*, 49.

Johann, E. (ed.), *Reden des Kaisers: Ansprachen, Predigten und Trinksprüche Wilhelms II* (Munich, 1966), pp. 86–88. Translated by R.S. Levy. http://www.assumption.edu/users/McClymer/hi119net/KaiserWilhelmIIBoxers.html.

Johnson, S. (2003). *Peace without justice: Hegemonic instability or international criminal law?* London: Ashgate Publishing.

Jonassohn, K. (1996). Before the Holocaust deniers. *Culture and Society*, *33*, 31–39.

Jonassohn, K. & Bjornson, S.K. (1998). *Genocide and gross human rights violations.* New Brunswick: Transaction.

Jones, J.R.W.D. (1998). *The practise of the international criminal tribunals for the former Yugoslavia and Rwanda.* Irvington-on-Hudson, NY: Transnational Publishers.

Jorgensen, N.H.B. (2000). *The responsibility of the states for international crime.* Oxford: Oxford University Press.

Junk, J. & Miner, J.M. (2004). Compensating historical injustice: More than just money. *Humanity in action. Reports of the 2004 Fellows in Denmark, Germany and the Netherlands.* New York, *6*, 43–47.

Kalshoven, F. (1987). *Constraints on the waging of war.* Dordrecht: Martinus Nijhoff.

Kalshoven, F. (1991). State responsibility for warlike acts of the armed forces: From Article 3 of the Hague Convention IV of 1907 to Article 91 of Additional Protocol I and beyond. *International and Comparative Quarterly*, *40*, 830.

Kamali, M. (2001). Accountability for human rights violations: A comparison of transitional justice in East Germany and South Africa. *Columbia Journal of Transnational Law*, *40*, 89.

Kamminga, M. (1996). State succession in respect of human rights treaties. *European Journal of International Law*, *7*, 469.

Kandetu, V. (2005). Namibia: Cold Discourse upon Chronic Pain. *New African*, *436*, 64–66.

Kastenberg, J. (2003–2004). The customary international law of war and combatant status: Does the current executive branch policy determination on unlawful combatant status for terrorists run afoul of international law, or is it just poor public relations? *Gonzaga Law Review*, 495.

Katjavivi, P. (1989). *A history of resistance in Namibia.* Paris, London & Addis Ababa: UNESCO.

Kaulich, U. (2003). *Die Geschichte der ehemaligen Kolonie Deutsch-Südwestafrika (1884–1914). Eine Gesamtdarstellung* (2nd ed.). Frankfurt am Main: Peter Lang.

Kaumbi, U. (2004). The land is ours. In Hunter, J. (ed.), *Who should own the land? Analyses and views on land reform and the land question in Namibia and southern Africa.* Windhoek: Namibia Institute for Democracy.

Keal, P. (2003). *European conquest and the rights of indigenous peoples: The moral backwardness of international society.* Cambridge: Cambridge University Press.

Keen, M.H. (1965). *The laws of war in the late Middle Ages.* London: Routledge & Kegan Paul.

Kelly, M.J. (2002). Can sovereigns be brought to justice? The crime of genocide's evolution and the meaning of the Milosevic trial. *Saint John's Law Review*, 257.

Kennedy, P. (1982). The Kaiser and German *Weltpolitik*: Reflections on Wilhelm II's place in the making of German foreign policy. In Röhl, J.C.G. & Sombart, N. (eds.), *Kaiser Wilhelm II, new interpretations: The Corfu papers.* Cambridge/New York: Cambridge University Press.

Kennedy, P.M. (1974). *The Samoan tangle: A study in Anglo-German-American Relations 1878–1900*. Dublin: Irish University Press.

Kenya: Ex-Mau Mau Set Date to File Case against UK. *The Nation*, (Nairobi), May 6, 2006.

Kerina, M. (1981). *Namibia: the making of a nation*. New York: Books in Focus.

Kesting, R.W. (1998). Blacks under the swastika: A research note. *The Journal of Negro History*, *83*, 84–99.

Kindt, L. (1905). Vom Aufstand in Ostafrika. *Koloniale Zeitschrift*, *XI* (25), 435–437.

Kitchen, M. (1968). *The German Officer Corps 1890–1914*. Oxford: Clarendon Press.

Kittichaisaree, K. (2002). *International criminal law*. Oxford: Oxford University Press.

Klinghoffer, A.J. (1998). *The international dimension of genocide in Rwanda*. New York: New York University Press.

Knoll, A.J. (1939). *Togo under imperial Germany 1884–1914*. Stanford, CA: Hoover Institution Press.

Knoll, A.J. & Gann, L.H. (eds.), (1987). *Germans in the tropics: Essays in German colonial history*. New York/London: Greenwood Press.

Knoops, G-J. (2003). *An introduction to the law of international criminal tribunals*. Ardsley: Transnational.

Kohut, T.A. (1991). *Wilhelm II and the Germans: A study in leadership*. New York: Oxford University Press.

Konrad-Adenauer-Stiftung/Namibia Institute for Democracy (1994). *Namibia: Views and perspectives since independence*. Windhoek: Konrad-Adenauer-Stiftung/Namibia Institute for Democracy.

Kooijmans, P.H. (1991). In the shadowland between civil war and civil state: Some reflections on the standard-setting process. In Delissen, A.J.M. & Tanja, G.J. (eds.), *Humanitarian law of armed conflict: Challenge ahead*. Dordrecht: Martinus Nijhoff Publishers.

Korman, S. (1996). *The right of conquest: The acquisition of territory by force in international law and practices*. Oxford: Clarendon Press.

Kossler, R. (2003). Public memory, reconciliation and the aftermath of war: A preliminary framework with special reference to Namibia. In Melber, H. (ed.), *Re-examining liberation in Namibia: Political culture since independence*. Uppsala: Nordic Africa Institute.

Krain, M. (1997). State-sponsored mass murder: The onset and severity of genocides and politicides. *Journal of Conflict Resolution*, *41*, 331–360.

Krautwurst, U. R. (1997). *Tales of the "land of stories": Settlers and anti-modernity in German colonial discourses on German South West Africa, 1884–1914*. PhD. (History) Connecticut: University of Connecticut.

Kriangsak, K. (2001). *International criminal law*. New York: Oxford University Press.

Krüger, G. (1999). *Kriegsbewältigung und Geschichtsbewusstsein: Realität, Deutung und Verarbeitung des deutschen Kolonialkrieges in Namibia, 1904 bis 1907*. Göttingen: Vandenhoek & Ruprecht.

Kunz, J.L. (1956). The laws of war. *American Journal of International Law*, *50*, 313.

Kuper, L. (1981). *Genocide: Its political use in the twentieth century*. New Haven, CT: Yale University Press.

Kuteeve, P. Herero Leader's Remains Returned, Reburied. *Africa News Service*, October 6, 2004.

Kwakwa, E. (1992). *The international law of armed conflict: Personal and material fields of application*. Dordrecht: Kluwer Academic.

Lambourne, W. (1999). The pursuit of justice and reconciliation: Responding to genocide in Cambodia and Rwanda. Paper delivered at the International Studies Association 40th Annual Convention, Washington, D.C., 16–20. Available at http://www.ciaonet.org/isa/sites/isa.html.

Lau, B. (1989). Uncertain certainties: The Herero-German war of 1904. *Mibagus*, 2.

Lau, B. (1990). Letter to the editor, *Southern African Review of Books*.

Lau, B. & Renier, P. (1993). *100 years of agricultural development in colonial Namibia: A historical overview of visions and experimenting*. Windhoek: The National Archive of Namibia.

Lauren, P.G. (1998). *The evolution of international human rights*. Philadelphia: University of Pennsylvania Press.

Lauterpacht, H. (1952). The problem of the revision of the law of war. *British Year Book of International Law*, *360*, 363–364.

Lazare, A. (1995). Go ahead, say you're sorry. *Psychology Today*, *28*, 40.

Lemarchand, R. (2003). Comparing the killing fields: Rwanda, Cambodia and Bosnia. In Jensen, S.L.B. *Genocide: Cases, comparisons and contemporary debates*. Copenhagen: Danish Center for Holocaust and Genocide Studies.

Lemkin, R. (1944). *Axis rule in occupied Europe: Laws of occupation - analysis of government—proposals for redress*. Washington D.C.: Carnegie Endowment for International Peace.

Lemkin, R. (1945). Genocide: A modern crime. *Free World*, April 4, 39.

Lemkin, R. (undated). Untitled and unpublished manuscript dealing with the Herero, Jacob Rader Marcus Center of the American Jewish archives Cincinnati; the Raphael Lemkin Papers, Box 6, Folder 12.

Lemkin, R. Undated and unpublished manuscript: The Germans in Africa. Jacob Rader Marcus Center of the American Jewish Archives, Cincinnati; the Raphael Lemkin papers, Box 6, Folder 9.

Leutwein, T.G. (1906). *Elf Jahre Gouverneur in Deutsch-Südwestafrika*, Berlin: Mittler.

Levene, M. (1994). Is the Holocaust simply another example of genocide? *Patterns of Prejudice*, *28*, 3–26.

Levene, M. (2000). Why is the twentieth century the century of genocide? *Journal of World History*, *11*, 305.

Levie, H.S. (ed.). (1987). *The law of non-international armed conflict, protocol II to the 1949 Geneva Conventions*. Dordrecht: Martinus Nijhoff.

Levin, N. (1968). *The Holocaust: The destruction of European Jewry 1933–1945*. New York: TY Crowell.

Levmore, S. (1999). Privatizing reparations: Changes, anticipations, and reparations. *Columbia Law Review*, *99*, 1657.

Lewin, E. (1915). *The Germans and Africa. Their aims on the dark continent and how they acquired their African colonies*. London: Cassell.

Lewy, G. (1999). Gypsies and Jews under the Nazis. *Holocaust and Genocide Studies*, *13*, 383–404.

Leys, C. & Saul, J.S. (1995). Introduction. In Leys, C. & Saul, J.S. *Namibia's liberation struggle: The two edged sword*. London: James Currey.

Liebenberg, J. Namibia's Dirty Little Secret Revisited, *Sunday Independent*, May 2, 2004.

Lindley, M.F. (1926). *The acquisition and government of backward territory in international law*. London: Longmans, Green & Co.

Lippman, M. (1985). The drafting of the 1948 Convention on the Prevention and Punishment of the Crime of Genocide. *Boston University Journal of International Law*, *3*, 62.

Lippman, M. (1994). The 1948 Convention on the Prevention and Punishment of the Crime of Genocide: Forty-five years later. *Temple International & Comparative Law Journal*, *8*, 1.

Lippman, M. (2002). Aerial attacks on civilians and the humanitarian law of war: Technology and terror from World War I to Afghanistan. *California Western International Law Journal*, 1

Louis, W.M.R (1967). Great Britain and German expansion in Africa 1884–1919. In Gifford, P. & Louis, W.M.R. (eds.), *Britain and Germany in Africa: Imperial rivalry and colonial rule*. New Haven: Yale University.

Louis, W.R. (1967). *Britain and Germany's lost colonies 1914–1919*. Oxford: Clarendon Press.

Lovejoy, P. (2000). *Transformation in slavery: A history of slavery in Africa* (2nd ed.). Cambridge: Cambridge University Press.

Lugard, F.D. (1922). *Dual mandate in British tropical Africa*. London/Edinburgh: William Blackwood & Sons.

Lundtofte, H. (2003). Radicalization of the German suppression of the Herero rising in 1904. In Jensen, S.L.B. *Genocide: Cases, comparisons and contemporary debates*. Copenhagen: Danish Center for Holocaust and Genocide Studies, 27.

Luttig, H.G. (1933). *The religious system and social organization of the Herero: A study in Bantu culture*. Utrecht: Kemink & Zoon.

Lyons, M.E. (2002). World Conference against Racism: New avenues for slavery reparations. *Vanderbilt Journal of Transitional Law*, *35*, 1235.

Macdonogh, G. (2000). *The Last Kaiser: The life of Wilhelm II*. New York: St. Martin's Press

MacEdo, S. (ed.). (2004). Universal jurisdiction: National courts and the prosecution of serious crimes under international law. Philadelphia: University of Pennsylvania Press.

Mackenzie, K. (1974). Some British reactions to German colonial methods 1885–1907. *The Historical Journal*, *17*, 165–175.

Macklem, P. (2005). Rybná 9, Praha 1: Restitution and memory in international human rights law. *European Journal of International Law*, *16*, 1–25.

Madley, B. (2004). Patterns of frontier genocide 1803–1910: The aboriginal Tasmanians, the Yuki of California, and the Herero of Namibia. *Journal of Genocide Research*, *6*, 167–192.

Mahoney, M.R. (2003). The Zulu Kingdom as a genocidal and post-genocidal society, c. 1810 to the present. *Journal of Genocide Research*, *5*, 263.

Maier, C.S. (1988). *The unmasterable past: History, Holocaust, and German national identity*. Cambridge, MA: Harvard University Press.

Malan, J.S. (1995). *Peoples of Namibia*. Pretoria: Rhino Publishers.

Maletsky, C. (1999). International Court Dashes Hereros' Reparation Hopes. *The Namibian*, September 8, 1999.

Maletsky, C. (2001). Hereros Temporarily Drop Claim in $2 bn Suit. *Business Day*, September 20, 2001.

Maletsky C. & Mokopanele, T. (2001). SA Refuses to Consider Reparation for Hereros. *Business Day*, September 28, 2001.

Maletsky, C. (2004) Germany Denies Herero Negotiations. *Africa News Service*, December 9, 2004.

Maletsky, C. (2005). Govt Ups the Pressure on "Reluctant" Farmers. *The Namibian*, 31 March 2005.

Mamdani, M. (1996). *Citizen and subject: Contemporary Africa and the legacy of late colonialism.* Princeton: Princeton University Press.

Mamdani, M. (2001). A brief history of genocide. *Transition*, *10*, 26–47.

Mamdani, M. (2002). Making sense of political violence in postcolonial Africa. *Identity, Culture and Politics*, *3*, 4.

Mande, M. & Edwin, E. (2006) Justice for Maji Maji. *The East African* (Nairobi), February 28, 2006.

Mann, M. (2000). Were the perpetrators of genocide "ordinary men" or "real Nazis"? Results from fifteen hundred biographies. *Holocaust and Genocide Studies*, *14*, 331–366.

Markovits, I. (2001). Selective memory: How the law affects what we remember and forget about the past. *Law and Society Review*, *35*, 513.

Marks, G.C. (1992). Indigenous peoples in international law: The significance of Francisco de Vitoria and Bartolome de las Casas, *Australian Year Book of International Law, 13*, 1–51.

Masson, J.R. (1995). A fragment of colonial history: The killing of Jakob Marengo. *Journal of South African Studies*, *21*, 247–256.

Masson, J. (2001). *Jakob Marengo: An early resistance hero of Namibia.* Windhoek: Out of Africa.

Matua, M. (1995). Why redraw the map of Africa: A moral and legal inquiry. *Michigan Journal of International Law*, *16*, 1113.

Matundu-Tjiparuro, K. Presumed apology. *New Era,* August 16, 2004.

Matundu-Tjiparuro, K. An open letter to Professor Hinz and fellow verkrampte academics. *Allegemeine Zeitung*, February 11, 2005.

Mazzeschi, R.P. (2003). Reparation claims by individuals for state breaches of humanitarian law and human rights: An overview. *Journal of International Criminal Justice*, *1*, 339.

Mbumba, N. (2004). Paper to the International Conference on the German-Herero War: One hundred years after Bremen. Germany.

McCormack, T. L.H. (1997). Selective reaction to atrocity: War crimes and the development of international criminal law. *Albany Law Review*, *60*, 681.

McCoubrey, H. (1998). *International humanitarian law* (2nd ed.). Williston, VT: Ashgate.

McGregor, L. (2001). Individual accountability in South Africa: Cultural optimum or political facade? *American Journal of International Law*, *95*, 32.

Meister, R. (2005). Never again: The ethics of the neighbor and the logic of genocide. *Postmodern Culture*, *15*, 22.

Melber, H. (1985). Namibia: The German roots of apartheid. *Race and Class*, *27*, 63–77.

Melber, H. (1984). Ein Bremer Kaufmann und die Folgen. Die Landgeschäfte des Adolf Lüderitz und die Proklamation "Deutsch-Südwestafrikas." Eine ideologiekritische Dokumentation. *Informationsdienst Südliches Afrika*, 6.

Melber, H. (1990). Genocide. *Southern African Review of Books*, 23.

Melber, H. (1991). *Krieg und Kriegsbewältigung in Namibia: Wir können vergeben, aber nicht vergessen.* Freiburg: Arnold-Bergstraesser-Institut, 38. Cited in Hunter, J. (ed.), *Who should own the land? Analyses and views on land reform and the land question in Namibia and southern Africa.* Windhoek: Namibia Institute for Democracy.

Melber, H. (2003). Namibia: Land of the brave. In Abbink, J., De Bruijn, M., & Van Walraven, K. *Rethinking resistance: Revolt and violence in African history.* Leiden: Brill.

Melson, R. (1992). *Revolution and genocide: On the origins of the Armenian genocide and the Holocaust.* Chicago: University of Chicago Press.

Menon, P.K. (1992). The international personality of individuals in international law: A broadening of the traditional doctrine. *Journal of Transnational Law and Policy*, *1*, 151.

Meron, T. (1992). Shakespeare's Henry the Fifth and the Hundred Years War. *American Journal of International Law*, *86*, 1.

Meron, T. (1995). International criminalization of internal atrocities. *American Journal of International Law*, *89*, 554.

Meron, T. (1997). Francis Lieber's Code and Principles of Humanity. *Columbia Journal of Transnational Law*, *36*, 269.

Meron, T. (2000). The Martens Clause, principles of humanity, and dictates of public conscience. *American Journal of International Law*, *94*, 78.

Meron, T. (2000). The humanization of humanitarian law. *American Journal of International Law*, 239.

Middleton, L. (1936). *The rape of Africa.* New York: Harrison Smith and Roman Haas.

Miller, J. Iraq Accused: A Case of Genocide. *N.Y. Times Magazine*, January 3, 1993, 13.

Miller, M.S. (ed.). (1993). *Cultural survival, state of the peoples: A global human rights report on societies in danger.* Boston: Beacon Press.

Mokopakgosi, B. (1988). *Review: The Namibian Herero: A history of their psychological disintegration and survival. African Affairs*, *87*, 480–481.

Mombauer, A. (1999). Germany's last Kaiser: Wilhelm II and political decision-making in Imperial Germany. *New Perspective*, *4.* Found at http://www.users.globalnet.co.uk/~semp/wilhelmii.htm.

Mombauer, A. (2003). Wilhelm Waldersee and the Boxer Rebellion. In Mombauer, A. & Deist, W. (eds.), *The Kaiser: New research on Wilhelm II's role in Imperial Germany.* Cambridge: Cambridge University Press, 91–118.

Morgenthau, H. (1918). *Ambassador Morgenthau's story.* New York: Doubleday.

Morris, V. & Scharf, M.P. (1998). *The international criminal tribunal for Rwanda*, 344.

Morton, J.S. & Singh, N.V. (2003). The international legal regime on genocide. *Journal of Genocide Research*, *5*, 47–69.

Moses, A.D. (2002). Conceptual blockages and definitional dilemmas in the "racial century": Genocides of indigenous peoples and the Holocaust. *Patterns of Prejudice*, *36*, 7–36.

Moyo, S. (2004). Socio-economic dominance of ethnic and racial groups: The African experience. *Human Development Report, Occasional Paper 8.* United Nations Development Programme.

Mugambwa, J. (1987). Treaties or scraps of paper? A second look at the legal character of the nineteenth century. British/African colonial agreements. *Comparative and International Law Journal of Southern Africa*, *20*, 79–93.

Muir, R. (1917). *The expansion of Europe: The culmination of modern history* (2nd ed.). Boston/New York: Houghton Mifflin.

Mukisa, L. Court clears UK on Bunyoro killings. *The Monitor*, August 24, 2005.

Mumbuna, M. Academics Dissect Herero Genocide. *Africa News Service*, September 16, 2004.

Murphy, J.F. (1999). Civil liability for the commission of international crimes as an alternative to criminal prosecution. *Harvard Human Rights Journal*, *12*, 1.

Nagan, W.P. & Rodin, V. F. (2003–2004). Racism, genocide, and mass murder: Toward a legal theory about group deprivations. *National Black Law Journal*, 133.

Naimark, N.M. (2001). *Fires of hatred: Ethnic cleansing in the twentieth century Europe*. Cambridge: Harvard University Press.

Namibia: Germany's Herero reconciliation efforts rebuffed. United Nations Office for the Coordination of Humanitarian Affairs Integrated Regional Information Network (IRIN), December 2, 2005.

Neier, A. (1998). War crimes: Brutality, genocide, terror and the struggle for justice. *New York Times Books*, 12.

Nelayeva, G. Development of treaties concerning punishment of individuals for unlawful acts of war committed by individuals in international law. Found at http://www.idebate.org/magazines/vol2issue3/058icc.pdf.

Nersessian, D.L. (2002). The contours of genocide intent: Troubling jurisprudence from the international criminal tribunals. *Texas International Law Journal*, *37*, 231.

New York Times current history: The European war, Vol. xxvii., New York: New York Times, 1920, 322.

Ngavirue, Z. (1972). *Political parties and interest groups in South West Africa: A study of a plural society*. PhD thesis. Oxford University.

Niekerk, C. (2003). Rethinking a problematic constellation: Postcolonialism and its Germanic contexts. *Comparative Studies of South Asia, Africa and the Middle East*, *23*, 58.

Nina, H.B.J. (2000). *The responsibility of states for international crimes*. Oxford: Oxford University Press.

Nobles, M. Official apologies and their effects on political membership in democracies. Paper prepared for presentation at the American Political Science Association Meeting, Philadelphia, PA, August 28–31, 2003. Available at http://web.mit.edu/polisci/research/mnobles/official_apologies_in_democracies.pdf.

Nollkaemper, A. (2003). Concurrence between individual responsibility and state responsibility in international law. *International and Comparative Law Quarterly*, *52*, 615.

Nordbruch, C. (2002). *Der Hereroaufstand von 1904*. Stegen am Ammersee: Kurt Vowinckel Verlag; and (2004). *Völkermord an den Herero in Deutsch-Südwestafrika? Widerlegung einer Lüge*. Tübingen: Grabert Verlag.

Nordbruch, C. (2004). Atrocities committed on the Herero people during the suppression of their uprising in German South West Africa 1904–1907? An analysis of the latest accusations against Germany and an investigation on the credibility and justification of the demands for reparation. Paper delivered to the European American Culture Council, Sacramento, April 25, 2004. Found at http://www.nordbruch.org/artikel/sacramento.pdf.

Nsereko, D. (2000). Genocide: A crime against mankind. In McDonald, G.K. & Swaak-Goldman, O. (eds.), *Substantive and procedural aspects of international criminal law: The experience of international and national courts, Vol. 1.* The Hague: Kluwer Law International, 129.

Nuhn, W. (2000). *Feind überall: Der grosse Nama-Aufstand (Hottentottenaufstand) 1904–1908 in Deutsch-Südwestafrika (Namibia).* Bonn: Bernard & Graefe.

Nujoma, S. (1986). Preface. In Dreschler, H. (ed.), *Let us die fighting.* Berlin: Akademie-Verlag.

Nujoma, S. (2001). *Where others wavered: The autobiography of Sam Nujoma.* London: Panaf Books.

O'Brien, W.V. (1957). The meaning of "Military Necessity" in international law. *World Polity, 1*, 109.

O'Connell, D.P. (1970). *International Law* (2nd ed.) London: Stevens.

O'Connor, R. (1973). *The Boxer Rebellion.* London: Robert Hale.

O'Donnell, K. (1999). Poisonous women: Sexual danger, illicit violence and domestic work in German Southern Africa 1904–1915. *Journal of Woman's History, 11*, 32–54.

Oermann, N.O. (1999). *Mission, church and state relations in South West Africa under German rule (1884–1915).* Stuttgart: Franz Steiner Verlag.

Oermann, N.O. (2003). The law and the colonial state: Legal codification versus practise in a German colony. In Eley, G. & Retallack, J. (eds.). *Wilhelminism and its legacies: German modernities, imperialism, and the meanings of reform, 1890–1930.* New York: Berghahn.

Ofcansky, T.P. (1981). The 1889–97 rinderpest epidemic and the rise of British and German colonialism in Eastern and Southern Africa. *Journal of African Studies, 8*, 31–38.

Ogden, T.H. (1994). *Subjects of analysis.* New Jersey/London: Jason Aronson.

Ögren, K. (1996). Humanitarian law in the articles of war decreed in 1621 by King Gustavus II Adolphus of Sweden. *International Review of the Red Cross, 313*, 438.

O'Hara, E.A. & Yarn, D. (2002). On apology and consilience. *Washington Law Review, 77*, 1121–1192.

Olusanya, O. (2004). *Double jeopardy: Without parameters.* Antwerp: Intersentia.

Omer-Cooper, J. (1994). *History of Southern Africa* (2nd ed.). London: James Currey.

Oppenheim, H. (1955). *International law: A treatise, Vol. 1: Peace* (8th ed.). New York: David Mackay.

Orenstein, A. (1999). Apology expected: Incorporating a feminist analysis into evidence policy where you would least expect it. *Southwestern University Law Review, 28*, 221.

Orentlicher, D. (1998). The law of universal conscience: Genocide and crimes against humanity. Paper presented at the Committee on Conscience conference *Genocide and crimes against humanity: Early warning and prevention*, at the United States Holocaust Memorial Museum. Available at http://www.ushmm.org/conscience/events/conference_98/orentlicher.pdf.

Orentlicher, D. Genocide. Available at http://www.atranaya.org/Articles/EngArticles/Genocide.htm (last accessed August 2, 2005).

Osterhammel, J. (1997). *Colonialism: A theoretical overview.* Princeton, NJ: Markus Weiner.

O'Sullivan, M. (2005). Past violations under international human rights law: The indigenous "Stolen Generation" in Australia. *Netherlands Quarterly of Human Rights, 23*, 243–272.

Otavi Mines Minerals 100th anniversary commemorative publication (1900–2000).

Packenham, T. (1992). *The scramble for Africa: White man's conquest of the Dark Continent from 1875–1912*. New York: Avon Books.

Paech, N. (2004). Der juristische Weg der Wiedergutmachung: Schadenersatz für Völkermord? In Böhlke-Itzen, J. (ed.), *Kolonialschuld und Entschädigung: der deutsche Völkermord an den Herero (1904–1907)*. Frankfurt am Main: Brandes & Apsel.

Pakendorf, G. (1987). The literature of expropriation: Peter Moor's journey to South-West and the conquest of Namibia. In Totemeyer, G., Kandetu, V., & Werner, W. (eds.), *Namibia in perspective*. Windhoek: Council of Churches in Namibia.

Palmer, A. (1998). Colonial and modern genocide: Explanations and categories. *Ethnic and Racial Studies, 21*, 89–115.

Palmer, A. (2000). *Colonial genocide*. Adelaide: Crawford House.

Pankhurst, D. (1995). Towards reconciliation of the land issue in Namibia: Identifying the possible, assessing the probable. *Development and Change, 26*, 551–585.

Paul, J.R. (2001). Holding multi-national corporations responsible under international law. *Hastings International and Comparative Law Review, 24*, 285.

Paust, J. (1995). Threats to accountability after Nuremberg: Crimes against humanity, leader responsibility and national fora. *New York Law School Journal of Human Rights, 12*, 545.

Paust, J.J. (2001). Dr. Francis Lieber and the Lieber Code. *American Society International Law Proceedings, 95* (April 4–7), 112.

Pauwelyn, J. (1995). The concept of a "continuing violation" of an international obligation: Selected problems. *British Year Book of International Law, 66*, 415–450.

Pendleton, W.C. (1976). Herero reactions: The pre-colonial period, the German period and the South African period. In Chanaiwa, D. *Profiles of self-determination: African responses to European colonialism in southern Africa*. Present, Northridge: California State University Foundation.

Penrose, M. (2000). It's good to be the king! Prosecuting heads of state and former heads of state under international law. *Columbia Journal of Transnational Law, 39*, 193.

Papazian, P. (1984). A unique uniqueness. *Midstream*, 14–25.

PCIJ *Chozrow Factory* case, *Publications of the Permanent Court of International Justice*, Collection of Judgments, Series A, No. 9, 21; Series A, No. 17, 29 (June 27, 1928).

Pease, K.K. & Forsythe. D.P. (1993). Human rights, humanitarian intervention, and world politics, *Human Rights Quarterly, 15*, 290–314.

Pendleton, W.C. (1976). Herero reactions: The pre-colonial period, the German period and the South African period. In Chanaiwa, D. *Profiles of self-determination: African responses to European colonialism in southern Africa*. Present, Northridge: California State University Foundation.

Pennington, R. & Harpending, H. (1993). *The structure of an Africanist pastoral community: Demography, history and ecology of the Ngamiland Herero*. Oxford: Clarendon Press.

Penny, H.G. & Bunzl, M. (eds.), *Worldly provincialism: German anthropology in the Age of Empire*. Ann Arbor: University of Michigan Press.

Penzler, J. (ed.). *Die Reden Kaiser Wilhelms II. Vol. 3: 1901–1905*. Leipzig. Found at http://www.zum.de/psm/imperialismus/wilhelm1905.php.

Perez, A. (2000). The perils of Pinochet: Problems for transitional justice and a supranational governance solution. *Denver Journal of International Law and Policy*, *28*, 175.

Perrin, W.A. (1999). The petition to obtain an apology for the Acadian deportation, *Southern University Law Review*, *27*, 1.

Peterson, M.D. (2004). *Starving Armenians: America and the Armenian genocide, 1915–1930 and after*. Charlottesville: University of Virginia Press.

Pfister, G. (2005). Sport, colonialism and the enactment of German identity: *Turnen* in South West Africa, 24. Paper delivered at the 20th International Congress for the Historical Sciences July 3–9, 2005, Sydney. Found at http://www.cishsydney2005.org/images/GertrundPfisterST25.doc.

Pictet, J. (1985). Development and principles of international humanitarian law. Dordrecht/Geneva: Martinus Nijhoff & Henry Dunant Institute.

Pienaar, H. (2005) A Massacre No One Seems to Want to Remember. *Weekend Argus*, August 27, 2005.

Pierard, R. (1971). The transportation of white women to German South West Africa, 1898–1914. *Race*, *12*, 317–322.

Pierard, R.V. (1964). *The German colonial society 1882–1914*. PhD thesis (Modern History). State University of Iowa.

Pierson, C. (2000). Pinochet and the end of immunity. *Temple International and Comparative Law Journal*, *14*, 263.

Pitswane, J. (1992). Namibia: Challenges of the first decade. In Benjamin, L. & Gregory, C. (eds.), *Southern Africa at the crossroads*? Rivonia: Justified Press.

Plattner, D. (1992). Assistance to the civilian population: The development and present state of international humanitarian law. *International Review of the Red Cross*, *288*, 246–263.

Poewe, K. (1985). *The Namibian Herero: A history of their psychosocial disintegration and survival*. Lewiston, NY: Edwin Mellen.

Pohamba, H., quoted in Hunter, J. (2004). Interviews on land reform in Namibia. In Hunter, J. (ed.), *Who should own the land? Analyses and views on land reform and the land question in Namibia and southern Africa*. Windhoek: Namibia Institute for Democracy.

Pool, G. (1991). *Samuel Maherero*. Windhoek: Gamsberg MacMillan.

Posner, E.A. & Vermeule A. (2003). Reparations for slavery and other historical injustices. *Columbia Law Review*, *103*, 689.

Prein, P. (1994). Guns and top hats: African resistance in German South West Africa 1907–1915. *Journal of African Studies*, *20*, 99–121.

Procter, R. (1988). *Racial hygiene medicine under the Nazis*. Cambridge, MA: Harvard University Press.

Pross, C. (1998). *Paying for the past: The struggle over reparations for surviving victims of the Nazi terror*. Baltimore: Johns Hopkins University Press.

Provost, R. (2002). *International human rights and humanitarian law*. Cambridge: Cambridge University Press.

Pustogarov, V. (1996). Fyodor Fyodorovich Martens (1845–1909): A humanist of modern times. *International Review of the Red Cross*, *312*, 300.

Rahn, W. (1997). Sanitätsdienst der Schutztruppe für Südwestafrika während der Aufstände 1904–1907 und der Kalahari-Expedition 1908. *Beiträge zur deutschen Kolonialgeschichte*.

Ramcharan, B. (2005). The United Nations High Commissioner for Human Rights and international humanitarian law. *Program on Humanitarian Policy and Conflict Research, Harvard University Occasional Paper Series, 3*, 1.

Randelzhofer, A. (1999). The legal position of the individual under present international law. In Randelzhofer, A. & Tomuschat, C. (eds.), *State responsibility and the individual: Reparations in instances of grave violations of human rights*. The Hague: Martinus Nijhoff, 231.

Rasulov, A. (2003). Revisiting state succession to humanitarian treaties: Is there a case for automaticity? *European Journal of International Law, 14*, 141.

Ratner, S. & Abrams, J. (1997). *Accountability for human rights atrocities in international law*. Oxford: Oxford University Press.

Ratner, S. & Abrams, J. (2001). *Accountability for human rights atrocities in international law: Beyond the Nuremberg legacy* (2nd ed.). Oxford: Oxford University Press.

Read, J.S. (1969). Kenya, Tanzania and Uganda. In Milner, A. (ed.), *African penal systems*. London: Routledge & Kegan Paul, 91–164.

Redfern, P. Colonialism: Britain faces lawsuits. *The East African* (Nairobi), January 26, 2004.

Redress report (2000). *Challenging impunity for torture: A manual for bringing criminal and civil proceedings in England and Wales for torture committed abroad*. London.

Rees, W.L. (1888). German conduct in Samoa. XXIV. *Nineteenth Century*, 734–752.

Rehm, P.H. & Beatty, D.R. (1996). Legal consequences of apologizing. *Journal of Dispute Resolution, 1*, 115–130.

Reparations Not on the Table. *The Namibian*, August 31, 2000.

Report of the British Consul, Roger Casement, on the Administration of the Congo Free State: British Parliamentary Papers, 1904, LXII, Cd. 1933.

Report of the International Commission to Inquire into the Causes and Conduct of the Balkan Wars, Washington 1914.

Report of the International Law Commission on the Work of its Forty-eighth Session, May 6–July 26, 1996, G.A.O.R., 51st session, Supplement No. 10 (A/51/10) 89.

Report of the International Law Commission on the Work of its Fiftieth Session, April 20–June 12, 1998, July 27–August 14, 1998, UN Doc. A/53/10.

Reydams, L. (2003). *Universal jurisdiction: International and municipal legal perspective*. Oxford: Oxford University Press.

Reyhan, P.Y. (1997). Genocidal violence in Burundi: Should international law prohibit domestic humanitarian intervention? *Albany Law Review, 60*, 771–800.

Rich, N. (1965). *Friedrich von Holstein: Politics and diplomacy in the era of Bismarck and Wilhelm II*. Cambridge: Cambridge University Press.

Richardson, H.J. (1984). Constitutive questions in the negotiations for Namibian independence. *American Journal of International Law, 78*, 76.

Riruako, K. Statement at the International Conference on the German-Herero War: One hundred years after Bremen. Germany.

Ritter-Petersen, H.G. (1991). *The Herrenvolk mentality in German South West Africa 1884–1914*. DLitt (History). Pretoria: University of South Africa.

Roberge, M-C. (1997). Jurisdiction of the ad hoc tribunals for the former Yugoslavia and Rwanda over crimes against humanity and genocide. *International Review of the Red Cross, 321*, 651–664.

Roberts, A. (2001). Traditional and modern approaches to customary international law: A reconciliation. *American Journal of International Law, 95*, 757.

Robertson, G. (2000). *Crimes against humanity: The struggle for global justice.* New York: New Press.

Robinson, R. (1986). The eccentric idea of imperialism, with or without Empire. In Mommsen, W.J. & Osterhammel, J. (eds.), *Imperialism and after: Continuities and discontinuities.* London: Allen & Unwin.

Rodley, N.S. (1999). *The treatment of prisoners under international law* (2nd ed.). Oxford: Clarendon Press.

Röhl, J.C.G. (1982). Introduction. In Röhl, J.C.G. & Sombart, N. (eds.), *Kaiser Wilhelm II: New interpretations. The Corfu Papers.* Cambridge: Cambridge University Press.

Röhl, J.C.G. (1994). *The Kaiser and his court: Wilhelm II and the government of Germany.* Cambridge: Cambridge University Press.

Röhl, J.C.G. (2001). *Wilhelm II. Der Aufbau der persönlichen Monarchie 1888–1900.* München: CH Beck Verlag.

Röhl, J.C.G. & Sombart, N. (eds.), *Kaiser Wilhelm II: New interpretations. The Corfu Papers.* Cambridge: Cambridge University Press.

Rohrbach, P. (1907). *Deutsche Kolonialwirtschaft, Vol. I: Südwestafrika.* Berlin /Schoneberg: Buchverlag der Hilfe.

Romano, C.P.R. (2002). International justice and developing countries: A quantitative analysis. *The Law and Practice of International Courts and Tribunals, 1*, 367–399.

Rome Statute of the International Criminal Court, U.N. Diplomatic Conference of Plenipotentiaries on the Establishment of an International Criminal Court, U.N. Doc. A/CONF. 183/9 (1998).

Roosevelt, T. (1904). State of the Union Message, December 6. Found at http://www.theodore-roosevelt.com/sotu4.html.

Rosenberg, T. (1999). *The haunted land: Facing Europe's ghosts after communism.* New York: Random House.

Rotberg, R.I. (1983). Political and economic realities in a time of settlement. In Rotberg, R.I. (ed.), *Namibia: Political and economic prospects.* Cape Town: David Phillip.

Rudolf, B. (1997). *Loizidou v. Turkey. American Journal of International Law, 91*, 532.

Rummel, R.J. (1996). *Lethal politics. Soviet genocide and mass murder since 1917.* New Brunswick: Transaction.

Sarkin, J. (1999). The necessity and challenges of establishing a truth and reconciliation commission in Rwanda. *Human Rights Quarterly, 21*, 767.

Sarkin, J. (2002). Finding a solution for the problems created by the politics of identity in the Democratic Republic of the Congo (DRC): Designing a constitutional framework for peaceful co-operation. In Konrad Adenauer Foundation (eds.), *The politics of identity.* Pretoria: Konrad Adenauer Foundation.

Sarkin, J. (2004). The coming of age of claims for reparations for human rights abuses committed in the South. *Sur International Human Rights Journal, 1*, 67–125.

Sarkin, J. & Binchy, W. (eds.). (2001). *Human rights, the citizen and the state.* Dublin: Round Hall, Sweet & Maxwell.

Sarkin, J., Van de Lanotte, J. & Haeck, Y. (eds.) (2001). *Resolving the tensions between crime and human rights: European and South African perspectives.* Antwerpen: Maklu.

Saunders, C. (2003). Liberation and democracy: A critical reading of Sam Nujoma's "autobiography." In Melber, H. (ed.). *Re-examining liberation in Namibia: Political cultures since independence.* Uppsala: Nordic Africa Institute, 87.

Sautman, B. (2001). Is Tibet China's colony?: The claim of demographic catastrophe. *Columbia Journal of Asian Law*, 81.

Scales-Trent, J. (2001). Racial purity laws in the United States and Nazi Germany: The targeting process. *Human Rights Quarterly*, *23*, 260–307.

Schabas, W.A. (1997). Conceptualizing violence: Present and future developments in international law. *Albany Law Review*, *60*, 733.

Schabas, W.A. (1999). The Genocide Convention at fifty. *United States Institute for Peace Report*. Available at http://63.104.169.22/pubs/Specialreports/sr990107.pdf.

Schabas, W.A. (2000). *Genocide in international law.* Cambridge: Cambridge University Press.

Schabas, W. (2000). Groups protected by the Genocide Convention: Conflicting interpretations from the International Criminal Tribunal for Rwanda. *ILSA Journal of International & Comparative Law*, *6*, 375.

Schabas, W.A. (2001). *Problems of international codification: Were the atrocities in Cambodia and Kosovo genocide? New England Law Review*, *35*, 287–320.

Schabas, W.A. (2003). National courts finally begin to prosecute genocide, the "crime of crimes." *Journal of International Criminal Justice*, *1*, 39–63.

Schafft, G.E. (2004). *From racism to genocide: Anthropology in the Third Reich.* Urbana: University of Illinois Press.

Schaller, D.J. (2005). Raphael Lemkin's view of European colonial rule in Africa: Between condemnation and admiration. *Journal of Genocide Research*, *7*, 531–538.

Scheper-Hughes, N. (1996). Small wars and invisible genocides. *Social Science & Medicine*, *43*, 889–900.

Schindler, D. (1982). Human rights and humanitarian law: Interrelationship of the laws. *American University Law Review*, *31*, 935.

Schindler, D. & Toman, J. (1981). *The laws of armed conflicts: A collection of conventions, resolutions and other documents.* Alphen aan den Rijn: Sijthoff & Noordhoff.

Schindler, D. & Toman, J. (1988). *The laws of armed conflict.* Boston: Martinus Nijhoff.

Schindler, D. & Toman, J. (2004). *The laws of armed conflicts: A collection of conventions, resolutions, and other documents* (4th ed.). Leiden/Boston: Martinus Nijhoff.

Schmokel, W. W. (1985). The myth of the white farmer: Commercial agriculture in Namibia 1900–1983. *International Journal of African Historical Studies*, *18*, 93–108.

Schnee, H. (1926). *German colonization past and future: The truth about the German colonies.* London: George Allen & Unwin.

Schneider-Waterberg, H.R. (2003). Konzentrationslager als Einrichtungen kolonialer Kriegsführung in Südlichen Afrika. Zum Bedeutungswandel eines Begriffes. *Befunde und Berichte zur Deutschen kolonialgeschichte*, *6*, 11–19.

Schnieder, T. (1967). Political and social development in Europe. In *The new Cambridge modern history, XI: Material progress and worldwide problems, 1870–1898.* Cambridge: Cambridge University Press.

Schöng, H. (1959). *Der Imperialismus und Chinas Politik*. Berlin (DDR) S. 144. Found at http://www.zum.de/psm/imperialismus/rums24/rums24_62e.php3.

Schrank, G.I. (1974). German *South West Africa: Social and economic aspects of its history 1884–1915*. PhD thesis (History), New York University.

Schulz, S. & Hamutenya, M. (2003). Juvenile justice in Namibia: Law reform towards reconciliation and restorative justice? Polytechnic of Namibia. Available at http://www.restorativejustice.org/resources/docs/Namibia.

Schuring, E. (2004). *History obliges: The real motivations behind German aid flows in the case of Namibia*. MA thesis (Law & Diplomacy), Fletcher School of Law and Diplomacy, Tufts University.

Schwabe, K. (1904). *Mit Schwert und Pflug in Deutsch-südwestafrika: Vier Kriegs- und Wanderjahre*, Berlin.

Schwarzenberger, G. (1947). The judgment of Nuremberg. *Tulane Law Review*, *21*.

Schwarzenberger, G. (1968). *International law as applied by international courts and tribunals, Vol. II: The law of armed conflict*. London: Stevens.

Schwelb, E. (1946). Crimes against humanity. *British Yearbook of International Law*, *23*, 178.

Schwerin, K. (1972). German compensation for victims of Nazi persecution. *Northwestern University Law Review*, *67*, 479.

Schwerin, K. (1995). German compensation for victims of Nazi persecution. In Kritz, N. (ed.), *Transitional Justice, Vol. II*. Washington, D.C.: United States Institute for Peace, 51.

Schwirck, H. (2002). Law's violence and the boundary between corporal discipline and physical abuse in German South West Africa. *Akron Law Review*, *36*, 81.

Scott, J.B. (1909). *The Hague Peace Conferences of 1899 and 1907*. Baltimore: Johns Hopkins.

Scott, J.B. (1934). *The Spanish origin of international law: Francisco de Vitoria and his law of nations*. London: Humphrey Milford, App. F, cxxiv.

Scott, M. (1958). The International Status of South West Africa, *International Affairs*, *34*, 318–329.

Sebok, A.J. (2001). Slavery, reparations, and potential legal liability: The hidden legal issue behind the U.N. racism conference. http://writ.news.findlaw.com/sebok/20010910.html (last visited on May 23, 2002).

Shamsey, J. (2002). The International Criminal Court and the 20th century's first genocide. *Journal of Transnational Law and Policy*, *11*, 327.

Shandley, R.R. (ed.) (1998). *Unwilling Germans? The Goldhagen debate*. Minneapolis: University of Minnesota Press.

Sharf, F.A. & Harrington, P. (2000). China 1900: The eyewitnesses speak; The experience of Westerners in China during the Boxer Rebellion, as described by participants in letters, diaries and photographs. Mechanicsburg, PA: Stackpole.

Shaw, M. (1986). Title to territory: African international legal issues. Oxford: Clarendon Press.

Shaw, M.N. (1989). Genocide and international law. In Dinstein, Y. (ed.), *International law at a time of perplexity: Essays in honour of Shabtai Rosenne*: Dordrecht: Martinus Nijhoff, 797.

Shaw, M.N. (2003). *International Law* (5th ed.). Cambridge: Cambridge University Press.

Shelton, D. (1999). *Remedies in international human rights law*. Oxford: Oxford University Press.

Shelton, D. (2003). The world of atonement: Reparations for historical injustices. *Netherlands International Law Review*, 289–325.

Shelton, D. (2004). The world of atonement reparations for historical injustices. *Miskolc Journal of International Law*, *1*, 259–289.

Shelton, D. (2005). *Remedies in international human rights law* (2nd ed.). Oxford: Oxford University Press.

Shigwedha, A. (2001). *Hereros v. Germany*. *New African*, 14.

Sieghart, P. (1983). *The international law of human rights*. Oxford: Clarendon Press.

Silvester, J. (1998). Beasts, boundaries and buildings: The survival and creation of pastoral economics in Southern Namibia 1915–35 In Hayes, P., Silvester, J., Wallace, M. & Hartman, W. *Namibia under South African rule: Mobility and containment 1915–1946*. Oxford: James Currey, 95–116.

Silvester, J., Hillebrecht, W., & Erichsen, C. (2001). The Herero Holocaust? *The Namibian Weekender*, August 10, 2001.

Simma, B. & Alston, P. (1988–1989). The sources of human rights law: Custom, *jus cogens*, and general principles. *Australian Year Book of International Law*, 82.

Simmons, D. (2003). Chivalry, "mutiny," and Sherlock Holmes: Three aspects of imperial grandiosity and rage. *Psychology of the Self Online*. Available at http://www.psychologyoftheself.com/papers/simmons.htm.

Simon, T.W. (1996). Defining genocide. *Wisconsin Law Journal*, *15*, 243.

Smith, H.W. (1998). The talk of genocide, the rhetoric of miscegenation: Notes on the debates in the German Reichstag concerning Southwest Africa, 1904–14. In Friedrichsmeyer, S., Lennox, S. & Zantop, S. (eds.), *The imperialist imagination: German colonialism and its legacy*. Ann Arbor: University of Michigan Press.

Smith, H.W. (1999). The logic of colonial violence: Germany in South West Africa (1904–1907), the United States in the Philippines (1899–1902). In Lehmann, H. & Wellenreuther, H. (eds.), *German and African nationalism: A comparative perspective*. Oxford: Berg.

Smith, R.W. (1999). State power and genocidal intent: On the uses of genocide in the twentieth century. In Chorbajian, L. & Shirinian, G. (eds.), *Studies in comparative genocide*. New York: St. Martin's Press, 3–14.

Smith, R.W., Markusen, E., & Lifton, R.J. (1995). Potential ethics and the denial of the Armenian genocide. *Holocaust and Genocide Studies*, *9*, 1–22.

Soggot, D. (1986). *Namibia: The violent heritage*. London: Rex Collings.

Sohn, L. (1982). The new international law: Protection of the rights of individuals rather than states. *American University International Law Review*, *32*, 1.

Sohn, L.B. & Buergenthal, T. (1973). *International protection of human rights*. Indianapolis: Bobbs-Merrill.

Sole, T.E. (1968). The Sudwestafrika Denkmunze and the South West African campaigns of 1903–1908. *Military History Journal*, *1*, 19–23.

Solf, W.A. (1983). The status of combatants in non-international armed conflicts under domestic law and transnational practice. *American University Law Review*, 33.

Spinedi, M. (2002). State responsibility v. individual responsibility for international crimes: *Tertium non Datu*. *European Journal of International Law*, *13*, 895.

Spraul, G. (1988). Der "Völkermord" an den Herero: Untersuchungen zu einer neuen Kontinuitätsthese. *Geschichte in Wissenschaft und Unterricht, 12*, 713–739.

Stals, E.L.P. (1984). *Duits-Suidwes-Afrika na die groot opstande*. Pretoria: Staatsdrukker.

Stannard, D.E. (1996). Uniqueness as denial: The politics of genocide scholarship. In Rosenbaum, A.S. (ed.), *Is the Holocaust unique? Perspectives on comparative genocide*. Boulder, CO: Westview Press.

Steer, G.L. (1939). *Judgement on German Africa*, London: Hodder & Stoughton.

Steinberg, J. (1965). *Yesterday's deterrent: Tirpitz and the birth of the German battle fleet*. London: Macmillan

Steinmetz, G. (2003). The implications of colonial and postcolonial studies for the study of Europe. *European Studies Newsletter (Council for European Studies), 32*, 1–3.

Steinmetz, G. (2003). The devil's handwriting: Precolonial discourse, ethnographic acuity and cross-identification in German colonialism. *Comparative Studies in Society and History, 45*, 41–95.

Steinmetz, G. (2005). From "Native Policy" to exterminationism: German Southwest Africa, 1904. In *Comparative perspective, theory and research in comparative social analysis, Paper 30*, 4–5. Los Angeles: Department of Sociology, UCLA, 1. Found at http://repositories.cdlib.org/cgi/viewcontent.cgi?article=1036&context=uclasoc.

Stephens, D. (2001). Human rights and armed conflict: The advisory opinion of the International Court of Justice in the Nuclear Weapons Case. *Yale Human Rights and Development Law Journal, 4*, 8.

Stevens, B. (2002). Translating Filartiga: A comparative and international law analysis of domestic remedies for international human rights violations. *Yale Journal of International Law, 27*, 1.

Stoecker, H. & Sebald, P. (1987). Enemies of the colonial idea. In Knoll, A.J. & Gann, L.H. (eds.), *Germans in the tropics: Essays in German colonial history* (2nd ed.). New York/London: Greenwood Press.

Stoecker, H. (ed). (1986).*German imperialism in Africa: From the beginnings until the Second World War*. London: C. Hurst & Co.

Stoecker, H. (1987). The position of Africans in the German colonies. In Knoll, A.J. & Gann, L.H. (eds.), *Germans in the tropics: Essays in German colonial history* (2nd ed.). New York/London: Greenwood Press, 119–129.

Stoett, P. (2004). Shades of complicity: Towards a typology of transnational crimes against humanity. In Jones, A. (ed.), *Genocide, war crimes, and the West*. London: Zed Books, 31–55.

Stone, D. (2001). White men with low moral standards: German anthropology and the Herero genocide. *Patterns of Prejudice, 35*, 33.

Stone, D. (2004). Genocide as transgression. *European Journal of Social Theory, 7*, 45–65.

Stratton, J. (2003). It almost needn't have been the Germans: The state, colonial violence and the Holocaust. *European Journal of Cultural Studies, 6*, 507–527.

Sudholt, G. (1975). *Die deutsche Eingeborenenpolitik in Südwestafrika: Von den Anfängen bis 1904*. Hildesheim/New York: Olms.

Sunga, L.S. (1992). *Individual responsibility in international law for serious human rights violations*. Dordrecht: Martinus Nijhoff.

Suzman, J. (2001). *Regional assessment of the status of the San in southern Africa*. Windhoek: Legal Assistance Centre (LAC).

Suzman, J. (2002). *Minorities in imperial Namibia.* London: Minority Rights Group International.

Swaak-Goldman, O. (2000). Crimes against humanity. In McDonald G.K. & Swaak-Goldman, O. (eds.), *Substantive and procedural aspects of international criminal law: The experience of international and national courts, Vol. I.* The Hague/London/Boston: Kluwer Law International, 143–168.

Swan, J. (1991). The Final Solution in South West Africa. *Military History Quarterly, 3,* 36–55.

Tan, C.C. (1967). *The Boxer catastrophe.* New York: Octagon Books.

Tapscott, C. (1993). National reconciliation, social equity and class formation in independent Namibia. *Journal of Southern African Studies, 19,* 29–39.

Tavuchis, N. (1991). *Mea Culpa: A sociology of apology and reconciliation.* Stanford, CA: Stanford University Press.

Thompson, L. (ed). (1969). *African societies in Southern Africa.* London: Heinemann.

Ticehurst, R. (1997). The Martens Clause and the laws of armed conflict. *International Review of the Red Cross, 317,* 125.

Tomuschat, C. (2002). Reparation for victims of grave human rights violations. *Tulane Journal of International and Comparative Law, 10,* 157–184.

Totten, S., Parsons, W.S. & Charny, I. W. (eds.), (1997). *Century of genocide: Eyewitness accounts and critical views.* New York/London Garland.

Traverso, E. Die Moderne und die Barbarei, *Sozialistische Zeitung,* December 7, 2000.

Triffterer, O. (1996). Prosecution of states for crimes of state. *Revue Internationale de Droit Penal, 67,* 341.

Troup, F. (1950). *In face of fear: Michael Scott's challenge to South Africa.* London: Faber & Faber, 63.

UN Commission on Human Rights. *Study concerning the right to restitution, compensation and rehabilitation for victims of gross violations of human rights and fundamental freedoms* (Van Boven Report), UN Doc. E/CN.4/Sub.2/1993/8, July 2, 1993.

UN HRC E. and A. K. v. Hungary, Decision of May 5, 1992. CCPR/C/50/D/520/1992.

UN HRC Malik v. Czech Republic, CCPR/C/D 669/1995, Decision of October 21, 1998.

UN Human Rights Committee, General Comment no. 18 (37th session, 1989). UN Doc. HRI/GEN/1/Rev.3.

United Nations Development Programme (2005). *Human Development Report,* 94.

United Nations Economic and Social Council Commission on Human Rights Sub-Commission on Prevention of Discrimination and Protection of Minorities Thirty-Eighth Session, Item 4 of the Provisional Agenda, E/Cn.4/Sub.2/1985/6-July 2, 1985. Review of Further Developments in Fields with which the Sub-Commission has been Concerned. Revised and Updated Report on the Question of the Prevention and Punishment of the Crime of Genocide. Prepared by Mr. B. Whitaker. (E/CN.4/Sub.2/416).

United Nations Office for the Coordination of Humanitarian Affairs Integrated Regional Information Network IRIN Africa English reports, 7/2/2003.

United States of America v. Alfred Krupp von Bohlen und Halbach (The Krupp Trial), *Law Reports of the War Commission, 10,* 69, 1949.

U.S. Abebe-Jira v. Negewo, 72 F.3d 844 (11th Cir. 1996).

U.S. Alejandre v. Republic of Cuba, 996 F. Supp. 1239 (S.D. Fla. 1997).

U.S. Cicippio v. Republic of Iran, 18 F. Supp. 2d 62 (D.D.C. 1998).

U.S. Department of State Office of the Spokesman, March 8, 2005. Statement by Richard Boucher (Spokesman). German foundation boosts payments to victims of Nazi medical experiments.

U.S. Flatow v. Republic of Iran, 999 F. Supp. 1 (D.D.C. 1998).

U.S. Rein v. Socialist People's Libyan Arab Jamahiriya, 995 F. Supp. 325 (E.D.N.Y. 1998).

U.S. Supreme. Court. *Argentine Republic v. Almerada Shipping Corp.*, 488 U.S. 428 (1989).

Uzoigwe, G.N. (1976). Spheres of influence and the doctrine of the hinterland in the partition of Africa. *Journal of African Studies, 3*, 183–203, 189–193.

Van Bueren, G. It's Britain's Guilty Secret, *Guardian*, May 25, 2001.

Van Bueren, G. (2004). Slavery as piracy: The legal case for reparations for slavery. In Walden, R. (ed.), *Racism and Human Rights*. Leiden: Brill, 41–53.

Van der Kiste, J. (1999). *Kaiser Wilhelm II: Germany's last Emperor*. Stroud, Gloucestershire: Sutton.

Van Dongen, Y. (1991*). The protection of civilian populations in time of armed conflict.* Groningen: Rijksuniversiteit Groningen.

Van Onselen, C. (1973). Reaction to rinderpest in Southern Africa 1896–97. *Journal of African History, 13*.

Van Schaack, B. (1997). The crime of political genocide: Repairing the Genocide Convention's blind spot. *Yale Law Journal, 106*, 2259–2291.

Vedder, H. (1966). *South West Africa in early times*. New York: Barnes & Noble.

Verdirame, G. (2000). The Genocide definition in the Jurisprudence of the ad hoc tribunals. *International and Comparative Law Quarterly, 49*, 578–598.

Verdun, V. (1993). If the shoe fits, wear it: An analysis of reparations to African Americans, *Tulane Law Review, 67*, 597.

Vetlesen, A.J. (1998). Impartiality and evil: A reconsideration provoked by genocide in Bosnia. *Philosophy & Social Criticism, 24*, 1.

Vetlesen, A.J. (2000). Genocide. A case for the responsibility of the bystander. *Journal of Peace Research, 37*, 519–532.

Vidal-Naquet, P. (1992). *Assassins of Memory: Essays on the Denial of the Holocaust.* New York: Columbia University Press.

Vienna Convention on the Law of Treaties, May 23, 1969, UN Doc. A/CONF. 39/27 (1969).

Vigne, R. 1990, February/May. Diary: Shark Island. *Southern African Review of Books*, 31.

Vigne. (1990). Genocide. *Southern African Review of Books*, 13.

Villa-Vicencio, C. (2000). Why perpetrators should not always be prosecuted: Where the International Criminal Court and truth commissions meet. *Emory Law Journal,* 214.

Voeltz, R.A. (1988). *German colonialism and the South West Africa Company, 1884–1914; Allies in Apartheid: Western capitalism in occupied Namibia* (Monographs in International Studies, Africa Series No. 50). Athens: Ohio University Center for International Studies.

Voeltz, R.A. (2000). Review of mission, church and state relations in South West Africa under German rule (1884–1915). *The International Journal of African Historical Studies, 33*, 153.

Vogt, A. (1995*). National monuments in Namibia.* MA, University of Stellenbosch.

Von Falkenhausen, H. (1906). *Ansiedlerschicksale: Elf Jahre in Deutsch-Südwestafrika 1894–1904*. Berlin: Reimer.

Von Francois, C. (1899). *Deutsch-Südwest-Afrika*. Berlin: Dietrich Reimer, 133. Quoted in Kienetz, A. (1975). *Nineteenth-century South West Africa as a German settlement colony*. PhD thesis, University of Minnesota.

Von Glahn, G. (1992). *Law among nations: An introduction to public international law* (6th rev. ed.) New York: Macmillan.

Von Trotha, T. (1994). *Koloniale Herrschaft: Zur soziologischen Theorie der Staatsentstehung am Beispiel des Schutzgebietes Togo*. Tübingen: J.C.B. Mohr.

Von Trotha, T. (1999). The fellows can just starve. On wars of pacification in African colonies of Imperial Germany and concept of total war. In Boemeke, M.E., Chickering, R., & Förster, S. (eds.), *Anticipating Total War: The German and American Experience 1871–1914*. Cambridge: Cambridge University Press, 415–435.

Waldron, J. (1992). Superseding historic injustice. *Ethics, 103*, 4–28.

Wallace-Bruce, N. I. (1985). Africa and international law: The emergence to statehood. *Journal of Modern African Studies, 23*, 575–602.

Wallenkampf, A.V. (1969). *The Herero rebellion in South West Africa: A study in German colonialism*. PhD thesis. Los Angeles: UCLA.

Wallimann, I. & Dobkowski, M.N. (eds.), (1987). *Genocide and the modern age: Etiology and case studies of mass death*. New York: Greenwood Press.

Walther, D.J. (2002). *Creating Germans abroad: Cultural policies and national indemnity in Namibia*. Athens: Ohio University Press.

Watts, N.H.Z. (1983). The roots of controversy. In Rotberg, R.I. (ed.), *Namibia: Political and economic prospects*. Cape Town: David Phillip.

Weeramantry, C.G. (2004). *Universalising international law*. Dordrecht: Martinus Nijhoff.

Wehler, H-U. (1985). *The German Empire 1871–1918*. Leamington Spa/Dover: Berg Publishers.

Weigend, G.G. (1985). German settlement patterns in Namibia. *Geographical Review, 75*, 156–169.

Weindling, P. (2002). *Epidemics and genocide in Eastern Europe, 1890–1945*. Oxford/New York: Oxford University Press.

Weitz, E.D. (2003). *A century of genocide: Utopias of race and nation*. Princeton: Princeton University Press.

Wellington, J.H. (1967). *South West Africa and its human issues*. Oxford: Clarendon Press.

Werle, G. (1997). Menschenrechtsschutz durch Völkerstrafrecht. *Zeitschrift für die Gesamte Strafrechtswissenschaft, 109*, 808–829.

Werle, G. & Jessberger, F. (2002). International criminal justice is coming home: The new German code of crimes against international law. *Criminal Law Forum, 13*, 191–223.

Werner, W. (1993). A brief history of land dispossession in Namibia. *Journal of Southern African Studies, 19*, 29–39.

Werner, W. (1997). From colonial pastures to enclosures: The development of land tenure in Herero reserves. Windhoek*: NEPRU Working Paper No. 60.*

Werner, W. (1997). *Land reform in Namibia: The first seven years*. Windhoek: Namibian Economic Policy Research Unit.

Werner, W. (1998). *No-one will become rich: Economy and society in the Herero reserves in Namibia 1913–1946*. Basel: P. Schlettwein.

Werner, W. (2000). Agriculture and land. In Melber, H. (ed.), *Namibia: A decade of Independence 1990–2000*. Windhoek: Namibian Economic Policy Research Unit, 29–48.

Westlake, J. (1904). *International Law: Part 1: Peace*. Cambridge: Cambridge University Press.

Whitaker Report: United Nations Economic and Social Council Commission on Human Rights Sub-Commission on Prevention of Discrimination and Protection of Minorities, Thirty-eighth Session, Item 4 of the Provisional Agenda, E/Cn.4/Sub.2/1985/6-July 2, 1985. Review of further developments in fields with which the sub-commission has been concerned: Revised and updated report on the question of the prevention and punishment of the crime of genocide. Prepared by Mr. B. Whitaker. (E/CN.4/Sub.2/416).

Whittle, T. (1977). *The last Kaiser: A biography of William II, German Emperor and King of Prussia*. London: Heinemann.

Wieczorek-Zeul, H. (2004). Speech delivered at the commemoration ceremony for the centenary of the battle at the Waterberg, August 14, 2004. Available at http://www.bmz.de/de/presse/reden/ministerin/rede20040814.html.

Wilcox, S.S (2004). The South West Africa People's Organisation 1961–1991: A guide to archival resources and special collections in the Western Cape, South Africa. *Occasional e-publications series*. Cape Town: University of Cape Town, 1.

Wildenthal, L (1996). She is the victor: Bourgeois women, nationalist identities and the ideal of the independent women farmers in German South West Africa. In Eley, G. (ed.), *Society, culture and the state in Germany 1870–1930*. Ann Arbor: University of Michigan.

Wildenthal, L. (2001). *German woman for Empire, 1885–1945*. London: Duke University Press.

Wilets, J.D. (2001): Introduction: The building blocks to recognition of human rights and democracy: Reconciliation, rule of law and domestic and international peace. *ILSA Journal of International and Comparative Law*, *7*, 597, 598.

Wilhelm II (1922). *The Kaiser's memoirs* (English translation T.R.Y. Barra). New York: Harper & Brothers.

Willis, J.F. (1982). *Prologue to Nuremberg: The politics and diplomacy of punishing war criminals of the First World War*. Westport, CT: Greenwood Press.

Wood, B. (ed.). (1988). *Namibia 1884–1984: Readings on Namibia's history and society*. London: Namibia Support Committee.

Woolsey, T. S. (1891). *Introduction to the study of international law* (6th ed.). New York: Charles Scribner's Sons.

Wright, Q. (1919). The legal liability of the Kaiser. *American Political Science Review*, *13*, 120–128.

Yablonka, H. (2004). *The state of Israel vs. Adolf Eichmann* (translated from Hebrew by O. Cummings with D. Herman). New York: Schocken Books.

Yacoubian Jr., G.S. (1997). Underestimating the magnitude of international crime: Implications of genocidal behavior for the discipline of criminology. *Injustice Studies*, 1. Available at http://www.habermas.org/yacoubiandoc.htm.

Zedlitz-Trutzler, R. (1951). *Twelve years at the imperial German court*. London: Nisbet & Co.

Zegveld, L. (2003). Remedies for victims of violations of international humanitarian law. *International Review of the Red Cross*, *85*, 497.

Zia-Zarifi, S. (1999). Suing multinational corporations in the U.S. for violating international law. *University of California Los Angeles Journal of International Law and Foreign Affairs, 4*, 81.

Zimmerer, J. & Zeller, J. (2003). *Völkermord in Südwestafrika. Der Kolonialkrieg (1904–1908) und seine Folgen.* Berlin: Christoph Links Verlag.

Zimmerman, A. (2001). *Anthropology and antihumanism in imperial Germany.* Chicago: University of Chicago Press.

Zimmerman, A. (2003). Adventures in the skin trade: German anthropology and colonial corporeality. In Penny, H.G. & Bunzl, M. (eds.), *Worldly provincialism: German anthropology in the Age of Empire.* Ann Arbor: University of Michigan Press.

Zirkel, K. (1999). Military power in German colonial policy: The Schutztruppen and their leaders in the East and South West Africa, 1888–1918. In Killingray, D. & Omissi, D. (eds.), *Guardians of Empire: The armed forces of the colonial powers, 1700–1964*. Manchester: Manchester University Press, 91–113

Zweig, R. (2001). *German reparations and the Jewish world.* London: Frank Cass.

Zweig, R.W. (1987). *German reparations and the Jewish world: A history of the claims conference.* Boulder: Westview Press.

Index

accountability, 2, 23, 65, 83–84, 94, 117, 134, 159–60, 163, 172, 175–76
acknowledgment, 24, 33, 60, 123, 133–34, 143, 156, 189
actus reus, 98, 100, 103
Aetna Inc., 176
affirmative action, 145, 166
African Americans, 87, 131, 145, 176–77
African Charter on Human and People's Rights, 168
African Commission on Human and Peoples Rights, 11, 127, 168–69; *Henry Kalenga v. Zambia*, 168; *Louis Mega Mekongo v. Cameroon*, 168; *Malawi Africa Association and Others v. Mauritania*, 169
African Court of Human Rights, 23, 128, 168–69, 192
African sovereigns, 32
Agricultural (Commercial) Land Reform Act (No. 6 of 1995), 54
aid distribution, 61
Alien Tort Claims Act (ATCA), 125, 150–51, 154, 191
Anglo-Boer War, 75, 120
anniversary, 8, 49, 56–57, 132, 134
apartheid, 3, 45, 51, 152, 154, 174–75
apology, 8–10, 23–24, 59, 120, 124, 126, 131–37, 144, 154, 158, 177–78, 189, 191–94; elements of, 133
applicant, 125, 150, 167, 171–72
Armenia, 8, 56, 87–88, 90, 94, 109, 178
Arthur Koppel Company, 7. *See also* Orenstein-Koppel
atrocities, 2, 4–5, 7, 9–10, 16, 21–23, 25, 56, 64–65, 77, 86, 94–95, 103, 108, 116–17, 119, 120, 132–33, 143–44, 149, 155–57, 162, 173, 182–84, 188
Australia, 110, 131, 155, 158, 178–79

Bank of America, 176
Belgium, 59, 65, 87, 155, 171, 192
Berlin, 15, 16, 37, 43, 59, 137
Berlin Anti-Colonial Africa Conference (2004), 130
Berlin Conference of 1884–1885, 15, 27, 32, 181
Berlin Conference Treaty of 1885, 33, 85, 114, 118, 143, 187
Berlin Wall, 3, 143
Bethanie Community, 36, 41. *See also* protection treaties; sovereignty

Bismarck, 30, 114
Blue Book, 9
Bremen Conference, 58, 139
British, 14, 19, 27, 29, 31, 41, 75, 118, 120, 156; army explosives, 179; colonies, 115; court decision, 179, 180; forces, 30; government, 9, 17, 33, 156, 178; legal aid, 179; Ministry of Defense, 179; Parliament, 120; reports of 1909 and 1918, 9 (*see also* Blue Book)
Brussels Conference (1874), 75, 77–80, 87, 114
burden of proof, 151

Canada, 110, 166, 178–79, 190
Cape Verde, 61
Caprivi Strip, 27, 184
cattle, 5, 9–10, 15, 25, 28, 44, 48, 55, 100, 102, 137, 144, 184
cause of action, 150, 153–54
Central American Court of Justice, 127
Central Association for Commercial Geography and the Promotion of German Interests Abroad (1878), 30
CERD. *See* International Convention on the Elimination of All Forms of Racial Discrimination Committee; treaties
civil action, 173
civil litigation, 147
claimant, 21–22, 76, 129–30, 145, 149, 152–53, 159, 162–63, 166, 172, 176, 179
claims, historical, 4, 9, 12, 21–22, 51, 54, 124–26, 135, 139, 145, 148, 189
codification, 12, 69–71, 80, 107, 111–12, 186, 189
collective group memory, 47
colonial: administration, 2, 42, 51, 53, 58; authorities, 7, 9, 16, 35; powers, 27, 42, 108, 119, 126, 155, 156–59, 169, 174, 181, 184, 192; territory, 14, 15, 42; wars, 20, 157
colonial wars, 1904–1908, 20, 135
colonialism, 1–3, 7–8, 20, 23, 25, 28–30, 32–34, 49, 51, 65, 114, 125, 132–33, 155, 179, 194
colonialists, 1–2, 4, 15, 23, 30, 33, 41, 50, 59, 61, 118, 133, 154, 157, 159, 181
combatant, 5, 13, 15, 66, 70, 76, 78, 81, 95, 115, 120–21
commemoration, 53, 55–58, 133–34
Commission for Compensation, 137
Commission on the Responsibilities of the Authors of War and on Enforcement of Penalties for Violation of the Laws and Customs of War, 89
community development, 158
companies, 7, 27, 38, 42, 102, 130, 137, 142–43, 146, 149–50, 154–55, 177–79, 191
compensation, 20, 23–24, 49, 54–55, 67, 126–33, 137–40, 142–45, 147, 154, 156–58, 166–68, 170, 178–80, 189–91, 193–94
complaints, 4, 126–27, 150, 153–54, 165–66, 168, 170–71, 175
concentration camps, 48, 56, 100, 103, 148–49
conduct: illegal, 193
Conference against Racism in Durban, South Africa, 133
Conference on Jewish Material Claims against Germany, 139
Congo, 3, 23, 32, 59, 87, 114, 118, 155
conspiracy, 99, 162
continuing situation, 171–72
control: effective, 31, 34, 73, 102, 166; overall, 101
Coordinating Committee for the Commemoration of the Ovaherero Genocide, 100 Years After, 57
corporations, 10, 23, 70, 140, 145–46, 148–49, 155, 176, 191–92
crimes against humanity, 2, 10–14, 64–67, 74, 77, 84, 86–90, 92–97, 105–11, 113, 122, 130, 148–49, 151, 153, 156–57, 161, 172–73, 182, 186
criminal law. *See* international criminal law
critical date, 170–71
Cuba, 115, 161
custom and usages, 120

customary law, 10–12, 17, 39, 64–67, 69–71, 74–77, 80, 82, 84, 89, 91, 93, 95, 97, 101, 109–15, 126, 129–30, 185–86
Czech Republic, 132, 167, 170
Czechoslovakia, 132, 167, 191

damages, 11, 24, 98, 124, 131, 147–48, 177–78, 189, 151, 153
Damara, 23, 26, 28, 38, 50–52, 58, 64, 135, 139, 184
Declaration of St. Petersburg (1868), 73, 75, 78, 80, 87, 122
democratization, 3, 47
dependency, 65, 159
descendants, 21, 58, 81, 137, 176–78, 180
Deutsche Afrika-Linien GmbH & Co. *See* Woermann Lines
Deutsche Bank, 146, 148–50, 153, 191
development aid, 23, 26, 50, 55, 60–61, 120, 133, 145, 157, 175, 191, 194
development partner, 50, 191
dignity, 48, 63, 70, 105, 134, 158, 193
Diplomatic Immunities and Privileges Act, 2001 (Act 37 of 2001), 176
discrimination, 54, 125–26, 130, 133, 140, 144, 165–68, 170, 191
disparities: in reparations, 144; in unemployment, 28; in wealth, 25, 28
documentation: historical, 151
domestic courts, 83–84, 129, 159, 189; Germany, 172–73; Namibia, 173–75; South Africa, 175–76
donor, 60

East Germany, 7, 125, 139, 143
economic relationship, 159
Egypt, 61, 68
Eichmann case, 103, 113, 161
enforcement, 68–69, 83–84, 86, 89, 115, 122, 147–48, 168, 186
equality, 31, 138, 166–67, 170
equitable tolling, 151–53, 178
eradication, 6
ethnic group, 28–30, 97–98, 100, 182–83, 187
European Convention on Human Rights, 127, 140, 169–70
European Court of Human Rights (ECHR), 12, 148, 168–70, 172, 191; *Broniowski v. Poland*, 171; *Chassagnou v. France*, 170; *De Becker v. Belgium*, 171; *Denmark v. Turkey*, 170; *Gratzinger and Gratzingerova v. Czech Republic*, 170; *Loizidou v. Turkey*, 171; *McDaid & Others v. United Kingdom*, 171; *Yagci and Sargin v. Turkey*, 170
European powers, 33, 42, 113, 156, 181
European states, 34, 41, 43, 84, 116
evidence, 16, 19–20, 43–44, 46, 69, 73, 77, 83, 85–86, 95, 101, 102, 104–5, 109, 116, 118–20, 122–23, 142, 151–52, 171, 184–86, 192
exhaustion of domestic remedies, 166, 168, 170–71, 173
expropriation, 49–50, 166
extermination order, 2, 5–7, 9, 48, 56, 58, 76, 80, 93–95, 100, 104, 108, 130, 135, 148, 153, 187

farmers, 109; black, 51; German, 23, 25, 50, 60, 133, 138, 175, 176; Masaai, 179; white, 49, 51, 54, 179
farms, 23, 27–28, 30, 49, 50, 51, 54, 60, 121, 138; commercial, 50–51; white, 50
Filartiga v. Pena-Irala, 146
forced labor, 67, 100, 105, 113–17, 140, 142–43, 148, 150–51, 153, 155, 193
foreign policy, 40, 144, 153–54, 185

Geingob, Hage, 55
General Act of the Conference Respecting the Congo (General Act of Berlin), 1885, 33, 114
Geneva Conventions. *See* treaties
genocide: Armenian, 8, 56, 178; classification, 104; conventions (*see* treaties); elements of, 99, 102, 160; definition, 5, 10, 97–99, 101, 104, 108, 109, 187; legal requirements, 104; means of committing Herero genocide, 7; order (*see* extermination order); origin of concept, 12, 64, 107–13

German: accountability, 134; aid, 55, 61; authorities, 13, 15–16, 41, 43–45, 53, 103, 143; business, 140, 142; citizens, 120; colonial abuses, 2; colonialism, 3, 7, 25, 49, 114; criminal law code, 173; government, 8, 29, 56, 58, 63, 122–23, 132–35, 137, 139–40, 144, 149, 173, 177, 190, 193; media, 16; Parliament, 119–20, 140; patrols, 19, 121; protectorate, 15, 44; settlers, 5, 25–26, 44, 137, 175–76, 188; territories, 15, 36, 130; troops, 5, 16, 18, 37–38, 45–47, 57, 96, 115, 121–23, 132, 142
German Army Manual on Land Warfare, 1902, 122
German Association for Colonization and Export, 30
German Association for Threatened People, 132
German Code of Crimes against International Law CCIL, 2002, 172–73
German Colonial Association, 30
German Foundation for Remembrance, Responsibility, and the Future, 2000, 140, 142
German History Exhibition, 59
German-Namibian Special Initiative Concept, 193
German-Namibian War, 15
German Social Democrats, 46, 119
German South West Africa (GWSA), 2, 4, 9, 38, 45, 62, 74, 82, 103, 116, 149, 183
German Supreme Court, 147
grave breaches, 71, 107
Greece, 65, 68, 74, 90, 107, 109, 112, 116, 147

Hague Conventions. *See* treaties
Hague regulations. *See* treaties
Herero: Chiefs' Council, 27, 41, 51–52; court cases, 8, 55–56, 148–59; identity, 46–48, 182; legal status of, 31–34, 185; population numbers, 10, 25–26; rebellion, 14–20
Herero People's Reparations Corporation, 148
Hero's Day, 55
Holocaust, 7–8, 22, 46, 109, 125–26, 133, 140, 143–46, 148, 191
humanitarian intervention, 1, 21, 86, 116, 186
humanitarian law. *See* international humanitarian law
humanitarian protection, 64, 75, 130
human rights. *See* international human rights
Human Rights Committee (HRC), 12, 126, 148, 165–66, 168; *Brok v. Czech Republic*, 167; *Diergaardt of Rehoboth Baster Community et al. v. Namibia*, 167; *Drobek v. Czech Republic*, 167; *E. and A.K*, 167; *Lubicon Lake* communication, 166; *Malik v. Czech Republic*, 167; *Simvnek v. The Czech Republic*, 167; *Somers v. Hungary*, 166–67

indigenous land title, 158
In re Austrian and German Bank Holocaust Litigation, 1999, 146
In re Holocaust Victim Assets Litigation, 1997, 146
Inter-American Court of Human Rights 146, 177; *Aloeboetoe v. Suriname*, 77
internal armed conflicts, 12, 35, 73, 91
International Agreement for the Suppression of the White Slave Traffic, 115
international agreements, 1, 82, 115. *See also* treaties
international armed conflict, 13–15, 31, 38, 45, 66, 72–74, 77, 91, 96, 185–86, 193
International Court of Justice (ICJ), 12, 13, 68–69, 79, 91, 93, 99, 155, 159, 164; *Advisory Opinion on the Legality of Nuclear Weapons of July 8, 1996*, 80, 91; *Ambatielos* case, 112; *Article 38*, 68; *Barcelona Traction* case, 129; *Bosnia v. Serbia*, 102; *Corfu Channel* case, 74, 93; *Legal Consequences of the Construction of a Wall in the Occupied Palestinian Territory*, 164; *Military and Paramilitary Activities in and against*

Nicaragua (Nicaragua v. United States of America) Merits, Judgment, ICJ Reports 1986, p. 14 (June 27), 76; *Preliminary Objections in the Application of the Genocide Convention* case, 161; *Western Sahara case*, 33–34; *Yugoslavia v. United Kingdom*, 102
International Covenant on Civil and Political Rights (ICCPR), 12, 111, 126, 140, 165–67
International Convention on the Elimination of All Forms of Racial Discrimination Committee (CERD), 126, 165
international crimes, 8–10, 22, 65, 71, 84, 89–90, 95–96, 98–99, 110–11, 113–14, 121, 123, 161, 165, 173, 190
International Criminal Court, 13, 95, 145, 148, 180, 190–91, 193
international criminal law, 1, 10–11, 63, 83, 117, 173; Lima Treaty to Establish Uniform Rules for Private International Law, 1878, 1; Montevideo Treaty on International Penal Law, 1889, 1
International Criminal Tribunal for Rwanda (ICTR), 13, 95, 98, 160; *Akayesu* decision, 99–100, 103, 113; *Kayishema and Ruzindana* decision, 103
International Criminal Tribunal for Yugoslavia (ICTY), 13, 95–96; *Jelisic* case, 100, 102; *Kristic* case, 101; *Kupreskic* case, 92, 106; *Martic* case, 92; *Sikirica* case, 101, 106; *Tadic* case, 74, 80, 96, 101–2, 106; *Vukovar Hospital* case, 95
international humanitarian law, 1, 10–11, 13, 21, 26, 63–64, 67, 70–78, 81, 83–84, 86, 88, 90, 92, 109, 124, 126, 128–30, 144, 186, 189, 192
international human rights, 1–4, 7, 10–13, 20–23, 63–64, 66–67, 70–71, 74–75, 77, 82–85, 91, 96, 108–9, 111, 116, 124–27, 130–31, 140, 143–48, 152–58, 163, 165–72, 175–77, 180–82, 185–88, 191–93
International Labor Organization, 127
international law: customary law, 3, 17, 21, 35, 63–65, 67–70, 72, 74–75, 77–79, 82–85, 89, 92–93, 96, 99, 107, 112–13, 115, 150, 153, 160, 186–87, 189; origins of, 67–70; sources of, 68, 91
International Law Association, 129
International Law Commission, 100, 159–60
international obligations, 12, 83, 111, 172–73, 190
International Prize Court, 127
investment, 50, 144–45
Iran, 147, 161
Israel, 103, 138–39, 141, 161, 164

Jackson, Robert H., 86
Jama v. I.N.S., 151
Japan, 32, 61, 65, 89, 129, 141, 178
Japanese Americans, internment of, 177
Jonker, Jan, 38
JP Morgan Chase & Co., 176
jurisdiction: universal, 78, 145, 147, 161, 165, 173; territorial, 147
jus cogens, 11, 115
justiciability, 151, 174

Kaiser, Wilhelm II, 5, 43, 59–60, 89–90, 103, 122, 125, 161–62, 187, 192
Kapuuo, Clemens, 52–53
Kenya, 23, 32, 148, 156, 179–80, 185
Kooper, Simon, 18–19
Krupp decision, 92
Kutako, Hosea, 52–53, 60

labor camps, 143
laborers, 140, 142–43, 146
land: access to, 3–4, 26, 48–49, 51, 104, 124; acquisition, 49; appropriation, 28, 46, 177; clearance, 44; confiscation, 25, 27, 48, 50, 118, 137, 167, 178; deprivation, 51, 166, 184; holdings, 5, 15, 23, 25, 51; ownership, 25, 49, 54, 62; policies of tabula rasa, 30; policy, 15, 30, 173; reform, 3, 25, 50–51, 54; repossession, 138; tax, 51;

transfer/redistribution, 50, 54, 138, 158; valuation, 51
Land Reform Advisory Commission, 54
laws of war, 11, 15, 21, 45, 65, 70–71, 73, 75, 79–80, 88, 93, 95, 109–10, 126, 143
legal continuity, 161
Lehman Brothers, 176
Leipzig War Crimes Court, 123
Lemkin, Raphael, 16–17, 104–5, 107–9
Leutwein, Theodor, 15, 19, 37, 43–45, 119, 121, 137
liability: civil, 11, 71, 98, 159–60, 172, 192; criminal, 11, 98, 113, 189; direct, 65; legal, 35, 65; retrospective, 11; state, 102, 129, 159, 161–62, 192
liberation, 4, 31, 46, 50–53, 56, 62, 120, 137
Libya, 161
Lieber Code, 1863, 71, 75–77, 80–81
limitation period, 152–53
litigants, 158

Mabo case, 158
Maherero, Samuel, 19, 38–41, 43–44, 48, 52–54
Maherero, Tjamuaha, 52–53
Maji Maji rebellion, 156
Mandates Commission of the League of Nations, 127
Maori, 131–32, 168, 180
marginalization: economic, 184; political, 48, 182
Marootian v. New York Life Insurance Company, 178
Marshall Plan (second), 194
Martens Clause, 12. *See also* Hague Conventions
martial law, 15
mass graves, 4, 136
Mau Mau freedom fighters, 156, 180
mens rea, 98, 102–3, 106
minority, 3–4, 21, 25–26, 28, 51, 54, 56, 61–62, 64, 83, 87, 93, 113, 116–17, 127, 132, 144, 174–75, 184, 188
Morenga, Jakob, 18
multinationals, 23, 145, 154–55, 161, 165, 169, 192

Nama, 5, 18, 23, 25–26, 28–32, 35, 37–39, 41, 50–51, 55, 59, 61, 64, 94, 104, 135, 139, 184
Namibia: constitution, 49; demography, 28–29; geographical location, 26–28; history, 29–31; National Assembly, 48, 56; National Unity Democratic Organization (NUDO), 27, 52; Parliament, 27, 49, 52–55, 60, 158
National Conference on Land Reform and the Land Question, 1991, 54
Native Americans, 177, 180
Nazi(s), 4, 56, 104, 108, 125, 139–41, 160, 163, 179
Nexus, 13–14
Nigeria, 23, 32, 42, 148
non-governmental organization (NGO), 76, 88, 148, 157, 169–70
non-state actors, 70, 155
Nujoma, Sam, 56–57
nulla poena sine lege praevia, 11
nullum crimen sine lege, 11
Nuremberg Charter, 13, 66, 95

Okereka Jeuangelie Joruuano (the Protestant Unity Church), 46
Omaruru, 39, 47–48
Ombara, 39. *See* paramount chief
opinio juris, 69, 74, 85
Orenstein-Koppel. *See* Terex
Organization of African Unity (OAU), 51
Otavi Mines and Railway Company (OMEG), 149
Otjiherero, 28
Ottoman empire, 65, 88, 116–17
Ovaherero Genocide Committee, 57, 136
Ovaherero/Ovambanderu Council for Dialogue on 1904 Genocide Technical Committee, 193
Owambo, 10, 13, 18, 27–29, 32, 37–38, 50–51, 54–56
Oxford Manual of the Laws of War on Land, 75, 79–80

paramount chief, 38–39, 48, 52–53, 58, 135–36, 139, 148, 173, 176, 193
Peace of Okahandja, 31
peace treaties, 13, 15, 19, 37, 40, 45

Permanent Court of International Justice 33, 162; *Opinion on the Jurisdiction of the Courts of Danzig*, 1928, 127
perpetrators, 7, 9, 11, 20–21, 23, 46, 96–97, 99, 101, 103–4, 131, 134–35, 144, 147, 159–60, 171, 176–77, 181, 189
plaintiffs, 27, 149–53, 159, 180
political ramifications, 50, 159
poverty, 20, 23, 25, 157
predecessor governments, 162
private individuals, 93, 99, 101–2, 126, 159
private law, 67, 147
propaganda, 5, 9, 16, 55, 138
property rights, 49, 130, 166–67, 170
prosecution, criminal, 98, 128, 156, 172, 189
Protection of Investment Agreement between Germany and Namibia, 1993, 50
protection treaties, 13–14, 17, 31, 33, 35, 39–42, 45, 173
protectorates, 15, 30, 33, 41–44, 119–20
public officials, 99, 102–3, 159, 161
public policy, 154

racism, 47, 125, 133, 144
railroad/railway, 141–42, 149–50, 178, 191
rape, 5, 88, 95, 156, 179
ratification, 78, 112, 127, 165, 167, 170–71
rebellion, 2, 14–15, 18, 37, 77, 105, 109, 121, 132, 150, 156
reciprocal criticism, 118
recognition, 7, 21, 48, 52, 55, 59, 60, 66, 70, 80, 83, 89, 113, 119, 123, 127–28, 130–31, 142–44, 147, 158, 184, 189–90, 192
reconciliation, 3–4, 20, 22, 26, 57–58, 60, 131, 135, 139, 156, 158
Red Band Organization (*Otjira Tjotjiserandu*), 46
red line, 50, 54
redress, 8–9, 21, 24, 54, 63, 85, 93, 98, 124, 126, 137, 140, 144–45, 148, 155, 165, 169, 176–77, 194
regional human rights instruments, 145
rehabilitation, 4, 24, 140, 145
Reichstag, 36, 109, 119, 137–38
remedies, 24, 98, 126, 134, 144–45, 153, 166, 168–71, 173, 193
reparations: for Aboriginal children, 178; for alleged killing of Ugandan prophet and people by British, 180; for detention of Ukrainian-Canadians, 178; for forceful removal of Maasai resulting in malaria, 179; for genocide, 180; for head tax on Chinese, 190; for Kenya-British army explosives, 179; for land possession by white farmers in Zimbabwe, 179; for slavery, 116, 176; future claims, 189; group, 177; IBM, gypsies suit of, 179; individual, 17, 63, 126, 128, 177; Kenyan charges of rape by British soldiers, 179; Pan-African Reparations Movement, 180; Rosewood Florida massacre, 180; symbolic, 158; Tulsa race riots, 180
repatriation, 49
reprisal, 71, 151–53, 175
res judicata, 150, 153
reservation, 9, 62, 110, 161, 163, 169–70
resistance, 16, 18, 46, 55, 62, 95, 123, 156, 177, 180
resolution, 8, 54, 79, 110, 112, 116, 124, 159, 193
resources, 9, 20, 47, 49, 104, 130, 155, 158, 168, 180
Re-Southern Rhodesia decision, 1918, 32, 33
responsibility, 11, 46, 84, 89, 99, 101–3, 120, 128–29, 131–34, 137, 140, 142–45, 159–64, 171, 177, 189
restitution, 4, 24, 54, 86, 127, 137–40, 145, 158, 167–68, 190–91, 193
retroactivity, 111–13, 167, 188, 191
retrospectivity, 110–11
revolt, 14, 18, 88
Rhenish missionaries, 16, 29–30, 45
Riruako, Kuaima, 52–53, 57–58, 139, 144, 148–49
Rome Statute. *See* treaties
Russia, 65, 77–78, 80, 89, 94, 116, 134

settlements, out-of-court, 22, 125, 146
settlers, 25–28, 30, 41, 44–45, 95, 97, 137–38, 145, 147, 150, 175–76, 184–85, 188, 191
signatories, 75, 85, 113–14, 118, 120–21, 186
si omnes clauses, 13, 74–76, 85
slavery, 7, 21, 23, 42, 64, 67, 77, 81, 83–85, 88, 93, 95, 103, 108, 113–17, 130–31, 133, 140, 142–43, 146, 149–51, 153, 155, 176, 182, 186–91, 193
Sosa v. Alvarez-Machain, 153–54
South Africa, 3, 4, 26–27, 29, 30, 47–50, 52–56, 62, 74–75, 109, 131, 133, 137, 148, 152, 154, 158–59, 163, 174–79, 191
South African Truth and Reconciliation Commission, 4
South West African National Union (SWANU), 51
South West African Peoples Organization (SWAPO), 4
sovereign immunity, 147, 159
sovereign right, 35, 85
sovereignty, 13–15, 17, 26, 29, 31–37, 40–43, 45, 63, 83, 116–17, 184–85, 188
specific intent, 99–103, 106
state practice, 12, 21, 32–33, 66, 69, 80, 89, 92, 128, 163, 190
state responsibility, 11, 102–3, 128, 160–63
state succession, 162–63, 177
statue(s), 59–60
statute of limitations, 151–52, 154, 172
successor government, 161
Superior Court of the District of Columbia, 150
survivors, 7–8, 48, 100–1, 141, 144, 146, 177, 180, 182
Syria, 116

Tanzania, 61, 119, 156, 179
Terex, 148–49
third-party beneficiary doctrine, 85
Tjiseseta, King Michael, 47
trade, 15, 35, 37, 42, 43, 50, 61, 63, 64, 68, 83, 85, 93, 113–15, 117, 146, 155
Traditional Authorities Act (Act 25 of 2000), 48
Traditional Authorization Act of 1995, 48
transitional justice mechanism, 184
travaux preparatoires, 111, 187
treaties: Annex to the 1899 Convention, 115; Anti-Slavery Convention, 1890 (Brussels Act of 1890), 84, 85, 187; Basic Principles and Guidelines on the Right to a Remedy and Reparation for Victims of Violations of International Human Rights and Humanitarian Law, 2005, 144; Berlin West Africa Convention, 84; CERD Convention, 71, 91–92, 129; Convention on an International Prize Court of October 18, 1907, 127; Convention on Land Warfare with Annexed Regulations, 1899, 128; Convention on the Non-Applicability of Statutes of Limitation to War Crimes and Crimes against Humanity of 1968, 11, 113; Convention Relative to the Slave Trade and Importation into Africa of Firearms, Ammunition, Spirituous Liquors, 1890 (General Act of the Brussels Conference), 114; First Optional Protocol to the ICCPR, 165–66; Geneva Convention for the Amelioration of the Condition of the Wounded and Sick in Armies in the Field of July 6, 1906, 12, 74; Geneva Conventions, 1, 12, 71, 73–77, 81–82, 91, 95, 121, 129, 186, 193; Optional Protocols to the Geneva Conventions, 71, 91–92, 129; Genocide Convention, 16, 65, 67, 97–102, 104, 108–13, 159, 161–63, 173, 187, 192; Hague Conventions, 12–13, 16–17, 63, 65–66, 69, 72–76, 78–82, 81, 84, 88–89, 93, 119, 122, 127–29, 150, 185–86, 189; Hague regulations, 72, 81; International Declaration Concerning the Laws and Customs of War,

1874, 78; London Treaty between Great Britain, France, and Russia for the Pacification of Greece, July 6, 1827, 116; Luxembourg Treaty, 1952, 139; May 1915 declaration from Great Britain, France, and Russia about the occurrences in Armenia, 89; Palgrave-Maherero treaty, 31; Paris Declaration Respecting Maritime Law of April 16, 1856, 74; Polish-Danzig Treaty, 127; Resolution of the Great Powers to intervene in the Ottoman Empire to halt the slaughter of Greek Orthodox Christians, 1827, 116; Rome Statute, 95, 97, 145, 147, 191; St. Petersburg Declaration Renouncing the Use, in Time of War, of Explosive Projectiles under 400 Grammes Weight, 1868, 75, 78, 80, 87, 122; Treaty for the Suppression of the African Slave Trade (Treaty of London), 114; Treaty of Kutchuk-Kainardi Russia, 116; Treaty of Lausanne, 1923, 90; Treaty of Sevres, 1920, 90; Universal Declaration of Human Rights, 69, 111; Versailles Treaty, 24, 62, 89; Vienna Convention on the Law of Treaties of 1969, 111; Vienna Declaration 1815, 113
Truppenspieler (troop players) movement, 46
truth commissions, 3–4, 23, 137, 156, 184
Tshekedi Khama and another v. The High Commissioner, 33

UN Commission on Human Rights, 111, 140
UN Commission on Human Rights *Study Concerning the Right to Restitution, Compensation, and Rehabilitation for Victims of Gross Violations of Human Rights and Fundamental Freedoms*, 140
UN Convention on the Non-Applicability of Statutory Limitations to War Crimes and Crimes against Humanity, 113
UN Convention on the Prevention and Punishment of the Crime of Genocide, 1948, 108, 111
UN Declaration on the Rights of Indigenous Peoples, 20
UN General Assembly, 20, 110, 112, 144, 164–65
United States, 10, 14, 22, 26, 47, 55, 61, 65, 76–78, 87–89, 94, 115–16, 125–26, 129, 141, 143, 145–48, 150, 154, 173, 176–77, 179–80, 189–91, 193
United States Federal Appeals Court for the 7th Circuit, 176
United States Supreme Court, 126
UN Sub-Commission on Prevention of Discrimination and Protection of Minorities, 1989, 144
UN Whitaker report on genocide, 1985, 98, 107
Upper-Silesian Arbitral Tribunal, 127
U.S. District Court for the District of New Jersey, 151–52, 154
U.S. Federal Courts, 150, 191

Velasquez–Rodriguez case, 146
victims, 1, 3–4, 7–9, 20–24, 56, 58, 76, 96, 98, 100, 103–4, 106, 124–25, 128–29, 131, 133–35, 139–41, 144–48, 151, 155, 163, 166, 168–71, 176–77, 180–82, 189, 191
Vienna Congress, 1815, 87, 116
violations, historical, 10, 124, 132, 140, 148, 155, 172
von Bulow, Chancellor, 93,
von Caprivi, Chancellor, 36
von Francois, Captain Curt, 38
von Trotha, Adrian Dietrich Lothar, General, 5, 14–16, 26, 45, 48, 65, 71, 82, 94, 102–5, 120–23, 133, 137, 162, 192

war crimes, 21, 64, 70–73, 77–78, 80, 86, 88–89, 93–94, 96, 107, 109, 111, 113, 121, 123, 130, 148, 172–73, 180
water, 5, 27–28, 44, 49, 121

Waterberg, 8, 29, 57–58, 95–96, 120, 133
welfare benefits, 145
West German Association for Colonization and Export, 1881, 30
Windhoek, 15, 38, 57, 60, 150
Witbooi Hendrik, Chief, 19, 36–38, 41, 44, 59
Witbooi tribe, 37
Woermann Lines, 148–51, 154, 191
World War I, 7, 9, 24, 29–30, 46, 83–84, 89, 94, 119, 123, 130, 162, 178
World War II, 11, 14, 21–22, 64, 70, 73, 83, 92, 130, 131, 134, 138–40, 143, 145–46, 156, 162–63, 167, 172–73, 175–78, 186, 190, 192
wrongs, historical, 131, 194

Zimbabwe, 23, 27, 29, 50, 179

About the Author

JEREMY SARKIN is Visiting Professor of Human Rights at the Fletcher School at Tufts University and Senior Professor of Law at the University of the Western Cape in Cape Town, South Africa. He is Special Rapporteur for Enforced and Involuntary Disappearances to the United Nations Human Rights Council. He served as an acting judge in the Cape High Court in South Africa. He is Legal Advisor to the Paramount Chief of the Herero people in Namibia. He has published over 100 articles and 12 books, including *Human Rights in African Prisons* (2008), *Reconciliation in Divided Societies: Finding Common Ground* (2007), *Carrots and Sticks: The Truth and Reconciliation Commission and the South African Amnesty Process* (2004), and *Human Rights, The Citizen, and the State: South African and Irish Perspectives* (2002).